Counseling and
Psychotherapy Essentials

Counseling and Psychotherapy Essentials

Integrating Theories, Skills, and Practices

GLENN E. GOOD, PH.D.

BERNARD D. BEITMAN, M.D.

W·W·NORTON

NEW YORK · LONDON

For information about permission to reproduce
selections from this book, write to
Permissions, W. W. Norton & Company, Inc.
500 Fifth Avenue, New York, NY 10110

Composition and book design by Viewtistic, Inc.
Manufacturing by Hamilton Printing
Production Manager: Leeann Graham

Library of Congress Cataloging-in-Publication Data

Good, Glenn E., 1954-
Counseling and psychotherapy essentials: integrating theories, skills, and practices/
Glenn E. Good & Bernard D. Beitman.
   p.   cm.
"A Norton Professional Book."
Includes bibliographical references and index.
ISBN-13: 978-0-393-70458-7
ISBN-10: 0-393-70458-0
1. Psychotherapy. 2. Counseling. I. Beitman, Bernard D. II. Title.
RC480.G658 2006
616.89'14—DC22   2006040056

W. W. Norton & Company, Inc., 500 Fifth Avenue, New York, NY 10110
www.wwnorton.com
W. W. Norton & Company, Ltd., Castle House, 75/76 Wells Street, London W1T 3QT
1 3 5 7 9 8 6 4 2 0

Contents

Preface

As teachers of counseling and psychotherapy we want our students to effectively learn its core principles in ways that can be adapted to their own individual styles and to the varying needs of their clients. Although most introductory texts emphasize "schools" over pragmatics, most practitioners utilize ideas from many sources within their own framework. The field needs a less ideological, more pragmatic introductory text.

Written with his colleague Dongmei Yue, Bernard Beitman's book *Learning Psychotherapy* (now in its second edition) has received two national psychiatric education awards and has been used in more than half of the 190 psychiatric training programs in the U.S. We decided to build upon its clear description of psychotherapy's core processes to create a more complete practical introduction to counseling and psychotherapy. Section II of this book holds closely to the core processes of engagement, pattern search, change, and termination. Section I describes the approaches of the schools and Section III focuses on common difficulties and therapeutic solutions. We clarify our presentation of information with case examples developed from composites of clients that we have seen. All together, this book provides the essential knowledge base for any beginning therapist.

Bernie and I (Glenn Good) ride bikes together, go on canoe trips together, and talk about psychotherapy together. We hatched this book while floating down the Jack's Fork River in the Ozark National Forest in southern Missouri, accompanied by our buddies Hank Schneider (a therapist) and Cap'n Bill Parks (an emergency room physician married to a therapist). Bernie and I argued over first authorship while Bernie was in a tree. The four of us have grown closer over the 13 years of annual floating and bike riding, peeling back the layers of our social selves to see a little more of what is underneath. We have tried to accomplish something similar with this book—to peel back the ideologies, the name-calling, the boasting, and the weaknesses to reveal to students the psychotherapy of real-world practitioners.

Glenn E. Good
Columbia, Missouri
May 2006

Acknowledgments

Many thanks to the editors at W. W. Norton, starting with Susan Monroe, who immediately saw the possible value of *Learning Psychotherapy*; then to Deborah Malmud, who encouraged us to write this book; and to Michael McGandy, who helped to shepherd it along; and finally to Andrea Costella, who saw it through to publication. Debby Burnley handled the massive detail of the reference section with her usual aplomb.

We also wish to express our appreciation to Dr. Chris Lawrence for her contributions to the Substance Abuse chapter, to Angela Soth for her contributions to the Therapeutic Communication chapter, and to Dr. Donna Sudak for her contributions to the Psychodynamic, Behavioral, and Cognitive Theories chapters and also to the Depression and Suicide chapter. We also express our appreciation to Michael Davidovits, Jessica Pue, Angela Soth, and David Tager, who provided feedback on one or more chapters.

Last, yet definitely not least, we would like to express our deep appreciation of the women, men, children, adolescents, couples, and families who have the courage to seek therapy. You have entrusted us with your secrets, hopes, doubts, and concerns. You also challenged us to meet you where you were and to understand your experiences and their meaning to you, and you allowed us accompany you on the journey. You were willing to risk trying new ideas, experiences, and behaviors—to risk imagining better lives, relationships, and futures.

Finally, you taught us how to serve you effectively and how to improve the services that mental health professionals provide to others. For all of this, we are most appreciative!

I (Glenn Good) would like to acknowledge the support of my immediate family—my wife, Dr. Laurie Mintz, and our delightful daughters, Jennifer and Allison—for their love, patience, and understanding during this time-intensive project. I am also grateful to my family of origin—Drs. Jeanne and Robert Good—for their nurturance and encouragement, and to my sister, Ellen Wakeman, who tolerated me during our upbringing. I would also like to express my gratitude to Bill Parks and Hank Schneider, who endured extended discussions of this project during our annual canoe trips on the Ozark waterways. I also want to thank my colleagues at the American Psychological Association for their friendship and intellectual clarity, and I am similarly appreciative of my colleagues and the graduate students at the Department of Educational, School, and Counseling Psychology at the University of Missouri-Columbia. They make each work day a pleasure. Finally, I would like to acknowledge my recognition of the fact that I have rarely made a more astute move than my entry into partnership with Bernie Beitman. It has been my distinct pleasure to experience Bernie's intellect, creativity, generosity, and commitment to improving psychotherapy.

I (Bernard Beitman) deeply thank my wife, Paula Levine, for her support and understanding through the intensities of this project and for her loving care for our children Arie and Karlen. Much appreciation also to the University of Missouri-Columbia Department of Psychiatry and its Medical School for providing the opportunity to study and write about psychotherapy in the fashion of Midwestern pragmatism. Thanks also to the American College of Psychiatrists and the Association for Academic Psychiatry, which have recognized the precursor of this book with their educational awards. Most importantly, thank you to the many teachers of psychotherapy who have used and extended the ideas in *Learning Psychotherapy* to help new generations of trainees become informed about this essential helping process. To Glenn Good, what a delight to work with you and feel your reliability, enthusiasm, intellect, and knowledge in the hand-to-hand combat that is book-writing collaboration.

Glenn E. Good and Bernard D. Beitman
Columbia, Missouri
May 2006

Counseling and Psychotherapy Essentials

A Contextual Overview
of Counseling
and Psychotherapy

Information is the difference that makes a difference.
— GREGORY BATESON (1972)

Students entering the mental health professions face daunting tasks. They must familiarize themselves with over 400 schools of counseling and psychotherapy; learn scores of elaborate theories on personality, human development, and cultural considerations; become well-versed in the many extensive theories on psychological difficulties, resilience, and resolution; master a vast array of in- and out-of-session therapeutic skills; be able to recall the many valuable psychoeducational and community resources available to assist clients in reaching their goals; and become self-aware as a counselor or therapist, including identifying their "hot" personal issues, their potential value to diverse clients, and their particular interactional talents, limitations, and preferences. No wonder the prospect of seeing one's first client provokes anxiety.

As therapists and educators ourselves, we have struggled to find a resource that provides students in mental health professions with what they actually need to both *understand* therapeutic practice and *implement* that knowledge. Because no such text exists, instructors in the mental health professions must typically "talk around" this void by using books that describe therapy theories but lack information on direct application in real-life therapy settings.

This book seeks to address this deficit. Our goal was to provide the essential *"information that makes a difference,"* to use the words of Gregory Bateson. We specifically tried to eliminate unnecessary jargon, clearly present central concepts, and equip students with the information and skills they need if they are to be as helpful to as many of their clients as possible. No book can replace the utility of personalized feedback from supervisors, colleagues, and clients. That said, we have attempted to provide as much crucial information as is possible to convey in written form.

We have divided the book into three sections. Section I, Foundations of Counseling and Psychotherapy, discusses the essentials of therapy theories, concepts, and terms. Chapter 1 presents the key concepts of psychodynamic, psychoanalytic, Jungian, Adlerian, ego psychology, object relations, self-psychology, behavioral, and cognitive approaches to psychotherapy and counseling. Chapter 2 outlines the central concepts from the broad categories of humanistic, existential, and interpersonal theories. Also described in this chapter are the essentials of multicultural and systems approaches, including brief, strategic, and solution-focused therapies, as well as therapies addressing culture and societal influences, such as multicultural, feminist, and gender-aware therapies.

Section II, Components of Effective Counseling and Psychotherapy, provides readers with an understanding of the core processes in counseling/therapy—in other words, *how to do* effective counseling and psychotherapy. Foundations of therapeutic communication (how therapists talk) are addressed in Chapter 3. Developing, maintaining, and repairing the therapeutic working alliance are discussed in Chapter 4. Identifying clients' patterns and planning treatment are described in Chapter 5. General strategies for helping clients effect change are examined in Chapter 6. Chapter 7 discusses strategies associated with different schools that focus on clients' emotions, cognitions, behaviors, interpersonal relationships, or systems (ECBIS). Potential barriers to change (including resistance, transference, and countertransference) as well as their paradoxical usefulness in promoting change are elucidated in Chapter 8. Chapter 9, the final chapter in this section, describes termination, in its may forms including therapy that never ends.

Beyond acquiring proficiency with the core processes of counseling and psychotherapy, therapists should know the specific skills required to address frequently encountered client concerns. Section III, Higher-Incidence Concerns and Effective Treatments, provides more specifics about what therapists need to know about common problems as well as what to do to help resolve these problems. To this end, a plethora of psychoeducational resources are provided in Chapter 10. Addressing clients' concerns about their mood, including sadness, dysthymia, depression, and suicide are discussed in Chapter 11. Helping clients with their fears, anxieties, panic, and posttraumatic stress is described in Chapter 12. The pervasive yet often hidden problems of substance use, abuse, and dependence are delineated extensively in Chapter 13. Couple, marital, and family therapy problems and techniques are presented in Chapter 14. Cutting-edge issues in coordinating care using psychotherapy and medications from an integrated mind-brain perspective are described in Chapter 15.

We repeat descriptions of different key concepts in the book's different contexts—for example, psychodynamic, cognitive, Rogerian, and emotion-focused ideas appear in both Section I and Section II. Section II is more pragmatic and builds upon the early descriptions of the schools.

Issues in the Contemporary Practice of Counseling and Psychotherapy

Clients seek effective, time-limited assistance. Health insurance companies seek to reduce healthcare costs. Insurers also prefer providers who offer cost-efficient treatments. Some researchers argue for adherence to a limited repertoire of "empirically supported treatments" (ESTs) whereas others contend that "all therapies have won and all deserve prizes" (Beutler, 2004; Luborsky, 1975). More broadly defined "evidence-based practices" (EBPs) have been proposed as a reasonable middle ground between excessively restricted manual-based interventions and excessively loose "going with your gut" approaches (Levant, 2004, 2005). This middle ground is supported by process research (e.g., the working alliance), which is also empirical (Norcross, 2002; Wampold, 2001).

To complicate matters further, some critics claim that therapy is ineffective (e.g., Dawes, 1996) despite volumes of research data to the contrary (Wampold, 2001). In addition, proponents of the over 400 different psychotherapy orientations insist that their approach is best. Further clouding these already murky matters is the role that multiculturalism (race, ethnicity, and gender) plays in therapy. No wonder the current state of affairs is so confusing to students of counseling and psychotherapy!

Keep in mind that counseling/psychotherapy is ever-changing and yet ever the same. Researchers continue identifying new aspects of "what works" and "what makes a difference" to clients and their concerns. Yet much is already known about what constitutes "good" counseling or therapy. This bedrock will endure. Counselors and therapists will continue seeking to address the unique needs of each client who enters their offices. Despite all the hype about new therapeutic orientations, contemporary counselors and therapists overwhelmingly endorse the "integrative" or "eclectic" theoretical orientation. Indeed, this approach is the most widely endorsed therapeutic orientation among *all* North American mental health professionals—counselors, social workers, psychologists, and psychiatrists (Bechtoldt, Norcross, Wyckoff, Pokrywa, & Campbell, 2001; Norcross, Hedges, & Castle, 2002; Prochaska & Norcross, 2002).

The popularity of the integrative approach is probably due to a number of reasons, including pressure from insurance companies for more cost-efficient interventions and the availability of empirically supported integrative approaches (e.g., Beitman & Yue, 2004). The growing popularity of the integrative approach signals that therapists are increasingly responding to the unique needs of their clients rather than pledging allegiance to particular theoretical orientations. Integrative therapists view theories and techniques as tools to draw from rather than as "banners to ride under" (Shoben, 1962, p. 621). This enables them to better match their interventions to clients' needs. Similarly, results from three decades of meta-analytic studies question the utility of relying excessively on empirically supported school-based treatments and underscore the importance of common therapeutic factors such as the therapeutic working alliance (e.g., Wampold, Ahn, & Coleman, 2001).

The Mission of This Book

This book seeks to integrate the best of all worlds, highlighting particular techniques as well as summarizing core components of effective therapy, all of which have empirical-support for their relationship to favorable outcomes. We wish to define the realities of psychotherapy so that you are not distracted by the latest theoretical hyperbole. What is the most important determiner of outcome in psychotherapy? The client! Specifically, the severity of the client's problem and the strength of the social network predict the likelihood of change (Beutler, Harwood, Alimohamed, & Malik, 2002). The second most important variable is probably related to factors associated with the individual therapist rather than the specific therapeutic approach (Wampold, 2001). The third most important predictor of outcome appears to be the strength of the working alliance (Wampold, 2001). Hence, we seek to help each student better understand and apply the knowledge, skills, and attitudes associated with being effective counselors and therapists by emphasizing the obvious, research-supported factors that influence outcome.

These chapters are designed for flexibility and innovation. Individual instructors and institutions may use the chapters as foundations upon which to build particular areas of interest. Additionally, the information presented in the chapters can serve as a reference with which to view videos, discuss current clients, or role play various situations and concerns.

It bears repeating that we are *not* introducing a new theoretical model of therapy. There are already too many divergent schools of thought, each grounded in one or another important element of human psychological function: emotions (emotion-focused therapy), thought (cognitive therapy), behavior (behavior modification therapy), interpersonal relationships (interpersonal therapy), systems (family therapy), or culture (multicultural counseling). Many efforts to launch new and overarching conceptualizations of psychological thought and treatment, like the "primal scream" and Ehardt Seminar Training (EST) enjoyed brief prominence among the lay public before effectively exiting the intellectual arena. Others, like Reichian Orgone therapy, survive only on the fringes of therapy among a few passionate supporters. More recently, eye movement desensitization and reprocessing (EMDR) appears to be losing its claim to unique effectiveness as research indicates that exposure to the feared memory remains fundamental to effective treatment for many clients with posttramatic stress. Many varieties and systems of brief therapy have come and gone over the years, very few with durable and consistently replicable results (Beitman & Yue, 2004).

Rather than suggesting that you adopt a particular therapeutic principle or system, this book encourages you to think for yourself within this rich and varied tradition. We hope to help you find a method or, more likely, a combination of therapeutic methods that works well for you and your clients, enables you to use your abilities, fits with your environment, and is based upon the core processes common to all effective psychotherapies.

The Process of Learning

The training upon which you are about to embark assumes your willingness to immerse yourself in learning. You do this in part by actively participating in discussions, exercises, and homework. Like your clients, your experiences with therapy in the classroom and clinic will foster change in you. Your transformation into a skilled and knowledgeable counselor or therapist is largely dependent upon your own motivation to learn, willingness to take risks, and preparedness to accept change in yourself. Learning how to do therapy means changing a great deal about the way you think about yourself, your relationships, and the processes of therapy. You should also understand that your development as a therapist will not be completed when you reach the last page of this book or when you graduate, become licensed, or even receive your first paycheck. The best therapists say that they learn something new about their craft almost every day of their careers. Be prepared to maintain lifelong commitment to learning and quality improvement.

During the learning process, allow yourself to be seen and heard, but also to watch and listen. We encourage you to be courageous, take risks, reveal your vulnerabilities, and help make it safer for others to take risks and learn. Enjoy practicing and learning therapy for the rest of your life!

Foundations
of Counseling
& Psychotherapy

CHAPTER 1

Psychodynamic, Behavioral, and Cognitive Theories
Concepts and Techniques

There is nothing so practical as a good theory.
–Kurt Lewin (1951)

It is important for therapists to be conversant in the various theories of therapy. Such knowledge provides a framework for understanding the history of the profession, a context for the use of concepts and techniques drawn from particular schools, and a way to communicate effectively with other therapists. To this end, the following two chapters provide an overview of the concepts and techniques associated with the primary theories of counseling/therapy. For heuristic purposes, these theories are sometimes clustered into four major historical *forces*: psychodynamic, cognitive-behavioral, existential-humanistic, and multicultural. We will loosely follow this organization, describing psychodynamic, cognitive, and behavioral theories in this chapter and humanistic, existential, interpersonal, systems, and multicultural theories in Chapter 2.

Psychodynamic Theory

Psychodynamic theory is based on the notion that tension exists between individuals' conscious and unconscious. "Psychodynamic" literally refers to dynamics of the psyche, with "psyche" referring to an individual's mind as the center of thought, emotion, and behavior. Psychodynamic theory arose from the psychoanalytic theory originated by Freud. Freud's work generated numerous followers and competitors, many of whom developed their own variations. These variations grew into a multitude of different therapies, which are grouped in the broader category of psychodynamic therapy. Thus, psychoanalytic therapy is considered one of the many types of psychodynamic therapies. Other psychodynamic therapies discussed in this chapter include Jungian, Adlerian, ego psychology, object relations, and self-psychology.

Psychoanalytic Therapy

Psychoanalytic approaches arose from the works of Sigmund Freud written from 1886 to 1939 (Strachey, 1953). Psychoanalysts view people as being influenced by factors and dynamics over which they initially may have little or no awareness. *Unconscious* influences are aspects of individuals' inner worlds of which they are not consciously aware. This can include material that is relatively easily brought to conscious awareness (preconscious), as well as material that is inadmissible to consciousness (unconscious). Inadmissible unconscious ideas and feelings are theorized to be dissociated from consciousness either by never having been allowed to become conscious or by having been repressed from consciousness. Unconscious material sometimes appears in individuals' everyday life via dreams, slips of the tongue, and odd behavior Freud (1900/1953). Biological instincts, including *Eros* (sexual and life instincts) and *Thanatos* (aggressive and death instincts) are viewed as basic dynamic forces motivating personality, with the term *libido* referring to sexual and life energy associated with Eros.

The psychoanalytic view of personality structure posits three components: the id, ego, and superego. The *id* is the primary source of psychic energy and of all instincts. Operating on the *pleasure principle*, the id seeks pleasure, avoids pain, and reduces tension. The id is the eternal inner child—illogical, amoral, and driven to immediately satisfy instinctual wants and needs. The *ego* serves as the mediator between the instinctual impulses of the id and the environment. Operating on the *reality principle*, the ego exercises adult-like executive functions, formulating plans of actions for satisfying needs via realistic and logical thinking. The *superego* is the internalized moral code of the personality. As the representation of internalized standards and morals of caregivers and society, the superego strives for moral and social perfection by inhibiting instinctual impulses.

Defense mechanisms serve as inner controls to restrain unacceptable impulses from being expressed in uncontrolled ways. They help individuals avoid experiencing condemnation for breaking familial and social rules, as well as avoid experiencing anxiety, guilt, and shame from their desire to break such rules. Everyone is presumed to experience unconscious conflicts and to employ defense mechanisms; however, individuals differ in the nature of their predominant impulses, rules, anxieties, and defense mechanisms. (See Chapter 5 for a more detailed discussion of defense mechanisms.)

> Defense mechanisms serve as inner controls to restrain unacceptable impulses from being expressed in uncontrolled ways. They help individuals avoid experiencing condemnation for breaking familial and social rules, as well as avoid experiencing anxiety, guilt, and shame from their desire to break such rules. Everyone is presumed to experience unconscious conflicts and to employ defense mechanisms; however, individuals differ in the nature of their predominant impulses, rules, anxieties, and defense mechanisms.

Freud also postulated that people's impulses, anxieties, and defenses are determined in part by their biological development through five critical *psychosexual stages*: the oral, anal, phallic, latency, and genital stages. Individuals whose needs are not adequately met during each stage can become *fixated* (stuck) at that stage. Freud theorized that individuals' personalities were formed primarily during the first three psychosexual stages (oral, anal, and phallic), with fixation at any of the three stages producing characteristic personality types.

During the *oral stage* (birth to year 1), the mouth is the prime source of pleasurable sensations and the instinctual urges strive to receive oral gratification from sucking (and later biting) on a gratifying object (e.g., the breast). These oral needs are perceived as urgent and intense, yet the child is dependent upon others to provide objects for adequate oral gratification. Caregivers can be overindulgent or depriving, either of which is theorized to increase the likelihood of the child becoming fixated at this stage. Overindulgence is theorized to contribute to traits such as optimism, gullibility, cockiness, manipulativeness, and admiration, with such individuals directing their energies toward trying to maintain or repeat the gratifying conditions. Conversely, deprivation is associated with traits such as pessimism, suspiciousness, self-belittlement, passivity, and envy, with individuals subsequently directing their energies toward finding oral gratification that was insufficient earlier in their lives.

During the *anal* stage (18 months to 3 years), the anus and rectum are the prime sources of pleasurable sensations, with the actions of retaining and releasing feces being the primary foci. Children whose caregivers are perceived as excessively demanding or permissive may develop *anal personalities*. Excessively demanding or controlling care-givers are theorized to foster development of characteristics associated with excessive "holding-on" traits. Such individuals may tend to be constricted (emotions), stingy (money), stubborn (personal relations), orderly (environment), hygienic (dirt), and punctual (time). Overindulgent caregivers are theorized to contribute to development of individuals who "let go" whenever pressure builds. Such individuals are theorized to be: expansive (emotions), wasteful (money), acquiescent (personal relations), messy (environment), unhygienic (dirt), and tardy (time) (Fenichel, 1945). Aggressive aspects of this stage can lead to development of various psychological defenses, including *reaction formation* (doing the opposite of what one desires to do). Psychological problems associated with obsessive-compulsivity and paranoia are theorized to arise from conflicts at this stage.

After mastery of toilet training, children enter the *phallic* stage (3 to 6 years) during which the penis or clitoris is the prime source of pleasure. Children at this stage gain manual dexterity, become interested in their genitalia, and increase their frequency of masturbation. They also become curious about the opposite sex, with games of "doctor-patient" becoming relatively common. During this stage, children are theorized to develop intense sexual feelings for the parent of the opposite sex. The *Oedipal complex* refers to children's attraction to the opposite-sex parent and their corresponding fears of the same-sex parent. (Originally, boys' experiences were referred to as *Oedipal conflicts* and girl's experience as *Electra conflicts*.) Due to their fear of the same-sex parent, children eventually *sublimate* their sexual attraction for their opposite-sex parent into nonsexual love, identify with their same-sex parent, and develop erotic preference for the opposite sex. Difficulties with resolution of this stage are theorized to result in sexual identity problems potentially affecting relationships with individuals of the same and opposite sex (Wolman, 1968).

Following resolution of the Oedipal conflict, individuals enter the *latency* period that lasts from about 6 until puberty. During this time, the sexual instincts diminish and children are encouraged to channel their energies into school, friends, sports, and activities. Sexually related memories remain present and may influence subsequent personality development (Freud, 1924/1961).

Finally, the *genital* stage (puberty onwards) is characterized by an investment of one's energy into socially acceptable endeavors such as forming romantic relationships, friendships, preparing for a career, and recreational activities.

Among Freud's most controversial ideas were the *Oedipal complex* (the notion that boys desire to possess their mother sexually and to exclude their fathers), the *Electra complex* (the notion that girls desire their fathers sexually), and *penis envy* (the notion that girls blame their mothers for their lack of a penis and associated loss of self-esteem). The debates continue: Most therapists seem to believe the Oedipal and Electra complexes are products of Freud's fantasies; others, in the quiet of their offices, confirm the possibility that for many children the battle for the sexual love of the opposite-sex parent seems quite real. Gender-aware therapists tend to take issue with the penis envy idea, pointing instead to male privileges within most cultures.

Jungian Therapy

Carl Jung believed that people journey toward *individuation*—complete-ness and authenticity. This journey involves recognizing our limitations and admitting them to ourselves. Dream interpretation and other methods of accessing unconscious processes can direct the journey by clarifying problems. As stated by Jung: *"The serious problems of life, however, are never fully solved. If ever they should appear to be so, it is a sure sign that something has been lost. The meaning and purpose of a problem seems to lie not in its solution but in our working at it inces-santly. This alone preserves us from stultification and petrifaction"* (Carl Jung, quoted in Campbell, 1971, pp. 11–12).

Jung also theorized that there was a *collective unconscious* con-sisting of universally shared myths, symbols, motives, urges, fears, and potentials. *Archetypes* are patterns of behavior within the collective unconscious from which each individual may take. Although Jung described many archetypes, his most widely used are the persona, shadow, self, and anima and animus. The *persona* is the mask that indi-viduals wear, or the set of behaviors they engage in, in order to accom-plish what is expected in particular social relationships. Jung theorized that healthy people adapt to the demands of their environment, with the persona enabling them to keep their inner selves together while responding to the world around them. The *shadow* is the part of the psyche that we are unaware of and have difficulty accepting. Our shadow is often reflected in the characteristics of others that bother us the most (or "push our buttons"). These individuals may display characteristics of ourselves that we seek to keep from our conscious awareness (such as the desire for attention, expression of anger or sexuality, desire to steal or be lazy).

The process of individuation involves learning to recognize and understand one's dark side. The *self* is the central organizing archetype reflecting awareness of being—an internal embodiment of truth and wisdom that helps connect individuals with larger spiritual truths. The self is our source of meaning in life. *Anima* and *animas* are archetypes similar to the Chinese concepts of *yin* and *yang*, the feminine and masculine aspects of all humans.

Jung believed that people spend approximately the first half of life individuating—finding out who they are and jostling for position. The task for the second half of life is integrating—pursuing their calling and gifts, not wasting their energies where they do not fit or are not welcome, and developing the complementary aspects of their personalities (Singer, 1973). Jung also encouraged people to attend to *synchronicity*—coincidences that result in an enhanced sense of meaning for those involved (Marlo & Kline, 1998; Singer 1973). An example of synchronicity might be when the problems of clients strongly resemble the problems of their therapists.

Adlerian Therapy

Alfred Adler posited that *striving for superiority* is humans' core motive. This striving for completion and improvement encompasses and powers other human drives. Conversely, individuals' feelings of *inferiority* (or an *inferiority complex*) can emerge from actual physical impairments or from subjective psychological or social weaknesses. Feelings of inferiority can lead to efforts at *compensation*, *basic mistakes*, and the construction of *maladaptive goals*. Healthy people display *social interest*, seeking to contribute to the common welfare of humanity. Adler also attended to *birth order*—the role that individuals' position in the family constellation may play in their life expectations (i.e., *style of life*). For example, oldest children may be more likely to assume responsible roles yet fear being dethroned as the center of attention by others. Middle children may choose an ambitious approach, striving to surpass the older sibling, and the youngest child, never risking being dethroned, may be more likely to live the life of an entitled princess or prince (see

Adler, 1917, 1929/1964a, 1929/1964b; Ansbacher & Ansbacher, 1964; Dinkmeyer, Dinkmeyer, & Sperry, 1990).

Ego Psychology

Whereas Sigmund Freud focused on the *id* (instincts and conflicts over impulses), his daughter Anna Freud (1936) and her student Erik Erikson focused more on individuals' ego development. Hence, ego theories incorporate a focus on later developmental stages in addition to the earlier ones addressed by psychoanalytic theories. Issues such as identity, intimacy, ego integrity and defense mechanisms are commonly addressed. Erickson (1950) posited eight stages ("ages") of psychosocial development throughout the lifespan, each having a characteristic challenge (or "crisis"). These stages are outlined in Table 1.1.

Object Relations Therapy

Object relations therapy is based on theories concerned with the relationships between and among people and how the history of interpersonal relationships is transferred from past to present behavior (Bowlby, 1969, 1988; Kernberg, 1975, 1976; Klein, 1975; Mahler, 1968; Winnicott, 1965, 1971). The major person (object) in clients' history is their primary caregiver.

John Bowlby's *attachment theory* posits that the primary task of the caregiver-child relationship is for the child to learn how to be securely attached to another. This secure attachment provides a safe base from which the child can explore and develop. A securely attached child is also able to *separate and individuate*. Bowlby surmised that there are three major patterns of attachment: securely attached, anxious-resistant (arising from an ambivalent and alternating accepting/rejecting primary caregiver), and anxious-avoidant (arising from a rejecting an impoverished primary caregiver–child relationship).

Donald Winnicott (1965, 1971) is associated with influential concepts like transitional objects, the good-enough mother, and the true

> According to attachment theory, the primary task of the caregiver-child relationship is for the child to learn how to be securely attached to another. Secure attachment provides a safe base from which the child can explore and develop. A secure attachment allows a child to separate and individuate. Three patterns of attachment are: securely attached, anxious-resistant, and anxious-avoidant.

TABLE 1.1   Erickson's Eight Stages of Life

1.	Infancy *(trust versus mistrust).* Developing trust in their primary caregiver to meet their physical and emotional needs is the challenge. Anxiety and rage may be experienced if their needs are insufficiently met, creating a possible subsequent mistrust toward others and the world.
2.	Early Childhood (*autonomy versus shame and doubt*). Gaining control of one's bladder and bowel in particular and developing self-reliance in general are the challenges. Caregivers who criticize excessively or who foster dependence produce doubt and shame in the child. Such children are hesitant to explore and interact with their world and may have difficulties with independence.
3.	Preschool Age (*initiative versus guilt*). Directing their energies into creative and social activities encourages development of a sense of initiative and competence. Children who are not encouraged (or are discouraged) from making their own decisions may develop a sense of guilt about taking the initiative and tend to allow others to decide for them.
4.	School Age (*industry versus inferiority*). In contrast to Freud, who saw this period (latency) as a quiet time in personality development, Erickson viewed this as a critical period in the development of real-world competence. Individuals' tasks are to develop skills for success in school and work, to set and attain personal goals, and to form their gender-role identity. If they fail to develop this sense of industry, they are likely to feel inadequate and inferior. Erickson noted that some individuals may fail to develop a sense of industry due to external environmental factors that discriminate against them rather than due to unresolved internal conflicts.
5.	Adolescence (*identity versus role confusion*). Developing an integrated sense of self that is personally acceptable and distinct from others is the challenge. Individuals create educational and career goals and begin to consider the meaning of their lives. If not satisfactorily resolved, individuals may feel confused, inadequate, isolated, and indecisive.
6.	Young Adulthood (*intimacy versus isolation*). Having attained a sense of personal identity, the challenge of this stage is to develop close and meaningful relations with others. Individuals learn to share themselves with others on emotional, cognitive, moral, and sexual levels. Those with difficulties at this stage may experience isolation, loneliness, and alienation.
7.	Middle Age (*generativity versus stagnation*). The challenge for this stage of adulthood is to look beyond oneself (and immediate family) and develop concern for the betterment of others and the world. During this period individuals may seek to reconcile discrepancies between their dreams and actual accomplishments. Individuals who fail to develop a sense of productivity may experience stagnation and apathy.

8. Later Life (*integrity versus despair*). The challenge of this stage is to view oneself as having a worthwhile life, as having generally accomplished what one wanted, as having relatively few regrets, and as having knowledge worth sharing with others. Individuals who appraise their lives in less favorable ways may be prone to resentment, guilt, hopelessness, and despair.

and false self. *Transitional objects* (such as stuffed animals, baby blankets, and other symbolic objects) may assist infants (or adults) with moving from a state in which they believe they are the center of the universe and control all aspects of the world around them to an awareness of the existence and needs of others. For example, transitional objects can help infants cope with fears during times when their primary caregivers are absent (Winnicott, 1953). The *good-enough mother* (caregiver) refers to primary caregivers who adapt their parenting style to meet their infant's developmental needs. Such caregivers completely meet the infant's needs during early infancy and then gradually help the infant develop greater independence over time. Caregivers need to be "good enough" to meet the infant's basic needs but not so perfect that the infant never learns to tolerate frustration. Winnicott theorized that children whose needs are not adequately met may develop a *false self* due to being inadequately separated from their caregiver. In this case, children comply with what they believe is expected of them by their caregiver. Alternatively, children whose needs are adequately met develop a *true self* featuring a sense of spontaneity and realness that includes a clear distinction between the child and caregiver (St. Clair, 2000).

Self-Psychology

Heinz Kohut (1971, 1977, 1984) emphasized people's need for relationships that provide certain types of experiences during development. Called *selfobject* experiences, these experiences include mirroring, idealizing, and twinship, and they allow the individual to feel valued and admired. Growing infants benefit from feeling a sense of value and worth when their caregivers joyfully accept and celebrate their mini-achievements. Hence, *mirroring* selfobjects are caregivers who serve as mirrors of the child's potential and greatness. Such caregivers are in tune with the child's inner life and desire for normal grandiosity, and they communicate delight in the child's presence. Later in life, children look up to their caregivers as strong, powerful, and affirming persons who provide the safety, security, and freedom they need to explore the world. In *idealizing relationships*, the developing person identifies a goal and seeks to become like his or her ideal person. Thus, idealizing relationships help inspire and motivate people to strive toward a goal. Relationships in which the person feels that he or she and the other person are essentially the same (i.e., are like "twins") are called *twinship* (or "alterego") relationships. In twinship relationships, there is little perception of distance between the person and the "twin"; the relationship is perceived as vitalizing because one joins with another with whom one shares an affinity (Bedi & Matthews, 2003; Patton & Meara, 1992).

Sufficient positive selfobject experiences during infancy and childhood are theorized to facilitate formation of a strong, cohesive self—the core of one's personality and character. *Healthy narcissism* is associated with a strong, vital, cohesive self that strives with ambition and ideals toward the realization of a person's skills and talents. In contrast, *pathological narcissism* develops from a weak, vulnerable self that attempts to maintain self-cohesion and bolster self-esteem. Narcissistic rage (uncontrolled anger), often triggered by minor interpersonal slights is theorized to arise from extreme fear of being perceived as worthless. The rage serves to bolster a threatened and vulnerable self, providing a temporary sense of strength, cohesion, and self-esteem.

Psychodynamic Therapy Techniques

Psychodynamic approaches are generally described as *uncovering therapy*. They try to help clients bring the unconscious into consciousness. Increasing consciousness/awareness is the primary goal of therapy. As awareness is gained, the ego is strengthened as it becomes more able to manage intrapsychic conflicts. Behavior then becomes more based on reality, more effective, and less often based upon instinctual cravings (e.g., id), irrational guilt (e.g., superego), problematic archetypes, excessive striving for superiority, or problematic selfobjects. Frequently used techniques include:

> Psychodynamic techniques encourage the activation of self-observation to explore both here and now experiences as well as subconscious and unconscious ideas and feelings. As these ideas and feelings reach surface awareness they are integrated into daily life by repetitive working through.

- *Free association*. This is a basic psychodynamic technique designed to access clients' unconscious and subconscious dynamics. Clients are encouraged to "say whatever comes to mind"—to express their thoughts, feelings, and reactions regardless of their content.
- *Confrontation*. This involves addressing something the client may not want to accept or is minimizing. It may concern how the client is affecting others or an emotion the client appears to be avoiding.
- *Interpretation*. This involves using clients' statements and reactions to identify and give meaning to their wishes, needs, fears, resistance, and transferences. Done properly, an interpretation helps to make the unconscious conscious.
- *Dream analysis*. This is a process in which clients free-associate to elements of their dreams. Clients should be active collaborators in interpreting their dreams in order to avoid excessive speculation on the part of the therapist (Levy, 1990). Freud contended that dreams were the "royal road to the unconscious." Morning dream diaries are valuable additions to unconscious exploration as dreams are usually quickly forgotten.
- *Working through*. This involves repetitions of the *disruption-restoration process* that allow clients' sense of self to change and develop.

Behavioral and Cognitive Theories

Behavioral theory focuses on the how theories of learning apply to observable behaviors. Cognitive theory focuses on the role individuals' thoughts and beliefs have in altering perceptions, appraisals, and reactions to situations. Behavior therapy is based on behavioral theory and cognitive therapy is based on cognitive theory, although the latter includes many of the ideas and interventions used in behavior therapy. Together behavioral and cognitive therapies are considered the "second force" of counseling/therapy, with cognitive-behavioral therapy being a combination of these two approaches.

Behavioral Therapy

Behavioral therapy draws from several different learning theories and techniques. In general, learning principles and procedures derived from scientific investigation are employed. Behavioral therapy exercises usually progress from easier to harder, from simple to complex, and from less threatening to more threatening behaviors. Therapy goals are refined so that they are clear, concrete, and observable. Traditional behavior therapists focus only upon the observable, considering the mind to be an unknowable "black box."

Respondent Conditioning

In respondent conditioning (also referred to as *Pavlovian* or *classical* conditioning), responses are elicited from an essentially passive organism (see the learning theories of Pavlov, 1928, and Hull, 1943). Wolpe, the founder of systematic desensitization, stated that learning has occurred when "a response has been evoked in temporal contiguity with a given stimulus and it is subsequently found that the stimulus can evoke the response although it could not have done so before" (1973, p. 5). He added: "If the stimulus could have evoked the response before but subsequently evokes it more strongly, then, too, learning may be said to have occurred" (p. 5). In other words, individuals are assumed to have learned anxiety when a previously neutral stimulus produces anxiety or when it produces greater anxiety than it did before the classical conditioning occurred.

Anxiety plays a central role in many disorders treated with behavior therapy. Anxiety is associated with a cluster of *sympathetic nervous system* responses to a perceived threatening stimulus. These physiological responses typically include: increased pulse rate and blood pressure, greater muscle tension, dilation of the pupils, increased blood flow to large voluntary muscles, decreased blood flow to stomach and genitals, and reduced saliva production (dry mouth).

Behavior therapists believe that because anxiety about particular situations, places or things develops through conditioning, it can be unlearned through counterconditioning (see Eysenck, 1959; Lazarus, 1971; Wolpe, 1973). *Counterconditioning* is based on the concept that some responses inhibit and eventually replace classically learned responses. Counterconditioning is composed of two important elements. First, it is essential to identify a response that is incompatible with anxiety and that can be paired with the stimuli that evokes anxiety. Responses that activate the *parasympathetic nervous system* (e.g., relaxation, exercise, assertion, or sexual arousal) tend to inhibit anxiety. In defining *reciprocal inhibition* Wolpe stated: "If a response inhibiting anxiety can be made to occur in the presence of anxiety-evoking stimuli, it will weaken the bond between these stimuli and anxiety" (1973, p. 17). Second, it is helpful to start with stimuli that are low on a person's hierarchy of anxiety-producing stimuli. This is important because it is essential that the counterconditioning be sufficiently powerful to overcome the sympathetic anxiety response (i.e., start with "baby steps").

> Positive and negative reinforcement both tend to increase the likelihood of a behavior being repeated. Positive reinforcement occurs when a specific behavior is followed by provision of something desired. Negative reinforcement occurs when engaging in the behavior is followed by removal of something unpleasant. Conversely, punishment, the administration of an aversive consequence after an undesired behavior, tends to *reduce* recurrence of the behavior.

Operant Conditioning

In *operant (Skinnerian) conditioning*, behaviors that are followed by reinforcement are likely to increase, and behaviors not earning reinforcement (or that earn punishment) are likely to decrease. The two types of reinforcement—positive and negative—both tend to *increase* the likelihood of a behavior being repeated. *Positive reinforcement* occurs when a specific behavior is followed by provision of something desired (e.g., praise, food, money). In a *negative reinforcement* paradigm, engaging in the behavior is followed by removal of something unpleasant (e.g., cessation of criticism or nagging). *Punishment*, the administration of an aversive consequence after an undesired behavior, tends to *reduce* recurrence of the behavior. In general, effective punishment is immediate, salient, intense, and delivered in a calm manner. Demonstration and reinforcement of the desired adaptive behavior should accompany the use of punishment. Punishment tends to produce imprecise (and sometimes undesired) learning due to the recipient's desire to avoid the unpleasant experience. It is recommended that punishment be used only when options to shape behavior using positive reinforcement have been exhausted, and even then with caution (in other words, above all, do no harm).

Behavioral Therapy Techniques

Behavioral (or *functional*) *analysis* can be used to identify the ABCs: *antecedents* (the stimulus situations that cue the behavior), *behaviors* (the behavior), and *consequences* (the reinforcement contingencies that follow the behavior). A *behavior chain* refers to this A → B → C sequence and is the foundation for both understanding and modifying behavioral contingencies. Results of behavioral analyses typically specify three types of behavioral problems: *excesses* (in which behaviors occur too frequently), *deficits* (in which behaviors do not occur frequently enough), and *inappropriateness* (behaviors that most adults would consider inappropriate to the context in which the behavior was performed).

Contingency management refers to efforts to shape the consequences of behavior so that desired behaviors are reinforced (hence engaged in more frequently) and undesired behaviors are either unrewarded or punished (hence more likely to extinguish). *Shaping* refers to the process of reinforcing clients' successive approximations to the desired behaviors. *Modeling* involves the therapist (or someone else) demonstrating the behavior that the client is seeking to acquire. *Rehearsal* refers to practicing desired behavior (such as in therapy) to improve skills, gain feedback, receive reinforcement, and increase the likelihood of successful subsequent performance.

Interventions based on *exposure* present clients with their anxiety-provoking stimuli while seeking to alter the learned pairing of the stimuli with anxiety. Through repeated successful pairing of anxiety-producing stimuli with the counterconditioning response, the stimuli-anxiety conditioned response is diminished or extinguished. Interventions that involve exposure include: exposure therapy, systematic desensitization, flooding, and EMDR. Exposure also desensitizes clients to the physiological effects of anxiety by habituation.

Exposure therapy involves intentional, prolonged contact (exposure) with feared stimuli combined with active *response prevention* (blocking of the undesirable avoidance behaviors). In the short term, clients experience increased anxiety, but through the process of habituation they learn that the feared stimulus is not dangerous. *Emotional processing*

via exposure in post-traumatic stress disorder is theorized to allow clients to realize that: (a) anxiety
does not remain indefinitely in the presence of
feared situations or memories, (b) experiencing
anxiety does not result in loss of control, (c) being in
a safe situation that reminds them of the previously
experienced trauma is not dangerous, and (d) remembering trauma is
not the same as experiencing it again (Foa & Meadows, 1997).

> The ABC model describes the temporal sequence of antecedents, behaviors, and consequences that are examined with functional (or behavioral) analysis.

Systematic desensitization applies classical learning principles.
Clients learn relaxation training, develop an anxiety hierarchy, and
then engage in graded exposure to the feared situation. Clients
imagine or directly experience (*in vivo*) successively more anxiety-
producing stimuli while they simultaneously engage in a behavior
that interferes with anxiety. Through this process, clients gradually
and systematically become desensitized to the anxiety-arousing
stimuli (Wolpe, 1958). Wolpe theorized that in order to successfully
counter-condition the stimuli paired with anxiety, clients must learn
to relax voluntarily. *Relaxation training* is sometimes referred to as
"the aspirin of mental health"—it has broad beneficial properties and
little risk for adverse consequences. Relaxation training involves
helping clients learn to effectively relax their muscles and to release
tension and anxiety. Learning to relax can be facilitated by a variety
of techniques, including progressive muscle relaxation, guided
imagery, meditation, yoga, and biofeedback (e.g., Davis, Eshelman, &
McKay 1995; Jacobson, 1938). When clients can initiate self-calming
responses, they may feel more confident in their ability to proceed
with exposure to their feared stimuli. That said, research indicates
that the primary essential component in systematic desensitization is
exposure, and that relaxation is not essential for favorable outcome
(Yates, 1970). Potential reasons for including relaxation training in
therapy are that it may help strengthen the working alliance, provide
clients with a sense of mastery, and strengthen clients' willingness to
face fears.

Flooding refers to either actual (*in vivo*) or imaginal exposure to
intense anxiety-producing stimuli for extended periods of time. In
flooding, clients are prevented from engaging in their usual maladaptive coping strategies, and their anxiety gradually decreases on its own,
thereby weakening the link between the stimulus and anxiety. Exposure and response prevention (ERP) is a mainstay for the behavioral

treatment of obsessive-compulsive disorder. Clients are exposed to the feared stimulus (e.g., dirt in a waste basket) and then try to stop themselves from engaging in compulsive behavior that responds to the obsession, thereby desensitizing the anxiety that accompanies the obsessive thought.

EMDR (eye movement desensitization and reprocessing) is a form of exposure therapy designed to assist people in dealing with traumatic memories (Shapiro, 1995). During the desensitization phase, clients are instructed to visualize the traumatic image, pay attention to physical sensations, and visually track the therapist's finger as it is moved rapidly back and forth across the client's line of vision 12 to 24 times. Clients are then instructed to block out negative experiences momentarily, breathe deeply, and report what they are imagining, feeling, and thinking. However, controversies about both potential unique components and effectiveness of EMDR remain (e.g., Davidson & Parker, 2001; Sikes & Sikes, 2003).

Cognitive Therapy

The Greek philosopher Epictetus noted that people "are disturbed not by things, but by the views they take of them." The basic assumption of cognitive therapy is that people's thoughts about events, situations, and encounters influence how they react, behave, and feel. In other words, how organisms (O) appraise stimuli (S) is critical in determining their response (R)—hence, the S-O-R paradigm. Thus, in cognitive therapy, it is individuals' thoughts, beliefs, and behavior that are of critical importance. More specifically, cognitive therapists view emotional difficulties as associated with people's *irrational beliefs* (Ellis & Harper, 1997) or *dysfunctional automatic thoughts* (Beck, 1976, 1995).

People (e.g., clients) often view *activating events* (A) as causing their emotional *consequences* (C). This notion is akin to behavioral stimulus-response (S-R) theory, which specifies that a particular stimulus produces a particular response in the organism. However, in Ellis' and Beck's cognitive model, *activating events* (A) are stimuli that people appraise with their *beliefs* (B) or automatic thoughts, which determine their emotional *consequences* (C), or behaviors or physiological responses. (Note: The ABCs of cognitive therapy differ from those of behavior analysis described earlier.)

One way of considering the course of cognitive therapy is to follow clients' experiences. First, clients typically enter therapy because they are experiencing some form of relatively intense unpleasant emotions such as depression, anxiety and worry, guilt and shame, or extreme anger and hostility. These are the emotional consequences (C) that prompted clients to enter therapy. In addition, clients also will present problems that they are unable to solve on their own. Often the key to a cognitive conceptualization is to consider why a client has not been able to solve his or her problems in view of his or her entire life history (Sudak, 2006).

The therapist forms collaborative relationships with clients by educating them about their disorder and teaching the cognitive model. Therapists conceptualize the client from a synthesis of the knowledge of the client's experience, the cognitive model for a particular disorder, and a biopsychosocial and interpersonal history of the client's current and past experience. In the process of therapy, therapists share and refine the conceptualization with the client and partner with him or her to attain focused and measurable treatment goals. A specific tool that therapists use is to collaboratively identify dysfunctional thoughts and beliefs (dBs) or irrational thoughts and beliefs (iBs) that prompted clients to experience their emotional consequences (Cs). (See Table 1.2 for a list of common dysfunctional beliefs.)

At a deeper level, cognitive therapy considers dysfunctional beliefs as sharing a demanding and absolute way of thinking. Desires, preferences, and wants become essential, absolute needs that must be met. Four major categories of dysfunctional beliefs or cognitive distortions as defined by Ellis include: *demanding* ("I must, should, have to, need to"), *catastrophizing* ("It's awful, terrible, catastrophic"), *overgeneralizing* ("I'll *always* be a failure; I'll *never* make it"), and *copping out* ("*You* make me angry; *It* upsets me"). In essence, these dysfunctional beliefs have rigid, dogmatic demands at their core (e.g., "I absolutely *must* have this important goal unblocked and fulfilled!"). Further, overgeneralized and unrealistic conclusions follow from that line of thought. Individuals may then make *catastrophizing* inferences about what happens if access to their perfect goal is thwarted (Ellis & Harper, 1997). Beck's cognitive therapy considers the beliefs of a client as following from the developmental history and that these beliefs must be altered to maintain the long-term goals of treatment.

TABLE 1.2   Common Dysfunctional Beliefs

I need the love and approval of every significant person in my life.
I must be competent and adequate in all possible respects.
People (including me) who do things that I disapprove of are bad people who deserve to be severely blamed and punished.
It's catastrophic when things are not the way I'd like them to be.
My unhappiness is externally caused; I can't help feeling and acting as I do and I can't change my feelings or actions.
When something seems dangerous or about to go wrong, I must constantly worry about it.
It is better for me to avoid the frustrations and difficulties of life than it is for me to face them.
I need to depend on someone or something that is stronger than I am.
Given my childhood experiences and the past I have had, I can't help being as I am today and I'll remain this way indefinitely.
I can't help feeling upset about other people's problems.
I can't settle for less than the right or perfect solution to my problem.

Cognitive Therapy Techniques

Cognitive therapists seek to assist clients in becoming more conscious of maladaptive cognitions, to recognize the problematic impact of such thoughts, and to collaboratively replace them with more appropriate and adaptive thought patterns based on evidence. In addition a specific focus on maladaptive behaviors and compensatory strategies (e.g., avoidance) is employed in a flexible way as dictated by the client's conceptualization. The evaluation of maladaptive cognitive patterns includes: (a) evaluation of underlying thoughts and beliefs, (b) evaluation of evidence for thoughts and beliefs, (c) instruction about refuting or reframing dysfunctional thoughts and beliefs, (d) collaborative practice in recognizing and altering dysfunctional thoughts and beliefs, and (e) homework (such as thought records in which clients identify beliefs, challenge dBs, and successfully dispute dBs). Criteria for evaluating the functionality of cognitions may include asking oneself:

> Cognitive therapists assist clients to become more aware of maladaptive cognitions, to recognize the problematic impact of such thoughts, and to replace them with more appropriate and adaptive thought patterns.

- What is the evidence that supports or refutes this thought?
- How useful is it to think this way?
- Is this thought likely to lead to action that destroys my life or health?
- Is this thought likely to interfere with my creating the kind of life I want to lead and the kind of world I want to live in?
- What is the best, worst, or most likely outcome that will occur in this situation? If the worst happened, how would I cope?
- What would I tell a friend in this situation?

Cognitive therapy is problem-oriented, present-focused, and psychoe-ducational, with clients often being expected to engage in homework outside of therapy sessions. Research in cognitive therapy suggests that homework compliance correlates well with outcome (Burns & Spangler, 2000).

Summary

This chapter provided an overview of the first two "forces" of counseling and psychotherapy: (a) psychodynamic and (b) behavioral and cognitive approaches. Psychodynamic approaches include: psychoanalytic, Jungian, Adlerian, ego psychology, object relations, and self-psychology. In general, psychodynamic therapies assist clients in gaining greater conscious awareness of their intrapsychic dynamics and conflicts. Behavioral therapy is based on learning principles designed to help clients shape their behavior. Behavior therapists often employ behavioral analysis, contingency management, and exposure to feared stimuli. Cognitive therapy focuses on the role of clients' cognitions to their concerns, with clients being assisted in identifying and altering their dysfunctional beliefs and thinking patterns.

CHAPTER 2

Humanistic, Multicultural, and Systems Theories
Concepts and Techniques

*Theories to be useful must be [viewed] as tools to work
with rather than as banners to ride under.*
—Edward J. Shoben, Jr. (1962)

This chapter continues the discussion of counseling theories, concepts, and techniques begun in the preceding chapter. First humanistic theories, including: person-centered, gestalt/experiential, emotion-focused, existential, and interpersonal therapies are described. Second, multicultural theories, including multicultural, feminist, and gender-aware therapies, are discussed. Third, systems theories, including strategic, structural, and solution-focused therapies are examined.

Humanistic, Person-Centered, Gestalt/Experiential, Emotion-Focused, Existential, and Interpersonal Theories

The group of theories described in this section is considered the humanistic or "third force" therapy theories. This cluster is humanistic in that they focus on the individual client seeking to become an authentic person, responsibly confronting existential issues, gaining emotional awareness, and maintaining healthy interpersonal relationships.

Person-Centered Therapy

Person-centered therapy is based on Carl Rogers's view that people are inherently *self-actualizing*–moving "toward greater order, complexity, and interrelatedness" (Bohart, 1995, p. 123). However, growth is interfered with by *conditions of worth* outside of their awareness. Specifically, as children grow up and seek positive regard from others, they experience conflicts between their inner wishes and those of their caregivers. Children gradually internalize their caregivers' appraisals of them, thereby developing conditions of worth (beliefs like "I am worthy when I do what others expect of me"). However, these conditions of worth occasionally are incongruous with people's true inner selves. Hence, conflicts and discrepancies develop between people's conscious, introjected values (taken in from others as one's own) and their unconscious genuine values. As an example, a child growing up in a racist/homophobic community may experience criticism if he or she does not reflect the views of those around them. The child may introject (take in) the discriminatory views of others as his/her own, even though such views conflict with his/her unconscious appreciation of diverse people.

In the words of Rogers and Wallen (1946):

> Counseling . . . [is] a way of helping the individual help [the] self. The function of the counselor is to make it possible for the client to gain emotional release in relation to . . . problems and, as a consequence, to think more clearly and more deeply about . . . self and . . . situation. It is the counselor's function to provide an atmosphere in which the client, through . . . exploration of the situation, comes to see . . . self and . . . reactions more clearly and to accept (personal) attitudes more fully. On the basis of this insight, [the client] is able to meet . . . life problems more adequately, more independently, more responsibly than before. (pp. 5–6)

Person-Centered Therapy Techniques

The primary task for therapists is to provide the right type of therapeutic relationship for their clients. Rogers held that "if I can provide a certain type of relationship, the other person will discover within himself the capacity to use that relationship for growth, and change and personal development will occur" (1961, p. 33). Many of the basic therapeutic communication skills described in Chapter 3 are technical manifestations of the person-centered view. As summarized by Rogers (1961), effective therapy occurs when:

The therapist has been able to enter into an intensely personal and subjective relationship with the client—relating not as a scientist to an object of study, not as a physician expecting to diagnose and cure—but as a person to a person. It would mean that the therapist feels this client to be a person of unconditional self-worth; of value no matter what his condition, his behavior, or his feelings. It would mean that the therapist is genuine, not hiding behind a defensive facade, but meeting the client with the feeling the therapist is experiencing. It would mean that the therapist is able to let himself go in understanding this client; that no inner barriers keep him from sensing what it feels like to be the client at each moment of the relationship; and that he can convey something of his empathic understanding to the client. It means that the therapist has been comfortable in entering the relationship fully, without knowing cognitively where it will lead, satisfied with providing a climate which will permit the client the utmost freedom to be himself. (pp. 184–185)

> Person-centered theory provides the basis for most therapeutic approaches to the establishment of the working alliance. Most beginning therapists find person-centered approach to be a safe and reliable foundation from which to build their own theory and intervention repertoire.

In essence, Rogers (1957) believed that effective therapists need to create and communicate three *core conditions*–congruence, unconditional positive regard, and accurate empathy. *Congruence* refers to therapists' authenticity, genuineness, and transparency, with congruent therapists being real, open, and honest. *Unconditional positive regard* refers to therapists' communicating warm regard, acceptance, or respect to their clients. By therapists' accepting all of who they are, clients are presumed to be freer to explore who they really are and what they really want, with less interference from conditions of worth. *Accurate empathy* refers to therapists' perceiving the emotional and cognitive internal frame of reference as if they were the client. At deeper levels of empathy, Rogers mentioned "sensing meanings of which the client is scarcely aware" (1980, p. 142).

More recently, *motivational interviewing* arose from person-centered traditions (Miller & Rollnick, 1991, 2002). In part, motivational interviewing can be viewed as "a way of being with people" that emphasizes collaboration, evocation, and autonomy. *Collaboration* refers to therapists communicating a partnerlike relationship that involves exploration and support.

> Carl Rogers emphasized the value of three core therapeutic conditions—congruence, unconditional positive regard, and accurate empathy.

Evocation refers to therapists' role of eliciting or drawing out clients' intrinsic motivation to change. *Autonomy* refers to therapists' affirming clients' right and capacity for self-direction and facilitating informed choice (Miller & Rollnick, 2002, p. 34–35). Motivational interviewing appears especially useful for clients with little initial motivation to change, especially those with addictions and those who seem stuck in their current predicament.

Gestalt/Experiential Therapy

The German word *gestalt* means "whole." In the therapeutic sense, gestalt refers to helping individuals become aware of, integrate, and own their entire selves, including their previously disowned and devalued parts. Fritz Perls (1973) likened the process of developing a healthy personality to the process of peeling an onion. In Perls's view, individuals peel off five superimposed layers of neurotic growth disorders—the phony, phobic, impasse, implosive, and explosive—to attain psychological maturity. The *phony* layer consists of stereotypic and inauthentic interactions with others in which individuals play games as if they were people whom they are not. The *phobic* layer reflects individuals' fears about the pain of facing the parts of themselves with which they are dissatisfied. This layer also includes the fear that if one were to recognize who he or she really is, others will surely be rejecting. The *impasse* is the place where individuals are stuck in their maturation. At this "sick point," individuals believe that they have no chance of survival because they cannot find the means within themselves to move ahead due to the threat of withdrawal of environmental support. Thus, they fear moving ahead because they fear that they cannot survive on their own. In addition, people with neurotic traits opt not to move ahead because they find manipulating and controlling their environment for support easier than becoming self-reliant. The *implosive* layer is the deadness, nothingness, or catatonia associated with one's disowned parts. As the phony and inauthentic characters are shed, individuals are theorized to experience the *explosive* layer—a freeing of pain and joy that allows them to be authentically alive.

Perls believed that by giving up the constant struggle for control and gaining integration, people could live by the message conveyed in "The Gestalt Prayer." This poem begins with the now famous line *"I do my thing and you do your thing"* (Perls, 1973, inner cover). Although potentially beneficial in helping free clients from excessive concerns regarding others' judgments (conditions of worth), this poem has also been characterized as epitomizing the self-centered "me generation." More specifically, it has been criticized for minimizing the extent to which healthy individuals *do* have responsibilities beyond themselves. Maintaining healthy relationships and communities do at times involve effort and personal sacrifice to support the welfare of others (e.g., children, partners, extended family members, neighbors, community, and country). Hence, contemporary therapists seek to assist clients in balancing their individual wants and needs (individualism) with those of others (collectivism; Sue & Sue, 2003).

Numerous additional concepts are central to Gestalt therapy. One contribution of Gestalt therapy is its emphasis on the present moment. By helping individuals be more aware of the *here and now*, individuals also become more aware of their *unfinished business*—unresolved feelings, issues, and relationships from the past that interfere with effective contact with oneself and others in present life. Gestalt and experiential therapists also attend to where individuals' energy is located, how it is used, and how it is blocked within individuals. Blocked energy can also be a form of resistance. It can be manifested in a variety of ways including tension in a part of the body, shallow breathing, repetitive body movements, body posture, and restricted voice.

Gestalt/Experiential Therapy Techniques

Experiments are therapeutic activities offered to help clients gain fuller awareness, resolve dichotomies and inconsistencies, experience internal conflicts, and work through impasses preventing completion of unfinished business. Levitsky and Perls (1970) described several Gestalt/experiential exercises, including: the empty chair, exaggeration, staying with the feeling, and reversal. The classic Gestalt technique of the empty chair is described here to illustrate the approach; the other techniques are described in Chapters 6, 7, and 8.

The *empty chair* (internal dialogue) exercise is based on the notion that people tend to incorporate ("introject") aspects of others (parents, critical peers) into their ego system. The empty chair technique is a way of helping clients become more aware of toxic messages from others that they have come to hold as true of themselves. Therapists conduct the technique using two chairs. Clients are instructed to sit in one chair and to fully become the critical other ("topdog" or critical self), badgering with "shoulds" and "oughts" and manipulating with threats of catastrophe. Clients then move to the other chair and fully become the victim ("underdog" or experiencing self): passive, weak, helpless, apologetic, defensive, excuse-making, emotional, needy, desiring and without responsibility. Moving back and forth between chairs (and poles of personality) provides greater awareness of introjects, conflicts, and fears, with the aim of furthering acceptance and integration of the whole person. This method can be used to clarify other internal polarities and help resolve unfinished business with others.

Emotion-Focused Therapy

Emotion-focused therapy (EFT) emphasizes the centrality of emotions in people's experience of distress and in therapy (Greenberg & Johnson, 1988; Johnson & Greenberg, 1994, 1995). EFT emerges from earlier Gestalt/experiential therapy and incorporates attachment theory (described later in the interpersonal therapy section of this chapter). EFT specifies four processes through which change in emotion occurs. The first process is clients' gaining awareness and acceptance of their feelings. The second process incorporates "regulation" into the process of healing, as clients must learn to tolerate those emotions and control any self-destructive behaviors that seriously interfere with their daily lives. Clients learn healthy methods of coping with their feelings, and how to prevent emotions from flowing out of control. The third process is transformation, and the final process is reflection. Initial studies of EFT are promising, particularly in the area of couple and marital concerns (see Chapter 14).

Emotion-Focused Therapy Techniques

Serving as an "emotional coach," therapists seek to enhance client's adaptive emotional processing. Beyond instruction in emotional skill acquisition, emotional coaching involves empathy. This empathy conveys understanding and promotes the discovery of new meaning, allowing clients to discuss and tolerate previously unexperienced or avoided feelings. Through expressing denied emotions, clients make positive behavioral changes. Clients are also assisted in identifying whether particular emotions are adaptive or maladaptive, and how to facilitate identification of beliefs that block their process of change. Change is facilitated when adaptive and beneficial emotions are accessed and integrated into daily life. Thus, a key technique of emotion-focused therapy is to leverage adaptive emotion to facilitate change. Specific emotion-focused techniques are discussed in greater detail in Chapter 7.

> Emotion-focused therapy seeks to enhance clients' adaptive emotional processing. Therapists convey deep understanding and promote discovery of new meaning, with clients being able to discuss and tolerate previously unexperienced or avoided feelings. Through expressing denied emotions, clients make positive behavioral changes.

Existential Therapy

Early existentialists (such as Soren Kierkegaard, Friedrich Nietzsche, Jean-Paul Sartre, Martin Heidegger, José Ortega y Gasset, Karl Jasper, Gabriel Marcel) wrote more than a century ago, and yet their concepts remain fitting today. They were concerned with rediscovering the living person amid the compartmentalization and dehumanization of modern culture. In the context of therapy, existential perspectives aim to understand the person in his or her world and to grapple with the conflicts produced by the ultimate concerns of life.

Existential concepts include the "I-am" (ontological) experience. This idea suggests that individuals will be victimized by others and circumstances until each realizes that "I am living, and I am responsible for my life." Another concept is "being-in-the-world" (Dasein), referring to the notion that the person and his or her phenomenal perspectives are inseparable. The person is aware of self and can make decisions. The person *has to be,* and thus has to choose, and has to make meaning out of nothingness. Choosing may entail *guilt* because some choices do not get made which results in failure to live up to one's expectations. For example, people may choose to live as conventional conformists; such individuals may experience guilt for "sinning against themselves" by missing the opportunity to live more authentically.

Anxiety arises from the personal need to survive, to preserve our being, and to assert our being (May, 1977). Existential perspectives differentiate normal anxiety from neurotic anxiety. As described in greater detail in Chapter 12, normal anxiety is proportionate to the situation confronted, does not involve repression, and can stimulate us to address the situation that triggered anxiety. In contrast, neurotic anxiety is not appropriate to the threat, may be repressed, and can be destructive. Existential perspectives do not aim to do away with anxiety, but rather minimize neurotic anxiety and enhance individuals' ability to tolerate the unavoidable existential anxiety of living.

Existential Conflicts and Ultimate Concerns

Existential conflicts and ultimate concerns include death, freedom, responsibility, isolation, and meaninglessness.

- *Death*. Conflict between awareness of death's inevitability and our wish to continue to live.
- *Freedom*. Conflict between groundlessness and our wish for grounding. "Human beings are condemned to freedom" (Sartre).
- *Responsibility*. People differ in the amount of responsibility they are willing to take for their own life situation.
- *Isolation*. Conflict is the tension between awareness of our isolation and our wish for contact and protection. Individuals must deal with the awareness that no matter how closely we relate to others, we are alone. We enter and leave the world alone.
- *Meaninglessness*. Conflict is the dilemma of being a meaning-seeking creature thrown into a world without meaning (Yalom, 1980). What possible meaning can life have? Why do we live? How shall we live? Individuals must create their own meaning in life. Can we do it? Do we merely succumb to accepting messages fed to us by our culture and advertising (e.g., meaning is earning enough money to buy marketed products)?

As May stated: "Life is not superficial. . . . How are you able to live in a world where we are all alone, where we all die?" (Rabinowitz, Good, & Cozad, 1989, p. 439).

Yalom (1980) described two psychological defense mechanisms individuals use to reduce their anxiety about the ultimate concerns, particularly about death.

> *Existential conflicts* and *ultimate concerns* include: death, freedom, responsibility, isolation, and meaninglessness.

- *Belief in existence of an ultimate rescuer.* Individuals may believe that there is a personal omnipotent servant (e.g., God) who eternally guards and protects our welfare. Individuals may seek to shore up this defense by "living for the dominant other" (Arieti, 1977, p. 864) via obedience, appeasement, dependency, passivity, or searching. In contrast to the Freudian view that basic human drives create anxiety that leads to psychological defenses, existentialists believe that awareness of the ultimate concerns creates anxiety that leads to psychological defenses (May, 1977; Yalom, 1980).

> Existentialism emphasizes the unique individuality of each person while also teaching us that ultimately we are each alone in the universe. The search for personal meaning can help to reduce the sense of isolation, despair, and fear of death.

- *Belief in personal specialness.* Individuals may seek to believe that they are unique and special. They defy the laws of biology that apply to others. They might think, "Bad things may happen to others, but not to me. I am invulnerable!"

Existential Therapy Techniques

The primary objective of the existential therapist is to understand the client as a being in the world. Via engaging the client in authentic interpersonal encounters, the therapist and client may become aware of ways in which the client seeks to avoid these real encounters (e.g., avoid responsibility). For example, a client might persist in responding in a passively compliant way, instead of as a free person participating in an authentic "I-Thou" encounter. Thus, rather than using techniques, existential therapists seek to aid clients in identifying their unconscious existential conflicts, maladaptive defense mechanisms, and damaging consequences. Therapists then assist clients in altering their restrictive ways of enacting themselves and of interacting with others, thereby reducing secondary anxieties and gaining greater responsibility and freedom in their lives.

Interpersonal Therapy

Interpersonal therapy arose from the interpersonal approaches of Harry Stack Sullivan (1953, 1972) and Adolf Meyer (1957), the attachment research of John Bowlby (1969, 1973, 1976), and the sociological theory of George Herbert Mead (1934). Although not everyone would view it as falling under humanistic theory, the numerous variations of interpersonal

> People tend to elicit predictable responses from others, although they may not be the types of responses that they desire. Interpersonal therapy focuses altering these undesired responses from others.

therapy focus on improving individuals' current interpersonal relationships and life situations.

Key concepts of interpersonal therapy include the principle of interpersonal *complementarity*—the notion that people in dyadic interactions negotiate the definition of their relationship using verbal and nonverbal cues (Carson, 1969; Kiesler, 1983; Wiggins, 1982). *Circular causality* refers to patterns in which individuals continually affect and are affected by others through their interactions. The concept of *reinforcing systems* describes how individuals' interpersonal behavior elicits restricted classes of self-sustaining behaviors from their interactional partners (Carson, 1969).

Introduced by Harvard professor and subsequent LSD experimenter Timothy Leary (1957), the *interpersonal circle* is based on the idea that correspondence tends to occur along the *Affiliation* (horizontal) axis and reciprocity tends to occur along the *Power* (vertical) axis (see Figure 2.1). On the hostile-to-friendly (Affiliation) axis, individuals' hostile responses elicit hostile responses from others, and friendly responses elicit friendly responses from others. However, on the dominant-to-submissive (Power) axis, dominant responses tend to elicit submissive responses, and submissive behaviors tend to elicit dominant responses (Kiesler, 1983; Leary, 1957, 1982).

Interpersonal therapists generally view relationship problems as arising from and being exacerbated by automatic, rigid styles of communicating that elicit inadvertent, unwished-for responses from others. Hence, therapists using interpersonal therapy ideas tend to closely examine communication patterns and assist clients in expanding their interpersonal repertoire of behaviors, balancing selective affiliation, interpersonal flexibility, and a sharing of responsibility in their current relationships.

Klerman and colleagues developed a specific version of interpersonal therapy (IPT) that seeks to integrate knowledge of the profound impact of early developmental experiences on later interpersonal relations while emphasizing "here and now" interpersonal relations and environmental stressors (Klerman, Weissman, Rounsaville & Chevron, 1984; Klerman & Weissman, 1993).

IPT has evidence supporting its effectiveness in the treatment of some forms of depression for which it was first developed. It involves three phases of treatment typically occurring over 12 to 16 sessions.

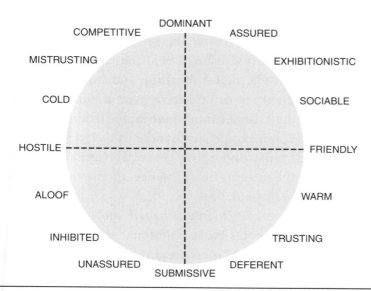

FIGURE 2.1   The Interpersonal Circle (Kiesler, 1983; figure from Gurtman, 1997). Reprinted with permission.

Phase 1. The initial phase of IPT has four broad components: (1) therapists review clients' symptoms, name the syndrome, assign clients the "sick role," and evaluate clients needs for psychotropic medications; (2) clients' problems are related to the interpersonal context by assessing the nature of the interactions, assessing the nature of significant others' expectations and whether these are being fulfilled, and identifying the nature of the changes that clients desire in their relationships; (3) the major problem areas associated with clients' syndromes are identified; and (4) IPT concepts and the therapeutic contract are explained.

Phase 2. The intermediate phase directly addresses clients' primary interpersonal problem areas: grief, role transitions, role disputes, or interpersonal deficits. Clients often have a number of problem areas. Although all problem areas are noted, IPT only addresses one or two of the most troubling problems due to time restrictions.

Phase 3. In the termination phase, progress is reviewed, remaining work is summarized, and clients' feelings about termination are discussed. As an intentionally brief therapy, IPT adheres to explicit arrangements for termination.

Interpersonal Therapy Techniques

Reparative relationship (positive working alliance) refers to helping clients improve their ability to form healthier interpersonal relationships and attachments via the establishing and experiencing of such a relationship with their therapist. *Corrective emotional experience* means "to reexpose the patient, under more favorable circumstances, to emotional situations which he could not handle in the past. The patient, in order to be helped, must undergo a corrective emotional experience suitable to repair the traumatic influence of previous experiences" (Alexander & French, 1946, p. 66).

Monitoring and responding to interpersonal "pulls." As part of interpersonal complementarity, clients evoke emotional and behavioral responses from therapists. By monitoring these responses, therapists experience the kinds of responses clients are likely to be eliciting from significant others. These here-and-now responses can be used to clarify and change the client behavior that elicits these responses (Kiesler, 1983).

Multicultural Theories

Initially, counseling and therapy were envisioned as providing universal solutions suitable to all individuals' psychological problems. However, it has become increasingly clear that therapy, like the individuals it serves, is inextricably culture-bound (Wohl, 1989). Clients develop their sense of themselves, their style of coping and interacting, and their perceptions of their life options within their cultural environment context. Similarly, therapists develop their sense of mental health, appropriate coping strategies, and acceptable interventions within *their* societal and cultural environments. Multiculturalism, viewed as the "fourth force" in therapy, arose from the awareness that therapists need to address culture, race/ethnicity, gender, acculturation, class, affectional preference, ability/disability, and spirituality in their therapeutic work with clients (e.g., Good & Brooks, 2005; Pederson, 1991; Sue & Sue, 2003; Worrell & Remer, 2003).

Although numerous theories describe factors associated with human development, Bronfenbrenner's (1979, 1989, 1994) ecological model of development is one of the more comprehensive (see Figure 2.2). This model views individuals as being at

> Multicultural perspectives equip therapists to address culture, race/ethnicity, gender, acculturation, class, affectional preference, ability/disability, and spirituality in their therapeutic work with clients.

the center of a series of concentric circles. The elements in each circle influence the circles inside it. Individuals—initially consisting of their biological makeup—are most directly influenced by their immediate environment (home, family, peers, and colleagues). The immediate environment is influenced by the social and economic context. For example, the home environment is influenced by the makeup of the neighborhood, including such factors as crime and neighborhood resources. Families are influenced by such factors as whether parents are able to find work permitting frequent contact with their children and the degree that parents feel satisfied with their work. The social and economic context is influenced by the cultural context—the beliefs, values, and guidelines that people in a particular society tend to share. Individuals interact with these contexts as part of a system: Individuals act on the context while the context acts on individuals. Thus, all the contexts interact with one another.

Multicultural Therapy

Multicultural counseling and therapy (MCT) arose from the awareness that there is no single model for a healthy personality. Each culture has

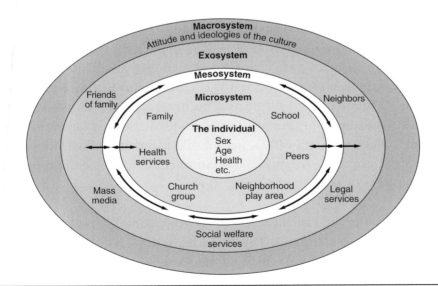

FIGURE 2.2   Bronfenbrenner's Ecological Model (Santrock, 2001, p. 83). Reprinted with permission.

its own norms, rituals, and expectancies that shape individuals and groups. In this sense, culture is defined broadly—including not just race and ethnicity but also gender, affectional orientation, age, and ability status. Like feminist therapists, mental health professionals recognized that early therapeutic theories included inherently ethnocentric values and biases (e.g., APA, 1991, 1993, 2000; Fabrega,1992). For example, excessive emphasis on individualism, rationalism, and self-determination reflect Eurocentric biases (Sue & Sue, 1999, 2003). Asian cultures may emphasize interdependence and filial piety, in which children are expected to subordinate their wishes for the needs of their family. Similarly, African-Americans may emphasize "groupness" and collective survival (Parham, White, & Ajamu, 1999). This notion is reflected in the Afrocentric idea "I am because we are; and because we are, therefore I am" (Mbiti, 1970, p. 141; Cheatham, 1990, p. 375).

As stated by Sue and Torino (2005):

> Multicultural counseling and therapy can be defined as both a helping role and process that uses modalities and defines goals consistent with the life experiences and cultural values of clients, recognizes client identities to include individual, group, and universal dimensions, advocates for the use of universal and culture-specific strategies and roles in the healing process, and balances the importance of individualism and collectivism in the assessment, diagnosis, and treatment of clients and client systems. (p. 6)

There are several major tenants of MCT. One is that clients' (and therapists') identities are formed on multiple levels of experience (e.g., individual, group, and universal) and context (individual, family, and cultural). Sue and Sue's (2003, pp. 12–13) tripartite model of personal identity development (Figure 2.3) illustrates this point using three concentric circles of personal identity:

- Individual level (in which all individuals are, in some respects, unlike other individuals)
- Group level (in which all individuals are, in some respects, like some other individuals)
- Universal level (in which all individuals are, in some respects, like all other individuals)

Additionally, the totality of experiences and contexts is a central focus of treatment. Cultural identity development is an important determinant of clients' and therapists' attitudes toward the self, others of the same group, others of a different group, and the dominant group.

Multiculturally-aware therapists possess competencies associated with three broad dimensions (Sue & Sue, 2003; Sue et al., 1982; Sue, Arrendondo, & McDavis, 1992). These dimensions are outlined in Table 2.1.

Models of identity can be useful tools for increasing therapists' knowledge, attitudes, and skills for working with diverse clients. Presentation of a general model of cultural identity development, and of a specific White/European-North American therapist identity development model follows.

Broadly stated, the premise of *cultural identity models* is that individuals have varying conceptions and levels of awareness of their cultural identities (e.g., ethnic/racial, gender, affectional preference, age, ability status). It is important that therapists be knowledgeable, aware, and skilled in interacting with clients in matters that pertain to the salient identity(-ies).

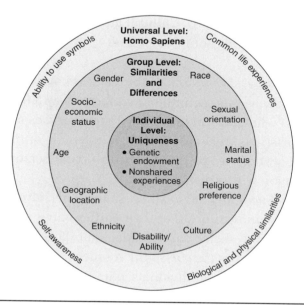

FIGURE 2.3   Tripartite Personal Identity Development Model (Sue & Sue, 2003, p. 12). Reprinted with permission.

TABLE 2.1   Dimensions of MCT Competencies

Knowledge of the manner in which "race, culture, ethnicity, and so forth may affect personality formation, vocational choices, manifestations of psychological disorders, help-seeking behaviors, and the appropriateness or inappropriateness of counseling approaches" (Sue, Arrendondo, & McDavis, 1992, p. 485). This dimension also emphasizes the need for therapists to understand how factors associated with discrimination and racist attitudes affect clients, therapists, and therapeutic encounters.

Attitudes/beliefs pertaining to the need for therapists to gain awareness of their racial/ethnic heritage, cultural attitudes, values and biases, and how they influence processes and interactions in therapeutic relationships with minority or dominant group members.

Skills that allow therapists to translate their knowledge and attitudes/beliefs into culturally appropriate interventions reflecting sensitivity to clients' experiences and values.

Racial/ethnic identity, gender-related identity, and affectional preference theories provide various models of cultural identity development (Bargad & Hyde, 1991; Cass, 1984; Cross, 1971; Fischer et al., 2000; Helms, 1990, 1995; Jackson, 1975; Jackson & Hardiman, 1983; Meyers et al., 1991; Sue & Sue, 2003). Cultural and gender-related development models generally include some version of:

> *Stage 1. Naïveté/Conformity*. Individuals have little awareness of themselves as cultural beings (e.g., as an African-American, as a white person of European ancestry; as a Buddhist, Christian, Muslim, or a Jew; as a female or male; as a heterosexual, gay, bisexual, or transsexual person; or as a person with a disability, etc.).
>
> *Stage 2. Encounter/Dissonance*. Individuals have an experience that demonstrates that their earlier naïve views of themselves and society were inadequate. This is sometimes referred to as *the click*—the moment when people gain initial awareness. Individuals' naming of the cultural problem can be transformative.
>
> *Stage 3. Immersion*. At this stage, individuals become keenly aware of a central aspect of their cultural identity—such as racism, sexism, homophobia, or able-ism. Individuals may

feel significant anger toward those viewed as cultural aggressors. For majority culture members, this stage is challenging, as aspects of themselves and their culture are viewed negatively by those who have been harmed.

Stage 4. Introspection/Reflection on Self as a Cultural Being. Individuals develop a greater awareness and valuing of what it means to be a member of their subculture. Their focus is on developing a consciousness of their culture, with the majority culture often being of little relevance.

Stage 5. Integrative Awareness. Individuals develop pride in themselves and awareness of others. They have access to the important aspects of the other developmental stages. They recognize and accept worthwhile aspects of the dominant culture and oppose those aspects that are racist, sexist, homophobic, ageist, ablistic, and otherwise discriminatory or oppressive. They are able to view the world through multiple frames of reference (i.e., through the eyes of others).

The White/European-North American, heterosexual (dominant culture) therapist identity development theory is particularly useful for majority culture therapists working with clients from other cultures (Helms, 1985; Ponterotto & Pederson, 1993). This model helps therapists anticipate ways in which their understanding of the world, clients, problems, and therapeutic processes may be culture-bound as outlined below:

Stage 1. Preexposure. Therapists at this stage have not considered therapy as a multicultural phenomenon. They may engage in racism and sexism without awareness, or they may try to treat all clients the same under the mistaken belief that "people are just people."

Stage 2. Exposure. When therapists learn about cultural differences, discrimination, and oppression, they may become confused or unsettled by the incongruities and incompleteness of their previous training.

Stage 3. Defensiveness or Zealotry. Therapists respond to the challenges of multiculturalism in various ways. Some therapists may get angry, some may be quietly defensive, some may be passive recipients of information, some may withdraw into the predictability of their culture, and some will become active proponents of multiculturalism.

Stage 4. Integration. Therapists acquire respect for and awareness of cultural differences. Therapists gain greater appreciation for personal, familial, and cultural histories, and how these may affect therapeutic work. Therapists recognize that they cannot know all aspects of MCT and make plans for lifelong learning.

Multicultural Therapy Techniques

At this point, MCT reflects highly diverse approaches to therapeutic techniques. Thus, therapists seeking to use MCT to optimally accommodate the needs of diverse clients face both challenges and opportunities. Nonetheless, the importance of MCT to the provision of effective therapy is likely to increase as individual countries and the world becomes increasingly global and multicultural. The key technique is an attitude toward seeking to understand and accept the cultural variations that are influencing each client's difficulties and the ways in which therapeutic interventions may build upon endowed cultural strengths.

Feminist and Gender-Aware Therapies

Gender roles are patterns defined by a particular culture as masculine or feminine. Conceptions of appropriate gender roles are deeply imbedded in the fabric of society. Individuals' acquisition of particular gender role patterns transpires primarily via social learning during their upbringing. Hence, societal expectations begin shaping children's gender-related beliefs from the moment they enter the world and may profoundly influence psychosocial development over the lifespan (Bem, 2003; Good, Wallace, & Borst, 1994; Meth & Pasick 1992). During adolescence and by adulthood, beliefs about appropriate gender-related behaviors are typically deeply ingrained. Through culture-specific *gender socialization*, girls often learn that they should be nice, emotionally expressive, considerate of others, and interpersonally sensitive. Concurrently, girls usually receive *gender-linked messages* that they are valued for their physical appearance and attractiveness (Worrell & Remer, 2003). Boys

> Both clients and their therapists have unique cultural identities. Multiculturally-sensitive therapists seek to be aware of their own cultural background, cultural identity, and gender identity, and also seek to acquire an understanding of other cultural backgrounds and the stages of cultural and gender-related identities.

typically receive gender-linked messages that they are expected to be competitive, stoic, instrumentally successful, and physically tough. Boys also learn to view women's bodies as objects for their pleasure and to avoid exhibiting characteristics potentially associated with girls or gays (Brannon & David, 1976; Good et al., 1994; Good & Sherrod, 2001; Levant & Pollack, 1995; Mahalik, Locke et al., 2003; Mahalik, Good, & Englar-Carlson, 2003; O'Neil, 1981). Girls and boys or women and men who deviate from their culture or peer group's conceptions of appropriate gender roles risk being shamed, ridiculed, humiliated, ostracized, assaulted, or even killed (Good & Brooks, 2005; O'Neil, Good, & Holmes, 1995; Perez, DeBord, & Bieschke, 2000; Worrell & Remer, 2003).

Along with biological factors, *gender socialization* affects the types of problems individuals experience. Girls and women are more likely to acknowledge depression, anxiety, phobia, obsessive-compulsivity, and eating disorders (primarily internalizing disorders), whereas boys and men are more likely to report alcohol and drug abuse, conduct disorders, and antisocial disorders (primarily externalizing disorders) (Mahalik, Good & Englar-Carlson, 2003). However, when men's higher rate of substance abuse and antisocial behavior is included, women and men have comparable rates of psychological distress. Gender socialization also affects people's willingness to use mental health services (Addis & Mahalik, 2003; Good & Wood, 1995). In the U.S., women seek psychological services approximately twice as often as men. Conversely, men are approximately twice as likely to end up in the correctional system (perhaps in part due to externalizing their distress into substance abuse, violence, and other antisocial activities) (Addis & Mahalik, 2003).

Feminist therapy arose during the late 1960s and 1970s from awareness of societal and mental health injustices that disadvantaged women, ethnic, and sexual minorities. For example, the methods for creating diagnostic criteria and categories in early editions of the *Diagnostic and Statistical Manual of Mental Disorders* (*DSM* published by the American Psychiatric Association Press) were found to overvalue masculine gender-linked traits of autonomy and emotional control and to excessively pathologize feminine gender-linked traits such as emotional expression and interpersonal connection (American Psychological Association, 1979; Caplan, 1991; Kaplan, 1983a, 1983b; Nikelly, 1996). Similarly, discrimination and diagnostic biases against gay, lesbian and bisexual individuals began improving when the American Psychiatric

Association removed homosexuality from its list of mental disorders in 1973. Feminist therapists also sought to raise awareness of women's issues (such as domestic violence, sexual assault and harassment) and to increase awareness of power issues in therapy and society (Worrell & Remer, 2003).

Gender-aware therapy (GAT) was developed to integrate knowledge of gender with feminist therapy techniques to facilitate clients' development through exploration of their unique gender-related experiences (Good, Gilbert, & Scher, 1990). Five principles of GAT include:

- Regarding conceptions of gender as integral aspects of counseling and mental health
- Considering clients' problems within their societal context
- Actively seeking to change gender injustices experienced by women and men
- Emphasizing development of collaborative relationships
- Respecting clients' freedom to choose

Key concepts of feminist and gender-aware therapies include consciousness raising and informed choice. *Consciousness raising* involves therapists helping clients understand their problems within the context of their gender-role socialization experiences and how their concerns may be associated with the gender-related beliefs of society. This may include exploration of socialization experiences or messages (*gender-role analysis*). For example, individuals who have learned to attend excessively to others' needs without recognizing their own needs may be assisted in understanding this dynamic within the context of gender-linked messages and societal expectations they experienced. Similarly, individuals who have learned to be unaware of their emotional experiences or to avoid forming close relationships with others may be assisted in understanding these dynamics within the context of messages and expectations they experienced. Via these methods, gender-aware approaches can assist clients in better understanding how gender-role expectations can restrict, devalue, and harm individuals and groups through everyday sexist events (*micro aggressions*). Previously personalized dysfunctional beliefs can be appropriately located within the context of harmful and conflicting messages within society by exploring the roots of shame, humiliation, blame, or guilt. The notion of *informed choice* refers to therapists' helping clients increase their awareness of self and self-in-society. Consequently, therapists support clients in expanding their options and in making informed choices to improve their lives.

Feminist and Gender-Aware Therapy Techniques

Feminist and gender-aware therapy techniques are based on the following principles.

- Collaborative and egalitarian therapeutic relationships. To the greatest extent possible, feminist and gender-aware therapists seek to develop egalitarian relationships with their clients. Power imbalances are minimized and clients are encouraged to recognize their power to shape their therapeutic experiences and their lives.
- Empowerment. As they become aware of their situation in its sociopolitical context, aware of their options, and aware of the likely consequences of their choices, clients can develop the skills and confidence to successfully enact their choices. Skill development (e.g., assertiveness, emotional awareness) helps clients reach their goals and may produce greater options and role flexibility for others. In this sense, the personal is political.
- Psychoeducational interventions. Therapists readily share information with clients. Therapists are expected to have knowledge of issues with which their clients are struggling and to provide resources and consultation with their clients about them (e.g., see Chapter 10 for an overview of psychoeducational interventions).

System Theories

Many individual therapies described earlier (e.g., psychodynamic cognitive, behavioral) are also represented in theories of couple, marital, and family therapy. However, the need for additional theories, terms, and techniques arises when therapists are working with more than one individual in therapy or with problems based in couple or family systems. This section will briefly introduce, strategic, structural, and solution-focused theories and techniques. Greater detail regarding additional systems theory concepts and techniques is provided in Chapter 14 (Couple, Marital, and Family Therapy).

Couples, marriages, and families are systems. Systems are more than just the sum of their individual components. Hence, couples and families are more than just the sum of the individual family members. More specifically, members of a system are interconnected (affect one another) and have varying boundaries between one another (e.g., characteristic ways in which they interact, control, and influence one another). Systems also have homeostatic mechanisms—self-monitoring mechanisms that resist change (Jackson, 1957)—with family rules reflecting inferred patterns of interaction that maintain the homeostasis (Jackson, 1965a).

Strategic, structural, and solution-oriented therapies arise from system theories. In general they are characterized by: (a) a relatively high level of therapist activity, (b) the establishment of specific but limited goals, (c) early, directive interventions, (d) the identification and maintenance of a clear focus therapy, and (e) a relatively shorter duration of therapy (Bloom, 2000).

Strategic Therapy

Not surprisingly, *strategic* therapy focuses on innovative strategies for achieving clients' goals (Simon, Stierin, & Wynne, 1985). Problems with individuals and families are viewed as being expressions of dysfunctional organizational patterns within the family. Strategic therapists see themselves as aggressive change agents (Goldsmith, 1986; Haley, 1973, 1987). Hence, strategic therapists might think, "These clients came here to change; I am going to change them." The *goals* of strategic therapy are generally phrased in concrete, behavioral terms and are sequenced in a manner to facilitate other therapeutic aims (Bodin, 1981).

Strategic Therapy Techniques

Rather than emphasizing collaborative relations with clients, strategic therapists often provide innovative directives and expect clients to carry them out. Based on the power of the therapist and the degree of anticipated client motivation or resistance, interventions may be either straightforward or paradoxical. In successful paradoxical interventions, the therapist changes the client (or system dynamics) by providing an explanation or task that produces change for reasons which differ from those the therapist provided the client(s) (paradoxical interventions and caveats are described in greater detail in Chapters 7 and 8).

> Structural, strategic and solution-focused therapies typically involve: the identification and maintenance of a clear therapeutic focus, establishment of specific but limited goals, a high level of therapist activity, and a shorter duration of therapy.

Structural Therapy

The word "structure" in the name structural family therapy refers to repetitive patterns of communication and interaction within family systems (Minuchin, 1974; Minuchin & Fishman, 1981). Thus, in structural family therapy at least as much attention is accorded to the patterns of interactions (how familial interactions occur) as is given to the content of the interaction (what they talk about). The general assumption is that positive change occurs through shifts in patterns of interaction among family members (and important people outside the family). To create these positive structural changes, therapists must be familiar with dysfunctional patterns in family transactions. Common structural problems include detouring spousal conflict through a child, cross-generational coalitions, and weak generational boundaries.

Structural family therapy also emphasizes the importance of assessing how families avoid or resolve conflicts, particularly when disagreements occur between the adults, such as mother and father, or parent and grandparent. Helping families learn to negotiate and resolve conflict, including doing so without therapists' assistance is a primary therapeutic objective. It is common for families to use a variety of mechanisms to avoid and defuse conflict, or to have conflict expressed openly but unproductively in stereotyped behavior patterns. In families with a low threshold for conflict expression, such as families with a member who has a thought disorder or psychosomatic child, conflict is usually expressed fleetingly and avoidance mechanisms are triggered rapidly.

Three concepts central to structural family therapy are (a) family subsystems, (b) boundaries, and (c) alliances and coalitions (Minuchin, 1974; Minuchin & Fishman, 1981). A *subsystem* is a part of a larger system that has organization and communication, and that performs some distinctive function. Typical family subsystems include spousal, parental, and sibling subsystems. Minuchin believed that a mother and father should constitute the parental subsystem—communicating primarily with each other around parenting (rather than others), performing most of the parenting tasks together, and creating problems in other subsystems when this subsystem is dysfunctional.

Closely associated with subsystems is the concept of boundaries. *Boundaries* are invisible lines that separate individuals or systems from one another. Boundaries range from being too diffuse (with family members being over involved [enmeshed] with one another) to excessively rigid (with family members being insufficiently connected [disengaged] from one another). Similarly, boundaries between the family system and the outside world can vary from closed (the family is cut off from influences from the outside world) to open (in which the family is open to information exchange with the outside world).

Alliances and coalitions refer to aspects of how individuals or subsystems work together. *Alliances* refer to relatively explicit and positive bonds between family members. In contrast, *coalitions* include the notion of a coalition against one or more people or subsystems. Members of the coalition are brought together by a common enemy, rather than because of positive bonds between them. The concept of cross-generational coalitions is particularly important in this context (e.g., father and child against the mother). Such coalitions are typically problematic and common targets for therapy.

Structural Therapy Techniques

Joining involves efforts by the therapist to behave in manners that let the family know that they are similar to the family (e.g., posture, style of speech). This is viewed as important because the family members need to feel that the therapist is with them and understands them before they are willing to accept any movement toward change. Structural family therapists also seek to "bring the symptoms into the room." As family members tend to be relatively poor observers of their own behavior (particularly non-verbal behavior), this technique provides the opportunity to observe actual behaviors related to the symptom (e.g., parents of a poorly controlled child can be invited to decide on an appropriate bed time for the child during the session). Therapists also "map" interaction patterns, and then plan therapeutic structural interventions accordingly. Finally, tasks for homework activities are designed to strengthen the desired structural changes. They should be well structured, easy to accomplish, and have a high likelihood of success.

Solution-Focused Therapy

While not everyone might opt to place solution-focused therapy under a systems theory umbrella, we view this as appropriate because, like other systems theories, solution-focused therapy seeks to identify exceptions "that make a difference" to clients' problems. The solution-focused therapist then seeks to amplify these exceptions into desired outcomes. Like strategic and structural, solution-focused therapists do not necessarily seek to gain clients' agreement about dysfunctional patterns but rather go directly to changes that will make the desired difference.

Solution-focused therapy begins with the observation that most psychological problems are present only intermittently. Consider, for example, that people with panic concerns do not spend every moment of every day in panic, and that people with depression usually notice that their depression fluctuates in severity. Additionally, solution-focused therapy seeks to increase clients' clarity of how they desire things to be. Thus, therapy focuses on clarifying clients' goals and enhancing solutions (*solution behaviors*) that are already available to clients (de Shazer, 1985; de Shazer & Berg, 1988).

Solution-Focused Therapy Techniques

Solution-focused therapy assists clients in becoming more aware of when their symptoms are diminished or absent and uses this knowledge as a foundation for improvement. If clients insist that their symptoms are constant and unrelieved, therapists work with them to find exceptions and then to make these exceptions more frequent, predictable, and controllable. Walter and Peller (1992) offered these suggestions for therapeutic choices: (1) If it works, don't fix it. Choose to do more of it; (2) If it works a little, choose to build on it; (3) If nothing is working, choose to experiment, including imagining miracles; and (4) Choose to approach each therapy session as if it were the last. Start change now, not later.

De Shazer (1985, 1988, 1994) offered numerous potential foci for constructing solutions:

- Goal focus. "What brings you here?" is an opening designed to elicit clients' present goals for therapy
- Problem focus. If clients respond by talking about problems and complaints, the therapist listens empathically. However, once the problem story is told, the therapist assists the client in finding a more productive focus.
- Solution focus. "When the problem is solved, what will you be doing differently?" is a question designed to help the client begin doing a small piece of the change now.
- Exception focus. "When isn't the problem happening" and "How is what you will be doing differently happening in some way now?" are exception finding questions that help bolster clients' awareness and use of their strengths.
- Spontaneity or choice. "When these problem-free moments happen, do they occur by deliberate, intentional choice, or rather by unpredictable, unintended accidents?" is a question designed to help clients gain greater awareness and control over the exceptions to their problems.

Systemic approaches seek to identify the "difference that makes a difference" in the interpersonal dynamics. In other words, therapists seek opportunities tip the interpersonal system into healthier equilibrium.

Summary

This chapter described humanistic, multicultural and system theories. Humanistic therapies (person-centered, gestalt/experiential, emotion-focused, existential, and interpersonal therapies), are part of the "third force" which focuses on assisting clients in becoming authentic, responsibly confronting existential issues, gaining emotional awareness, and developing healthy interpersonal relationships. Multicultural theories (the fourth force) focus on societal/cultural influences on the psychological issues of groups and individuals. Particular attention is given to diversity in terms of race/ethnicity, gender, affectional preference, ability/disability, and spirituality, with therapists having responsibility for understanding their own cultural views and how they are likely to influence their work with diverse clients. Systems theories focus on creating change via various methods. Strategic therapy relies upon the therapist's use of creative interventions to change client or system.

Structural family therapy focuses on patterns of interactions, and seeks to change dysfunctional patterns of interactions within or between family subsystems. Solution-focused therapy emphasizes identifying clients' positive exceptions to their problem(s), enhancing clients' strengths and better moments as pathways to improvement.

Components of Effective Counseling & Psychotherapy

CHAPTER 3

Foundations
of Therapeutic
Communication

Communication works for those who work at it.
—JOHN POWELL (1995)

Sam has felt increasingly down for the last several months, unable to fall asleep at night, losing motivation at work, experiencing irritability, isolating himself from others, and feeling hopeless about the future. After receiving strong encouragement from family and friends, he reluctantly decided to give therapy a try. When he informs his therapist about his concerns, the therapist rolls her eyes and replies, "You think you have it bad?! Suck it up!"

Cara seeks therapy because she feels she needs assistance in adjusting to recent developments in her life. A 20-year-old college student, Cara shares that she has been put on academic probation at the university, sprained her ankle dancing at a rock concert, and was recently told by her romantic partner that he wants to end their relationship. When Cara looks expectantly at her therapist for a reaction, the therapist sighs and asks her, "Do you always whine like that?"

These case vignettes illustrate the potential negative impacts of therapeutic communication. The practitioners in these situations are clearly not responding therapeutically; in fact, their abrasive,

This chapter was cowritten with Angela M. Soth.

uncaring, and brash comments to Sam and Cara are inappropriate, unethical, counterproductive, and likely to be detrimental. Trainees enter the role of therapist with varying abilities to become open to the experience of others, accurately perceive the impact of another person on themselves, and express certain communication styles. For therapists, the key to working effectively with clients is developing expertise in the basic skills of therapeutic communication. Although it takes considerable effort, this expertise can be learned through formal instruction, professional training, and clinical supervision. This chapter introduces the basic interviewing and therapeutic communication skills that represent the foundation for a career-long commitment to excellence (see Hill & O'Brien [2004]) for a more thorough review).

Therapeutic communication, including tone, timing, feeling, and content, reflects a unique form of relating to others. Unlike the typical forms of communication in one's life, such as the unstructured and spontaneous nature of everyday conversation with family and friends, therapeutic language is characterized by different formats, levels of intensity, and therapeutic objectives. Such communication may be verbal or nonverbal. Therapeutic verbal communication styles, or *verbal response modes*, have to do with the grammatical structure of a therapist's response, independent of the topic or content of speech (Hill, 1982). *Nonverbal communication* consists of interactional signals not explicitly coded in language, such as posture, facial expression, and pauses between words. The communication style used varies according to therapeutic intention. A therapeutic *intention* is defined as the therapist's rationale for selecting a specific response mode, technique, or intervention to use with a client at any given moment within a session (Hill & O'Grady, 1985). In other words, intentions are based on the responses the therapist wants to explore with the client. Therapeutic intentions should be developed in light of the client's desired future. Whereas verbal and nonverbal response

> Therapeutic language is characterized by different formats, levels of intensity, and professional goals. Such communication may be verbal or nonverbal. Therapeutic verbal communication styles, or *verbal response modes*, have to do with the grammatical structure of a therapist's response, independent of the topic or content of speech (Hill, 1982). *Nonverbal communication* consists of interactional signals not explicitly coded in language, such as posture, facial expression, and pauses between words. The communication style used varies according to therapeutic intention. A therapeutic *intention* is defined as the therapist's rationale for selecting a specific response mode, technique, or intervention (Hill & O'Grady, 1985).

modes help therapists answer the question "What do I do in session?", intentions help them answer "What do I want to accomplish in session?"

Verbal responses and nonverbal cues are generally used to help clients feel validated, supported, and empowered. Specifically, these communication variables encourage clients to open up, explore, clarify, risk self-expression, experience catharsis, feel understood, identify maladaptive patterns in thoughts, emotions, and behaviors, believe in their ability to change, and gain hope for the future. These and other therapeutic intentions were described by Hill and O'Brien (1999) and are listed in Table 3.1.

Therapeutic intentions and communication modes are structured to assist clients during and through the stages of psychotherapy: engagement, pattern search, change, and termination (Beitman & Yue, 2004), which are described in subsequent chapters of this book. These core therapy processes may be used as a framework for understanding the intentions, selection, and use of various communication skills. The verbal and nonverbal response modes and intentions discussed in this chapter are primarily employed in the engagement and pattern search stages of therapy. Strategies more commonly used during the change stage will be discussed in later chapters.

Verbal Response Modes During Engagement

The main purpose of the first stage of therapy, engagement, is to establish a solid working alliance. This involves providing a safe and supportive interpersonal environment conducive to clients' exploring their inner and outer world. The primary therapeutic intentions during this phase are: support, validate, set limits about relationship parameters, instill hope, identify and intensify feelings, and encourage catharsis. The following nonverbal and verbal response modes (*attending, active listening, silence, observing nonverbal cues, open questions, restatement,* and *reflection of feelings*) may be used to carry out these intentions.

Attending

Effective therapists are sensitive to the fact that clients read the nonverbal cues of helpers. With the aim of providing nonverbal communication, therapists orient themselves physically toward, or *attend* to,

TABLE 3.1   Therapist Intentions

1. **Set Limits.** Structure, make arrangements, establish goals and objectives of treatment; outline methods to attain goals; correct expectations about treatment or establish rules or parameters of relationship (e.g., time, fees, cancellation policies, homework).

2. **Get Information.** Find out specific facts about history, client functioning, future plans, relationships, work.

3. **Give Information.** Educate, give facts, correct misrepresentations or mis-information; give reasons for therapist's behavior or procedures.

4. **Support.** Provide a warm, supportive, empathetic environment; increase trust and rapport and build relationship; help client feel accepted, understood, comfortable, reassured, and less anxious; help establish a person-to-person relationship.

5. **Focus.** Help client get back on track, change a subject, channel or structure the discussion if he or she is unable to begin or has been diffuse or rambling.

6. **Clarify.** Provide or solicit more elaboration, emphasis, or specification when client or therapist has been vague, incomplete, confusing, contradictory, or inaudible.

7. **Hope.** Convey the expectation that change is possible and likely to occur; convey that the therapist will be able to help the client; restore morale; build up client's confidence to make changes.

8. **Cathart.** Promote relief from unwanted feelings; allow client a chance to talk through feelings and problems.

9. **Cognitions.** Identify maladaptive, illogical, or irrational thoughts, self-talk, automatic thoughts, attitudes, or beliefs.

10. **Behaviors.** Identify and describe client's inappropriate or dysfunctional behaviors or their consequences; analyze the stimulus-response sequences of dysfunctional behavior; describe dysfunctional interpersonal patterns.

11. **Self-Control.** Encourage client to take responsibility or gain a sense of mastery or control over dysfunctional thoughts, feelings, behaviors, or impulses; help client become more responsible for interpersonal effects rather than blaming others.

12. **Feelings.** Identify intense feelings or enable acceptance of feelings; encourage or provoke client to become aware of underlying or hidden feelings and to experience feelings at a deeper level.

13. **Insight.** Encourage understanding of the underlying reasons, dynamics, assumptions, motivations, history or meaning of cognition, behaviors, attitudes or feelings; may include an understanding of client's reactions to others' behavior.

14. **Change.** Encourage the development of new and more adaptive skills, behaviors, or cognition in dealing with self and others; may offer new, more adaptive assumptive models, frameworks, explanations, views or conceptualizations; may offer new options for behavior or self-view.

15. **Reinforce Change.** Offer positive reinforcement or positive feedback about behavioral, cognitive, interpersonal or affective attempts at change to enhance the probability that changes will continue or be maintained; encourage risk taking and new ways of behaving. Review new changes; understand the reasons for them; and increase the likelihood that new changes will be maintained.

16. **Resistance.** Overcome obstacles to changes or progress by discussing them; may also discuss failure to adhere to therapeutic procedures in the past to prevent possibility of such failure in the future.

17. **Challenge.** Jolt client out of a present state; shake up current beliefs or feelings; test validity, reality, or accuracy of beliefs, thoughts, feelings, or behaviors; help client question the necessity of maintaining old patterns.

18. **Relationship.** Resolve problems as they arise in the relationship in order to build or maintain a smooth working alliance; heal ruptures in the alliance; deal with issues appropriate to stage in treatment; identify and resolve distortions in client's thinking about the relationship that are based on past experiences and patterns rather than on current reality.

19. **Therapist Needs.** Protect, relieve, or defend the person of the therapist; alleviate therapist's anxiety; may try excessively to persuade, argue, or feel good or superior at the expense of the client; may be done more in the service of the therapist's needs than the client's.

20. **Interpersonal.** Clarify the client's reactions, attitudes, thoughts, behaviors, and feelings toward another person and sometimes the other person's reactions to the client in order to understand the client's interpersonal schema.

clients (Hill & O'Brien, 2004). In many ways, what therapists communicate nonverbally may be more important than what is verbally spoken, particularly early on in the helping relationship. Most clients can discern when a therapist is not completely "present" in a session. Therapists that do not look at the client or doodle on a pad of paper are transmitting disinterested nonverbal cues, conveying a message that what the client is saying is unimportant. Such inattention leads most clients to feel less trusting of the therapist, which interferes with the helping process. By maintaining an attentive presence, therapists communicate therapeutic intentions of support, encouragement, empathy, and hope. Attending to clients conveys interest and investment, which facilitates clients' willingness to talk about their vulnerabilities and problematic issues.

One of the chief means of prompting clients to continue opening up is the use of *minimal encouragers*. Nodding, leaning forward, and non-language sounds such as "uh-huh," "mm-hmm," "yeah," and "sure" communicate attentiveness, provide noninvasive support, and monitor the flow of conversation. These subtle signs of approval imply that therapists empathize with and understand clients. Reassurance that problems are normal and that the client is having an expected response can be validating and empowering. Although excessive use of minimal encouragers can be distracting and seem insincere, tempered use of this type of attending behavior, such as occasional use at the ends of client comments or speaking turns, typically enhance clients' willingness to continue to open up and explore (Hill & O'Brien, 1999).

Acronyms have been developed to aid in the mastery of appropriate attending behaviors. One such acronym is SOLER: (face the client *squarely*, adopt an *open* posture, *lean* toward the client, maintain moderately consistent *eye* contact, and try to be relatively *relaxed* and natural) (Egan, 1994). Hill and O'Brien (1999) offered another acronym, shown in Table 3.2.

These prescriptions of skill sets are only *guidelines* for how to attend actively to clients. Trainees are encouraged to try such attending behaviors and modify them according to what feels comfortable and natural, while being simultaneously aware of the effects of these nonverbal behaviors on clients. Hill and O'Brien (1999) encouraged therapists to ask themselves, "How much does my present behavior communicate openness and availability to the client?"

Active Listening

Listening is fundamental to psychotherapy. All aspects of treatment depend upon what the therapist learns about each client. This learning occurs through grasping a client's verbal and nonverbal expressions. To listen to another person is to pay attention to his or her words, tone of voice, facial expressions, and body language. Listening is a basic

TABLE 3.2   Encourages

E:	Maintain moderate levels of *eye* contact (avoiding looking away frequently or staring).
N:	Use a moderate amount of head *nods.*
C:	Maintain a respect and awareness of *cultural differences* in attending behaviors.
O:	Maintain an *open stance* toward the client (do not keep arms closed tightly, lean toward and face the client squarely).
U:	Use acknowledgements and minimal encouragers such as "*umm-hmm.*"
R:	*Relax* and be natural.
A:	*Avoid distracting behaviors* (e.g.; too many adaptors, too much smiling, giggling, chewing gum, or playing with hair or objects.)
G:	Match the client's *grammatical style* (use the same language style as the client within the limits of one's own style).
E:	Listen with a third *ear* (listen attentively to verbal and nonverbal messages).
S:	Use *space* appropriately (do not sit either too close or too far).

skill that therapists use throughout the entire helping encounter to receive and understand messages that clients directly and indirectly communicate.

Research shows that clients speak 60–70% of the time during a counseling session; in contrast, nontherapeutic dyads are marked by both individuals' speaking an equal amount (Hill, 1978; Hill, Carter, & O'Farrell, 1983). Therapists actively listen to clients in an effort to communicate that they are attentive, interested, and empathetic. When clients feel they are worth being listened to, they are implicitly encouraged to continue speaking in an open and nondefensive way. This sense of being valued facilitates clients' feeling safe and more deeply exploring their thoughts and feelings.

When listening to clients speak, therapists focus on the client, freeing their minds from distraction. Rather than receiving a client's messages through the filter of the therapist's cultural lens, active listening involves genuine efforts to understand the client's subjective worldview and to experience the world as the client does. A crucial component of active listening is to be present with the client without formulating a next response. By being fully open to the client's world, therapists are better positioned to accurately learn about the client's thoughts, feelings, and experiences.

A warning: Some therapists, in their eagerness to enter clients' worlds, overdo their efforts, becoming too deeply involved for too long. Ideally therapists strive to enter the world of the other for a little while and then regroup by coming back into themselves. Active listening can be tiring! Conversely, some therapists go to the opposite extreme, tentatively and only briefly touching the mind of the other and losing much potential to assist.

In addition to listening to words, therapists must also listen to what is not being directly spoken. Clients may verbally express their ideas incompletely, transmit subtle meanings, or omit details even though their language initially seems well-formed and ordinary. Therapists cannot accept at face value everything clients explicitly say. The concept of hidden content was introduced by Freud (1913) with the notion of latent meanings in dream material. Covert messages are also quite common in everyday communication, particularly therapeutic communication.

Clients' hidden intentions can be deciphered through noticing incomplete speech and detecting masked content in surface speech. They can also be detected through therapists' observing their effect on themselves—for example, therapists' noting intense feelings of empathetic sadness during a client's neutral speech. Effective listeners become sensitized to such "unfinished" communication in order to help clients illuminate what they may be trying to convey. For example, a client might state, "Everyone hates me," or "Whatever I do turns out wrong." A therapist might ask, "Who is everyone that hates you?" or "What are the things you have done that have turned out wrong?" Another client with two young children who was experiencing significant financial difficulties said in reference to her sister, "She has so much going for her—wealth, status, and prestige. I wish I

> When listening to clients speak, therapists focus on the client, freeing their minds from distraction. Rather than receiving a client's messages through the filter of the therapist's cultural lens, active listening involves genuine efforts to understand the client's subjective worldview and to experience the world as the client does. A crucial component of active listening is to be present with the client without formulating a next response. By being fully open to the client's world, therapists are better positioned to accurately learn about the client's thoughts, feelings, and experiences.

had happiness too." The therapist might detect and process with this client her veiled message equating mental well-being and economic status. Therapists seek clarification of concepts that are abstract, vague, generalized, or not rooted in specific real-world people or events. Reik (1948) referred to the importance of listening to clients with a "third ear," putting together verbal messages, covert messages, and body language to capture what clients really mean and feel.

Silence

Along with active listening, silence can be useful in encouraging clients during the exploration process. A silence is a pause of at least 5 seconds that may occur after a client's statement, within a client's statement, or as a client digests a therapist's statement (Hill & O'Brien, 1999). Rather than interrupting a client or immediately continuing the therapeutic dialogue, therapists may demonstrate their support and attentiveness by simply allowing clients space and time. Silence may allow clients to think through what they want to say, process feelings, expand on an idea, recognize patterns, celebrate insight, or even cry. At other times, silence may be disorienting or anxiety-producing for clients who feel disconnected from their therapists or do not know what is expected from them. Therapists should evaluate the impact of silence for each of their clients to determine its potential therapeutic value.

Observing Nonverbal Cues

Both when speaking and listening, clients and therapists disclose through bodily communications. Such nonverbal cues have several purposes, including conveying emotions, regulating conversations, modifying or emphasizing verbal messages, and providing clues that people may not be saying what they are thinking or feeling (Highlen & Hill, 1984). Egan (1994) suggested that effective helpers are able to identify and interpret the following nonverbal communications:

- Bodily behavior (e.g., posture, gestures, movement)
- Facial expressions (e.g., smiles, frowns, raised eyebrows, pursed lips)

- Voice-related behavior (e.g., tone of voice, pitch, volume, intensity, inflection, spacing of words, pauses, fluency)
- Observable autonomic physiological responses (e.g., blushing, quickened breathing, turning pale, pupil dilation)
- Physical characteristics (e.g., fitness, weight, complexion)
- General appearance (e.g., grooming, dress)

Nonverbal behaviors are typically characterized as *eye contact, facial expression, physical proximity, paralanguage,* and *kinesics*. Each culture develops rules for nonverbal communication, which are usually outside of conscious awareness. Nonverbal behavior that is appropriate in one culture may not be appropriate in another. Therapists need to adapt their style to each client's nonverbal style, taking cues from clients as to what makes them feel at ease and comfortable (Hill & O'Brien, 1999).

Eye Contact

Eye contact is an important nonverbal therapeutic behavior used to initiate communication, monitor speech, provide feedback, signal understanding, and regulate turn taking (Harper, Wilens, & Matarazzo, 1978). In everyday conversation, speakers tend to look at listeners 40% of the time and listeners tend to look at speakers approximately 70-75% of the time (Nelson-Jones, 2000). In therapy, clients may look at therapists less often when they are anxious, bored, or discussing topics that particularly distress them. On the other hand, clients' pupils tend to dilate when they are engaged and find a topic interesting or useful. While an excess of eye contact by the therapist can make a client feel intruded upon or uncomfortable, a lack of eye contact may communicate disinterest. Sustained eye contact is often considered a sign of interest in British and European-North American middle-class culture; however, direct eye contact, particularly if done by a young person to an elder, is a sign of disrespect among some Native American and Latino/a groups (Ivey & Ivey, 2002). Individuals from Asian cultures may avoid eye contact with authorities, such as professional figures (Ivey, 1994). Therapists need to observe clients for discomfort related to eye contact, noting the context of the session and cultural differences.

Facial Expression

Facial expressions also offer clues about the meaning of verbal and nonverbal messages. The face, in fact, represents the most important source of information for inferring how a person feels (Keats, 1993). While more than 1,000 facial expressions have been identified, Ekman, Friesen, and Ellsworth (1972) have found that there are seven main facial expressions: happiness, interest, surprise, fear, sadness, anger, and disgust. Although these facial expressions appear to have similar meaning to people all over the world, cultures differ in

> Nonverbal behaviors include *eye contact, facial expression, proxemics, paralanguage,* and *kinesics.* Nonverbal behaviors appropriate in one culture may be inappropriate in another. Therapists need to adapt their style to each client's nonverbal style, taking cues from clients as to what makes them feel at ease.

when, how, and the degree to which these facial forms express emotion. For therapists, key facial expressions are friendly and relaxed, conveying interest, attention, and concern.

Physical Proximity

Physical proximity refers to use of space in interpersonal interactions. Research on space patterns show four general zones: intimate (0–18 inches), personal (1.5–4 ft), social (4–12 ft), and public (12 ft or more) (Hall, 1968). These physical zones vary according to the nature of the relationship. The personal to social distance is typically considered appropriate for seating arrangements in therapeutic relationships (Hill & O'Brien, 1999), although individuals have different personal preferences. Differences also exist between and within cultures that may affect clients' comfort with physical closeness. For instance, whereas a comfortable conversational distance for North Americans is slightly more than an arm's length, many Latino/as prefer half that distance (Ivey & Ivey, 2002), and Arabs and Israeli Jews predominantly prefer closeness (Hill & O'Brien, 1999). Therapists should be aware of cultural differences without making assumptions about individual clients.

Paralanguage

Paralanguage refers to the manner in which things are said. This category of communication includes emotion-reflecting behaviors such as non-language sounds (e.g., moans, sighs, sniffs) and non-words (e.g., "er," "ah," "ahem"), along with speech deviations such as stutters and vocal style (e.g., volume, pitch, rate) (Hill & O'Brien, 1999; Nelson-Jones, 2000). Ivey and Ivey (2002) emphasized the therapeutic utility of *verbal underlying,* when increased volume or vocal emphasis is given to certain words and short phases of particular importance. Therapists may use a client's paralanguage to note verbal underlying or to identify discrepancies (such as gently pointing out how a client is speaking loudly and quickly but saying that she feels calm) to encourage exploration into how the client might be really feeling.

Kinesics

The communicative properties of the moving body, such as arm movements, leg movements and head nods, are referred to as kinesics. This category also includes *gestures* or physical movements that can frame or illustrate words, such as a clenched fist or shrugging shoulders. Kinesics and gestures not only serve to emphasize and give additional information about verbal messages, but also communicate feelings and attitudes. In fact, excess display of kinesics is often a sign of "nonverbal leakage": there is a feeling that the person is trying to conceal (Hill & O'Brien, 1999). If clients repeatedly tap their feet, shift in posture, scratch their heads, or play with a pencil, the possibility of nonverbal leakage should be considered and explored.

Clients' nonverbal behaviors do not have fixed, standard "meanings," but are rather dependent upon context. To facilitate the effectiveness of a session, therapists need to continually monitor the verbal and nonverbal communication of the client, using this feedback to hypothesize about what a client might be feeling, which may be further investigated by gathering more data to determine its accuracy (Hill & O'Brien, 1999).

Open Questions

Asking questions to clients seems a natural skill for a therapist. However, asking relevant, purposeful, and insightful questions requires dexterity, knowledge, and proficiency. Open questions tend to be broad and general, and phrased so that they encourage the client to answer in long phrases or full sentences. Instead of purposefully soliciting a specific, limited answer from clients, such as a "yes" or "no," open questions are armed with the therapeutic intent of encouraging clients to explore what comes to mind around the content of the question. As such, open-ended questions facilitate clients sharing their internal perspectives without curtailing their options (Nelson-Jones, 2000). This verbal response mode may be phrased as a directive ("Give me an example of what you do when you're angry"; "Tell me about your panicky feelings") or a query ("How do you feel about the roommate situation?"; "What do you think of your new class?"). Once a therapist has an overview of the situation, asking more specific questions will assist in gaining context (e.g., "You mentioned that you are quite nervous about being here in therapy. What aspects of being here trouble you the most?"; Sevel, Cumins, & Madrigal, 1999).

> Open-ended questions cannot be responded to by a simple "yes" or "no" response, but rather encourage clients to explore their experiences and inner perspectives.

To formulate open questions, effective therapists consider the purpose, focus, tense, and object of the question. Hill and O'Brien (1999) discussed eight types of open questions:

- Encouraging exploration ("How has this past week been for you?")
- Exploring helping expectations ("What would you like to happen in this session?")
- Exploring different parts of the problem ("How would you like your relationship with your sister to be in the future?")
- Requesting exploration ("Tell me more about that")
- Encouraging clarification and focus ("What is your role in those conflicts?")
- Encouraging exploration of thoughts ("What did you really want to tell her?")
- Encouraging exploration of feelings ("When I said that, how did you feel?")
- Requesting examples ("What happened the last time you felt out of control?")

In asking open questions, therapists should maintain the appropriate attending behaviors, such as keeping the voice low to convey concern, using a slow rate of speech, and tentatively phrasing questions to avoid sounding interrogating and judgmental. In addition, open-minded questions should follow from the clients' prior statements without an abrupt change of topic and deal with content that the client can comfortably handle given the level of trust established and depth of client self-understanding. Effective open questions facilitate exploration of thoughts and feelings, encourage clients to clarify when they are unclear, focus clients who are rambling, and support clients in telling their stories.

Closed Questions

A therapeutic closed question asks for a brief response, such as a "yes," "no," or confirmation of the therapist's previous statement. These inquires are typically limited and specific, such as "How old were you when this trauma happened?"; "Does that sound right to you?"; and "I'm sorry I missed that, what did you say?" Closed questions enable therapists to check details of the client's narrative for accuracy, pinpoint the details of a situation, gather small pieces of information, and bring into focus a particular issue (Sevel et al., 1999). Closed questions, however, have a limited role in therapy; they are primarily only used when helpers are seeking particular answers rather than encouraging clients to explore their thoughts or feelings. Beginning therapists often use closed questions excessively, perhaps because this verbal skill is a familiar mode of relating to others. Use of multiple closed questions can lead therapists to slip into the interviewer role, starting a cycle in which clients expect or depend on their therapist for the next question.

Restatement

Restatements are a repeating or paraphrasing of the content or meaning of a client's dialogue. They typically are more clear and succinct than the client's original statement. Restatements may be used to confirm what a client has just articulated or what was discussed earlier in session. To avoid redundancy, therapists can vary the format of restatements. There are several ways to introduce restatements, such as "I hear you saying . . ."; "It sounds as though . . ."; "I wonder whether . . ."; and "You're saying that . . ." (Hill & O'Brien, 1999). Tentative language should be used so that clients can reject restatements that do not seem accurate. Ivey and Ivey (1999) encouraged therapists to check the accuracy of their restatements by briefly inquiring whether or not the paraphrase was correct and useful, such as asking "Am I hearing you correctly?"

By focusing on the content of client messages, restatements confirm the importance clients have attached to the statement. Restatements help clients perceive clearly what they are experiencing and offer an opportunity to reconsider issues from a different perspective (Hepworth, Rooney, & Larsen, 1997). Restatements allow clients to hear how their concerns sound when stated by another person. Restatements also help clients explore their concerns more deeply, reevaluate their thinking, clarify when they are unclear, and sharpen when they are vague (Hill & O'Brien, 2004). Nonetheless, excessive use of restatements should be avoided, as it can give the impression that therapists are simply mimicking what the clients are saying. Paraphrasing should be used in conjunction with other methods of facilitating clients' responses, such as minimal encouragers, reflection of feelings, and interpretation (Hepworth et al., 1997).

Restatements can be particularly useful in three instances: at the beginning of a new session, in the course of a session that is unfocused, and when a client gets stuck (Egan, 1994). In the first case, restatements offer a starting point for new clients who are in a first session and are struggling with what to discuss. In the second instance, restatements model paraphrasing skills for particularly rambling, talkative clients by helping them regain their bearings and focus on the implications of what they have said. In the final case, restatements can be useful when clients seem to have exhausted everything they have to say about a particular issue. The restatement lets them know that they were being listened to carefully, that they provided enough information, and that perhaps there is a different way of looking at what was stated (Egan, 1994).

Summaries, which are often given at the end of sessions, are a type of restatement. Summaries tie together several ideas, highlighting the and general themes of the content expressed by clients. For example, "Today we seemed to cover important concerns you have about quitting your job, including financial anxiety, fears about disappointing your partner, and having feelings of being selfish." By consolidating what a client has said, summaries help organize a series of scattered ideas and clear the way for new ones (Sevel et al., 1999). Summaries offer yet another way to show clients that they have been heard. It also can be effective and empowering to ask the client to provide a summary; in asking clients to recap the major points of a session, therapists facilitate clients' investment in and owning of the therapeutic process. This response mode also lets therapists know whether their conclusions about the material presented are similar to those of the client. Finally, having clients summarize their own words provides an opportunity to practice self-reflection that is useful in other parts of the therapy process (Beitman & Soth, in press; Egan, 1994).

Reflection of Feelings

Reflection of feelings is a rephrasing of the client's statements with an emphasis on the client's emotions. The client may have directly stated the feeling or the therapist may have inferred the feeling from the context of the client's message or nonverbal behavior. Reflection of feelings involves accurately understanding clients' flows of emotions and sensitively communicating one's understanding back to them. Because individuals respond differently to events, therapists need to know how experiences are interpreted and felt by individual clients. Reflected feelings assist therapists as well as clients in understanding how clients respond emotionally to life (Cormier & Cormier, 1991).

Clients frequently experience a wide range of feelings and may have difficulty separating them and considering how they are related to one another (Sevel et al., 1999). In most situations, therapists should encourage clients to express as many of their feelings as possible without worrying if they are contradictory. If clients have difficulty expressing a particular feeling, therapists may want to offer several affective (feeling) words with similar meanings, so that clients can select the ones that best fit (Kadushin & Kadushin, 1997). This process enables clients to confirm their feelings without experiencing the pressure of identifying emotional states.

Reflections of feelings are generally formatted as "You feel . . . because . . . ." For example, "You feel sad because he disappointed you," "You feel anxious in response to her indecisiveness," or "I'm sensing you feel concerned about the upcoming holiday season." Therapists should select what they perceive to be the most salient feelings rather than trying to reflect all the client's feelings. Paying attention to clients' non-verbal reactions and to what parts of their verbal messages have the most or least energy behind them can help therapists detect what feelings to reflect (Hill & O'Brien, 1999).

Therapists typically use reflection of feelings to help clients identify, clarify, and explore feelings. By encouraging clients to experience their emotions, therapists may provide cathartic relief or clarification of blocked emotions. Other therapeutic intentions of the reflection of feelings include the promotion of self-control and instilling of hope through helping clients learn to express and manage their feelings. When therapists reflect feelings, they give clients the opportunity to get more in touch with their feelings. Clients may be best able to resolve issues when they have access to all their feelings (Good, 1998; Hill & O'Brien, 1999).

Cultural differences influence the expression of emotion and the degree to which clients open up about personal experiences. Although individuals in North America are generally encouraged to share their feelings, other cultures, such as Asian groups, are often more reserved in expressing emotions (Ivey, 1994). In addition, therapists should be sensitive to socialization experiences; some people, particularly men, may feel threatened if asked to articulate what they are feeling (Good et al., 1995). Clients who exhibit *emotional competence*—who are able to experience, identify, accept, label, and discuss their emotions—can make more informed choices about what to do with their feelings and the useful information they often provide (Good, 1998).

Pattern Search

Pattern search, the second primary stage of therapy, aims to help clients gain insight into their dysfunctional and maladaptive patterns. The goal of this phase is to define the patterns of thought, feeling, and behavior that the client is able to influence and that, if changed, would lead to a desirable outcome (Beitman, 1987). These patterns are identified from limited samples of information that the client presents in verbal or nonverbal cues during the session. Helpful verbal response modes during this phase include *interpretations*, *challenges*, *immediacy*, *self-disclosure*, *giving information*, and *direct guidance*. The therapeutic intentions behind these communication techniques are to focus and clarify; encourage catharsis; identify maladaptive affect, cognition, and behavior; challenge; promote insight; and encourage self-control.

Interpretations

Interpretations go *beyond* what the client has overtly said to present a new meaning, reason, or explanation for behaviors, thoughts, or feelings (Hill & O'Brien, 1999). Interpretations may establish connections between seemingly isolated statements or events; identify themes or patterns in the client's behavior, thoughts, or feelings; explain the meaning of defenses, resistance, or transference; or provide an alternative framework for looking at an issue, concern, or problem (Beitman &

Yue, 1999; Hill & O'Brien, 2004). In other words, interpretations often allow clients to see problems in a new light.

The verbal response mode of interpretations can be effectively paired with reflection of feelings, empathy, and restatements to provide support to clients in dealing with new introspections (Hepworth et al., 1997). Interpretations may be phrased as a direct statement ("I wonder if feeling insecure about your ability to be a loving partner is related to feeling like an inadequate daughter?") or through a question ("Might you be angry because your current relationship does not match your expectations of what a family should look like?"). Effective therapists offer interpretations in tentative language, gauging the client's reaction to find out if the assumptions seem to resonate. Therapists may also use interpretations with an aim of encouraging and empowering clients to embark on their own interpretative quests.

Therapists use interpretations to promote insight and help get beneath the surface of the problem as envisioned by the client (Cormier & Cormier, 1991). In this sense, interpretations aim "to explain rather than merely describe a client's behavior and to change a client's frame of reference in a therapeutic direction" (Clark 1995, p. 484). Interpretations can assist clients in learning about themselves—the motivation and reasons behind their thoughts, feelings, and behaviors. Interpretations may also increase clients' sense of security, mastery, and self-efficacy by providing a label and name for experiences that seem confusing and inexplicable (Frank & Frank, 1991).

Challenges

Challenges, or confrontations, are used by therapists to point out discrepancies, contradictions, or omissions in clients' thoughts, feelings, and behaviors. Therapist may use challenges with clients to confront the use of unhealthy defenses, contest self-defeating or irrational ideas, or juxtapose two elements to highlight the contradictions between them (Hill & O'Brien, 2004). As discrepancies and contradictions are often signs of unresolved issues, ambivalence, or suppressed feelings, challenges invite clients to become more aware of themselves, their problems, feelings, thoughts, and behaviors. Additionally, pointing out discrepancies may help reduce ambiguities and incongruities in clients' experiences and communication, thereby assisting them in becoming more self-accepting and fully functioning (Carkhuff & Berenson, 1967).

Hill and O'Brien (1999) listed eight types of therapeutic challenges intended to highlight discrepancies:

- Between two verbal statements ("You mentioned that you don't have a preference where you and your partner move, but you also say you want to live closer to the South.")
- Between words and actions ("You say you want to spend more time getting in shape, but you indicate that you spend your free time watching television.")
- Between two behaviors ("You are laughing, but your hands are clenched.")
- Between two feelings ("You feel pleased that you were invited, but have doubts about the reason.")
- Between values and behaviors ("You say you believe strongly in gender equality, but you make sexist jokes.")
- Between one's self and experience ("You say that that no one finds you attractive, but earlier you mentioned that an old friend complimented you on your appearance.")
- Between one's ideal and real self ("You say you want to attend professional school, but you also doubt that you can accomplish this feat.")
- Between the therapist's and client's opinions ("You say that you are not making progress in therapy, but I see you gaining important insights, learning new skills, and changing your behavior.")

For challenges to be used effectively in a helping relationship, therapists must first establish a strong working alliance and a safe, trusting rapport with the client. The strong alliance helps reduce clients' tendencies to react defensively or to feel attacked (Sevel et al., 1999). It is helpful for therapists to bear in mind that all confrontation is *for* and *with* the client, not *to* or *against* the client.

Immediacy

Immediacy refers to the current interaction of the therapist and the client in the relationship and processing of the here-and-now in session. This occurs when therapists disclose how they are feeling about themselves in relation to the client or about the client, the overall session, a specific event in session, or the therapeutic relationship (Egan, 1994). For example, a therapist might state, "You seem to think that because I am young, I won't be able to help you," "I feel honored that you are sharing deep and personal feelings with me," or "I feel as through we are circling around the theme of your relationship without really focusing." These present-tense, immediate disclosures are typically made to promote insight, to challenge, to identify and intensify feelings, or to identify maladaptive behaviors (Hill & O'Brien, 1999). Given that many clients have difficulties with interpersonal relationships, the therapeutic relationship provides a microcosm of how clients relate in the real world (Teyber, 2000). Discussing problems in the immediate therapy relationship often results in clients' coming to a deeper understanding of how they behave in relationships.

Self-Disclosure

Self-disclosures reveal something personal about the therapist. Several types of self-disclosure are used by therapists: disclosure of history and credentials, disclosure of immediate experiences in the therapeutic relationship, disclosure of strategies, and disclosure to stimulate insight (Hill & O'Brien, 1999). When using personal self-disclosure, therapists present a personal experience they view as relevant to the client's concerns. Although clients report that they highly value self-disclosure (Hill, Helm, Spiegel, & Tichenor, 1988), therapists must remain vigilant about not gratifying their own needs through inappropriate self-disclosure, projecting their own issues onto clients, or satisfying their desire to be liked. It is important for therapists first to examine their intentions for self-disclosing ("How would this disclosure be helpful for my client?") and then to self-disclose in a respectful manner that suggests (rather than asserts) that this experience might be relevant for the client. Self-disclosure should be done in a manner that allows clients freedom to seek out their own truth. Ivey and Ivey (1999) recommended the "1-2-3" model for self-disclosure: (1) attend to your client's story, (2) assess the appropriateness of your disclosure and briefly share it, and (3) return the focus to the client—note how he or she receives your story.

> Self-disclosure by therapists should be clearly in the interest of assisting the client, rather than to meet therapists' needs.

In addition to serving as a modeling device, self-disclosures can alter the power dynamic of the relationship and lead to greater and higher-quality client participation. When therapists offer self-disclosures, they de-emphasize the therapist-as-expert, client-as-dependent dynamic and indicate instead that both they and the client are humans who wrestle with important life concerns. Feminist-oriented therapists advocate the use of self-disclosure as a means to prevent replaying unhealthy power dynamics in the outside world (Worell & Remer, 2003).

Giving Information

Information giving provides clients with specific facts, data, resources, and answers to questions (Hill & O'Brien, 1999). Therapists may use their knowledge, experience, and expertise to provide education to clients. For example, therapists often provide information about psychological concerns, diagnoses, effective treatments, psychosocial skills, and psychoeducational resources. Information giving may also take the form of giving clients feedback ("You seemed to nervously fidget during our assertiveness training session"). Concretely given feedback can build clients' self-awareness (Brammer & MacDonald, 1996). The therapeutic intent of relaying information to clients is to instruct, teach, and empower clients to know facts, to make decisions, and to be prepared for action. Prior to giving information, it may be helpful for a therapist to inquire about how much knowledge a client has about whether he or she would be interested in hearing more about the topic. Providing too much information prematurely can create dependency or resistance rather than enhance self-efficacy. Considerations regarding psychoeducational interventions are described in greater detail in Chapter 10.

Direct Guidance

Direct guidance provides directions for clients' behavior or for the therapeutic interaction through suggestions, directives, or advice. Direct guidance may take the form of process advisement (such as asking a client to replay an interpersonal interaction), participation in the empty chair technique, assertiveness rehearsal, completion of homework (such as keeping a dream diary, symptom record, or thought log), seeking information on the Internet, or reading a psychoeducational book. As clients often receive advice from others about what they should do about their concerns, therapists are cautioned to use direct guidance judiciously. As with providing information, it is desirable for therapists to assess clients' motivation before offering direct guidance. In general, therapists are encouraged to collaborate with their clients in terms of supporting the changes that clients seek to make.

Research on Therapist Verbal Response Modes

Empirical studies have shown that verbal response modes affect therapeutic outcomes. Clients and therapists differ in their opinions regarding which communication formats are most helpful. Although interpretation received a "strongly helpful" rating by both clients and therapists and restatements were rated as moderately helpful by both groups, self-disclosure was rated by clients as the most helpful of all response modes but received very different ratings by therapists. In addition, open questions and confrontation were rated as moderately helpful by therapists but less so by clients, and direct guidance was rated least helpful by clients and moderately helpful by therapists (Hill, Helm, Spiegel, & Tichenor, 1988).

In Hill and colleagues' (1988) study, therapist intentions accounted for more outcome variance than therapists' modes of response. The research indicates that therapists and clients concur that the most helpful interventions are those in which the therapist helped the client explore feelings and behaviors. When therapists intended to gain information and clarify, clients reported no reaction and fewer feelings of being understood and supported. In other research, clients' ratings of helpfulness were highest for therapists' intentions involving addressing resistance, cognition, and relationships, and lowest for setting limits, getting information, supporting, and focusing (Fuller & Hill, 1985).

Common Pitfalls

Effective use of communication skills provides the foundation for the therapeutic relationship. Developing this competence is a learned process and being aware of the mistakes and pitfalls commonly experienced by beginning therapists may help avoid potential problems that can hinder or damage the therapist-client relationship (Sevel et al., 1999). The first common pitfall is not allowing for silence. Trainees, often nervous about providing therapy, feel the need for verbal communication through the entire session. Silences, however, can allow a client to reflect on prior comments, make mental connections, or build courage for a future disclosure. Giving advice or telling the client what to do to solve problems is a second pitfall. Therapists may feel pressured to provide answers, rescue clients, or apply a "quick fix" to a problem situation. However, offering advice to clients can foster unhealthy dependence or resistance and does not help clients take responsibility for their solutions. Helping clients discover options for probable solutions on their own empowers clients as active participants who are responsible for their life choices.

A third mistake is interrupting the client and asking irrelevant questions. Excessive interruptions cause clients to lose focus and feel like the therapist does not care about them or their problem. Asking too many questions may make the session feel like interrogation rather than counseling (Egan, 1997). Although therapists may be curious about the story beyond what is relevant to therapy, only questions pertinent to the therapy process should be asked. Asking questions unrelated to the problem can lead to clients feeling misunderstood, disconnected, or believing that the problem-solving process is ineffective (Sevel et al., 1999). Premature confrontation, the fourth pitfall, occurs when therapists do not allow for the natural development of a trusting and safe relationship. Challenging clients too early tends to alienate them or make them skeptical about whether the confrontation is in their best interest.

When pitfalls are encountered during a session, the therapist's goal should be to learn from the experience so that when similar situations occur in the future, the therapist will be prepared to respond more appropriately (Sevel et al., 1999). In addition, directly admitting and discussing errors with clients usually strengthens the working alliance (Safran & Muran, 2000). Through practicing the communication skills discussed in this chapter and maintaining an awareness of common pitfalls, therapists will enhance their skills and build positive therapeutic relationships with their clients.

Summary

Therapeutic communication is central to working effectively with clients. The verbal and nonverbal response modes presented in this chapter, along with therapeutic intentions and rationales for selecting specific modes, are the basic therapeutic interactional tools and reasons they are used. During the engagement phase, attending, active listening, silence, observation of nonverbal cues, open questions, restatements, and reflection of feelings are important in facilitating a strong therapeutic rapport and encouraging clients to open up and explore. Within pattern search, interpretations, challenges, immediacy, self-disclosure, giving information, and direct guidance are often useful in assisting clients in identifying maladaptive feelings, thoughts, and behaviors and gaining insight. All of these communication modes may also be used in the final therapeutic phase, change, which will be discussed in later chapters. Therapists should seek to adapt their communication to individual client considerations, including different interpersonal styles, emotion states, expectations, problems, and cultural worldviews. Although expertise with these communication techniques is fundamental to developing an effective therapeutic style, therapists should also still be themselves. Authenticity and adaptability are vital to effective communication and promotion of client change.

CHAPTER 4

Engagement
Establishing, Maintaining, and Repairing Therapeutic Working Alliances

The essence of good therapy is to be able to descend with people into their hell and at the same time keep one foot in the land of hope and possibility.
—BILL O'HANLON (2003)

The goal of the engagement stage is to establish a strong working alliance: a trusting, confiding, and collaborative therapeutic relationship. This chapter examines the concept of the therapeutic working alliance, reviews the research supporting the central importance of the working alliance, describes how to establish effective working alliances, and offers suggestions about what to do when alliances falter. The chapter concludes with a discussion of therapeutic formulation. Formulation pertains to broadly understanding clients and their problems in their environments, and it is relevant to both forming effective therapeutic alliances and to identifying clients' patterns (which is the focus of Chapter 5).

The Therapeutic Working Alliance

Different theoretical approaches to counseling and therapy give various emphases and meanings to the therapeutic working alliance (e.g., Bordin, 1979; Goldfried & Padawer, 1982). Proponents of psychoanalysis address the positive attachment between client and analyst, which provides the latter with authority, strengthens the client's belief in the analyst's interpretations, and gives the client the personal strength and confidence to deal with painful experiences. Greenson (1967), another analyst, defined the working alliance as a relatively nonneurotic, rational rapport clients have with their therapists. The relationship is viewed as essentially realistic and reasonable, and largely based on the client's acceptance of and agreement with the therapist's approach. Some behavioral therapists perceive the function of the working alliance as creating an environment of safety and trust, conditions that are necessary in order to learn, implement, and practice the techniques that are ultimately responsible for therapeutic change (Horvath, 1995). According to Strong (1968), the strength of therapeutic relationship largely depends on the degree to which a client believes that the therapist is expert, attractive, and trustworthy, whereas Rogers (1957) defined the components of the positive therapeutic relationship as empathy, unconditional positive regard, and congruence. It is evident that the therapeutic relationship, although conceptualized differently through the primary theoretical schools, is a significant and central component of the healing process.

Bordin's (1979) widely accepted definition of the working alliance emphasizes collaboration between therapist and client and highlights three interrelated components: tasks, goals, and bonds. Horvath and Greenberg (1989) clarified the meaning of these three terms. *Tasks* refer to the in-therapy behaviors and cognitions that form the substance of the therapy process. In a well-functioning relationship, both persons perceive these tasks as relevant and potentially efficacious. Furthermore, each accepts the responsibility to perform these acts. A strong working alliance is also characterized by the therapist and client mutually endorsing and valuing the *goals* (outcomes) that are the targets of the given interventions. The concept of *bonds* encompasses the complex network of positive personal attachments between the client and therapist, and includes issues such as mutual trust, acceptance, and confidence.

Again, Bordin's concepts of tasks, goals, and bonds emphasize *collaboration* between therapist and client. This stance differs from alternative orientations, such as Rogers's (1957) therapist-offered relationship, which relies on the therapist's ability to offer a specific context, and Strong's (1968) client-determined relationship, which depends on the client's perception of the therapist's qualities and attitude. Bordin (1979) stated explicitly

> Bordin's (1979) view of the effective working alliance emphasizes collaboration between therapist and client and highlights three interrelated components—tasks, goals, and bonds.

that the quality of mutuality and collaboration in the working alliance is a primary ingredient for effective outcomes. Rather than viewing the working alliance as a therapeutic intervention in and of itself, Bordin perceived it as a vehicle that enables and facilitates therapeutic techniques. In other words, the working alliance provides the optimal context for the therapist's strategies and techniques.

Each school of psychotherapy suggests a particular sequence regarding the way in which the therapeutic relationship should unfold: how clients should be engaged, how maladaptive patterns should be defined, and how change should occur (see Table 4.1).

Consider your development as a therapist from now into the future as you consider the kinds of relationships you will try to develop with your clients. Younger therapists may be drawn to a specific school of therapy and tend to rigidly know "what kind of psychotherapist I am." In contrast, an older therapist, when asked, "What kind of therapist are you?" replied: "Twenty years ago I know how I would have answered that question. Now my clients no longer see ghosts of Carl Rogers or Alfred Adler. All I can say is that I try to apply what I have learned personally and professionally to help each client in front of me."

As therapists become older and more experienced, they are likely to be increasingly influenced by the clients whom they have helped (and not helped) as well as by their own personal experiences with crises and adaptation. The therapeutic practices of older therapists tend to be more similar than those of younger therapists (Blagys & Hilsenroth, 2000, 2002).

Content of Engagement

Clients enter therapy because they are experiencing intense negative emotions, distress, and confusion, because they need to make a difficult choice, or because they want to change something. Usually the ongoing problems have recently been made worse (the precipitating event), prompting the phone call for professional assistance.

What do clients and therapists discuss during the early phases of therapy? Clients are in the office with some kind of emotional pain and want relief. Many clients will want to talk about it; others, for example,

TABLE 4.1   Therapeutic Relationship Plans

SCHOOL	RELATIONSHIP PLAN
Psychoanalytic/psychodynamic	Provide safe environment to explore client's mind in presence of therapist; manage and utilize contract and boundary violations; define encoded behavioral communications, especially emotion, to clarify repeated dysfunctional patterns; focus on transference expression of these patterns.
Cognitive	Develop a collaborative-empiricist style of relationship; educate about clients' issues and corresponding thoughts/schemas, use thought record as a means to identify and change automatic dysfunctional thoughts and cognitive schemas; help client apply cognitive change techniques.
Behavioral	Serve as behavioral/learning consultant; use behavior analysis to identify problematic learning patterns.
Interpersonal	Adapt therapists' interpersonal styles to that of clients; monitor client impact on the therapist including "interpersonal pulls."
Family	Serve as family consultant depending on specific family treatment orientation.
Multicultural, feminist, and gender-aware	Demonstrate respect, knowledge, understanding, and openness to sociocultural-spiritual beliefs; utilize these beliefs and methods as part of the process of facilitating change; acknowledge and resolve differences between therapist and client involving socio-cultural beliefs.

more traditional men, may be quite reluctant and uncomfortable. What pain they describe and how they talk about it is partially determined by their cultural view. This role conception is also formed by their previous experiences with how others have helped them, as well as by movies, television, newspapers, the Internet, and how friends and acquaintances have reported their therapeutic experiences. If they have been in therapy before, their previous therapy experiences will strongly influence their expectations. Be sure to ask what they want from this new therapeutic encounter. At the outset, clients

> Experienced therapists tend to develop and employ a variety of relationship building plans. In so doing, they become increasingly similar in their therapeutic styles as they incorporate additional effective approaches based upon personal experiences, new training, and the lessons gained from their clients.

seek to know what content the therapist wants to know. They also may know what they want to say and are looking for the interpersonal safety in which to say it.

In the beginning, several simultaneous pressures guide therapists' investigation into the experiences and mind of each client: (1) relating the precipitating events to dysfunctional patterns, (2) defining clients' explanations for the problems and what they think should be done (the explanatory model), and (3) conceptualizing and diagnosing the concerns. The events that prompt clients to seek therapy often provide clues to the basic dysfunctional patterns to be uncovered. As therapists consider the precipitating event, they also take into consideration four important aspects of the client's life: age, sex, race/culture, and family relationships. These biographical facts help define the client's developmental stage and the issues the person is now probably having trouble mastering.

For example, consider a 19-year-old single, white female college student who seeks counseling because she feels sad, lonely, and confused. What would be typical problems of a 19-year-old unmarried white woman in her first year of college? The simplest and culturally most consistent answer would be difficulty transitioning to college, including difficulty in developing and enacting a personal vision that includes her primary relationships as well as her academic major and postcollege life.

What if the same woman were black and attending a predominantly white college? It would be appropriate to wonder if her experiences of being black at a predominantly white institution added to the challenges she was experiencing in transitioning to college, establishing relationships, and developing a sense of her academic and postcollege plans. One might also want to consider her past experiences with racism, her stage of racial identity development, the racial development views of those with whom she interacts, and the racial climate of her college environment.

Therapists must ask themselves what content in the wide array of ideas and feelings that make up the human psyche they value as most helpful to each client in the process of confusion reduction, choice, and change. Therapists' empathic reflections tend to reinforce production of specific content from the client. Even Carl Rogers, proponent of "client-centered" therapy, struggled with this dilemma. For example, studies of Rogers's recorded therapy sessions demonstrated that he selected certain content areas for his empathic reflections (Truax, 1966). The content areas that Rogers responded to became the focus of the client's discussions, whereas other content areas diminished.

Therapists clearly have many different content areas from which to choose. Each school of therapy encourages discussion of certain areas (see Table 4.2).

TABLE 4.2   Emphasized Content Areas

SCHOOL	CONTENT AREA
Psychodynamic	Childhood development history; intense and missing emotions, specifically anger and anxiety, especially related to therapist.
Cognitive	Distorted logic, unrealistic beliefs, and automatic thoughts.
Behavioral	Relationship between stimuli and consequences, including phobic stimuli.
Interpersonal	Current dyadic relationships, abandonment or fear of being controlled by others, interpersonal role conflicts, grief, role shifts.
Family	Dynamics and social role in current family as well as in family of origin.
Multicultural, feminist, and gender-aware	Values and expectations of clients' culture and influences of dominant culture.

Clients' Explanatory Models

Therapists seek to identify three aspects of clients' explanatory models: the client's explanation of the problem, the desired outcome and the means to get there, and the perception of the role of the therapist in the resolution of the difficulty. Occasionally, therapists are surprised by the disjunction between their views of these aspects and the client's views. For this reason, it is worthwhile to clarify each of these aspects of the explanatory model in order to avoid a rupture or tear in the relationship based on differing or conflicting expectations. Clients seek relief from confusion, distress, and uncertainty. But what do they expect from their therapist? Some want you to help them solve their problems, develop alternatives, make decisions, and act on them. Most clients, but not all, come with this general intention. Some clients want you to help define what "causes" their problems and perhaps seem less interested in doing something about them. Others want a relationship with you because they need a human connection and have not been able to create one in their outside-the-office world. Clients also may want a particular type of relationship. Some may want you simply to listen, nod, and appear to understand. They may not want you to help them change, only to listen and let them decide whether or not to do anything.

A 45-year-old highly educated, intelligent woman with an 8-year-old child had lost her third job. She was again living with her parents, depending on them for financial support. Her parents, in their early eighties, were losing their strength and health and arranged a separate meeting with the therapist pleading for assistance in helping their daughter become financially independent. The inheritance she would receive would last but a few years. The therapist had been listening intently to the client for several sessions before the parents had made their plea, trying to evoke a desired outcome from the client, who seemed to prefer to talk and be heard without having any clear outcome in mind. After the parents' visit, the therapist focused on what had been obvious—the highly intelligent woman needed to try again in the workplace. As the therapist encouraged the client to consider this option, the client became indignant and stormed out, never to return, saying that she only wanted to be heard.

> Therapists seek to identify three aspects of clients' explanatory models: the client's explanation for the problem, the desired outcome and the means to get there, and the perception of the role of the therapist in the resolution of the difficulty.

This client clearly had a particular type of relationship in mind. The therapist, by responding to the aging parents' plea, inadvertently ruptured the therapeutic relationship with the client. The client might have reacted more favorably and been better served by motivation enhancement approaches in which discrepancies between her long-term goals and current behavior were identified. Perhaps she was conflicted about being away from her child? Unfortunately, the therapist missed the opportunity to find out. With gender-aware and motivation enhancement approaches, clients are encouraged to consider taking steps *of their selection* to reach *their* long-term goals (rather than risking feeling misunderstood by an overly directive therapist).

Other clients want you to engage them, to interact with them, and to be actively involved with them during each session. They may also expect you to be responsive to their phone calls and e-mails. What types of responses and interactions are you willing to provide and what are you not willing to provide?

A therapist perceived one client to be a delightful person who well could have been a friend. The therapist looked forward to their meetings and enjoyed the details of the client's life and the manner in which the client described them. The client had minor anxiety, mild depressive symptoms, and some relationship concerns, but was content to enjoy the therapeutic relationship without having to work on more thorny issues. The client paid the therapist's full fee out of pocket (which is a plus for the therapist). The therapist had to consider whether or not their close bond was a sufficient reason to continue therapy.

Sometimes clients are happy to continue meeting but do not desire to make any changes. Should therapy continue under these circumstances?

Clients usually have some idea about how they want their therapist to act. Clients may think the therapist will function in a certain, specific role and be dismayed to discover they were mistaken. For example, the therapist may display too much or too little reflection, direction or self-disclosure. Some clients need their therapists to demonstrate their trustworthiness in many different ways before they can feel safe. Beginning therapists may inappropriately ignore the need to engage with their clients at all, focusing exclusively on assessment and interventions, such as assisting the client to be more assertive or to end a problematic relationship. Conversely, some action-oriented clients perceive a mismatch when they come in seeking to develop and implement a concrete plan of action to address their concerns, only to find their therapist too focused on how they feel and the therapeutic relationship. Clients who feel "missed" by their therapists are more apt to not return or terminate early. Clients often have an idea about what they need to change and how to go about it. Therapists need to help discover this information.

Engagement Methods

Engagement techniques include basic listening skills (especially the expression of empathic understanding described in Chapter 3), specialized knowledge, and useful suggestions, as well as therapist reliability and consistency (Beitman, 1987). Psychotherapy training builds primarily upon the methods for developing relationships that therapists bring into the educational and training experiences. You must ask yourself: "What engagement methods are most compatible with my own interpersonal style?" Do you easily track shifts in emotional tone, try to guess what the person is feeling, and then try to put those feelings into words? Do you prefer to be a fountain of knowledge, delivering answers to direct and indirect questions about how to think, feel, and act? Do you specialize in being able to explain? Do you enjoy the intensity of psychologically intimate, ongoing relationships that allow you to peer into the lives of others without revealing yourself? Your basic skills in engaging people in relationships become the foundation upon which you graft and develop therapeutic techniques for engagement. As you find your own style you will also be working with your clients' interpersonal styles and worldviews to find a mutually comfortable, workable interactions.

The various schools offer a variety of helpful engagement techniques that are relatively school-specific (see Table 4.3).

Therapists often use provision of information, psychoeducational interventions, and skills training to both engage clients in therapy (process) and to assist them in reaching their goals (outcome). (This is described in greater detail in the third section of this book.) By providing information, interventions, and recommendations that help

TABLE 4.3   Engagement Techniques

SCHOOL	ENGAGEMENT TECHNIQUE
Psychodynamic	Past/present interpretations (therapist demonstrates specialized knowledge)
Cognitive	Explanation of how changing thinking can change feelings (therapist demonstrates specialized knowledge and effective suggestions)
Emotion-focused	Empathic reflections (therapist demonstrates emotional empathy)
Behavioral	Suggestions for mastery and pleasure; relaxation techniques (therapist offers effective suggestions and specialized knowledge)
Interpersonal	Explanation of relationship between symptoms and interpersonal difficulties (therapist demonstrates specialized knowledge)
Family	Demonstration of how relationship dynamics can influence difficulties of family members (therapist demonstrates specialized knowledge)
Multicultural, feminist, and gender-aware	Demonstration of how societal and cultural factors contribute to clients' issues (therapist demonstrates specialized knowledge)

address clients' concerns, therapists demonstrate that they both care about and can help their clients.

Managing Boundaries

All therapists are responsible for managing the therapeutic relationship, particularly therapeutic boundaries. Although the therapeutic contract may be implicitly managed by therapists, it is clear that therapists are legally and ethically obligated to fully inform every client. As initially emphasized by feminist principles and now the Health Insurance Portability and Accountability Act (HIPAA) requirements, therapists must be clear about their expectations so that clients can be clear about what they should and should not expect. The following information should generally be included in mental health professionals' written informed consent and other relevant documents to underscore important aspects of the therapeutic contract:

- Fees and billing arrangements
- Potential meeting times for sessions (e.g., Monday–Friday 9am–5pm)
- How long sessions will last (e.g., 45–50 minutes)
- How frequently sessions will occur
- What happens if clients are late or if sessions are missed
- What clients should expect in the way of confidentiality
- Situations requiring the breaking of confidentiality
- How potential out-of-office encounters will be handled
- How therapeutic goals will be determined
- What is expected of clients
- What types of behavior are not acceptable (threats, yelling, property damage, assault)
- How to contact the therapist (emergency and after-hours procedures)
- Grievance procedures

Of the many potential boundary violations, sexual involvement is typically the most serious and damaging to clients (and potentially to therapists). Therapists should be alert to the warning signs: excessive interest in a client, dreaming about or having fantasies about a client, and wanting to touch or looking seductively at a client. Be particularly vigilant if your relational or sexual desires are not being well met in your personal life. Every year therapists are disciplined for sexual misconduct, with penalties including suspension, loss of professional license to practice, and legal costs and settlements that can exceed one million dollars. (Most malpractice insurance policies exclude coverage for sexual misconduct with clients.) In states that have criminalized sexual contact with clients such misconduct can result in imprisonment. Further, all professional organizations regard sexual contact with clients as *highly* unethical (American Psychological Association, 2002; Gutheil & Appelbaum, 2000).

Defining Roles

Research literature supports the notion that the clearer the understanding clients have about their therapeutic role, the longer the clients are likely to stay in therapy (Frank, Hoehn-Saric, Imber, Lieberman, & Stone, 1978; Garfield, 1978; Parloff, Waskow, & Wolfe, 1978; Richert, 1983). Psychoanalysis emphasizes therapeutic neutrality, whereas cognitive therapists prize collaborative empiricism. Clients want to know, without directly asking, the complementary role they are expected to play with you. Are they to be "equal" to you and call you by your first name? Or should they act as if you are an authority to whom they must be respectful?

You should also know your "stimulus value." People often make attributions about people based on their age, sex, race, size, and other aspects of their appearance. How do people generally react to the way you appear or the way you talk and move? Your clients are likely to react similarly. For example, some clients may like a soft-spoken, gentle manner, whereas others may find it irritating and want their therapist to speak more loudly, clearly, and directly. As described earlier in Chapter 3, you need to recognize other variations in what can be termed *intentional accommodations*—molding your behavior to the interactional demands of clients to enhance engagement. Being a good therapist means attending to and adjusting your behavior to meet the needs, interpersonal style, and worldview of your clients.

It is also important for therapists to know how they tend to respond to others. On a broad level, what types of biases and stereotypes do you hold in terms of race, sex, religion, disabilities and physical appearance? On a more psychological level, what kinds of people intimidate you? How do you tend to respond to anger directed at you from others? Do you tend to respond to others' aggression with quick anger of your own? Do you tend to back away and become "silenced" by others' anger and as a result not tell such clients things that they need to hear? Alternatively, what characteristics in others do you find particularly attractive? Someone whom you perceive as beautiful, handsome, sexy, or wonderful may walk into your office. You may be susceptible to "intoxicatation" by the intense interpersonal chemistry of the interaction. Be prepared to maintain neutrality, boundaries, and define role relationships as you would with any other client. Also seek consultation from trusted colleagues at the earliest opportunity. In general, peer consultations and case staffings are particularly valuable when we have strong reactions (positive or negative) to a client.

Research on Therapeutic Working Alliances

The strength of the working alliance strongly correlates with psychotherapy outcomes (Gelso & Carter, 1985; Horvath & Greenberg,

1989; Moras & Strupp, 1982; Wampold, 2001). Researchers have consistently found support for the alliance-outcome relationship despite variations in how the alliance and the outcomes were measured, who measured them, and what psychotherapeutic school of thought was being studied (Henry, Strupp, Schacht, &

> Client variables (symptom severity, strength of social network, expectancy) account for the most variance in outcome. The strength of the working alliances correlates more highly with outcome than do specific therapeutic techniques.

Gatson, 1994). Researchers have studied the impact of the alliance in psychodynamic, cognitive, and Gestalt experiential therapy (e.g., Greenberg & Webster, 1982, Luborsky, 1976; Rounsaville et al., 1987), across a wide range of client problems (e.g., Frank & Gunderson, 1990; Gomes-Swartz, 1978; Hovarth & Greenberg, 1989), in short- and longer-term interventions (Frank & Gunderson, 1990; Kokotovic & Tracey, 1990), from clients', therapists', and observers' perspectives (Marziali, 1984; Tichenor & Hill, 1989), and in relation to outcome measures from qualitative reports to behavioral performance indices (Horvath, 1981; Luborsky, McLellan, Woody, O'Brien, & Auerbach, 1985). Meta-analytic studies have further substantiated the relationship between the quality of the therapeutic working alliance and therapy outcomes (Horvath & Symonds, 1991; Martin, Garske, & Davis, 2000; Wampold, 2001).

Despite the recent emphasis on evidenced-based practices (e.g., empirically supported interventions), therapists should bear in mind some central research findings regarding predictors of therapy outcome. Carefully consider the question, "What best predicts how clients will be functioning at the termination of treatment?" The best predictor is *not* the therapists' use of specific therapeutic techniques; rather it is extratherapeutic factors, such as how well clients were functioning before they entered therapy (accounting for 40% of variance in therapy outcome). The next best predictor is the strength of the therapeutic relationship (30% of variance in therapy outcomes). Clients' expectancy, hope, and placebo are roughly equal to therapists' use of specific schools and techniques, accounting for about 15% each (Hubble, Duncan, & Miller, 1999; Lambert & Bergin, 1994; Miller, Duncan, & Hubble, 1997; Wampold, 2001). Wampold summarized these findings with the statement: "The relationship accounts for dramatically more of the variability in outcome than does the totality of specific ingredients" (2001, p. 158). Stated another way: "Research carried out with the intent of contrast[ing] two or more bona fide treatments shows surprisingly small differences between the outcomes for patients who undergo

Factors affecting therapy outcome are, in order of significance: client characteristics ("extratherapeutic" factors) (40%); the therapy relationship (30%); expectancy, hope, or placebo (15%); and structure, model, or technique (15%).

a treatment that is fully intended to be therapeutic" (Lambert & Bergin, 1994, p. 158). Hence, given the central role of therapeutic relationships to therapeutic outcomes, wise students will make developing their skills in forming and sustaining therapeutic relationships a significant focus of their training.

Establishing Effective Therapeutic Alliances

Because good working alliances are characterized by mutual endorsement of tasks and goals and by an interpersonal bond, therapists should directly attend to collaborating with their clients in developing these key components. Some studies have explored therapist's technical contributions to the working alliance. For instance, in general, therapist's use of greater amounts of data collection and assessment techniques are negatively related to the strength of the working alliance (Kivlighan, 1990). Also, there may be a relation between therapists' technical contributions and client characteristics. Specifically, when clients were highly motivated, an examination of negative transference strengthened the alliance. However, when clients were poorly motivated, the alliance was strengthened by a consistently positive therapist attitude (Horowitz, Marmar, Weiss, Dewitt, & Rosenbaum, 1984).

Therapists must attempt to both intuitively and objectively grasp the role-relationship model most appealing or familiar to the client. In other words, how does the client conceptualize the role of the other person in a close, trusting, and confiding relationship? Clients from different cultures often have alternate worldviews, with correspondingly different expectations of the nature of the working alliance. For example, individuals from Asian cultures may have greater faith in the wisdom of older therapists (their elders), be more comfortable with hierarchical relationships, and seek more direct guidance than would be typical of individuals from the dominant culture in the U.S. From another perspective, clients who are highly reactant (rebel against direction from others) may best engage by empathic understanding, therapist self-revelation, and gentle questioning, whereas less reactant clients may more easily engage through direct guidance, direct questioning, and possibly confrontation. Therapists' self-observing behaviors and thoughts associated with the tasks, goals, and bond may provide useful ongoing feedback. Similarly, clients' self-observations regarding the working alliance may also facilitate establishing and maintaining a good relationship. For example, perhaps a client doesn't want to take responsibility for a task that the therapist and client had mutually agreed would be useful. Helping the client observe this discrepancy could lead to a self-evaluation that produces the desired results, contributes to the development of a more appropriate task to perform (e.g., a more useful homework assignment), or stimulates a new awareness of how this situation illustrates a general pattern of behavior (e.g., agreeing but then failing to carry out the agreement).

To look at the therapeutic relationship from another perspective, clients generally want answers to three questions: (1) Does my therapist like and value me? (2) Can my therapist be trusted to understand me? (3) Can my therapist help me? In order to trust a therapist, clients usually must feel that the therapist wants to help them, the therapist will not hurt them, and the therapist is consistent. The ability to confide in the therapist gradually emerges from increasing belief in the therapist's trustworthiness. The realization that the therapist will not cause harm is primarily dependent upon the client's previous experiences in interpersonal helping. Individuals with little experience in being helped or who have been harmed by people who were supposed to be helpful (e.g., parents and other adult caregivers) usually take more time and require more evidence to believe that the therapist will not be harmful (Sifneos, 1972). On the therapist's part, the ability to listen empathically and to demonstrate understanding of the client's experiences and life in a caring and gentle context helps accelerate approval of the therapist.

The therapist's willingness to be helpful is most effectively demonstrated by actually being helpful! How clients experience helpfulness is, again, in great part a product of their personal history. The therapist may clearly establish role relationships and foster articulation of the client's expectations of therapy and make specific effective suggestions. The collaborative aspect of the relationship emphasizes to clients that they are working together with their therapist to reach their goals. These actions help to demonstrate the therapist's willingness and ability to be of assistance. Consistency can be demonstrated by the therapist's predictable responses to the client's activity. If, for example, a client is discussing an emotionally laden subject and the therapist responds with an empathic reflection on several different occasions, the therapist is demonstrating consistency.

The engagement stage elicits from the therapist role relationship models previously developed in the therapist's personal and professional life for establishing close relationships (Luborsky & Crits-Christoph, 1990). Therapists tend to rely upon what they have already experienced and utilize those experiences as they attempt to engage clients in therapy. Many therapists were excellent listeners in their outside-therapy-life—people whom others naturally sought out when they needed someone to share their problematic experiences. Therefore, students might ask themselves by what means they establish trusting and confiding relationships with their friends, peers, and others.

Although there are many things therapists can do to successfully engage clients in therapy, the primary determinant of a strong working alliance during the engagement phase is the client's experiences with previous intimate relationships (Luborsky & Crits-Christoph, 1990; Sifneos, 1972). Clients with limited or no positive experiences confiding to a helpful other tend to be much more tentative in their abilities and willingness to engage in a therapeutic relationship. Conversely, clients who have enjoyed and benefited from confiding relationships will more readily engage with the therapist. An additional and sometimes overlapping factor is clients' motivation to use the therapeutic relationship as a mechanism for change (Prochaska & Norcross, 2002). Some clients come to therapy under duress and with no interest in changing, whereas others may appear to want to change but are very doubtful or dismissive of the potential value of the interpersonal helping relationship in assisting with this effort.

Repairing Tears and Ruptures in Therapeutic Alliances

Much like real-world relationships, therapeutic relationships can be strengthened when individuals honestly work out their differences. In fact, better therapy outcomes often include one or more incidents in which the therapeutic relationship experienced a "tear and repair"— that is, the therapeutic alliance was ruptured and mended (Safran & Muran, 2000). Tears, including strains, often occur somewhere in the middle of the therapeutic relationship (however that might be defined by the length of therapy). During this phase, therapeutic alliances often become strained because clients are conflicted because they want to please their therapists (by acting for their own betterment) but they are also reluctant to make changes. Therapists may be seen as a threat to the status quo and the relationship may become strained as a result. (Therapists typically experience this phenomenon as client "resistance," which is described in Chapter 8.)

> Repairing a ruptured alliance often strengthens the alliance and results in a better therapy outcome.

Research has repeatedly shown that the working alliance is fairly well set after three to four sessions. Differences between measures taken early in therapy and those taken later in therapy tend to be very small (Horvath & Symonds, 1991; Wampold, 2001). However, good alliances can be strained and may begin to tear or even rupture. No matter how skilled the therapist, things sometimes go wrong. The client is angry, dissatisfied, anxious about therapy, uncertain of its value, or may feel harmed by the therapist. Rather than viewing these experiences as indications of failure, look at them as opportunities. For many clients, therapists model conduct for ideal relationships: the commitment by each participant to the relationship encourages each member to find ways to heal the breach. Healing the breach then strengthens the alliance. You may have already noticed this in your personal life as well. When we successfully resolve a difficult issue with someone, our trust in the relationship typically grows stronger.

Two general categories of rupture have been identified: (1) the client avoids participating in therapy (withdrawal rupture) and (2) the client expresses frustration (confrontation rupture; Safran & Muran, 2000). After you have established a baseline of your client's responses, watch for signals of withdrawal, including denying an obvious emotion, responding minimally, shifting the topic, becoming too intellectual, adding too much detail to stories, and talking about other people excessively. Signals of frustration can be easier to notice: Clients may complain about the therapist's behavior or ability, about the activities of therapy, about being in therapy, or about the rate or degree of progress. Therapists first need to recognize the problem and then begin discussion of what is happening and not happening. What is missing? What did the therapist do or not do that contributed to the problem? Indeed, you may have done something wrong; if so, own it and apologize! A heartfelt apology can help solidify a relationship.

The way clients create a breach in the relationship can provide valuable information about basic maladaptive patterns (Safran, 1993). For example, a therapist attempted to be self-revealing early in therapy about his responses to a female client. Shortly after beginning his self-disclosure the client became upset and angry. After several sessions of discussion, including an apology on the part of the therapist about not accurately predicting his impact, the client described her intense fear of finding out what other people really think of her because she believed people found her silly, stupid, unattractive, and not worth knowing. Later, as they explored the client's relationships with her parents, they clarified the extensive emotional and physical abuse from both parents that led her to not want to imagine what they were thinking as they abused her. As described in Chapter 5, the therapeutic rupture became an "inducing point" for a basic maladaptive interpersonal pattern—her fear of knowing what others were truly thinking of her (i.e., knowing the mind of the other person).

Despite therapists' best efforts, working alliances sometimes get off to poor starts. Foreman and Marmar (1985) found that in cases with improving alliances, therapists were more likely to address the client's defenses, guilt, and problematic feelings in relation to the therapist, as well as link the problematic feeling with the therapist to the client's defenses. Additionally, therapists whose working alliance improved were relatively more challenging and here and now-oriented (rather than there and then-oriented), compared to therapists whose working alliance did not improve (Kivlighan & Schmitz, 1992). Although more studies are needed to understand the relation between therapist techniques and the strength of working alliance, these findings provide some of the information we need to consider in establishing, maintaining, and repairing working alliances.

Changes in the Therapeutic Relationship Over Time

The therapist-client relationship provides the foundation for therapeutically induced psychological change. Further, as the relationship and the client's therapeutic journey evolve, the therapeutic relationship can help buffer the client's experience of intense negative emotions (e.g., abandonment, isolation, hopelessness) and other stressors. Psychological change moves through stages like any problem-solving sequence. First, it is helpful to define the problem in a way that also includes options to resolve it, and then identify the steps that will be taken toward solving the problem. The routes to change may be foggy and strewn with impediments, but the more clearly therapists are able to imagine this progression, the more effectively they can assist their clients in their journey. When possible, therapists can serve as effective guides and allies by accurately predicting and assisting clients in preparing for experiences and barriers that they will probably encounter during their journeys.

What are some of the major characteristics of the evolving therapeutic relationship? Most therapeutic relationships are relatively brief, lasting from 1 to 8 sessions. Although the influence of psychoanalytic lore has made it appear that therapeutic relationships last much longer, research studies have reliably demonstrated their relative brevity over the past 50 years (Lambert & Bergin, 1994). Another factor skewing popular perception of the length of therapy comes from experienced therapists themselves, who, like everyone else, see most clients for a relatively short number of sessions but over their years of practice have accumulated a number long-term clients.

When therapists' control over the therapeutic relationship is diagrammed on a coordinate system with the vertical axis representing therapist control and the horizontal axis representing duration of treatment, a U shape is typically generated. In other words, therapists tend to direct the therapeutic relationship more at the beginning and end of treatment and less during the middle "working" phase. During engagement, therapists help define the relationship, their respective roles, the boundaries, and the therapeutic contract. During pattern search and change (discussed in Chapter 5), clients are freed to think, feel, and explore alternatives; therapists become observers, guides, collaborators, and commentators. Clients often have limited experience with successfully drawing relationships to a close, especially as this applies to a client-therapist relationship. Hence, as time for termination approaches, some clients know when and how to leave, whereas others require therapists' support, encouragement, and direction regarding termination.

How are therapists to know when to end the relationship? Some clients will, in one way or another, declare that their goals have been reached, or that sufficient time, energy, or money has been spent. It is time to stop. Other clients will simply drop away. Still others will leave "prematurely." When clients terminate prematurely, the therapist may, depending on the client's issues and dynamics (the client's needs should come first), opt to contact the client and discuss the reason for termination. If you do call, you may be surprised to find that one session actually helped (Malan, Heath, Balal, & Baltour, 1975). You may also discover that something good or bad happened that prevented further sessions. Or your worst fears may materialize: You acted in a way that prevented the client from continuing. In these cases, it is important to remember that *all* therapists occasionally act in ways that do not resonate with a particular client. When possible, learn from these experiences.

Assessment and Early Formulation

During engagement, therapists assess clients for their mental and emotional functioning within their social environments. They systematically gather information to develop clear descriptors of the basic difficulties, which may include symptom severity, diagnosis, readiness to change, and the social network strength. Assessment forms the foundation of formulation, which organizes the content of conceptualization, places the details into an expectation about what needs to change and can change, and defines how the client can create the change and what the therapist can do to assist (Sim, Gwee, & Bateman, 2005). Formulation is rarely rigidly fixed; rather, it is flexibly responsive to new information.

Assessment

During assessment, therapists clarify the client variables that will influence outcome. Among the first questions that therapists ask themselves during the initial assessment is: Is psychotherapy the best way to help this person? For some clients, food, clothing, and shelter are the most pressing problems; in such cases, social or case workers are more critical than personal therapy. Perhaps clients' symptoms are caused by biomedical problems like thyroid disease (with symptoms of restlessness, depression, or anxiety) or a hereditary susceptibility to depression (e.g., both biological parents experienced depression that successfully responded to antidepressants). In such cases referral to a primary care physician or psychiatrist would be appropriate, with the possible option of continuing therapy. Finally, some clients, such as individuals with long standing interpersonal issues or personality disorders, may be better served by group therapy than individual therapy.

Diagnosis

Standard assessments require diagnosis according the DSM IV-TR (American Psychiatric Association, 1994). Insurance companies typically reimburse for Axis I disorders (e.g., anxiety, depression, bipolar disorder, schizophrenia, and adjustment disorders) but not for Axis II (personality disorders) or marital and family therapy. Diagnosis can guide therapeutic treatment (discussed in Section III). Most schools of therapy tend to apply their approach no matter what the diagnosis (Prochaska & Norcross, 2003), whereas cognitive therapists explicitly vary their concepts and techniques depending on the diagnostic problem (Freeman, Simon, Beutler, & Ackowitz, 1989).

Severity of Problems

The most important factor predicting outcome is the severity of clients' problems (Beutler et al., 2002). For example, like all problems, depression varies in severity, with many forms responding very well to therapy. However, some forms of depression may require medication, and the most extreme and treatment-resistant forms may require electroconvulsive therapy (ECT).

Some problems almost always require medications—schizophrenia and bipolar disorder being the two prime examples. Mild to moderate anxiety or depression respond well to either medications or therapy (Beitman, Blinder, Thase, Riba, & Safer, 2003), with a combination of the two providing the most favorable outcome for clients with more severe problems. Additionally, the client's belief in a particular way of helping (type of interaction with the therapist, type of therapy, and view of medications) strongly influences outcome. Because the client has come to you, you will typically try therapy first.

Client Motivation

How motivated is the client to change? As noted in the Chinese saying *"in crisis there is opportunity,"* crises present opportunities for change in part because the status quo has been upset. There is the opportunity for clients to try something different. What good reasons does the client have for change? Clients' readiness to change is an important outcome predictor (Prochaska & Norcross, 2002).

Client Strengths

What previous experience and strengths does the client bring to the current set of problems? One of the more surprising findings comes from research comparing interpersonal therapy and cognitive therapy in the treatment of depression. Clinicians tend to think that interpersonal psychotherapy works best for people with interpersonal difficulties whereas cognitive therapy works better for people who have dysfunctional thought patterns. Quite the opposite was found: clients with good interpersonal skills responded well to interpersonal therapy and clients with good cognitive skills responded well to cognitive therapy (Elkin et al., 1989; Watkins et al., 1993). This research implies that therapists should generally seek to use clients' strengths to work around their weaknesses rather than try to directly fill in deficits. For example, therapists might best help clients who have relative strengths in rationality but weakness in interpersonal relationships by assisting them in thinking through how they might improve their relationships with others.

Social Network

The strength of the social network is also a strong predictor of outcome (Beutler et al., 2002). Change takes place within a social network, with social networks supporting change, inhibiting change, or having little influence. Clients with a close confidant and less family conflict experience better outcomes with brief therapy; clients without a close support figure and with greater family conflict experience better outcomes with longer-term treatment (Moos, 1990).

Resiliency

As these questions are being asked another one looms: How resilient is this client? How well has this person been able to handle difficulties in the past? Resiliency refers to people's ability to recognize that experiences recorded in memory can be altered to create new versions of these experiences, which leads to more effective adaptation. Highly resilient people know that their inner maps of the world are not the actual territory, and that maps can be altered. Characteristics associated with successful adaptation include: strong intellectual functioning, effective self-regulation of emotions and attachment behaviors, a positive self-concept, optimism, altruism, a capacity to convert traumatic helplessness into learned helpfulness, and an active coping style in confronting a stressor (Charney, 2004).

Goals

Therapy is future-oriented. Despite sometimes glorified emphasis on the past, current emotions, what goes on in the office, what clients think, or their current interpersonal relationships, therapists ultimately help clients plan to act differently when they leave the office. Everything that goes on in the office is directly intended to help clients think, feel, and behave differently in the world outside the therapist's office (Beitman, Soth, & Bumby, 2005). Goals for therapy evolve from the client's current and past levels of functioning. People who were once high-functioning can be expected to return to high functioning. Conversely, those who have followed a gradual downward course over years of treatment (such as recurrent major depression requiring longer hospitalizations) may use therapy to help slow the rate of their decline.

Formulation

Formulation puts form to the therapeutic information and is used to direct the client and therapist toward a desired outcome. Formulation gives structure to complex data by identifying maladaptive patterns to be changed and providing the means to change them. Effective formulation is less a product of theory and therapist bias and more a good fit with the client's way of understanding problems and methods of change. More accurately it can be called *reformulation* of the client's existing explanations and problem-solving methods.

Formulation has two parts related to the middle stages of therapy: definition of the problem in ways that suggest solutions (pattern search) and potential change strategies and techniques (change). These two aspects of formulation reciprocally influence each other as therapy proceeds: Attempts at change can sharpen or revise the conception of dysfunctional patterns; reworking dysfunctional patterns can reshape potential techniques and strategies.

The two aspects of formulation (pattern definition and change strategies) create tension between theory and technique. Theory tends to define *causes* of psychological dysfunction, whereas strategy and technique seek *solutions* to problems. Change techniques may have little relationship to theories of causality. A tension is created because theories tend to be about the past whereas change strategies are about the future. In the practicalities of the therapist's office, theory and strategy come close together in the search for patterns to change.

What needs to change to reduce symptoms, strengthen social and work functioning, and improve general well-being? What reactions, to what situations, need to be altered? What mediating factors will optimize the effort? Should the client be changing thoughts, emotions, behaviors, relationships, systems, or contexts? How does one define the patterns to be changed? What strategies and techniques should be used? The following chapters explore the answers to these questions.

Summary

This chapter focuses on the important tasks associated with seeking to engage with clients to develop and maintain effective therapeutic working alliances. The working alliance is of primary importance to therapy outcome, accounting for approximately 30% of variance in client outcome from therapy. Bordin's (1979) definition of effective working alliances as featuring client-therapist agreement on (a) goals and (b) tasks occurring in the context of a (c) positive interpersonal bond was described. Therapists' responsibility and methods for initiating, maintaining, repairing, and concluding therapeutic relationships were examined. The chapter concluded with a discussion of early formulation, which involves seeking to fill the gaps between diagnosis and interventions, seeking to integrate the explanatory, prescriptive, predictive, and therapist aspects of assisting clients' in addressing their concerns.

CHAPTER 5

Pattern Identification and Treatment Planning

In all chaos there is a cosmos, in all disorder a secret order.
—CARL G. JUNG

Therapists carry with them a set of patterns against which to match clients' individual difficulties. These patterns form the basis for discrepancies between "normal" and "abnormal" responses from their clients. Therapists seek to identify deviations from the standard: Intuitively we know that ideal mental functioning is neither excessive nor insufficient but rather somewhere in the middle (e.g., Trull, Widiger, Lynam, & Costa, 2003). This balanced middle perspective may be difficult to achieve. For some clients, finding and maintaining a sense of balance requires development of new skills. Therapists search for ways to assist their clients in moving out of their difficult situations. Clients are often caught between a rock and a hard place, between two or more undesirable options with no effective exit in sight. They are confused, often knowing that something must change, and yet not knowing how to decide what option to select or how to develop options. The therapist's quiet faith in yet-to-be discovered solutions is supported by well-established methods to discover and change pivotal dysfunctional patterns. These methods rely upon a simple formula: examine the odd, unwanted responses (e.g., feelings, thoughts, or behaviors), define the events that triggered the symptom, and then identify the intervening factors that connect the symptoms with the stimulus (e.g., thoughts, schemas, conflicts, role relationship models). The unwanted response can be represented with an R, the triggering event or stimulus can be represented with an *S*, and the intervening connection between the S and R may refer to the person or more generically to the organism, which can be represented with an *O*. The basic formula for pattern search, then is: S→O→R as described earlier. The desired outcome for therapy becomes an alteration in the manner in which the client responds to similar stimuli in the future, which can also include responses designed to alter their environment and thereby create different new stimuli in the future.

From individual examples of S→O→R, therapists "induce" general maladaptive patterns. In other words, therapists use *inductive reasoning* to generalize from specific bits of information to broader patterns that persist across situations. These specific pieces of information are called *inducing points*. By forming tentative generalizations from several inducing points, therapists can develop *well-formed patterns*. *Well-formed* means that the pattern (1) appears to fit the client well, (2) is viewed by both the client and therapist as needing to be changed, (3) includes sufficient details to suggest what needs to be changed, and (4) will, once changed, lead to the desired outcome. The development of a pattern or set of patterns usually requires an iterative process: The therapist infers the broad outlines of a pattern from an inducing point and waits for confirmation or disconfirmation from subsequent including points.

The hypothetical pattern may be presented directly to the client, who then confirms or disconfirms, sometimes adding nuances. The more experienced the therapist, the more quickly patterns can be defined. (Unfortunately experience may lead the therapist to select a pattern before the pattern has been clearly supported by data.) As part of this process the client and therapist reach a consensus about a pattern that seems to underlie many other dysfunctional symptoms and patterns. If the basic pattern is changed, the client will benefit with symptom reduction and an increase in social and work functioning. Some may argue that accurate selection of a pattern is less important than agreement that the pattern should be changed, so that the words describing the pattern provide a means, a fulcrum, around which change can take

---

Inductive reasoning involves generalizing from specific bits of information to broader patterns that persist across situations. The specific bits of information are called *inducing points*. By forming tentative generalizations from several inducing points, therapists can develop *well-formed patterns*. *Well-formed* means that the pattern (1) appears to fit the client well, (2) is viewed by both the client and therapist as needing to be changed, (3) includes sufficient details to suggest what needs to be changed, and (4) will, once changed, lead to the desired outcome.

place. In this view, the pattern is a metaphor rather than an accurate and complete depiction of reality.

If clients agree that a pattern should change, the next step is to help them define the reasons they have not changed it. This step leads to change strategies, which are explored in the following two chapters.

> Descriptors of dysfunctional patterns range in their level of detail from very general to very specific. The most general patterns are the "personality trait level," the second level is the "psychotherapy school level," and the third is "personal level." The more general patterns encompass the more specific ones.

Dysfunctional Patterns

Dysfunctional patterns have been defined at different levels of detail from very general to very specific. The first or most general level can be labeled the "personality trait level," the second is the "psychotherapy school level," and the third is the "personal level." The most general patterns encompass the less general ones.

The Personality Trait Level

The most abstract patterns provide a general picture of the client but do not suggest any specific ways to change. They include: submissive, perfectionistic, self-defeating, irresponsible, dependent, aggressive, paranoid, avoidant, self-aggrandizing, low self-esteem, codependent, passive, grandiose, hypersensitive, obsessive, unassertive, impulsive, indecisive, and self-depreciating. Related general terms include: dysfunctional family and maladaptive communication. These are terms used by both therapists and the general public in an attempt to categorize but are also often used as a way to blame.

The Psychotherapy School Level

At this level, the patterns are derived from attempts of various psychotherapeutic approaches, with their respective theoretical perspectives, to describe and understand pathology or dysfunction. Each approach uses its own theoretical terms to describe dysfunctional patterns.

Psychodynamic Therapy
- Reenactment from past to present
- Unconscious conflicts

- Inadequate ego development
- Immature defense mechanisms
- Human developmental stages and crises

Interpersonal Therapy
- Role transitions
- Role conflicts
- Unresolved grief
- Core conflictual relationship themes
- Interpersonal skill deficits

Behavioral Therapy
- Inadequate stimulus control
- Problematic conditioned responses
- Problematic modeling
- Neurotic paradox
- Behavioral excesses and deficits

Cognitive Therapy
- Dysfunctional automatic thoughts
- Negative cognitive schemas
- Cognitive distortions

Person-Centered Therapy
- Conditions of worth and negative self-concept

Existential Therapy
- Fear of responsibility and freedom
- Fear of death
- Existential isolation
- Meaninglessness

Emotion Focused Therapy
- Avoidance of emotional awareness
- Conflict splits
- Unfinished business

Family Therapy

- Triangulation
- Boundary problems
- Disturbed homeostasis
- Circular causality

These concepts are defined in the last section of this chapter.

The Personal Level

At the third level, dysfunctional patterns are more concrete and can be observed both clinically and in daily life. They often provide sufficient detail to point the way toward change. This level uses descriptive patterns specifically defined for individual clients. These patterns, or parts of them, usually appear in therapist reflections and restatements of what clients say and differ from client to client. For example, consider Ralph, who often felt frustrated, irritable, and angry in communicating with others in his life because he thought they neglected his needs. The therapist explored the way he communicated with others and found that he always assumed others knew his needs or feelings without his having made himself sufficiently clear. His third-level pattern might be: "You incorrectly assume that you have already communicated your wants and needs. You expect others to be able to read your mind."

Behaviors can be interpreted on all three levels. For example, Jan never confronted her partner when blamed for things she did not do (the personal level). Her failure to respond assertively might be due to a school-level pattern, such as a maladaptive cognition ("If I confront someone, I will lose him or her"), a reenactment from past to present (she never confronted her mother's controlling behavior because she was afraid of being abandoned by her), or negative modeling (her parents divorced after her mother was critical and her father became withdrawn). On the personality trait level we might say that she is passive, submissive, and dependent.

The therapist's presentation of a hypothetical pattern provides a stimulus for clients to join in an interactive process. Clients may agree, add to, reject, or revise a suggested pattern until it fits well. Positive feeling grows as the therapist and client collaborate in building the hypothetical pattern that appeals to both of them.

Therapeutic training and experience quickens therapists' ability to generalize from individual observations and reports to broader patterns. Which events of therapy, then, should therapists scan for patterns as they listen to and observe their clients? Following is a partial list of inducing points. Direct your attention first to things that differ from expectations about what is generally considered normal and adaptive.

- Verbal reports (of dysfunctional response to specific stimuli)
- Thought records (e.g., showing cognitive distortions)
- Behavioral observations in the office (incongruence between words and nonverbal behavior)
- Reports of unusual behavior from relatives and friends
- Unusual interpersonal interactions. These may be observed in the office, with the therapist, between members of a couple, family, or with office staff (e.g., one member talks for another person).
- Therapeutic contract-related behaviors (e.g., failure to keep appointments, excessive emails or phone calls, attempts to see the therapist outside of sessions or the office, failure to pay bills)
- Unusual responses to therapists' interventions (e.g., agrees to do a homework activity but then does not do it)
- Countertransference signals (e.g., irritation; see Chapter 8)
- Unusual reaction to or behaviors associated with pharmacotherapy (e.g., failure to take prescribed medications; see Chapter 15 and Beitman et al., 2003)

Therapists work backward from the noted difference from expectations to the event that triggered it to the possible intervening variable to induce a possible pattern. For example, suppose Jen, a 28-year-old female client, describes a panic attack that occurred while she was drying dishes in her boyfriend's apartment as he was washing them. She reports that she has had other panic attacks and wants them to stop. She desires therapy but not medication. What can the panic attack signal? Rather than being bad feelings to suppress and forget, unwanted reactions like this can be viewed as messages from the mind's interior. Developmentally Jen is probably being urged by culture and biology to get married and have children. Does she want to be involved with a man? Yes. Then what might be the problem? Doing the dishes together (the stimulus) can feel like domestic intimacy (a potential intervening variable or meaning). Might she be frightened of becoming too close to him? Has he given mixed signals about whether he is willing to commit to an egalitarian relationship with her? Her father dominated her mother and, according to the client, ruined her mother's career by insisting that they move from the place in which her career was advancing.

Jen's therapist decides to further explore the issue by asking the client to create a cognitive thought record. In this thought record, Jen describes a panic attack that occurred as she read to her 4-year-old niece and another during sexual contact with her boyfriend. For Jen, reading to the child is an emotionally charged, family-like situation. Sexual relations with her boyfriend evoke emotional intimacy and vulnerability. Thus, the therapist might deduce that Jen has apprehensions about being emotionally involved and vulnerable with this man. This hypothesis could be then presented to Jen to see how it fits her.

Presenting patterns like these to clients is not unlike helping a friend buy shoes or a hat. Indeed, therapists should almost never give a "hard sell" to convince clients of their hypotheses; clients must somehow see the pattern (or explanation) as "fitting" them in order for them to "buy" it. Reasoning inductively requires the selection of a small number of possible patterns based upon a salient S→O→R sequence; hypotheses must then be confirmed by additional individual situations.

Some patterns threaten the establishment and maintenance of the therapeutic relationship; these patterns can also be identified by inductive reasoning based on deviations from expected behaviors or responses. For example, consider Jerry, a 30-year-old man with depression, anxiety, and substance abuse problems. Jerry had previously seen three different therapists. During the initial interview with the new therapist, Jerry mentioned that he fired his previous therapists because "they just listened and had me talk—they didn't do any good." This response could happen again. The therapist observed that Jerry talked nonstop and even talked over the therapist when the therapist tried to break in. The therapist hypothesized that Jerry sought control of the discussion and the relationship. He could examine this hypothesis by exploring what else was going on in these interactions and how often this type of interaction takes place in the client's life outside of therapy.

The ability to induce dysfunctional patterns is related to the therapist's knowledge of various patterns from clinical and personal experience.

Experiences with previous clients facilitate discovery of patterns in current clients; personal experiences help therapists anticipate details that would confirm a pattern. For example, a therapist familiar with depression can more quickly grasp the client's hopelessness about the future, lack of confidence in self, and fear of abandonment by others. Therapists who have had paranoid experiences can understand clients who feel distrust, are overly cautious about the meaning of interpersonal reactions, and are afraid of some unnamed negative consequence.

The Human Life Cycle and Dysfunctional Patterns

Client problems often grow out of life cycle challenges. Adaptive and maladaptive patterns are learned in the emotional cauldron of early upbringing. We learn to function in these early environments and then continue to act as if we are still in them because our early adaptations are familiar or seem to still work. But the world and our expected interactions within it have changed. We have grown up and left that early environment. Clients' acceptance of their current life situation and their subsequent willingness to make changes is often facilitated by their getting the sense that their pattern of responding (e.g., the way they learned to cope with emotional disappointments or interpersonal conflicts) made perfect sense (i.e., was highly adaptive) when they developed it. Clients might then see how they tend to continue to use their characteristic method of coping in later contexts even if it is no longer adaptive.

Neurosis has been defined as doing the same thing over and over again and expecting different results. Dysfunctional responses result from a mismatch between expectations and experience. The basic pattern for change is: Change the expectations (and corresponding behavior) or change the environment. For example, Frank entered individual therapy after more than 20 years in a "good marriage." He believed that he and his wife were "friends," but he felt an intense desire for a "soul mate," which he was convinced his wife could not become. If his wife could not change, he could change either his expectations about his wife or soul mate, or he could change his environment (leave his marriage).

> *Neurosis* can be defined as doing the same thing over and over again and expecting different results. People's dysfunctional responses result from a mismatch between their expectations and experiences. The basic process for altering neurotic patterns is to change the expectations (and corresponding behavior) and/or change the environment.

Each of us journeys along the human life cycle from birth to death. The challenges of human development are formed by the confluence of biology and culture within a social structure (usually transmitted through a family). Many client problems are created by failure to negotiate developmental expectations. Therapists help clients reclaim their normal developmental progression.

Following are some examples of *normal* developmental difficulties:

- A child having trouble setting aside what he or she wants when learning to share toys while playing with others
- A child finding it challenging to consider the perspective of others
- Children and young adults wrestling with self-regulating their activities to advance their physical, emotional, and interpersonal well-being (making the self-directed effort to complete school/work/home obligations, exercise, sleep, eat properly, express anger and sexuality appropriately, and avoid addictions)
- Adolescents struggling with simultaneously striving to be themselves and to fit into their peer social environment
- Adolescents and young adults experiencing confusion and uncertainty about who they are, what they should do with their lives, and whom they should do it with
- A person feeling like an imposter when he or she enters a new interpersonal environment and tries to project an image of "having it all together"
- Individuals experiencing restriction, oppression, discrimination, or harassment based on some aspect(s) of their identity (e.g., race, sex, affectional preference, spiritual beliefs, ability, status, appearance) and deciding how to cope with it
- Individuals being confused about what they should focus their life energies toward in terms of academic studies and career
- Individuals feeling unsure about what characteristics are important and seeking to find their optimal significant relationship/marriage partner
- Members of a couple wondering if they made a mistake after the initial period of intense fusion ("the honeymoon period")

wears off and they become acutely aware of their differences ("the period of intense pulling"; see Chapter 14.)

- Parents struggling to balance the demands of raising an infant (or young child) and meeting work and home demands
- Members of a couple experiencing stress and tension in their relationship due to the loss of individual and couple time after having a child and during subsequent childrearing
- Individuals experiencing strong emotions (grief, anger, sadness, isolation) when a relationship ends or someone dies
- Individuals reflecting on the meaning of their life (commonly with milestones like marriage, contemplation of having children, midlife, children leaving home, change of relationship status, health concerns, and retirement)
- Older adults experiencing sadness and loss associated with physical weakening of themselves and people they care about
- Grief and loss associated with the death of friends and family members
- Older adults seeking to remain valuable and contributing (feelings of worth)

Life however, often does not proceed as it we think it should. Consider the following events and how most people would react, keeping in mind that age, sex, ethnicity race, family, and work status may affect individuals' responses.

- A child in elementary school witnesses physical violence between his or her parents. How might he or she cope?
- A boy in elementary school is ridiculed, taunted, and shamed by his peers because he cried. What might he learn from this?
- A child's parents announce their divorce. How might the child react?
- A 12-year-old girl is fondled by her stepfather. How might this affect her life?
- A 13-year-old boy develops insulin-dependent diabetes. How will he relate to his peers?

- Members of a 14-year-old's peer group start experimenting with tobacco, alcohol, and marijuana. How might he or she respond?

- An adolescent girl going through puberty enjoys compliments and positive attention but not the harassment and threats of sexual aggression she receives. What is she to make of this?

- A 15-year-old has strong and persistent attraction to members of his or her sex. What challenges might this teenager anticipate?

- An ethnic/racial minority teenager leaves his or her community to attend a predominantly white college where he or she encounters disparaging stereotypes, insults, and threats. How would you expect this person to react?

- A 21-year-old college student is drinking alcohol and smoking marijuana daily and has few friends. What is happening to his or her academic performance?

- A man in his late twenties accepts a job as an elementary school teacher. He is a very good teacher, but is the only male teacher at the school and must endure regular derogatory comments about his masculinity by others outside of his work setting. How might this affect his choice of life partner and friends?

- A 35-year-old devoutly religious woman has wanted children all her life but has not been in a sustained relationship. How might she be feeling?

- A bright and hard-working 38-year-old minority group member realizes that he or she has been repeatedly passed over for advancement in comparison to less competent majority group peers. The company has placed him or her in a highly visible but little utilized dead-end token diversity-related position. How might this affect the person?

- A 40-year-old woman with three school-aged children has metastatic breast cancer. What might she be thinking?

- A couple has been married for many years when one partner comes home and announces that he or she has been having an affair and wants a divorce. How would the other partner react?

- A couple in their forties has their prized teenage child die in a motor vehicle accident. How might they react and what influence might this death have on the marriage?
- A 45-year-old married man who has prided himself on his masculine virility loses his ability to obtain an erection. How might he react?
- The factory at which people in their late fifties worked their entire adult life closes. What would be their normal reactions?
- The last child of highly involved parents grows up and leaves home. What would the parents typically feel and what challenges might their marriage face?
- An aging parent becomes demented and moves in with his or her children's family who provide care. How might family members typically react?
- A 60-year-old is forced to retire from a job he or she loved. How might this person feel?
- A 78-year-old witnesses his or her 80-year-old partner stop breathing and then be resuscitated. What might the person fear about his or her partner's health?

Not everyone has a major problematic response when faced with these circumstances, and the mismatch between expectations and experience can often be managed without therapy. Yet, for those who appear in therapy, these major stimuli can be considered the first possible trigger for their presenting symptoms.

Interpersonal Mismatches

What expectations make interpersonal relationships difficult? Most people fear both being abandoned and being dominated by another to the extent that self-identity is lost (Melges, 1982). They then develop strategies that help keep them in the relationship but maintain enough distance that they are neither abandoned nor subsumed by the other person (Cashdan, 1973). Although these strategies are effective in maintaining relationships, they compromise true self-expression of each

> Fear of abandonment and fear of being dominated by another personal characterize most interpersonal relationships. To counter these fears, most people develop strategies that maintain the relationship but avoid intimacy.

partner. This compromise can often lead to emotional pain even though the relationship is being maintained, because ideal interpersonal relating is being sacrificed. To prevent threatened interpersonal loss or engulfment, clients may utilize the following strategies:

- The addicts' strategy: Go away if you won't keep using this substance with me.
- The high ambition strategy: Adore my competitive drive; it is the way I am and great for you to know me.
- The constant traveler strategy: I must be on the road to support you.
- The enabler's strategy: I'll give you something that you need so you can't leave me.
- The dependent strategy: I am weak and vulnerable; I will fall apart or die if you leave me. Or: I am safe for you to get involved with because I need you and could not leave you.
- The rescuer strategy: I will take care of you so you can't leave me.
- The martyr strategy: I am sacrificing myself for you.
- The sexual strategy: I will provide great sex so you will stay.
- The attractive strategy: I am so beautiful/handsome that you will always want to be with me.
- The dominant/aggressive strategy: I'll kill, destroy, or conquer you if you leave me.
- The financial strategy: I am such a good provider that you have to stay with me.

Some people are able to perform several of these strategies with the same partner. When the strategies stop working, the pair is set adrift either to separate or to find a more honest way of relating.

Creating Unintended Responses

People often inadvertently create the responses others give them. What prevents people from gaining what they want from others? A common reason is illustrated by the story of Jack, a highly intelligent and motivated businessman. Jack scowled and grimaced when people said "hi" to him in the hallway at work. He often asked difficult questions or criticized what they were telling him. He told a colleague, "The people

> People often elicit responses form others that they may not truly want. Hostile, aggressive and avoidant interpersonal styles tend to elicit unpleasant reactions from others.

around here aren't very friendly." Apparently, Jack did not know that the negative interpersonal messages he sent out were coming back to him. Hostile, aggressive, and avoidant interpersonal styles tend to elicit unpleasant reactions from others (see Figure 2.1).

Patterns Can Be Described in Many Different Ways

In most cases there is no single "right way" to describe a pattern; there are often many different words that could convey the same idea. It is crucial that therapists learn to describe patterns in ways that are most useful to each client, using the idiosyncratic words and sentence structures most familiar to the client. Therefore, therapists must be flexible when they describe patterns. As noted earlier, no research clearly demonstrates that accuracy of pattern definition is highly correlated with outcome. What is most important is that the pattern makes sense to clients and helps clients reach their therapeutic goals.

It seems clear that effective therapists are not restricted to either "one client/one pattern" or "one pattern fits all clients" strategies. For certain clients there may be a "right" pattern; for others the discussion of several possible patterns may provide the springboard for change. This might explain the apparent equivalence of effect in the treatment of depression by cognitive therapy, behavior therapy, and interpersonal therapy (Wampold, 2001). The self-confidence that emerges from simply naming the problem may in itself suggest avenues for change.

Pattern induction is related to but differs from verbal response modes and intentions. Therapists may use open questions, closed questions, restatements, reflections, confrontations, or other verbal response modes to uncover the client's patterns. The therapist's intentions relating to cognition, behaviors, feelings, interpersonal interactions, and the therapy relationship are used in the process of inductive reasoning to define patterns associated with these areas.

Homework

Homework allows clients to practice skills and therapists to obtain more information. The thought record (Beck, Rush, Shaw, & Emery, 1979) provides a useful way to induce client patterns (see Table 5.1).

TABLE 5.1   Thought Record

Name _Joe Accountant_

Case Summary—46 year old man presents with panic attacks and alcohol abuse.

DATE/TIME	SITUATION	NEGATIVE EMOTIONS OR BEHAVIORS	AUTOMATIC THOUGHTS
Tues 10am	Major task at work	Panicky	I can't do this project right
Thurs 8pm	Drinking at home—wife critical, threatens divorce	Anger	Drinking calms me down; she doesn't understand

Pattern—Wife threatened to leave him if he continued drinking. He panicked at work projects because failure at work leading to job loss would increase likelihood of her leaving. Work anxiety increased his need to drink making her more critical.

The first column describes the situation and context in which the symptom or dysphoric event is taking place. The second column describes the type and intensity of the emotion associated with each event. The third column contains the "automatic thoughts" that link the situation to the consequence. Automatic thoughts, like flying fish, emerge suddenly into consciousness and then quickly disappear below the surface. By paying attention they can be caught and recorded.

Assigning homework is no simple matter; clients have a great many reasons for not completing assignments. For example, clients may fear that others will see their diary or think that the therapist will criticize them, may not understand the directions, or may be ambivalent about exploring what their writings might reveal. The failure to complete assignments becomes, then, an inducing point.

School-Based Perspectives on Patterns

A list of the various school-based perspectives on patterns was given earlier in this chapter. This part of the chapter goes into more detail about each of these theoretical approaches. Tentatively fitting your observations into these molds can provide another way to understand clients' patterns.

Psychodynamic Therapy

Pschodynamics alert us to the formative influences of childhood relationship experiences, the influences of the out-of-awareness mental forces, our multiple intrapsychic conflicts and multiple challenges of human development.

Reenactment From Past to Present

The psychodynamic approach advocates understanding the client's present problem in terms of the client's past experience. Clients' emotional, cognitive, or interpersonal patterns are reflections of the past experiences and relationships. Clients will often repeat these patterns in current relationships, including in the relationship with the therapist.

Unconscious Conflicts

As noted earlier, Freud's *topographic model* divides the mind into three systems: the unconscious, the preconscious, and the conscious. Conscious awareness is only a small part of mental functioning. It does not fully determine people's behaviors. The preconscious consists of experiences, thoughts, and memories that can be easily brought into conscious awareness. The unconscious consists of needs, motivations, and instinctual impulses that may conflict with each other or with those in the conscious mind. In order to avoid the distress resulting from these conflicts, people repress them into the unconscious. Although these repressed materials are out of awareness, they still influence behaviors and are at the root of neurotic symptoms. Unconscious conflicts become one of the explanations for the client's behaviors and symptoms.

Inadequate Ego Development

In order to describe the dynamic interaction between unconscious and conscious, Freud developed his theory of the structure of personality. He divided the "self" into three parts: the id, the ego, and the superego: As described in Chapter 1, the id, which represents instinctual energy and inherited urges, seeks its gratification without considering the constraints of social reality (pleasure principle). The id is modified after birth by the experiences with parents, the social value system, and the culture. The ego is developed during this process of socialization. It represents the part of the personality responsible for coordinating internal and external reality. It allows some drives of the id to be gratified and suppresses others. This decision depends on the constraints of external reality (reality principle). The superego is developed as the child becomes socialized, meaning that the values and taboos of society are internalized into the child's thought processes. The superego is the part of mind that rewards one for being "good" and reproaches one for being "bad" (conscience principle). Guilt is often evoked when values of the superego have been contravened. Because of its asocial nature, the id continuously conflicts with the superego while the superego attempts to repress the id. Excessive or inadequate superego development can lead to a variety of symptoms and dysfunctional patterns. It is the task of the ego to reconcile the demands of the id with the injunctions of the superego.

Immature Defense Mechanisms

Defense mechanisms are generally defined as repetitive, stereotyped, automatic thought patterns used to cope with anxiety and prevent being overwhelmed. Defense mechanisms serve the ego in muting the anxiety generated by conflicts between the id and superego. Defense mechanisms are not always pathological; in fact, in many instances they are a part of normal adaptation. However, because defense mechanisms protect people by keeping the conflicts out of awareness, they can in some cases help to perpetuate the psychological disturbance by allowing it to remain unexamined.

Following are brief descriptions of some common mechanisms:

- *Repression*. Most defense mechanisms repress unwanted thoughts and feelings from conscious awareness, much as censorship by repressive governments keeps certain ideas from public awareness. Outside of awareness, the individual removes unwanted thoughts, memories, and feelings from consciousness.

- *Denial*. Unlike repression, which operates outside of awareness, denial may be conscious or preconscious. It simply distorts reality to fit the individual's needs. For example, people may use denial to avoid acknowledging and expressing anger at an important other person (such as a boss or parent). In the short run this defensive response prevents the expression of anger

> Defense mechanisms are thought patterns used to cope with anxiety and prevent feeling overwhelmed.

and subsequent interpersonal conflict, thereby keeping the relationship intact. However, in the long run the person may feel silenced and mistreated. Denial is useful in some cases, such as when a client is recovering from a heart attack, and harmful in other cases, such as when the partner of an alcoholic refuses to see how the alcoholism is destroying their family.

- *Projection.* Rather than admitting that they have an unwanted attribute, people may project this characteristic onto someone else. The other person becomes a blank screen onto which the attribute is projected like a filmstrip for a movie. For example, a self-defined highly moral person may accuse his boss of being dishonest and unethical when actually he was the one who had recently done something dishonest. Similarly people who are paranoid may ascribe the anger and mistrust that they experience on to others in their environment ("others are angry at me").

- *Rationalization.* Many people are adept at manufacturing "good" reasons to explain their own questionable attitudes and actions. Rationalizations help explain away bad decisions, losses, or hurtful behaviors, and they allow people to minimize their responsibility for what they do and think.

- *Conversion.* A distressing idea or feeling can be turned into a physical disorder. For example, a woman working as the only crew member on her husband's fishing boat might develop foot pain for which physicians can find no cause. When interviewed, she states, "I never want to set foot on the boat again." The foot problem provides her a means of accomplishing what she could not directly request.

- *Regression.* Some people under various stresses revert to former behavior that characterized them at an earlier developmental phase. It is as if the newer, more mature levels of development are less well-established and break down under duress, permitting less adaptive patterns to emerge. For example, a husband, recently able to reduce his physical assaults on his wife, hits her again after being fired from his job and not sleeping for 24 hours (Corey, 1996).

- *Displacement.* Individuals may shift an emotion from one idea or person to another that resembles the original idea or person. For example, a person who is angry at his/her boss may come home from work and yell at his/her partner and children, or kick the dog, when his/ her anger is really at the boss.

Other defense mechanisms include: reaction formation (doing the opposite of what we feel impelled to do), sublimation (diverting unacceptable impulses into socially acceptable or admirable directions), interjection (incorporating the values and standards of others), and compensation (hiding perceived weakness by developing positive attributes to make up for the perceived deficits).

Human Developmental Stages and Crises

Several psychoanalytic models address the ever-evolving nature of the human psyche from birth until death. Although most people tend to believe that something constant about themselves remains with them throughout their lifetimes, all of us proceed through predictable stages and challenges that repeatedly reform who we are and what we can do.

The developmental models vary in the challenges selected and the names chosen for stages, yet they all hold in common two related principles: (1) The manner in which certain developmental challenges and stages are confronted can have lasting influence on subsequent psychological functioning, and (2) each stage provides a window of opportunity for the creation of specific abilities and functions, which, if not mastered within a relatively specific time frame, can create lingering issues later on. Nevertheless, therapists strongly believe in the plasticity of the mind-brain to overcome developmental deficiencies. For example, during our early upbringing we learn to trust ourselves and others and how to love and feel close to others. As children, we also learn to recognize and express feelings of rage, anger, hostility, and hate, through which we discover our own autonomy and power as a person. We learn who we are in relationship to others by the way we are treated by parents and siblings. These early experiences, as well as schooling, work, and later social and family relationships, shape our identities in the world. These experiences provide lasting imprints on our lives.

Much has been written on this subject because developmental challenges and stages can be viewed from many perspectives. One helpful perspective is offered by self-psychology and object-relations approaches. (For a more comprehensive discussion of this subject, see Erik Erikson,

1963.) These approaches posit individual development as the process by which individuals separate and differentiate themselves from others. Mahler used the following terms to describe four developmental stages: *infantile autism*, *symbiosis*, *separation/individuation*, and *self–other constancy* (Hedges, 1983).

In the first months of life the infant is thought to be responding to physiological rather than psychological states (infantile autism). In this undifferentiated state there is no whole self or whole others; the infant responds to perceived parts of the other—breast, face, hands, mouth—rather than to a unified self or other.

From the 3rd to approximately the 8th month, the infant is intensely dependent on the primary caregiver. No longer an interchangeable part, the caregiver is expected to provide a high degree of emotional attunement with the infant (symbiosis).

The child then moves through several subphases involving differentiation and separation from the caregiver and then returning for a sense of confirmation and comfort. The toddler who proudly demonstrates self-sufficiency and then runs back to a welcoming parent can be said to illustrate the main issues of this period (separation/individuation). Other significant people are looked to as approving mirrors for the child's sense of self in order to help with the development and maintenance of self-other boundaries.

By the 36th month the child has usually entered the fourth and final stage by moving toward a sense of self and other constancy. Others are seen more fully as separate from the self because the self has firmer boundaries that protect against being overwhelmed through fusion with others. But the separation/individuation process does not stop here. Throughout the life span of each individual, the twin processes of joining with another in close relationships and pulling back into the sphere of oneself drives the ever-changing process of differentiation from others and clearer definition of the self (Corey, 1996; Erikson, 1963; Hedges, 1983). The description of role transitions in the following section on interpersonal psychotherapy continues this developmental theme.

Interpersonal Therapy

Most problems presenting to psychotherapists are easily related to some interpersonal disturbance. This section describes several common patterns to consider.

Role Transitions

Role transitions occur as individuals progress through the stages of the life cycle. Biological maturation transitions individuals through infancy, childhood, adolescence, early adulthood, later adulthood, and the decline of physical capacity with aging. Social transitions, which are greatly influenced by social class and historical events, may include events such as beginning school, leaving home, graduating from college, joining the military, marriage, divorce, job promotion or loss, and retirement. Many life cycle challenges, such as the death of a child, divorce, major disease, and trauma, are unexpected and catastrophic. Both biologically and socially determined role transitions require people to manage the loss of familiar social supports and attachments and develop new sets of social skills. Problems arise from role transitions bidirectionally (for instance, the transition may trigger depression, or depression may lead to an unexpected transition like divorce). Many transitions can be called "partial deaths," as the person permanently loses a social role that was expected to go on indefinitely. The divorced, non-custodial parent who rarely sees his or her children, the athlete who has a permanant injury, the person forced to retire— all experience the death of part of themselves (Klerman et al., 1984).

Role Conflicts

Role conflicts refer to situations in which the client and at least one significant other person have nonreciprocal expectations about their relationship. For example, a wife may expect her husband to take care of the children with her, whereas the husband thinks that is the wife's responsibility; a husband may expect his son to join the family business but the son has other ideas; or a daughter may want to marry someone outside her religion, race, or nationality, and her parents threaten to reject her (Klerman et al., 1984).

Unresolved Grief

Grief associated with the death of a loved one can be divided into normal or abnormal. Abnormal grief may be delayed or distorted. In a delayed reaction, the grief is experienced long after the loss, and it therefore may not be recognized as a reaction to the original loss. A distorted grief reaction is devoid of sadness or dysphoric mood. It manifests instead with nonaffective symptoms immediately following the loss or possibly years afterward (Klerman et al., 1984).

Core Conflictual Relationship Themes

Each person develops a set of expectations about his or her relationships to other people. These interpersonal expectations can be analyzed by examining reciprocal interactional sequences and explicating the pattern that emerges. The first step in the sequence asks: "What does the client want from other people?" The second step asks: "How do other people react to the expression of the client's wish?" The third step asks: "How does the client react to this reaction?" The underlying assumption is that each person develops a basic set of interactional patterns that emerge from the core conflict (Luborsky & Crits-Christoph, 1990).

Interpersonal Skill Deficits

Optimal social functioning requires establishing and maintaining some close relationships with family members or intimate friends, less intense friendships and acquaintances, and adequate handling of work or school roles. Socially isolated people lack relationships with intimates or friends or may have no work role. Such people may have long-standing or temporary deficiencies in social skills. Those who are severely isolated socially tend to be more severely disturbed (Klerman et al., 1984).

Behavioral Therapy

Therapists often attempt to assist clients to change what they are doing. By controlling the stimulus or the impact of the responses, behavior can be influenced. Systematic use of moderately effective models also may provide substantial leverage for behavior change.

Inadequate Stimulus Control

We are bombarded each day by stimuli that create a variety of effects on us based upon our previous experiences with them. From some we recoil, to others we are attracted, and the majority we ignore. A stimulus may be more than a single sound or sight. Various contexts, or social and physical environments, influence our behavior. For example, the recovering addict who visits the neighborhood in which his addicted friends live will be more likely to return to substance use, because the environment elicits behaviors associated with that place.

Problematic Conditioned Responses

Behavior is conditioned by its consequences. In other words, the events that follow a specific behavior influence the probability that this behavior will be repeated. A rewarding event increases the probability that the behavior will be repeated, whereas a noxious event decreases the likelihood that the behavior will be repeated. The consequence *operates* on the behavior.

A problem in connecting consequences with specific behaviors arises from people's differing interpretations of the same consequence. For example, being intoxicated might be fun for one person and horrible for another. If an action leads to a desirable, pleasurable outcome, the person or animal is likely to repeat it. Operant conditioning has been extensively researched in animal laboratories. One set of studies examined animal behaviors using a wooden box with a door that could be opened by pulling a loop. When a cat was placed within the box it first made a number of ineffective movements but eventually pulled the loop accidentally and escaped. Gradually the animal decreased the length of time before it pulled the loop and escaped. (In behavioral terms the cat learned that pulling the loop was followed by escape. In cognitive terms the cat learned to expect the door to open when the loop was pulled.) Operant conditioning can explain some clients' maladaptive behaviors or dysfunctional patterns. For example, avoidance of phobic stimuli usually yields a reduction in anxiety. This relief from anxiety reinforces avoidance behavior. All of us strive to reduce anxiety. Anything that reduces it becomes reinforcing (Sullivan, 1996).

Problematic Modeling

Individuals learn social behavior socially—by watching and imitating how others behave. Attractive, successful models are more likely to be copied than those who are unattractive and unsuccessful. Also, if the model is less than perfect, individuals are more likely to learn from the person, as the behavior may appear more attainable or achievable. Problematic modeling may occur when individuals observe others displaying a problematic behavior (e.g., aggressive acts) and subsequently do it themselves.

Neurotic Paradox

The *neurotic paradox* describes how individuals' use of some coping strategies may yield short-term relief from anxiety but have greater

The *neurotic paradox* describes how individuals' use of some coping strategies may yield short-term relief from anxiety but have greater long-term self-defeating consequences. Because of the immediate relief they provide, these detrimental patterns can be very difficult to alter or extinguish.

long-term self-defeating consequences. For example, procrastination, excessive passivity, and substance abuse may reduce anxiety in the short term but have deleterious long-term consequences. Because of the immediate anxiety relief they provide, these detrimental patterns can be very difficult to alter or extinguish (Mowrer, 1948).

Behavioral Excesses and Deficits

Individuals may engage in specific behaviors too often or intensely (e.g., tantruming, over eating, excessive hand-washing) or with insufficient frequency, intensity, or skills (e.g., not doing tasks, work, or physical exercise; insufficient assertion of wants and needs; or not performing activities involved in initiating and maintaining interpersonal relationships).

Cognitive Therapy

Humans think. Thinking influences emotion and behavior. Cognitive therapists work directly on thoughts and beliefs to facilitate behavior and emotion change.

Dysfunctional Automatic Thoughts

Cognitive therapy is based upon the idea that cognitions are "mediating events" between stimulus and response. As discussed earlier, an activating event (A) triggers a belief (B) that leads to a consequence (C). This is the ABC of cognitive therapy.

The belief (or attitude, construct, schema) emits a brief statement to the self (self-statement) that proceeds quickly through preconscious thinking, rarely reaching consciousness. This "automatic thought" is a reflex thought stimulated by the activating event. It becomes a clue to the content of the underlying cognitive schema that created it. For example, each time a student arrived late for a seminar, the student apologized excessively. The automatic thought experienced, slightly out of awareness, was that the student was offending the others and was about to be criticized. This automatic thought led the student to apologize. The student's underlying belief contained a fear of not living up to others' expectations.

Dysfunctional automatic thoughts associated with depression can be defined as spontaneous self-statements characterized by the cognitive triad of: negative views of self, negative interpretation of on-going experiences, and negative view of the future. Cognitive therapy involves training clients to observe and record these dysfunctional automatic thoughts, helping them learn to discriminate between these thoughts and actual events, and to understand the relationship between these thoughts, affects, behaviors, and environmental events (Beck et al., 1979; Merluzzi & Boltwood, 1989).

Negative Cognitive Schemas

Many different terms have been used to describe the filters human beings use to interpret their realities: *attitudes*, *beliefs*, *worldviews*, *maps of reality*, *constructs*, and *schemas*. Schemas determine the manner in which individuals respond to their world and are in turn altered by these experiences. General cognitive schemas for common psychological disorders appear in Table 5.2.

TABLE 5.2   Cognitive Profile of Psychological Disorders

DISORDER	SYSTEMATIC BIAS
Depression	Negative view of self, experience, and future
Suicidal behavior	Hopelessness
Hypomania	Positive view of self, experience, and future
Anxiety disorder	Physical or psychological threat
Phobia	Threat in specific, avoidable situations
Panic disorder	Catastrophic misinterpretation of bodily or mental experiences
Paranoid state	Attribution of negative bias to others
Hysteria	Belief in motor or sensory abnormality
Obsession	Repetitive warning or doubting about safety
Compulsion	Rituals to ward off doubts or threat
Anorexia nervosa	Fear of appearing fat (to self or others)
Hypochondriasis	Belief in serious medical disorder

(Beck & Weishaar, 1989; reproduced with permission)

Cognitive Distortions

Cognitive distortions are misinterpretations of reality that reinforce negative conclusions, or dysfunctional cognitive schemas. Beck (1976; Allen, 1996; Beck & Weishaar, 1989) described specific kinds of cognitive distortions, including:

- Overgeneralizing: formulating a general rule based on a single or a few isolated instances and applying the rule in a wide range of situations (e.g., a man might say after his girlfriend leaves him, "No one will ever love me")
- Dichotomous thinking: categorizing experiences in only extremes or in black or white (e.g., "I am the most worthless person in the world")
- Selective abstraction: conceptualizing a situation only on the basis of negative aspects (e.g., "My boss doesn't like me because he didn't ask about my work yesterday")
- Personalizing: attributing external events to oneself without any causal connection (e.g., "She looks unhappy today; I must have done something wrong")
- Arbitrary inference: drawing a conclusion without evidence or despite contradictory evidence (e.g., after making a speech that received long applause from the audience, a person might say, "It must have been an awful talk")
- Catastrophizing and minimizing: emphasizing negative outcomes and downplaying positive outcomes (e.g., after being separated from her abusive husband, a woman might think, "I can't survive without someone's support" while ignoring that she is no longer abused)

Person-Centered Therapy

Self-concept refers to a person's conceptual construction of him or herself, including perceptions, attitudes, and feelings about the self and the perceptions of the relationships of the "I" with others.

From earliest infancy, everyone has a strong need for positive regard or approval from others. The self-concept is developed through the process of socialization and is heavily dependent on the attitude and evaluation of those who constitute the individual's significant others.

Conditions of Worth and Negative Self-Concept

Individuals can internalize significant others' criticism and develop a negative self-concept. In person-centered therapy, the disturbance is conceptualized in terms of the degree of success or failure experienced by the individual in resolving these conflicts. Once caught in a negative self-concept, the person is likely to grow more disturbed, because the negative self-concept often induces behaviors that reinforce the image of inadequacy and worthlessness (Thorne, 1996).

Existential Therapy

Existential therapy is not a specific technical approach that presents a set of rules for therapy. Rather, as noted in Chapter 2, it asks deep questions about the nature of human beings and the nature of anxiety, despair, grief, loneliness, isolation, freedom, creativity, and love. It emphasizes that we are not the victims of circumstances; rather, we are what we choose to be.

Fear of Responsibility and Freedom

In answer to the question, "Are we victims of our circumstances or creators of our own lives?" existential therapists insist that our lives are the products of our own decisions, including our own failures to decide. No matter how awful or wonderful the circumstances, we can choose how to respond—whether it is positively or negatively. Therefore, people should come to realize that they are responsible for their lives, actions, and failures; they direct their lives. Fear of responsibility is evident in the search for causes outside the self for one's situation. Blaming others reduces self-responsibility but also reduces personal freedom.

On the other hand, many clients blame themselves excessively, rather than blaming others. This excessive self-blame contains a hidden and exaggerated sense of power, as if "I can change everyone else's life." Ironically, such a view of the self leads to paralysis of decision-making and helplessness in being responsible for the self. Freedom to choose is then strongly inhibited.

We experience anxiety when we use our freedom to choose to move out of the known and into the realm of the unknown. People try to avoid this anxiety by denying their creative ideas, by avoiding risk, by failing to learn from mistakes, by being frightened to choose, or by having somebody else decide for them (Corey, 1996; Yalom, 1980).

Fear of Death

Death is the most obvious ultimate concern; nobody escapes it. From the existential point of view, a core inner conflict involves awareness of death and a simultaneous wish for eternal life. People, at the deepest level, respond to death with terror. To cope with this terror, individuals employ defenses against awareness of death. To experience existential anxiety is to confront the emptiness of the universe, helplessness in the face of awesome and impersonal power, and the foundational terror of self-annihilation. Some panic attacks are triggered by this terrifying confrontation with nonexistence (Corey, 1996; Yalom, 1980).

Existential Isolation

Each of us is alone in the universe. Our individual uniqueness carries with it the realization that our own consciousness cannot be fully shared with anyone else. Occasionally, however, people experience those rare and special moments, sometimes referred to as "existential encounters," when they seem to share the same space and time with someone else. In our ordinary existence individuals achieve various degrees of attachment and involvement with others. For some, terror lies in isolation, as if the self will disintegrate without someone else present. This intense fear unleashes the impulse to attach to others. Others may flee from connection through counterdependent isolation, risking meaningful attachments with no one.

Existential therapists believe that no relationship can eliminate isolation but that experience can be shared with others in such a way that the pain of isolation is reduced. Some people, such as individuals with borderline traits, may experience intense existential anxiety when they are alone. They begin to believe that they exist only in the presence of another, that they exist only as long as they are responded to or are thought about by another. People may attempt to deal with isolation by fusion, such as fusing with a lover ("I" disappears into "we"), a group, or an organization (Corey, 1996; Yalom, 1980).

> A fundamental fulcrum of therapeutic change lies in client's realizing that they are responsible for directing their lives and actions. Searching for causes outside of the self and blaming others are common manifestations of the fear of responsibility.

Meaninglessness

Human beings struggle for a sense of significance and purpose in life. Without a sense of purpose, life has no pull toward the future. Religious beliefs, political causes, athletics, parenting, learning, and helping others provide some of the many ways of making life meaningful. Without meaning, people tend to dissolve into hedonistic pursuits or existential despair. Meaninglessness may arise as people disregard the old or traditional value systems without finding or building other suitable ones to replace them. Some believe that each person has a "mission in life" or a "great work" to accomplish—that part of life's odyssey is to find the purpose and strive to fulfill it. Sometimes meaninglessness arises when individuals are "not true to themselves": when what is of utmost significance is ignored in favor of another pursuit more congruent with society's expectations or the prized goals of others.

Emotion-Focused Psychotherapy

Emotions drive us to act and to think. Discovering how they are being avoided, misdirected and under-utilized can point toward useful change.

Avoidance of Emotional Awareness

Awareness is noticing, recognizing, and being in touch with the potential object of focused consciousness. *Avoidance* refers to the means people use to keep themselves from awareness of unfinished and negative emotions we do not wish to acknowledge and unresolved interpersonal difficulties that are too painful to face.

In emotion-focused therapy, emotional awareness is emphasized in maintaining one's health and integration. The avoidance of emotional awareness limits our full experience of internal and external reality, which can be a major impediment to managing ourselves effectively in the world (Corey, 1996; Parlett & Hemming, 1996).

Conflict Splits

The human condition has often been described as containing conflicts between two alternatives. Emotion-focused therapy emphasizes the common tension between emotion and cognition, which can be played out in many different ways. Some clients "know" what is right but cannot "believe" it because of their strong emotional investment in the belief. Said in many ways by representatives of other schools (for example, superego versus id), conflict splits can also be described as deeply felt emotions in conflict with externally derived standards that oppose desires or needs. For example, "I think that I should be involved more with other people but I want to stay home alone because I hate being around them." Emotion-focused therapists isolate these splits in order to better define their origins and attempt to resolve them.

Unfinished Business

Feelings that arise from painful, overwhelming experiences can be held back from conscious awareness and yet impede full or normal functioning because the needs from which these feelings emerge are blocked. Unresolved grief and feared anger expression are common examples. The "working through," resolution, or letting go of these feelings has not yet taken place. By providing situations in which clients catch glimpses of their underlying turmoil, therapists encourage expression and resolution.

Family Therapy

No person is an island. No couple exists in interpersonal isolation. Each is part of larger social systems of which the family unit, in all of its many forms, is primary.

Triangulation

As suggested by Murray Bowen (1978), anxiety can easily develop within intimate relationships. Under stressful pressures two people might recruit a third person to whom each can direct their anxious energy and tension. This redirection reduces anxiety within the system and leads to stability. However, triangulation does not necessarily lead to resolution of the conflicts in the dyad and, in the long run, the situation is likely to worsen. For example, a married couple may focus their attention on a problematic child instead of fighting with each other. If the child's problem resolves or the child leaves home, then the couple must either confront their unresolved conflict, live with intense anxiety, leave each other, or find another person or subject with which to form a triangle.

Boundary Problems

Family structure is maintained by appropriate boundaries between subsystems. A clear and effective boundary indicates that individuals can interact with the subsystem at a regulated and optimal degree.

There are two ineffective types of boundaries. *Rigid* boundaries are overly restrictive and restrain contact to outside systems, resulting in individuals or subsystems being disengaged and isolated from each other. Conversely, with *enmeshed* boundaries, family members are overly involved with and usually overly responsive to one another. Distances between subsystems are decreased and boundaries are blurred and diffused. A common boundary problem within the family involves an alliance between a parent and a child against another parent or stepparent (the cross-generational alliance), which can stabilize family dynamics but create symptoms or problems.

Disturbed Homeostasis

Homeostasis is a term borrowed from biology and systems theory. It refers to a balanced, steady equilibrium in a system. Families are described as homeostatic systems that maintain relative constancy of their internal functioning. The concept of homeostasis is relevant not only to functional families but also to dysfunctional ones. Family therapists often conceptualize family problems as the tendency to maintain the family's equilibrium in spite of developmental and unexpected events. The "identified client" (or "symptom bearer") in family therapy may be regarded as the person to restore the homeostasis. For example, a child's symptomatic behavior may be a response to parental discord. The child's problem distracts the parents from their interpersonal difficulties as they become concerned about the "identified client." On the other hand, the tendency toward homeostasis may inhibit a family system from adjusting to developmental events, such as a parent continuing to treat a child like a preschooler even after the child has begun elementary school.

If one member of a couple changes or improves in some way, perhaps by becoming more assertive or by giving up drug abuse, the marital balance can be disrupted, leading the other spouse to become symptomatic or leave—unless that spouse adapts to the new behavior by also changing. The newly assertive partner is now making more demands. The drug free partner may desire more attention and understanding (Nichols & Schwartz, 1991).

Circular Causality

In contrast to linear causality, which focuses on how A's response causes B's response, circular causality focuses on the reciprocal influence of A on B and B on A. In a relationship things do not necessarily occur because one partner has "caused" them but rather because of the complex cycle of interactions in which both partners actively participate. Moreover, a person's actions within a relationship stem not from a single cause, either in the immediate or remote past, but from a continuing chain of causation in which both partners are initiators and recipients. Thus, family therapists may not focus on one of the protagonists, but rather pursue change in which both partners contribute actively to facing and solving the problem.

Circular questioning refers to the therapist's asking one family member about an interaction, then asking another family member to respond to the first person's answer, and then asking a third person to respond to the second person. This concept relies on the fact that family members reciprocally influence each other, with the pattern of responses providing an example of the manner in which that influence takes place (Growe, 1996).

Summary

Despite numerous claims that specific techniques foster specific outcomes, clients respond to the core processes (Wampold et al., 2001). The benefits of treatments are probably due to the pathways common to all bona fide psychological treatments, such as the healing context, the belief in the rationale for and efficacy of therapy by the client and by the therapist, the therapeutic alliance, the use of procedures that are consistent with the client's understanding of his or her problems, the development of increased self-efficacy to solve one's problems, and strengthening of hope (Ahn & Wampold, 2001, p. 255). Nonetheless, therapists and their clients need to believe in what they are doing.

Search for maladaptive patterns by starting with undesired responses that seem to illustrate the pattern (inducing points) by working backward from the response to the stimulus and then to the psychological mediating variables (S→O→R). Using personality trait and school based-patterns, attempt to articulate the pattern(s) in personal terms that imply how to change. The predicable events of the human life cycle provide a context for likely patterns as do our common fears of interpersonal abandonment and enmeshment.

Through dialogue, an iterative process is initiated that sharpens the pattern definition leading to possible ways to change. Inducing points are gleaned from verbal reports, thought records, behavioral observations, reports from others, deviations from the therapeutic contract, transference and countertransference as well as idiosyncratic responses to medications. School-based patterns provide a rich source of templates for defining patterns which suit the individual.

CHAPTER 6

General Strategies
for
Facilitating Change

When all you own is a hammer, every problem starts looking like a nail.
—ABRAHAM MASLOW

Psychotherapy does not "cure" clients; rather it helps them to change (Kleinke, 1993). "Cure" implies that the problem will never recur—a questionable claim for any helping professional. Therapists help clients realize that change is possible, encourage them to take responsibility for change, and facilitate new emotional experiences, thinking, or behaviors. Therapists seek to help clients decrease symptoms (anxiety, depression, substance abuse), increase social functioning in work or school and relationships, and improve their general sense of well-being. These general objectives can be achieved by many different and overlapping processes that include the strategies and techniques offered by the different schools of psychotherapy as well as general principles embedded in the therapeutic relationship itself (Lambert, 1992; Wampold, 2001). This chapter describes what we mean by change and outlines the core change processes common to all counseling and psychotherapy approaches.

What Is Change?

Change may be the goal of therapy, but the concept is multilayered and complex. The presocratic philosopher Heraclitus proclaimed that "*the only constant is change,*" and that "*no man ever steps in the same river twice, for it's not the same river and he's not the same man.*" Others have paradoxically stated that reality is *"ever-changing yet ever the same."* Resolution of these apparent contradictions lies in the therapist's ability to recognize how clients are ever-evolving while also following fixed patterns, some of which are unchangeable, some of which are useful, and some of which can be altered to improve functioning.

For a mechanic, change means fixing or replacing the broken part. For an information technologist, change means installing and mastering new software and hardware. For a surgeon, change means excising diseased tissue or facilitating repair of the damaged tissue. For a physician treating an infection, change means eliminating the effects of noxious bacteria. But for the therapist, change means collaborating with clients to better serve the client's best interests. Therapists do not "make" clients change. Change instead occurs as a result of what clients do in conjunction *with* what therapists do. Although therapists' techniques provide a means to change, clients sometimes change before therapists have the opportunity to try their favorite methods. Indeed, for many individuals, significant change occurs when they make the decision to seek the assistance of a mental health professional. For example, for some individuals and couples, the mere act of scheduling an appointment provides enough emphasis on their problem for them to make needed changes before they ever see a therapist. More commonly, the psychotherapeutic situation itself, which includes expectations for change and a supportive, collaborative relationship, may accelerate change without the introduction of a specific change technique.

Basic Change Processes

Change takes many forms: stopping, starting, decreasing, increasing, eliminating, modifying, and maintaining. Some changes appear and disappear whereas others are more enduring. *Pattern change* refers to modifying dysfunctional (maladaptive) patterns by reducing their intensity and frequency or initiating functional (adaptive) patterns by increasing their intensity and frequency. An example of initiating a functional pattern might be a couple who fights regularly and then retreats from each other for days. This

> Change takes many forms including: beginning, ending, reducing, increasing, altering and continuing. Maladaptive patterns may be relinquished, replaced and the new pattern may be initiated and strengthened.

couple could first modify their pattern by talking about the fight sooner after the fight occurred. They then may find themselves catching their arguments before they escalate. Then they may be able to anticipate the fight and together agree to avoid the argument completely. An example of modifying a dysfunctional pattern might be a person who believes he is responsible for many negative events happening around him. After modifying his pattern he might still believe that he is responsible for negative events but experience less guilt, certainty, or distress.

Pattern change has three substages:

1. *Relinquishing dysfunctional patterns* (e.g., less frequent thoughts of self-harm, substance use, avoidance, blaming, or binge eating)
2. *Developing (initiating) functional* patterns and increasing their duration, intensity, or frequency (e.g., becoming better able to relax when facing fears, increasing confidence when asserting one's wants to others, initiating social interactions more frequently, or increasing cardiovascular exercise)
3. *Maintaining new functional patterns*

Although new awareness experiences (insights, "clicks," and "ah-ha" experiences) do occur, new patterns rarely materialize suddenly and then endure. Instead, changes in patterns usually develop in fits and starts, with clients progressing and then slipping back to old patterns, but perhaps not as far back as before (Beitman, 1987).

Orders of Change

Change can take place at three levels or orders. *First-order change* is more superficial, less enduring, and more likely to be initiated during crisis intervention. It is often a simple solution to a current problematic situation such as giving hungry people a fish to eat. *Second-order change* involves changing a pattern or set of patterns. An example might be providing hungry people with fishing poles and instructions on how to use them. *Third-order change* offers a still more extensive means to change and represents the desired outcome of long-term therapy and personal growth: learning how to change patterns. An example of third-order change would be helping hungry people start a fishing pole manufacturing business, allowing them not only to feed themselves but also to teach others how to fish who then, in turn, purchase the fishing poles.

First-Order Change

Therapists help clients do something different in the very near future in a single instance. For example, an abused person might decide to enter a shelter; an alcoholic might go to an AA meeting; a social phobic might fill out a job application; a distraught spouse might consult a lawyer. No new patterns are necessarily initiated. The system does not change. The abused person might return to the abusive partner, the social phobic might decide not to go to the interview, the alcoholic might continue to drink, and the distraught partner might not change the marital relationship.

Second-Order Change

Therapists help clients alter their pattern within the situation in which the dysfunctional pattern is occurring. In systems theory, a change in the system leads to new rules for behavior. For example, the abused person may obtain an apology from the abusive partner for his or her cruel behavior; the social phobic might apply for a job, receive an offer, and accept the position; the alcoholic in AA might more closely examine his or her emotional reactions before reaching for a drink; and the distraught partner might learn to become more assertive in asking to have his or her needs met, with the other partner perhaps accepting the new behavior by changing as well.

Third-Order Change

The client learns how to recognize and change patterns without the ongoing help of the therapist—the psychological equivalent of "learning how to learn." For example, clients who learned how to disengage from their excessively anxious thoughts about their biomedical health might also learn how to disengage from their reactivity to their irritable employer. Therapy contains many implicit principles of third-order change toward which clients are guided. The fundamental psychotherapeutic principle is to learn to activate self-awareness when undesired outcomes occur and, in the future, recognize similar situations and activate self-awareness so that one can respond more effectively.

This principle is based upon clients' willingness to recognize those aspects of their area of influence that can be altered

> When clients learn how to recognize and change their patterns without assistance from their therapists, they have gained third-order change. A central aspect of this type of change typically involves activating their self-awareness when undesired outcomes occur and, in the future, recognizing similar situations or dynamics and activating their self awareness so that they can respond more effectively.

to achieve desired results—the willingness to take responsibility for change. This means not taking excessive or insufficient responsibility—sometimes not an easy judgment to make. It also requires a practical optimism: being able to look at the cold, hard facts realistically while also believing that a way out of the problem can be found.

Learning when to activate self-awareness and then what to look for takes practice and persistence. Other principles help fashion the effective use of self-awareness:

- When an unwanted emotional response occurs, try to notice it and stop to examine its source before responding. Take a deep breath, relax. Think about the consequences of the reaction versus a more thoughtful response. Recall the expression "A good night's sleep is often the best therapist."
- Embrace negative emotions as signals to examine patterns and their associated expectations.
- Learn from past mistakes by noticing how the current situation appears to be part of a familiar sequence that has led to difficulty. The analysis of problematic patterns can be aided by knowledge that past experiences shape these patterns but no longer need to dictate their recurrence.
- Allow new solutions and new responses to emerge into your consciousness and practice intuitive ranking of the probability of specific responses that may yield the desired results. Learn how to make good decisions and to trust your ability to do so.

When using a particular strategy or technique, it is important to pay attention to questions like:

- What is the likely impact of this strategy or technique on the client?
- How did the client perceive what I said?

It may be difficult for therapists to know which part of what they say is useful for a specific client. Some clients will pick up what the therapist intended. Others will hear something quite different. Consider an analogy to music. Different listeners are touched by different parts of a piece of music—melody, lyrics, or rhythm. Sometimes, when a therapist expects a client to change in response to an intervention, the client does not respond at all. Other times the therapist may expect little change but see great changes occur.

As noted earlier, specific therapeutic strategies and techniques contribute to a smaller proportion of the outcome of therapy than is generally believed—only about 15% (Lambert, 1992). Mental health professionals generally believe that the wider the range of therapists' strategies and techniques, the more options are available for adapting them to the specific needs of individual clients. None the less, it may occasionally be true that certain combinations of techniques are less effective than one clearly defined strategy (Lazarus, 1996). In the treatment of panic disorder, for example, adding relaxation training to behavioral-cognitive therapy produced fewer positive outcomes than behavioral-cognitive therapy alone (Barlow, 1990). Thus, more is not necessarily always better.

Some strategies and techniques for change are common among most therapy approaches, whereas some are limited to a specific approach. For example, clarification and confrontation might be used by therapists with knowledge of a variety of therapy orientations, whereas the "empty chair" is more likely to be utilized by Gestalt or Emotion-focused therapists.

> The wider the range of strategies and techniques, the greater number of options therapists have available to respond to the specific needs of each client.

General Strategies for Facilitating Change

General change strategies are listed in Table 6.1 and grouped under the various substages of change from relinquishing dysfunctional patterns to maintaining functional patterns.

The Substages

The substages have heuristic value in that they help us conceptualize the progression of change. In reality, however, the simple recognition of a modest dysfunctional pattern or a modest change in one area can initiate a cascade of events leading to new patterns and their maintenance. This cascade of events can occur without a clear demarcation between relinquishing an old pattern and initiating a new one, or between initiating and maintaining a new pattern. Similarly, although some strategies are directly associated with a specific substage, others may be used in multiple substages. For example, "therapist self-disclosure," "empathic reflections," and "role playing" are equally useful in all substages and therefore is placed at the bottom of the table. Following is a more detailed description of each of the strategies.

Defining Dysfunctional Patterns

Through confrontation and clarification, the therapist helps the client to define a well-formed pattern. The newly defined pattern implies what needs to be done to bring about change. By defining the pattern and seeing what needs to be changed, the client begins the process of relinquishing it.

Separating Past from Present Relationships

Individuals often react to present circumstances with past response patterns. When the old response does not fit current circumstances, the past pattern can be distinguished from the current response repertoire. "That was then and this is now." For example, intense emotion in the present may appear to be triggered by a current event but the excess is likely to originate from a similar emotionally laden past set of experiences.

Challenging Dysfunctional Beliefs, Behaviors, and Emotions

Dysfunctional patterns are usually composed of dysfunctional beliefs, behaviors, or emotions. Defining these patterns often requires highlighting one or several of these elements for the client to consider.

TABLE 6.1   General Change Strategies (by substages of change)

RELINQUISH DYSFUNCTIONAL PATTERNS	PREPARE TO CHANGE	INITIATE FUNCTIONAL PATTERNS	MAINTAIN FUNCTIONAL PATTERNS
Define dysfunctional patterns	Generate alternatives	Suggest how to change	Work through
Separate past from present relationships	Decide what to change	Turn stumbling blocks into stepping stones	Positive reinforcement
Challenge dysfunctional beliefs, behaviors, and emotions	Take responsibility	Alter expectations	Practice
	Explore the disadvantages and advantages of change	Practice in the session	
		Face fears	
		Reframe	
		Resolve conflicts	
Empathic reflection	Empathic reflection	Empathic reflection	Empathic reflection
Therapist's self-disclosure	Therapist's self-disclosure	Therapist's self-disclosure	Therapist's self-disclosure
Role play	Role play	Role play	Role play

Therapists may make a challenge in the form of an interpretation, question or statement. The challenge underscores the importance of the pattern, encouraging the client to consider what the therapist is describing.

Generating Alternatives

Clients and therapists collaboratively develop a list of possible responses (thoughts, behaviors, emotions) that could lead to desired change. Pros and cons may be formally defined. Skills to carry out change may be clarified and impediments faced. To increase motivation, clients may also be asked (a) how important it is for them to make the desired change, and (b) how confident they are that they can make the desired change (see Miller & Rollnick, 2002).

Deciding What to Change
As change alternatives are generated, one alternative is selected for action.

Taking Responsibility
As an alternative is selected, clients come to accept that carrying out this alternative is primarily up to them. Clients do not necessarily have to assume responsibility for the creation of the dysfunctional pattern. Rather, they take responsibility for maintaining the old pattern when more adaptive alternatives are available. Taking responsibility, or owning, accepting one's own part, or recognizing the "ability to respond" differently, is central to psychotherapeutic change.

Exploring the Disadvantages and Advantages of Change
Therapists *help* clients notice how change has been or will be beneficial. Therapists, may also increase motivation by examining the pros and cons of remaining the same and of change (Miller & Rollnick, 2002).

Suggestions of How to Change
In various forms, therapists help clients generate an alternative response(s) and support clients in trying it. Therapists usually co-imagine new futures with their clients and may see ways to reach them. Suggestions can be direct but more often are indirect—stated in terms of questions, possibilities, and even relevant therapist self-stories (self-disclosure).

Turning Stumbling Blocks into Stepping Stones
There is a Chinese expression that states, "In crisis, there is opportunity." To instill hope, therapists typically need to remain optimistic in the face of turmoil and impossibility. Turning lemons into lemonade, finding the silver lining in a storm cloud, looking at how to use the bad for good—this type of mental agility involves converting obstacles, problems, and difficulties into opportunities. For example, a job loss could be an opportunity, or the symptoms of an anxiety attack could be a clue to examine a situation more carefully rather than something to

be eradicated. Of course, sometimes awful is just awful, and nothing can be done but to accept the new, harsh reality.

At times therapists can be too optimistic, even Polly Anna-ish. Yet assisting clients in finding ways out of their dilemmas by using the negative aspect of their situation is central to the psychotherapeutic scientific art. Classic examples are clients who emerge from destruction and despair and find ways to help both themselves and then others in similar situations (e.g., become AA sponsors, volunteer or work in domestic violence shelters or hotlines, write a book for others recovering from similar situations). Therapists are resiliency consultants, looking with each client at the cold hard facts, and using available resources to find a good way out of the dilemma.

Altering Future Expectations

With the therapist's help, clients come to realize that a new and better future is more likely than the one they had in mind. Human distress is usually triggered by mismatches between expectations and experiences. If clients change their expectations of others and themselves to better match their current realities, a reduction in negative emotion and an increase in adaptation is likely.

Practice in the Session

Rather than risking a new response in the "real world," clients practice in the office with the therapist. The practice may take many forms: rehearsing assertiveness or other desired new behaviors, expressing difficult emotions, or discussing their perception of how the therapist was hurtful to them.

Facing Fears

A high percentage of clients' problems are related to excessive anxieties and fears that cause them to avoid the feared stimuli. These fears are not only external (e.g., spiders, blood, interpersonal performance, shopping malls, closed places) but also cognitive (thinking one must do something perfectly, believing it would be awful if one is abandoned), emotional (doubt, shame, humiliation, hopelessness, anger, love, dependence), behavioral (avoiding feared stimuli, not managing anxiety, not asking for what one wants), and related to memories (posttraumatic memories, grief).

Reframing

The therapist helps to create an alternative, more constructive view of current circumstances. Related to "turning stumbling blocks into stepping stones," reframing alters the negative event into an opportunity for constructive change.

Resolving Conflicts

The therapist defines two polarities by clarifying the perspectives of each side and beginning the work of mediating their differences and similarities. This principle may be most dramatically applied by putting each of the clients' alternatives in separate chairs and having them talk with each other by asking about "shoulds" versus "wants" and by labeling the separate parts as clearly as possible. This helps clients gain greater perspective and flexibility.

Working Through

Once a maladaptive pattern is defined and better alternatives are generated, the client must repeatedly unlearn the old patterns and learn the more adaptive patterns until they are ingrained. One major insight rarely brings lasting change; instead, clients enter situation after situation in which they need to recognize, adapt, and apply their new responses—sometimes falling into the old pattern and then attempting to reinstate the new one.

Research on brain functioning indicates that people's characteristic psychological responses have a basis in the neural circuitry of their brains (Beitman, 2005). Hence, clients seeking to develop new ways of responding typically need to repeat and relearn (i.e., strengthen) activation of the new response in place of the earlier and more established neural circuit response. In other words, therapists seek to assist clients in learning to intentionally and habitually activate different, more adaptive neural circuits. This point also applies to systems functioning. To use an example mentioned earlier, a couple's fights usually escalate into battles where each retreats to safe isolation. Working through begins when they decrease the time between the fight and making up with each other. Working through continues as they shorten their arguments and start looking for better ways to discuss issues. Working through concludes when they both recognize and accurately anticipate "hot" topics over which a fight is likely to start, and then find better interactional patterns and ways to resolve their differences before conflicts escalate. In most cases, various circular processes involving insight, memory, cognitions, behavior change, and interpersonal relationships are set in motion. Clients practice maintaining new ways of being in their lives, which strengthens the likelihood that more adaptive neural circuits and subsequent desired responses will occur with greater frequency in the future.

Positive Reinforcement

If behavioral responses are followed by generally rewarding events, the behaviors tend to be strengthened and occur more frequently. Praise, interpersonal gratification, and various forms of success can serve this purpose. Many different forces can act as reinforcers, including the therapist (praise, encouragement), self-talk, self-rewards, and social network responses.

Practice

Practice can improve skills, increase comfort, and maximize the effectiveness of performing the desired behavior. It also strengthens the desired underlying neural circuits described earlier.

Empathic Reflection

Usually considered an essential technique for establishing the therapeutic alliance, empathic reflection can increase clients' awareness of their inner states, motivations, and typical reactions, as the therapist acts as an external observer of clients' inner processes. This new awareness can lead to change, and help maintain it.

Therapist Self-Disclosure

Therapist's self-revealing can assist clients during all subphases by some element of their history or current responses. The client's best interests, not therapists' desire to talk about themselves, should be the primary reason for therapist self-disclose.

Role Playing

Two kinds of role play are commonly used: (1) interaction with the therapist or an empty chair as a way to practice new behaviors, and (2) interaction with an empty chair (where the chair represents a part of themselves or an important other) to resolve intrapsychic conflicts.

Caveats

Counselors and therapists tend to blur the meanings of *strategy* and *technique*. The problem arises because some strategies imply specific technical behaviors and some techniques incorporate a general plan of approach. For example, the strategy "face fears" implies a direct behavioral confrontation with a feared stimulus, and the technique "changing self-talk" can imply a search for the cognitive schemas generating maladaptive self-talk. For the purposes of these discussions, a *strategy* is defined as a plan, expectation, or guideline for accomplishing a goal, whereas a *technique* is a specific behavior or set of behaviors used to carry out a strategy.

Summary

Therapists facilitate change by providing a context, a relationship, observations and ideas which help clients find their ways out of predicaments. Usually, unwanted patterns must be relinquished, new patterns initiated and then maintained. Change has several orders: (1) handling the immediate crisis, (2) changing a dysfunctional pattern, and (3) learning how to change without the therapist. Find the strategies and techniques with the highest probability of facilitating client change, keeping in mind that the primary change variables lie with the client. Among the many change strategies common to all schools of psychotherapy are: empathic reflections, separating past from present, taking responsibility, reframing, altering expectations, facing fears, role playing and practicing new patterns.

CHAPTER 7

ECBIS Strategies for Facilitating Change

The capacity to tolerate uncertainty is a prerequisite for the profession. Though the public may believe that therapists guide patients systematically and sure-handedly through predictable stages of therapy to a foreknown goal, such is rarely the case: Instead . . . [t]herapists frequently wobble, improvise, and grope for direction. The powerful temptation to achieve certainty through embracing an ideological school and a tight therapeutic system is treacherous: Such belief may block the uncertain and spontaneous encounter necessary for effective therapy.
—IRVIN YALOM (1989) FROM *LOVE'S EXECUTIONER AND OTHER TALES OF PSYCHOTHERAPY*

D ifferent schools not only have different strategies for change but also emphasize different features of the psychological field: Cognitive therapy emphasizes changing distortions of thought; behavioral therapy focuses on modifying dysfunctional actions; emotion-focused therapy concentrates on changing dysfunctional emotional schemes; interpersonal therapy aims to change maladaptive schemes in human relationships; and systems therapies examine ways to alter the rules according to which multiple people interact. In other words, school-based change strategies have as their targets: emotion, cognition, behavior, interpersonal relationships, and systemic interactions (ECBIS). Although we may talk about these target areas as if they were entities, they actually are mutually influential and intersect with each other. If one element changes, the other elements usually (though not always) follow suit. Figure 7.1 illustrates this interrelationship. The ECBIS categories represent the general areas toward which change can be directed; they are five conceptual handles by which to grasp client patterns. Different therapists, or the same therapist for different clients, might start with different foci. Cognitive therapists prefer to concentrate on clients' thoughts, behavioral therapists focus on clients' behaviors (as well as stimuli and reinforcers), and emotion-focused therapists seek emotional expression. Because the interpersonal component is built upon a combination of these first targets, some therapists believe that interpersonal conceptualizing is an easy way to organize the three more elementary parts. Others think more easily in terms of family and social systems. All therapists attempt to comprehend individuals' functioning in their social fields. Where to begin the process (thoughts, feeling, behaviors, interpersonal relationships, or systemic interactions) is often a matter of individual preference.

It is useful to note that the therapist becomes part of the client's system and that the therapist's behavior can reverberate in the client's system for both good and ill. For example, a new insight, a useful coping strategy, or an invitation to bring in the client's spouse or partner can spur positive changes in the system, whereas inattention, inadequate support, excessive challenge, fostering of dependency, and exploitation can have a lasting negative impact on the client's world outside of therapy. Even "successful" therapy can have ill effects. For example, clients in unsafe environments who become confident, assertive, or outspoken about their views without making changes can experience devastating consequences (e.g., clients in violent relationships, in reactive work environments, in strict spiritual or cultural communities, or in racist, sexist, or homophobic, environments).

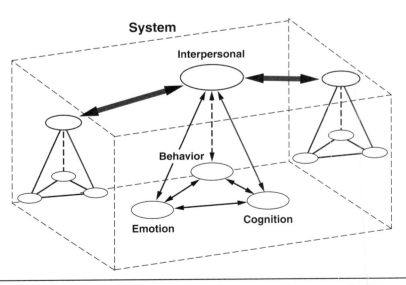

FIGURE 7.1   Interactions Among ECBIS Categories. Reproduced with permission from Beitman & Yue, 1999b.

The relationship between strategies and techniques varies. The same strategy can be implemented using a variety of techniques. For example, the techniques of questioning the evidence and reality-testing can be used both to identify and challenge distorted beliefs. Furthermore, one technique can be used to carry out various strategies. Assertion training, for example, can be used to change behavior, modulate emotion, modify anxiety-provoking thought, and alter system dynamics.

Strategy Selection

The most straightforward way to select a strategy is to decide which is most likely to achieve the goal the client desires and which the client is most likely to accept. At the moment of strategy selection, therapists must consider the most efficient path to the most comprehensive change for the specific client. Information influencing this decision may include: the client's goals, the nature of the dysfunctional patterns, the client's cultural beliefs, the strength of the therapeutic relationship, and the client's readiness to change. Therapists attempt to predict and thereby guide creation of the client-desired future through the strategies they select.

Ideally, therapy researchers would provide practitioners with answers to the question: What strategy, for what person, with what problem, at what time? (Meehl, 1954). Some evidence-based studies have been undertaken, but many have studied only highly selected, diagnostically homogeneous clients able to follow research protocols, and recruited through advertising. The degree to which these studies generalize to clinical populations is not well-established (Westen, Novotny, & Thompson-Brenner, 2004). Nevertheless, the results of these studies deserve careful consideration in strategy selection. Therapists should consider evidence-based practices for specific problems, such as behavior therapy for phobias and cognitive or interpersonal therapy for depression. Generally these strategies must be adapted to the needs and abilities of the client, as well as to the client's cultural worldview and to the therapist's strengths and predispositions.

> Select the strategy that is most likely to achieve the goal the client desires and that the client is most likely to accept. At the moment of strategy selection, therapists must consider the most efficient path to the most comprehensive change for the specific client. Information influencing this decision may include: the client's goals, the nature of the dysfunctional patterns, the clients' cultural beliefs, the strength of the therapeutic relationship, and the client's readiness to change. Therapists attempt to predict and thereby guide creation of the client-desired future through the strategies they select.

Evidence-based practices are not the only source of data-based guidance for therapists. Other researchers have paid less attention to diagnosis and more to client variables. Their conclusions offer useful guidelines for strategy selection. Some encouraging results have emerged from attempts to match three client variables (motivational stress, external coping style, and resistance to interpersonal influence) with three different strategies (group cognitive therapy, emotional-focused expressive therapy, and nondirective self-awareness procedures; Beutler, Mohr, Grawe, Engle, & MacDonald, 1991). For example, clients who are highly reactant (rebellious toward directives) were more successfully treated with nondirective self-awareness procedures. They reacted against the directive qualities of cognitive and emotion-focused approaches. There is even some evidence that excessive direction in highly reactant people can foster deterioration. Externalizers (clients who looked outward rather than inward for problems and solutions by avoidance and blaming others) responded more positively to a directive, symptom-focused cognitive therapy approach.

Many therapy dilemmas have escaped research scrutiny, leaving therapists without clinically developed guidelines for strategy selection. Simple problems, for example, should respond to simple techniques, but some do not, requiring the use of a second and often third strategy. Complex problems may require multiple, simultaneous strategies.

Finally, despite all the clever research and clinical innovations, individual therapists find that their personal predispositions influence treatment selection. Therapists who have personally benefited from, for example, facing fears, changing cognitions, and clarifying past/present relationships are likely to use those strategies when they are unsure of what to do. Practitioners may also be influenced by training programs as well as by the therapy book they most recently read or the last workshop they attended. Of course, client preference should also influence strategy selection. Some clients want therapy but not psychoactive medications, or vice versa. Interventions are typically only effective if clients elect to participate, so clients should be consulted regarding the selection of techniques. Indeed, therapist-client collaboration in selection and engagement in therapy activities (tasks) is a vital aspect of the therapeutic working alliance. As discussed earlier, task selection is one of the three components in Bordin's (1979) model of the therapeutic working alliance.

ECBIS Strategies

Knowledge of the ECBIS approaches provides therapists with a clear idea of the breadth of therapeutic possibilities and the opportunity to identify those that will best resonate with them and their experience. Within each ECBIS category (emotion, cognition, behavior, interpersonal relationships, systemic interactions), change strategies are presented that focus on assisting clients to give up old patterns and initiate and strengthen new patterns.

Emotion

Emotional awareness can lead to recognition of patterns of emotional distress which can be more adaptively regulated and maintained.

Evoking Emotion in the Session

During sessions therapists help clients access and reexperience emotion in order to define and restructure dysfunctional emotional schemas.

Catharsis.   This term originated from Freud's use of hypnosis in treating hysterics. He noticed that after clients discharged their strangulated emotions during hypnosis, their symptoms were reduced. However, symptoms often returned. Freud then found that therapeutic results could be obtained without hypnosis by permitting the client to talk freely and experience whatever ideas came to mind (free association). Catharsis is not only associated with hypnosis and free association, however. A client's verbal expression (with or without the help of the therapist) of traumatic experiences or of suppressed feelings such as guilt, fear, anger, or suffering can also be called catharsis.

Enactment of Conflict Splits: Two Chairs.   Two-chair dialogue is generally used to explore two aspects of the self that are in opposition. The two chairs represent the two conflicted parts or the "split." Any conflict is based on cognitive-emotional schemas representing two polarities. One is derived from deeply felt emotions, desires, and needs; the other is derived from externally derived standards that oppose the emotions, desires, and needs. The first one can be called "experiencing self" and the second "the critical self." Failure to recognize needs and wants generally leaves the person unclear and confused, whereas failure to meet the standards and values produces negative self-evaluation and loss of self-worth. The two-chair technique is used to evoke these two aspects simultaneously in the session. Therapists help clients role play and explore the "critical" aspect of the self, identifying its harsh, negative evaluations of the "experiencing" aspect of the self. At the same time, therapists also help clients to express the experiencing part's affective reactions to the harsh criticism. In this process, the critical part moves from general statements to more concrete and specific criticism of the person and situation, while the experiencing part begins to react in a more differentiated way that is expressed to the critic as a want or a need. Two-chair dialogue can lead to a negotiation between or integration of the two parts (Greenberg, 1995a; Greenberg, Rice, & Elliott, 1993).

Exploring Unfinished Business: The Empty Chair. *Unfinished business* refers to emotional experiences that are so overwhelming, painful, or frustrating that they are held back from conscious experience. The expression of the feelings and of the underlying needs is blocked. Those unmet needs do not, however, fully disappear. Rather, they and the situation become encoded in memory and remain as "unfinished business" that sometimes arises without awareness into the current moment and distorts clients' responses. The empty chair represents the significant others with whom the client has "unfinished" feelings. The client addresses the empty chair as if the significant other is present and sitting in it. This dialogue is used to evoke the unfinished business in the session in order to help the client reprocess and reconstruct the blocked emotional schemas (Greenberg, 1995a; Greenberg, Rice, & Elliott, 1993).

Evoking Problematic Reactions. Interactions with other people and difficult situations may trigger "markers" for problematic reactions. Markers for these events have three identifiable features: (1) a stimulus situation, such as "When I saw them walking down the hall"; (2) an emotional or behavioral reaction on the part of the client, like "I wanted to run"; and (3) an indication that the client views the reaction as puzzling, inappropriate, or in some way problematic. The therapist helps clients vividly evoke the incident and then reprocess it more slowly and completely. Clients discover that their problematic reaction was a direct consequence of their views of the eliciting stimulus. This, in turn, can stimulate further exploration, which may lead to recognition that the particular problematic reaction was an example of a broader pattern that is interfering with meeting the client's goals and needs (Greenberg, 1995a; Greenberg, Rice, & Elliott, 1993).

Exaggeration. To foster people's awareness of the signals they send through body language, clients are asked to exaggerate their movements, gestures, or postures repeatedly. This helps to intensify the feeling associated with the behavior and thereby makes the underlying meaning clearer. Therapists may also ask clients to give voice to their gestures or moving body parts (Levitskky & Perls, 1970).

Restructuring Emotional Schemas

A basic assumption of emotion-focused therapy is that the barriers to current healthy functioning result from dysfunctional, emotion-laden cognitive schemas. In other words, key cognitions are usually "hot."

Helping Clients Access New Information through Emotional Awareness. Some dysfunctional emotional schemas are beyond clients' conscious awareness. Helping clients to become aware of and experience these emotions is a prerequisite to the emotion-cognition reconstruction process. As clients directly experience their warded-off emotions, the therapist helps them access new information that has been beyond their awareness.

Reversal. Some concerns represent reversals of underlying (latent) impulses. Hence, therapists can suggest that clients consider playing the aspect of themselves that they have attempted to deny and submerge. For example, people who are excessively considerate of others ("nice" people) can be directed to be selfish and mean; excessively inhibited ("up tight") individuals can be directed to be exhibitionistic. This activity can help clients become more comfortable with parts of themselves that they have sought to disown (Levitskky & Perls, 1970).

Confronting Feared Emotions. Clients generally try to avoid experiencing feared emotions. Dysfunctional patterns result from this avoidance. In confronting feared emotions, therapists help clients to access emotions in a safe, supportive therapeutic environment and then to change their responses to them.

Staying with the Feeling.   People typically try to avoid or escape from unpleasant feelings. However, at critical times, therapists may encourage clients to "stay with feelings" and to "go deeper into the feeling" that they may be inclined to avoid. Movement into previously avoided emotional experiencing takes courage and emotional strength and reflects a willingness to endure the pain sometimes necessary for resolving emotional blocks and promoting further growth (Levitskky & Perls, 1970).

Practicing Emotional Awareness

Practicing emotional awareness can be done both in and out of the office. With the therapist's encouragement, clients repeat helpful exercises learned in the office. Clients are also encouraged to "try out" the new awareness in outside situations by noticing emotions, allowing them to rise fully into awareness and seeing where they lead.

Cognition

Interventions in this area involve identifying distorted beliefs, creating new alternatives, and then practicing them in the real world.

Identifying and Challenging Dysfunctional/Distorted Beliefs

The primary foci of cognitive therapy are dysfunctional/distorted beliefs. Therapists help clients identify, challenge, and change these beliefs. Between stimulus and response there is mind. In mind is our power to choose our response. Our ability to choose a response creates and our freedom.

Understanding Idiosyncratic Meaning. Therapists should not assume they completely understand the terms used by clients without asking for clarification. Therefore, it is essential to clarify the meaning of clients' verbalizations. In this way, therapists can make sure that they are on the right track. Clients often understate, exaggerate, or overgeneralize their problems. Just as often they may omit some information. Therapists should not, for example, take every self-criticism or every negative statement about others as true; instead, they should help clients define more explicitly what they mean. If, for instance, clients claim that they are "losers," therapists should explore what they mean rather than simply accepting the idea that nothing they do ever suc-ceeds (Freeman & White, 1989).

Reality-Testing and Questioning the Evidence.   Clients often use cer-tain evidence to maintain and support their distorted thoughts and beliefs. An effective way to challenge these dysfunctional thoughts is to examine the extent to which they are supported by the available evi-dence and whether other explanations fit the evidence better. It is essen-tial for therapists to show clients how to identify and then question the evidence they use to maintain or strengthen a belief if they are to find a way to let go of that belief (Freeman & White, 1989).

Guided Association/Discovery.   Guided association differs from the free association of psychoanalysis. In guided association/dis-covery, therapists ask guided questions as clients let ideas come to mind. This helps clients explore and expand their personal under-standing of specific experiences. Therapists' questions may focus on clients' distorted ideas, thoughts, and images. Key therapist questions include:

- "Then what?" (if the client stops to let the therapist draw a conclusion)
- "What would happen then?" (if the client does not complete the pattern being described)
- "What if . . . ?" (when the client fails to consider another possible environmental response) (Freeman & White, 1989).

The "Columbo approach" (after the bumbling TV detective), is a version of guided discovery that involves therapists' expressing confu-sion about clients' distorted but closely held beliefs. Therapists might say, "I'm confused. Can you help me understand how, if you are a ter-rible mother [distorted client belief], you have managed to raise two children who have successful careers and relationships [evidence to the contrary of the view]?" This approach often allows clients to be guided to discovery of their own dynamics and strengths and avoids problems frequently associated with direct confrontation or instruction.

Creating Adaptive and Reasonable Beliefs

This aim is accomplished by processing new information that is discrepant with previous beliefs. After the dysfunctional thoughts are identified, therapists help clients create functional thoughts and beliefs by providing new information, broader perspectives, and new ways to think. Clients use this new information to develop more adaptive responses.

Developing Alternatives. Some dysfunctional thoughts result from clients' limited options for interpreting situations. They simply have only one way to understand what they see. For example: "I think people do not like me because one day when I started to talk with one of my coworkers, he hurriedly left." The therapist must help clients generate additional options. When clients can see other options, they begin to replace dysfunctional thoughts with more adaptive ones. In response to the client whose coworker abruptly left, the therapist may say: "Perhaps he did not like the topic you brought up," or "He may have had an appointment with someone," or "Perhaps he needed to use the restroom," or "He may have been having a bad day."

Fantasizing About Consequences. Clients are asked to imagine a situation in their lives and to fantasize about the consequences. For example, suppose a client is afraid that someone will reject his invitation for a date. The client would be asked to fantasize about the consequences of having the person decline his invitation. By imagining and verbalizing their fears, clients can see their irrationality as well as their real concerns. This technique allows clients to bring into the consulting room unclearly imagined events, situations, or interactions that they believe will happen in the future. When clients clarify the imagined consequences, their concerns and fears become more rational, realistic, and addressable (Freeman & White, 1989).

Listing Positives and Negatives of Change. This technique helps clients move away from an all-or-nothing position to one that explores the possibility of new experiences, feelings, thoughts, or behaviors that have both negative and positive qualities. When the client examines both disadvantages and advantages, a broader perspective can be achieved. This approach is most often used in helping clients to resolve ambivalence and conflicts about change and to relinquish dysfunctional thoughts and behavior (Freeman & White, 1989; Miller & Rollnick, 2002).

Reattribution.   There are two common dysfunctional patterns concerning responsibility. Some clients take responsibility for events and situations that are only minimally attributable to them; other clients externalize blame excessively and take insufficient responsibility. Reattribution means helping clients distribute responsibility reasonably among the relevant parties. Therapists should typically avoid taking a position of total support ("It wasn't your fault at all") or total blame ("It is all your fault"). Rather, they should usually assume a supportive middle ground with clients assuming appropriate responsibility for their actions and outcomes (Freeman & White, 1989).

Turning Adversity Into Advantage.   Turning adversity into advantage is like turning stumbling blocks into stepping stones. There are times when an apparent disaster can be used to one's advantage. For example, divorce may be the starting point for a new life; pressure from a boss can be used as a motivator for finding a better job. Looking for the positive aspects in a negative situation is initially difficult for clients, and they may respond to the therapist's effort to point out the positive with greater negativity and opposition. In these cases the therapist can point out that the view being offered is no less realistic than the client's negative view (Freeman & White, 1989).

Editing Self-Talk.   People talk to themselves. They comment, criticize, and direct their own thinking and emotions. Cognitive therapy contends that the imprecise language with which clients talk to themselves is one of the causes of distorted thinking processes. Changing self-talk means that the therapist pays attention to the client's imprecise (e.g., exaggerated, minimizing) language patterns, noticing, for example, too many "shoulds," "musts," or "oughts." Therapists help clients to employ new self-statements to substitute for the old language. For instance, instead of saying, "It would be awful if . . .," they can learn to say "It would be inconvenient if. . . ." Through the process of changing their language patterns and making new self-statements, clients come to think and behave more rationally (Corey, 1996).

New Self-Instruction.   We all give ourselves the orders, directions, instructions, or information necessary to solve problems. Therapists can assist clients in their efforts to learn to control dysfunctional thoughts by introducing more adaptive instructions or directions. Therapists teach clients to start with direct verbalization of self-instruction aloud; then, with practice, clients learn to say the instructions silently. Gradually the instructions become more automatic. New instructions also can be introduced by clients themselves (Freeman & White, 1989).

Thought-Stopping.   Clients' dysfunctional thoughts often have a snowball effect. Once they start, they are hard to stop. Thought-stopping is used to inhibit their progression. Clients can be taught to picture a stop sign, to "hear" a bell, or to think the command "Stop!" Some clients wear a rubber band around their wrist that they snap to weaken dysfunctional patterns and to orient themselves toward new patterns. Any of these procedures can help stop the progression of a dysfunctional thought (e.g., disrupt a dysfunctional neural circuit). It is important to find a thought-stopping technique that is right for the client and practice it in the session. The memory of the intervention can then be used by clients to assist their thought-stopping between sessions (Freeman & White, 1989).

Disputing Irrational Beliefs.   Therapists actively dispute clients' irrational beliefs and teach them how to challenge their own thinking. These challenges take two general forms: (1) the logical debate, and (2) testing by comparing the beliefs with external evidence. The logical debate may take the form: "What does it matter if life is not exactly as you want it to be?" The testing approach involves quickly challenging irrational beliefs by asking questions like, "Where is the evidence of your beliefs?" Through a series of logical and empirical refutations, therapists help clients develop more rational and adaptive beliefs. This technique may be used when it is clear that there is a strong working alliance between the therapist and the client (Corey, 1996; Freeman & White, 1989).

The Four-Column Thought Record.   The thought record (see Figure 5.1) is widely used to identify clients' dysfunctional thoughts. It singularly separates cognitive interventions from other therapies. The four-column technique can help both clients and therapists identify connections between when and where the symptoms occur and what feelings and thoughts the client has at that time. The fourth column (the list of more functional thoughts) begins the process of change (Beck et al., 1979).

Repeating or Practicing the Modified Beliefs in Various Situations

In order to maintain clients' more adaptive thoughts or beliefs, therapists need to help clients practice these new thoughts and beliefs in different situations. One major task in this process is for therapists to provide positive reinforcement and teach clients how to positively reinforce the change on their own. As mentioned earlier, there is evidence that people develop habitual neural pathways. Practicing new patterns (as may occur in therapy) appears to help clients develop and strengthen new, more adaptive neural circuits (Beitman, 2005).

Behavior

Behavioral change starts with defining the behavior to change, initiating a new behavior and then finding ways to change it.

Defining the Maladaptive Behaviors

Behavior therapy focuses on clients' maladaptive behaviors. In order to change these behaviors, therapists need to identify them.

Description of Presenting Problems and Maintaining Variables. Therapists and clients should collaborate in describing behaviors targeted for change and the stimuli or reinforcers that are maintaining them.

Behavioral Observation by the Therapist and Significant Others. Direct observation of maladaptive behavior generally is clinically useful during assessment. These observations may be made by the therapist or by significant others. Clients' interaction with therapists during the session may provide a sample of their problem behaviors. The observations by others in the client's life, including the client's parents, spouse, friends, and the therapist's office staff, can be very informative because they provide additional perspectives and sources of information that can be used to better understand the client's behaviors in various situations.

Observations can provide valuable descriptive information connecting stimuli or reinforcers to behaviors targeted for change (Goldfried & Davison, 1976).

Self-Report and Self-Monitoring.   Self-report and self-monitoring also provide a window into the real-world correlates of symptomatic behavior. Clients are asked to observe their own targeted behaviors in particular situations and to record them. For example, if clients desire to reduce or eliminate a behavior (such as smoking), monitoring and recording each episode where the behavior occurs provides information about the behavior (and also tends to reduce the frequency of the undesired behavior by increasing the client's awareness that it is occurring).

Changing Behavior Directly

Behavior can be changed directly in many ways including controlling reinforcers and stimuli as well as forms of relaxation and planning.

Changing Reinforcers to Change Behavior.   The use of reinforcement to change behavior is the cornerstone of modern behavior therapy. Changing reinforcers to control behavior comes from the theory of operant conditioning, which proposes that behavior can be changed by manipulating its consequences. Reinforcers increase the probability of the behavior they follow. They can be positive or negative. As described earlier, a positive reinforcer is something positive that is given to the individual (e.g., praise, candy, money). A negative reinforcer decreases or eradicates something discomforting (e.g., the cessation of criticism). Both positive and negative reinforcements increase the likelihood of the behavior. For example, if a therapist is approving (positive reinforcer) of a client who reports that he went for a walk when he became angry with his wife instead of threatening her, the client will probably be more likely to "cool off" in the same way the next time he gets angry. If an irritated wife stops nagging her partner (negative reinforcer) about helping with the housework after he has done the dishes and cleaned the kitchen, the husband will be more likely to clean the kitchen in the future. In general, small, immediate reinforcements (e.g., small amounts of money provided at short intervals for desired behavior versus large amounts at one time well after the desired behavior) are more effective in promoting learning than large, delayed ones (Logue, 1995).

Self-Reinforcement.   Self-reinforcement can include a variety of pleasurable activities (e.g., praising oneself, doing something enjoyable, buying something for oneself). Ideally, self-reinforcement leads to the automatic implementation of the desired behavior.

Stimulus Control. Certain stimuli (cues) trigger unwanted responses. These cues may include places, people, sounds, smells, and touch. For example, people with addictions may lose control over their abstinent behavior if they receive a phone call from a person with whom they used to engage in their addiction. Smokers who associate smoking with drinking will have difficulty resisting the desire for a cigarette when they have a drink in their hand. Trauma and combat survivors often develop elevated reactivity to cues associated with their trauma. Returning to an old neighborhood, a certain glance from an important person, or even a long-forgotten song can trigger their old unwanted response. Learning to recognize the stimulus or stimuli and how to control or alter the response to it can be very helpful.

Relaxation Training.   There are many relaxation training methods, including breath control, meditation, visualization of pleasant scenes, and progressive muscle relaxation (see Chapter 10 for a sample progressive muscle relaxation script). An effective and simple method requires gentle focus of attention on the mechanics of breathing. For example, clients can be instructed to focus their attention on the rise and fall of their abdomen with each breath. As their attention inevitably drifts to other thoughts, they are instructed to gently return their attention to their breathing. Mindfulness practice is emerging as a potentially useful component of therapy not only because of its ability to provide relaxation but also because of its activation of self-awareness, which emphasizes allowing "hot cognitions" to pass through the mind rather than letting them get stuck in consciousness (Kabat-Zinn, 1990).

Biofeedback.   Individuals can learn to control the activities of their autonomic nervous system. Biofeedback machines help them become aware of their own biological rhythms and functions. These biological functions include skin temperature, heart rate, muscle tension, blood pressure, and brainwave activity. Clients are taught to reduce symptoms and reach a desired physiological state by regulating one or more of these biological states through feedback from the monitoring machine. For example, learning to raise the temperature of one's hand can be used to reduce the frequency of migraine headaches because it teaches clients how to alter regional blood flow.

Systematic Desensitization. The basic assumption underlying systematic desensitization is that anxiety responses are learned (conditioned), and can be inhibited by substituting an activity that is antagonistic to it. It includes three steps: (1) helping clients analyze stimuli that evoke anxiety in order to construct a hierarchy of situations that can be arranged in order of increasing aversiveness, (2) teaching clients relaxation techniques, and (3) encouraging clients to pair relaxation with imagined scenes from the hierarchy, beginning with the least fear-provoking item. The anxiety-producing stimuli are repeatedly paired with relaxation until the connection between those stimuli and the anxiety response is eliminated. Systematic desensitization can be conducted in session, where clients imagine each situation under conditions of deep relaxation, so that they are able to tolerate greater and greater levels of anxiety. Or it can be conducted between sessions, where clients use the learned relaxation to reduce their anxiety while directly confronting stimuli in the real world. The central change mechanism appears to be exposure to the feared stimulus (Goldfried & Davison, 1976).

Assertion Training. Assertion training is one form of social-skill training. The basic assumption underlying assertion training is that people have the right to express their wants and needs directly to others. There are many assertion training methods, most of which focus on the client's negative self-statements, self-defeating beliefs, and faulty thinking. Assertion training includes two parts: (a) challenging the beliefs that inhibit self-assertion, (b) providing skills and techniques for dealing with situations in which clients/people are better served by stating their beliefs and desires. Assertion training can be useful for clients who cannot express anger or irritation, who have difficulty saying no, who are overly polite and allow others to take advantage of them, who find it difficult to express affection and other positive responses, or who express their wants too aggressively (Corey, 1996).

Modeling.   The terms *modeling*, *observational learning*, *imitation*, and *social learning* are used interchangeably to refer to the process by which the observer learns to perform the model's desired thoughts, attitudes, and behaviors. Several types of models are used in therapeutic situations. A live model can teach clients appropriate behavior, influence attitudes and values, and teach social skills. Sometimes therapists can serve as live models for their clients. Behavior therapists also use symbolic models. A model's behaviors can be shown on film or videotape. Multiple models are especially relevant in group therapy. Clients/observers can alter their attitudes and learn new skills through observation of successful peers in the group. As noted earlier, people seem to learn better from models who are imperfectly successful than from ones who perform tasks perfectly.

Behavioral Rehearsal.   Behavioral rehearsal is used primarily to help clients learn new ways of responding to specific life situations by selecting a target situation, simulating the situation in the session, initiating new behavioral patterns, and carrying out this new role with its specific new behaviors in real-life situations. Sometimes this term is used interchangeably with *role playing*; however, behavioral rehearsal is more specifically focused on training new response patterns.

Practicing Modified Behaviors in Various Situations
In order to maintain the new behavioral patterns, therapists need to encourage clients to practice these new behaviors in real-life situations until they can carry them out on their own.

Interpersonal Relationships

Interpersonal relationship patterns can be identified through numerous techniques, mapped out for change and then practiced to maintain the change.

Identifying Maladaptive Interpersonal Schemas
Interpersonal therapy regards clients' problems as a function of disturbed interpersonal relationships. In the interpersonal approach, clients' intrapsychic conflicts, problematic attachments, and dysfunctional

thoughts, emotions, and behaviors impinge on relationships with significant persons in the client's life. Therefore, maladaptive interpersonal patterns (role relationship models, the way clients view their intimate and
important relationships) involve thoughts, emotions, and behaviors. Both
transference and current relationship patterns, coupled with patterns
developed in the family of origin, can clarify patterns to be changed.

Interpretation.   This term was used by Freud to describe attempts
to translate the potential hidden meanings of dreams into the language
of ordinary consciousness. This idea was then applied to the psychoanalytic relationship, in which analysts "translated" the hidden meanings
in clients' words with reference to transference reactions. Translation
gradually took on a causal quality, as interpretation came to suggest
how early childhood events influenced or "caused" the pattern in the
present, especially with the analyst. Interpretation also became associated with understanding resistance, as the therapist and client looked
for reasons (e.g., fear) behind reluctance to continue the therapeutic
process. Interpretation then came to mean a variety of things, including
probing for the history, cause, purpose, or meaning of a repeated dysfunctional pattern.

The interpretation of a resistance or transference reaction usually
contains three elements: (1) an empathic summary or confrontation, (2)
a clarification of the pattern, and (3) a suggestion or guess about its origins. For example, suppose a client becomes silent. An interpretation
might be: "It seems very difficult for you to talk about your feelings"
(empathic reflection); "You have had similar problems with your spouse
as well as your boss" (pattern reflection); or "Perhaps you are afraid that
people will take advantage of you if they know how you are feeling"
(avoidance because of a fear) (Greenson, 1967).

*Enacting and Identifying the Client's Interpersonal Patterns Within the
Therapeutic Relationship.*   The client repeats with the therapist patterns
from current and past relationships in a safe environment. These patterns are usually repeated to some extent no matter what the therapist
does. However, the longer the therapeutic relationship and the less
active the therapist, the more likely that details of the client's adaptive
and maladaptive interpersonal schemas with intimate others will be
enacted with the therapist. There are times when discussion of this

enactment is irrelevant to the client's purpose in seeking help. At other times, the repetition provides another example of the problems the client must overcome. Therapists can welcome these real-life imitations or divert attention away from them, depending upon their relevance to the therapeutic aim. For beginning therapists and for therapeutically unsophisticated clients, bringing the therapeutic focus into the office and into the relationship between the participants (the "here and now") can be highly anxiety-provoking. Beginners must learn to be effective users of their observing selves so that they can "step back" from the interaction to observe their own responses as well as those of the client. With a well-activated observing self, therapists can help clients step back to observe the interactional patterns and explain how the therapist's office can be a laboratory in which to study and learn to alter the maladaptive patterns. Clients might then be able to observe and describe the patterns in ways that suggest possible change.

Examining Interpersonal "Pulls" from the Client by Being Both a Participant and Observer.   This technique for identifying patterns is related to the previous one. Clients (like everyone else) usually attempt to elicit responses from others that fit their consciously or unconsciously desired role relationship models. The observing self of the therapist asks: What does the client expect me to do? What am I expected to be? What response is the client trying to "pull" from me? What reciprocal role does the client wish to assign to me? (See Chapter 8 for more on this subject.) (Kielser 1983; Strupp & Binder, 1984).

Cyclical Psychodynamics.   From a cyclical psychodynamic perspective, the psychodynamic process is not located in the past's reemergence in the present. Instead, the maladaptive process is understood as a vicious cycle generated both by clients and the reactions of others. Like the problem of which came first, the chicken or the egg, therapists and clients may have difficulty deciding what starts the vicious cycle. The key, however, is not in identifying a single initiating source but in helping clients identify points in their interaction patterns at which they can intervene. Clients treat themselves in the same way that they see others treating them. For example, clients who are highly self-critical often feel as if others are critical of them or induce others to be critical of them. Similarly, clients whose identity seems to be determined by the expectations of others are usually unable to define and respond to their own wishes and needs. Clients unconsciously shape their relationships with others to confirm their intrapsychic view of themselves (or because this particular neural circuit tends to get activated and feels familiar). This concept can be useful in identifying a dysfunctional pattern, as the same pattern gets played out in three different arenas: intrapsychic, interpersonal, and transference (Strupp & Binder, 1984; Wachtel & Wachtel, 1986).

Analyzing Interpersonal Transactions. Analyzing interpersonal transactions involves focusing on the contributions of clients' thoughts and feelings to relationships with others and the behaviors that result from those thoughts and feelings. This analysis takes into account the expressed or imagined actions (thoughts, wishes, fears, motives) as they form individuals' role relationship models. For example, a client is looking at the wall in the therapist's office and says "That is a pretty painting." This statement does not describe an interpersonal event, but this sentence does: "When he saw that I was drunk again, he got angry and slammed the door, and I imagined that I would never see him again." The action of drinking is understood as evoking the other person's anger, as demonstrated by slamming the door, which in turn evokes imagining the final separation (Strupp & Binder 1984).

Analysis of Faulty Communication.   Faulty communication may be responsible for failure in interpersonal relationships. Communication analysis is used to examine and identify these communication failures, which often result from one partner's mistaken assumptions about the other's thoughts, feelings, and intentions. Some common communication failures include: expecting the other person to "read my mind," ambiguous statements, nonverbal communication that contradicts verbal communication, incorrectly assuming that one has communicated clearly, and abrupt silence that closes off communication (Klerman et al., 1984).

Monitoring Examples of Faulty Interpersonal Transactions Through Diaries.   Repetitively studying the situations in which clients respond in ways that are ineffective and self-defeating can foster relinquishing these responses. Asking the client to keep a diary facilitates this analysis.

Modifying Role Relationship Models and Altering Interpersonal Scripts

After identifying the dysfunctional interpersonal schemas and their associated behaviors, therapists assist clients to reconstruct, modify, and change these schemas by incorporating more reasonable and adaptive thoughts, feelings, and behaviors.

Corrective Emotional Experience. Some therapists believe that what the client understands intellectually is far less important than what the client experiences emotionally in the context of the psychotherapeutic interaction. The term *corrective emotional experience* initially referred to the positive effects of clients emotionally sensing the discrepancy between (a) how they had expected the therapist to react to them about some important issue in their life (typically negatively based on prior experience with caregivers or others), and (b) the therapist's actual response to the client about that issue or event (typically supportive) (Alexander & French, 1946).

The term now has a more general meaning; it refers to all aspects of the therapeutic encounter that enable clients to experience an unexpected form of interaction that leads to a change in dysfunctional patterns. Therapy is a specialized subset of human relationships. A therapist's basic attitudes toward the client, such as caring, empathy, interest, and positive regard, can be corrective in themselves. Therapists may be able to bring about corrective emotional experiences through active understanding of clients' interpersonal expectations. For example, if clients expect to be dominated by a punitive authority figure, the therapist may assume a warm and permissive manner (Alexander & French, 1946; Beitman, 1987; Strupp & Binder 1984).

Rewriting, Modifying, and Correcting the Assumptions Underlying Interpersonal Scripts. Any intense relationship can provide an opportunity to begin modifying clients' role relationship models and scripts. *Role relationship models* refer to the concepts or schemas clients have about specific interpersonal roles. They start usually with one person being dominant and the other submissive. The roles carry with

> Corrective emotional experience has come to mean aspects of the therapeutic encounter that allow clients to experience an unexpected form of interpersonal interaction that helps heal a formerly dysfunctional pattern. Therapists may create corrective emotional experiences through active understanding of clients' specific interpersonal expectations, as well as through more general aspects of the therapeutic relationship such as caring, interest, empathy, and positive regard.

them implied descriptions of how they are to be played out (scripts). Some interpersonal approaches use the "here-and-now" therapy relationship, especially when the client reacts to the therapist with characteristic maladaptive scripts. This interaction in the therapist's office provides a model for clients' interactions with others. It also provides access for both participants to unrealistic concerns, distorted views of others, faulty assumptions, and unrealistic scripts and expectations. The enactment of more adaptive responses in the office provides a template for similar responses in clients' interpersonal environment. Similar changes can be initiated outside the therapeutic relationship. For example, clients can ask friends, "Am I being too sensitive or does that person really dislike me?" The answer can lead to a new set of response patterns.

Guiding Toward More Effective Communication.   Sometimes clients' problems result from their faulty communication. Therapists guide them to initiate effective communication, to practice these communication skills within the session, and then to try them out in various interpersonal situations.

Practicing Modified Roles

New interpersonal patterns need to be practiced or worked through in different contexts if they are to be maintained. Although they can be reinforced within the therapeutic relationship, the degree of generalization to other relationships varies. The factors that promote generalization from the therapeutic relationship (e.g., from therapist to husband) or from any other relationship (e.g., from wife to mother) remain to be studied.

Maintaining Consistent and Reliable Behavior to Disconfirm the Client's False Assumptions About the Interpersonal Reality.   Interpersonal and psychodynamic therapists believe that clients change through experiencing a new interpersonal relationship. In the context of that experience, clients come to understand the meaning of their prior faulty learning. In order to maintain client change, the therapist must maintain consistent and reliable behaviors (by not being drawn into the client's attempts to recreate old roles). The new human experience helps the client repetitively understand (work through) the differences

ECBIS STRATEGIES FOR FACILITATING CHANGE 177

between beliefs, feelings, and behavior patterns generated from the past and the beliefs, feelings, and behavioral patterns currently being established (Strupp & Binder, 1984).

Reinforcement from New Interpersonal Success. New interpersonal behavior is often rewarded in clients' lives and leads to increases in the desired direction. As happens often with successful adaptation, success breeds success. However, some interpersonal change can lead to negative responses in others. For example, the changes one spouse makes during therapy can disrupt a comfortable equilibrium for the other spouse, who then attempts to dampen the client's change. Therapists may need to be vigilant for negative reinforcement of change. In addition, the spouse may find him or herself experiencing anxiety or depression with the new equilibrium, requiring the therapist to be vigilant for the emergence of problems in the spouse that lay hidden because of the apparently bigger problems of the client. There are other situations where family members commonly resist disturbances of their system— for example, when a passive, compliant spouse or child starts to become assertive.

Systemic Interactions

Each person is entwined in a web of relationships within which are patterns to identify for change, to change, and then to maintain the new, more functional dynamics.

Identifying the Dysfunctional Dynamic Interactions among System Members

Several tool are available to define interpersonal sequences among system members.

Circular Questioning. Circular questions are systemic questions that link one member of the family to another. It is a technique for interviewing families: One person is questioned about the relationships among others. The responses are then utilized by therapists to introduce new formulations. Circularity is based on the idea that family members are connected to each other in particular patterns through time and that the problem in the family system often results from these

Therapists using circular questioning invite the family to access their curiosity and join them on a research expedition regarding their problem. This helps create an interpersonal atmosphere in which the family arrives at new understandings of their situation.

interacting patterns. In order to perceive the architecture of the system, therapists use circular questioning to define and clarify the interacting patterns and specific connections, as well as to introduce information back to the family in the form of new questions. Circular questioning is also regarded as a change strategy, because it allows families to get a comprehensive systemic view of their situation in the context of history and environment. This enables the family to open up new patterns and new levels of meaning in the system. In the following example of circular questioning, the therapist asks the son in the family:

Q: Who is the most upset by the problem?
A: My mother.
Q: What does your mother do about it?
A: She tries to motivate John to go to school.
Q: Who agrees with your mother?
A: The school psychologist.
Q: Who disagrees?
A: My father.
Q: Why do you think he disagrees?
A: He thinks they are pushing John too hard.
Q: Who feels the same as your father?
A: My grandmother.
(Boscolo, Cecchin, Hoffman, & Penn, 1987).

Enactments. The conflict situations and problems in the family are reproduced in the session. In order to identify interactional patterns in the family, family therapists often try to initiate the interaction between family members rather than simply listening to their reports. Therapists may have spouses talk to each other, have a parent negotiate with the child, or have the family enact interacting patterns associated with the presenting problems. The therapist becomes an observer and director for in-session interaction. These in-session interactions usually reproduce out-of-session patterns. Family therapists may emphasize different content areas—for example, distorted boundary patterns, transgenerational patterns, ineffective communication patterns, or distorted beliefs, ideas, and attitudes in the family culture (Griffin, 1993).

Analysis of the Sequence of Communication.   Ineffective communication between family members creates problems in the family system. Common ineffective communication patterns include withholding information, expecting the other to read one's mind rather than informing directly, sending vague and double messages, as well as attacking and defending. This analysis also includes identifying complementary relationships and symmetrical relationships. *Complementary relationships* are defined by the taking of reciprocal roles, the simplest example being one person dominant and the other submissive. *Symmetrical relationships* are characterized by similarity of response, the simplest example being the escalation of an argument in which each person retaliates with something similar to the last statement of the other. *Punctuation* refers to turn taking in communication; it is when one person stops talking and the other begins. One example of punctuation might be when a family member begins to speak and another one regularly interrupts (Sherman, Oresky, & Rountrees, 1991).

Genogram.   A genogram is a structural diagram of a family's three- or four-generational relational system. Through the creation of the genogram, therapists and clients may identify patterns that repeat across generations, such as infidelity, mental illness, substance abuse, premature deaths, and alternately aggressive and passive generations.

Narrative.   A story told by an individual about his or her perspective on selective experiences within the family will reflect the patterns of this person living in this family. The narrative can, like many stories, contain multilevel meanings of the family as a unit in society as well as its internal modes of operation.

Changing Interactional Patterns

Intervening in a system can produce sometimes dramatic results using one of several available methods.

Paradox.   A paradoxical intervention is one that, if followed, will accomplish the opposite of what it is seemingly intended to accomplish.

This technique, also called "prescribing the symptom" is based on the following assumption: Symptoms or problems in the family act as a mechanism for regulating the dysfunctional parts of the system and maintaining family homeostasis. The pull toward homeostasis explains why families are very resistant to change, even when they are seeking therapeutic help. Paradoxical techniques address this homeostatic resistance and can initiate change in the system. The three major techniques used in designing and applying systemic paradoxes are: redefining, prescribing, and restraining.

The purpose of redefining is to change the perception of the problem. Behavior that maintains the symptom is defined as positively motivated to preserve family stability; for example, anger could be defined as caring and distancing as a way of reinforcing closeness. Then the symptom-producing interaction is prescribed to the family. The key in doing this is to ask the family not only to continue to believe what they are doing is right, but to also dramatically exaggerate or increase the behavior. The third step is to insist that change be restrained when the family shows signs of changing. If the paradoxical prescription is successful, the family will rebel against the therapist and decrease the behavior. An important criterion for its use is based on the evaluation of the degree of resistance to change. Generally, paradoxical intervention is used for covert, longstanding, repetitious patterns of interaction that do not respond to direct interventions such as logical explanation or rational suggestions. Paradox must be used carefully, and it is usually employed by more experienced clinicians (Boscolo et al., 1987; Minuchin & Fishman, 1981; Sherman et al., 1991.)

Changing Rigid or Enmeshed Boundaries.   This strategy comes from structural family therapy, which assumes that dysfunctional behavior reflects an inadequate structure in the family system. Family structure is maintained by appropriate boundaries between subsystems. Therapists help to establish clear and effective boundaries that individuals can cross to an optimal degree. Rigid boundaries are loosened and overly flexible or enmeshed boundaries are defined and strengthened. Therapists help the family to change inappropriate boundaries by restructuring relationships and setting tasks that force new interactions between and among subsystems. This leads to a realignment of the subsystems (Griffin, 1993; Minuchin & Fishman, 1981).

Task-Setting.   In order to alter the structure of the family, the therapist increases the likelihood of new transactions by making specific suggestions about how to behave differently. For example, a disengaged parent may be directed to perform some tasks with a child. In doing so, an enmeshed parent may also regain better balanced boundaries with the same child.

Communication Skill Training.   Changing communication patterns between the family members can change the structure of the family. Ineffective communication can be changed through many techniques, such as having the members be aware of their ineffective communication patterns, direct instruction and coaching, blocking specific types of communication, task-setting, avoiding counterattacking and defensive talk, and having members keep a diary of their communication patterns (Kramer, 1985; Sherman et al. 1991).

Ritual Prescriptions.   While their specific definitions and intentions vary somewhat among various family theorists, rituals are ceremonial acts that mark activities of a family and provide meaning and an atmosphere of security. Ritual prescriptions are intended to begin the establishment of acts that assist the family in working through their difficulties. For example, a family characterized by disengagement and negativity may be given the prescription to meet together over Sunday dinner, with each person given the opportunity to share something that he or she appreciates about the family.

Practicing Functional Interactions to Create a Virtuous Cycle
The family is instructed to practice new behaviors in the office as well as at home. If effective, the new patterns will reinforce themselves. The spiral of change ideally creates more benefits until a better functioning equilibrium is reached.

Summary

Strategies for facilitating change have evolved from the five basic elements of the psychological field: emotions, cognitions, behavior, interpersonal relationships, and systems. These elements interact with each other within the client while the therapist also becomes part of the client's interpersonal system. Evidence from controlled clinical trials and from process research may help in strategy selection; yet therapists must, in the heat of the office interaction, make probability estimates for the intervention most likely to produce the desired outcome. Emotional awareness helps to identify maladaptive patterns and may provide the motivation for change. Defining distorted thought processes and beliefs may expose them for cognitive editing by deleting some, rephrasing others and replacing still others. By defining specific behaviors to change, clients and therapists may select from a variety of methods to alter them and in so doing change emotional reactivity and distorted cognitions. Emotions, cognitions and behaviors comprise interpersonal relationships which are vital to psychological stability. By clarifying problematic interpersonal patterns, several change strategies may applied to improving the manner in which our clients relate to others. And each person is part of a larger social system which strongly influences emotions, behavior and cognitions as well as interpersonal relationships. Changes in the client can influence either positively or negatively the systems of which the client is a part and these changes may feed back onto the client. Maintenance of change involves ongoing awareness and application of strategies acquired in therapy. This phase of therapy deserves additional attention from our profession.

CHAPTER 8

Resolving Resistance and Negotiating Transference and Countertransference Issues

*What is needed, rather than running away or controlling or suppressing or any other resist-
ance, is understanding fear; that means, watch it, learn about it, come directly into contact
with it. We are to learn about fear, not how to escape from it.*
—JIDDU KRISHNAMURTI

Many therapeutic relationships create useful challenges in
which the client or therapist does not meet the other's expectations or does not respond with thoughts, feelings, or behaviors that are expected from his or her role. These challenges are called
resistance, *transference*, and *countertransference*. This chapter describes
ways to predict and recognize these difficulties and gives suggestions on
generating alternative responses.

Resistance

In the therapeutic context, the term *resistance* originally referred to
forces within the client that opposed the recollection of repressed memories. Greenson broadened the concept, defining it as "all those forces
within the client which oppose the procedures and processes of analysis"
(1967, p. 45). Although it began as a psychoanalytic concept, resistance
is now clearly recognized in numerous forms of therapy (Leahy, 2001,
2003; Miller & Rollnick, 2002; Prochaska & DiClemente, 1983). Called by
many names including *constraints*, *blocks*, *impediments*, and *ambivalence*, resistance is common to all processes of human psychological
change. *Ambivalence* is emerging as the most useful term.

In clinical practice, a client's failure to meet the therapist's expectations may have a variety of reasons. For example, inappropriate

interventions can lead to failure to do homework; poor support from clients' social network can lead to missed appointments. To recognize resistance, therapists should maintain clear and reasonable expectations of client behavior. Not uncommonly, therapists recognize resistance first by sensing internal responses of frustration, anxiety, or discomfort. Of course, both the obvious failure of clients to do the expected and feelings of frustration may occur simultaneously. After recognizing the appearance of resistance, the usual human response might be anger or irritation. At this point, therapists have the opportunity to exercise their unique role by exploring the origin of the blocks and remembering that resistances may represent individual examples of maladaptive patterns. Resistance can activate the therapist's observing self—"What is going on here? Why am I feeling frustrated? What is going on in the client that is causing me to respond this way?" This last question directs the therapist's attention to the client's internal workings—"What is lacking in this person? What is motivating this person to respond in this self-defeating way? How can I activate the client's observing self to examine this reaction? What content should we explore? Does this resistance represent a discrete example of a wider problematic pattern? Or am I expecting too much of this person at this point?" This process of "stepping back" from resistance makes the therapist's role unlike most other social functions.

Sources and Forms of Resistance

Although resistance manifests itself as the *client's* failure to follow the therapist's various expectations, it does not always originate with the client. Resistance has three potential sources (1) the client, (2) the therapist, and (3) the client's social network (see Table 8.1).

Client-Originated Resistance

Client-originated resistance, which is the most common, occurs when ideas and feelings within the client block the process of therapy. Common sources of client resistance are fear of change, lack of necessary information, and dysfunctional patterns. Clients' *fear of change* is a major source of resistance during all stages of psychotherapy. The usual response to fear is avoidance, and avoidant behaviors in therapy often cause resistance. If clients are afraid to talk about a spe-

TABLE 8.1   Sources of Resistance

CLIENT	THERAPIST	SOCIAL NETWORK
Ambivalence or low readiness to change	Inappropriate expectations	Criticism of the client for being in counseling/therapy
Lack of necessary information or understanding of how to implement the therapist's expectations	Poor techniques	Criticism of the therapist
Fears associated with each stage of therapy	Countertransference	Fear of changes in client that might point to the need for changes by others in the client's social network
Dysfunctional patterns expressing themselves during therapy	Poor working alliance	Antagonism toward any changes that might disturb the equilibrium of the social network
Transference	Poor relationship-building skills	
Fear of becoming vulnerable to therapists' judgments, criticism	Lacking awareness of cultural considerations	
Fear of trusting therapist		

cific content area, for example, they can avoid this fear by keeping silent, talking about irrelevant topics, or missing an appointment.

A second source of resistance, *lack of necessary information*, can take many forms. For example, clients who have trouble expressing emotions like anger may never have learned how to recognize and label such feelings. Another example might be a the therapist's saying to a client: "I wonder if you might consider asking the person you are attracted to do something with you sometime?" The client may not act on this suggestion due to lacking the social skills necessary to implement it.

Common sources of client resistance are *ambivalence*, *fear of change*, *lack of necessary information*, and *dysfunctional patterns*. Clients' fear of change is a major source of resistance during all stages of therapy. The usual response to fear is avoidance, and avoidant behaviors in therapy often cause resistance.

Clients' *dysfunctional patterns* may interfere with the process of therapy in the same way that they interfere with other relationships. Clients who attempt to please others by never saying "no" and by rarely talking about what they want or experience may believe their therapist would be critical if they did so. Their fears may be related to the fact that their parents and partner criticize them whenever they talk about themselves.

Resistance can merge with transference. Generally *transference* refers to the distorted reactions toward the therapist, whereas *resistance* refers to the client's interference with the process of therapy. Because transference often becomes an obstacle in the process of therapy, it can also be considered a source of resistance. For example, a client who distrusts the opposite sex may fail to complete an assigned diary of thoughts and behaviors, fearing that the opposite-sex therapist may use the information to do harm. Or, a client's need to appear strong and in control may prevent the client from starting treatment, staying in treatment, or describing emotional pain.

Therapist-Originated Resistance

Therapist-originated resistance is associated with inappropriate expectations, ill-advised interventions, and countertransference. Therapists usually expect clients to follow indirect and direct instructions and advice. Sometimes, however, *therapist expectations* may exceed the client's ability to accomplish them. When confronted with resistance, therapists should examine their own expectations, keeping in mind clients' motivation, the degree of fear, the strength of the working alliance, and the client's functional level and social network. When clients are resistant, sometimes it means that they are being treated incorrectly.

Therapists may use *ill-advised interventions* because of their lack of experience. Beginning therapists are more likely to encounter resistance than experienced therapists. For example, a 19-year-old woman presented with agoraphobia and panic attacks. An inexperienced therapist moved quickly to develop a behavioral hierarchy designed to enable her to gradually face her agoraphobic fears. The client became uncomfortable, distracted, and did not participate in the hierarchy development. Unbeknownst to the therapist (because he did not inquire), the client had recently been raped by an ex-lover, something she felt understandably ambivalent about discussing. Once again in this situation she was being pushed into something to which she had not agreed.

Because *countertransference* can create inappropriate expectations for the client and lead to ineffective interventions, it too becomes a source of resistance. A female therapist who thought her husband was responsible for their divorce, for example, was treating a male client who was in the process of a divorce. The therapist directed the client to describe his responsibility for the marital difficulties as a homework assignment. The client did not return for the next appointment. The therapist had not discovered that the clients' wife was seriously abusing alcohol and had physically assaulted him when he had expressed his concerns about her drinking.

Social Network–Related Resistance

Resistance may emerge from the client's social network, including family members and coworkers who oppose the process or potential outcome of therapy. For example, depressed spouses may not accept therapeutic changes because their partner (perhaps unconsciously) resists their improvement. If the client were to become less symptomatic, he or she might make greater demands upon the partner for assistance with household tasks or involvement in decision making, possibly upsetting the partner's comfortable equilibrium. Furthermore, the spouse's own issues might become more apparent, with concurrent expectations for uncomfortable changes being made.

Recognizing Resistance

To recognize resistance promptly, therapists must be clear about what to expect from clients and familiar with various forms of resistance. The stages of therapy described in Table 8.2 provide a structure for what therapists need to do and expect. During the engagement phase, for example, the goal is to establish a good working alliance; therapists expect clients to trust them and actively collaborate. If clients fail to develop trust or collaborate, that suggests resistance. During pattern search,

> Therapist-originated resistance is associated with inappropriate expectations, ill-advised interventions, and countertransference.

TABLE 8.2   Therapist Expectations During Different Stages of Therapy

ENGAGEMENT	PATTERN SEARCH	CHANGE	TERMINATION
The goal is to establish a good working alliance. Therapists expect clients to trust them, keep contracts, and become active participants in the collaborative process.	The goal in this stage is to define well-formed dysfunctional patterns. Therapists expect clients to join with them to observe clients' dysfunctional patterns, to report their experiences, and to do homework.	The goals include relinquishing old patterns and initiating and maintaining new ones. Therapists expect clients to use their guidance in change, assume responsibility, take risks, and practice new patterns.	The goal is to maintain clients' gains and terminate therapy. Therapists expect clients to leave therapy without increased difficulty and with maintenance of change. If clients have trouble separating, therapists expect them to be willing to discuss it.

therapists expect clients to participate in observing their dysfunctional patterns. If clients are reluctant to do so, therapists may be dealing with resistance.

Table 8.3 details some of the many forms of resistance commonly encountered during the various stages of therapy.

During *engagement*, resistance occurs around issues of trust, role definition, contract agreements, and belief in the therapist's competence. Common resistances in this stage concern the therapeutic contract. Failure to appear for an appointment without prior notification, especially because the client "forgot," may be a nonverbal statement about the therapeutic relationship. Requests for reduced fees or time shifts may hide attempts by the client to test the therapist's "flexibility" and willingness to accommodate. Deeper still, these maneuvers may conceal attempts to probe the therapist's ability to manage and maintain the therapeutic contract.

Resistance during the pattern search stage may reflect client discomfort in observing and exploring dysfunctional patterns. The prerequisite for pattern search is the client's willingness to report personal experiences to the therapist and to join the therapist in exploring the client's dysfunctional patterns. Clients may fear they will reexperience pain, provoke their therapists' critical judgment, or that therapists will violate confidentiality. Additionally, clients may not know what thera-

TABLE 8.3   Forms of Resistance During Different Stages of Therapy

ENGAGEMENT	PATTERN SEARCH	CHANGE	TERMINATION
Resisting the establishment of the working alliance by:	Failing to report information relevant to identifying patterns, as seen in:	Failing to generate or implement alternatives by:	Terminating prematurely or failing to terminate therapy such as:
Having difficulty in trusting the therapist	Excessive silence	Agreeing to initiate a new pattern but failing to do so	Missing or canceling sessions
Doubting the effectiveness of psychotherapy collaboration	Withholding important information	Refusing to comply with the therapist's suggestions	Terminating prematurely
Failing to appear for an appointment	Becoming evasive when asked critical questions	Discussing terminating treatment before changing	Continuing to contact the therapist
Requesting reduced fee or appointment time changes	Lying		Visiting the therapist without appointment after termination
Criticizing the therapist's age, sex, inexperience, training, race, or religion	Talking about topics irrelevant to pattern definition		Experiencing symptom recurrence that prevents termination
	Providing excessive detail for pattern definition		
	Refusing to do role playing or homework		
	Attacking the therapist's questions or empathic statements		

pists want reported or how to report it. Resistant clients may remain silent, tell lies, withhold important information, become evasive when asked questions, refuse to role play or complete homework, or attack the therapist's questions, empathic statements, ability, or credentials.

Failure to do homework is one of the more common forms of resistance. Exploring the potential reasons for not doing homework helps therapists move the process of therapy. For example, clients with depression may be asked to record the situation, thoughts, and feelings associated with each time they feel upset, angry, or very sad. At the next appointment, therapists may find that clients have not completed the assignment as agreed. What could account for this behavior? Clients may:

- Have been afraid to experience their intense feelings of sadness even more strongly by writing about what they were feeling and thinking
- Have been fearful of reactivating painful memories of trauma associated with their depression
- Have been afraid that they would do the task incorrectly and get criticized by their therapist
- Not have understood the instructions but feel apprehensive about requesting clarification
- Have thought that they needed to describe every situation in great detail and felt too overwhelmed by the task to try it
- Have had insufficient time to complete the task
- Have been afraid that someone would encounter them working on it or would find their diary and ask them to explain what it was about and why they were doing it
- Have a substance abuse or cognitive functioning problem that interferes with following through on things they agree to do. A depressed person just may be too exhausted to complete the task.
- Think that it is a stupid assignment that won't help them get better but not want to say that to the therapist

Direct discussion will usually reveal and resolve these problems. Some resistances to homework are due to unconscious motivations and may illustrate a general dysfunctional pattern. For example, clients with depression may:

- Be afraid that if they get over the depression, their marriage might dissolve, as much of their involvement with their partner revolves around that partner taking care of them and the things that they feel unable to do

- Feel resentment toward the therapist for focusing too quickly on depressive problems when the client thought anxiety was the key issue
- Feel helpless about the depression and believe that nothing can change it

Change is often the most challenging stage for clients. From the beginning of therapy, some clients avoid having to change themselves. Even when they ask for help, they want the therapist to take away their symptoms or to make others change. Clients may disagree with the therapist's interventions, refuse to comply with the therapist's suggestions, miss appointments, refuse to take medication, or terminate treatment.

Change is a boundary experience (Yalom, 1980)—an event that defines one's own limitations by clearly defining losses as well as gains. To change is to lose one's identity and adopt a new one, to risk the unknown, and to become transformed. Consequently, change may create a sense of danger, even though new patterns promise a better life. The threat of change may trigger intrapsychic conflict about the past and the future, about the tried and untried ways of living. Clients may be afraid to become more assertive with their partner or spouse because they fear they will lose the person. Children may be afraid to leave home or assert themselves because their parents might withdraw their love. Clients may appear to avoid change, but have just not grasped what must be done to accomplish what they wish.

Resistance is less important in the *termination* stage of brief therapy than it is in long-term psychotherapy. It may occur around the fear of separation from the therapist and lack of confidence to handle situations unassisted. Clients may refuse to terminate therapy and activate new problems or symptoms. Therapists must be alert to the possibility that the termination process itself can engender new problematic behaviors. Additionally, termination can be more difficult for therapists than for clients (see Chapter 9).

Although resistance may occur at any stage of therapy, research shows that it seems to become more prominent in the middle period of treatment than during the beginning or termination stages (Orlinsky & Howard, 1979). This may suggest that resistance is lowest when interpersonal threats are low (e.g., when establishing an initial relationship or reviewing the whole progress of treatment) and highest when the client is being challenged to change (during the middle sessions).

Addressing Resistance

After recognizing resistance, therapists must proceed to manage it. Although resistance is an obstructionist force, quickly overcoming it may not be the most effective way to dilute its power. Resistances often must be understood and respected by both therapists and clients. The management of resistance requires looking at it objectively and attempting to connect it to the process of change. Metaphorically, view resistance as a stumbling block that can be turned into a stepping stone. Rather than blaming the client for an unconscious desire to subvert therapeutic change, therapists will be more successful if they take an optimistic, cooperative approach.

First, they should clarify the source of the resistance, including the client's difficulty in recognizing and handling unconscious or environmental blocks. Does the client's resistance originate from the therapist's inappropriate expectations? Are these expectations a manifestation of countertransference? If the resistance does not originate from inappropriate therapist expectations, discussion of resistance with the client is necessary. Not all clients, however, are willing to reveal or explore their reluctance to change. In that case, therapists must find alternative ways to work with clients' resistance or wait until clients are ready. Table 8.4 lists seven general ways to respond to resistance.

Empathically Honoring the Resistance

One way of responding to the fear of engaging in therapy is quiet, empathic verbal acknowledgment of how the client is probably feeling about entering therapy. Putting clients' feelings into words will help them feel safe, accepted, and understood by the therapist, and it will usually accelerate engagement in therapy. Client challenges to a therapist's ability can be unnerving at any stage of therapy, particularly for young therapists, but such questions generally reflect client fears of not receiving proper assistance. Therapists do not have to defend themselves. Offering the client empathic reflections and demonstrating that the therapist has the strength to deal with the client's

TABLE 8.4   Seven General Ways to Respond to Resistance
1. Empathically honoring the resistance.
2. Interpreting the cause, reason, or pattern suggested by the resistance.
3. Dancing with resistance.
4. Moving around the resistance.
5. Going with the resistance.
6. Reframing.
7. Ignore the resistance or accept it without comment.

problems can increase the confidence and trust essential to the therapeutic relationship.

Acknowledging with the client that resistance exists is one way of honoring resistance. This act of communication strengthens the relationship by acknowledging the reality of this aspect of the therapeutic relationship. Acknowledging resistance might be as simple as saying, "I am aware that you did not do the homework that we agreed upon last session. Perhaps you are trying to tell us something?"

Describing resistance is another way of honoring it. In describing resistance, therapists seek to have clients become more aware of their internal experiences. If a therapist offers some comment to which a client replies "Yes, *but* . . . ," the therapist may state, "Let's replay this interaction, and please pay particular attention to your internal world." The therapist then gives the same talk again, but pauses at the point at which the client said "yes, *but*." The client is then asked, "What are you aware of internally?"; "Do you feel any tension?"; or "What stands out for you?" These awareness exercises tend to bring internal tensions into greater awareness.

Interpreting the Resistance

For resistances that indicate basic dysfunctional patterns, therapists may opt to help clients step back, observe, and become aware that what they are doing is among the reasons they entered therapy. Such clients are trying to guard a vulnerable area of their emotional life and protect

> Four of the options for responding to resistance include: honoring the resistance, "dancing" with the resistance, moving around the resistance, and going with the resistance.

themselves from further pain. The therapist's task is to acknowledge the legitimacy of clients' apprehensions while also helping clients become free from rigid dysfunctional patterns.

All people use a variety of measures to ward off embarrassment, guilt, fear, and pain. These protective behaviors can become the problematic aspects of ineffective patterns. Most clients will not easily relinquish these coping mechanisms. Clients often bring these protective tactics into therapy and display them in their interactions with the therapist. No matter how inappropriate, nasty, sarcastic, and demanding clients' behaviors can be, therapists should remain aware that self-protection is probably the motivation. Maintaining emotional distance is therefore an important component of the intervention.

Therapists can use the resistance behaviors displayed in therapy as samples of ineffective patterns in client's lives. Once this assumption is confirmed, therapists should help clients activate their observing self by encouraging them to examine the resistance as an example of these maladaptive behavior patterns. Therapists can provide feedback about the behavior and its consequences, provide explanations for the pattern, or report their own reactions to the resistance behaviors.

Many clients fear the consequences of change. At the very least, their current social and psychological functioning could be disrupted, stimulating new and unknown experiences. The simple fear of the unknown often affects decisions to change. Acknowledging the fear and examining the feared consequences (like divorce, finding a new job, anger toward significant others) encourages clients to decide whether the risk of change exceeds the pain of continuing familiar but unsuccessful patterns.

Dancing with Resistance

Clients often get "stuck." They want to change on the one hand, and they aren't able to change on the other. Splitting ("I'm so torn I can't decide"), ambivalence or polarities ("The two parts of me want different things"), and unfinished business ("I'm mad at my mother for abandoning me when I was a child") are forms of resistance that lend themselves to exploration via "split work." Clients are encouraged to explore the polarities or unfinished business in greater depth (e.g., via the emotion-focused empty chair technique).

Moving Around the Resistance

At times, clients have experienced such emotionally traumatic experiences, especially those occurring early in their lives, that they have difficulty accessing the core emotional schemas underlying their fears. Their fixed core beliefs (e.g., "If I let anyone get close to me I will hurt again") are often fused with painful feelings such as fear of abandonment, terror, and vulnerability. Because even accessing the belief touches on the concomitant unprocessed raw feelings, it is understandable that clients would avoid "going there." In cases such as this, healing can frequently be accomplished through the use of metaphors, stories, and quotes that have a message parallel to that with which the client is wrestling. Metaphors, stories, and quotes may allow clients to incorporate the message in less threatening ways. Sometimes the intervention offers a new way of viewing the issue, a more objective perspective, or a different emotional attachment. In this way, it is sometimes possible to "slide around" the point at which clients are otherwise stuck. As they progress further in other areas, clients may come back to this particular issue to seek further resolution at a later time.

Going with the Resistance

There are times when clients are so deeply stuck that change seems impossible. When more collaborative approaches are ineffective, it is sometimes necessary to "go with the resistance." This typically involves paradoxical interventions such as prescribing clients' symptoms. As described earlier, prescribing the symptoms involves instructing clients to do exactly what they are already doing or even to increase the undesired behavior. The desired outcome of this is that clients realize that they do have control of their behavior. The case of Jim is a good example.

Jim came to therapy at the insistence of his family and friends. He was experiencing severe depression and persistent overwhelming grief over the loss of a loved one who had died a year earlier. After repeated unsuccessful collaborative attempts to alter Jim's depression, the therapist suggested that

Jim should seek to feel the grief more intensely during the coming week. This successfully broke his ruminative cycle. Jim was able to recognize his deep but objectively unfounded sense of responsibility for the death, and he moved on to adopt the perspective that this beloved person would have wanted him to continue embracing life in her absence.

Reframing

Another way of dealing with resistance is *reframing*. It can be useful for both issue-related resistance and for stage-related resistance. Reframing shifts the meaning of the clients' behavior. The case of James, described by Good and Mintz (2005, p. 259), illustrates reframing.

James, a bright but troubled 16-year-old, was having multiple problems. He had dropped out of high school, was socially isolated, was abusing alcohol and drugs, and was not maintaining steady employment. He was in therapy at his mother's insistence. (Family therapy was not an option due to blended family issues.) Although he always arrived early for his appointments (dressed in black with body-piercing jewelry prominently displayed), he tended to be surly and showed little effort to become less depressed or isolated. Indeed, when shown a cartoon-style diagram of the stages of change, he indicated that he was between "precontemplative" and "contemplative." Not surprisingly, efforts to facilitate change using more straightforward collaborative approaches yielded little progress. However, when the therapist reframed his problematic behaviors as reflecting his desire to anger his parents and wondered aloud if there might be other ways that he could let them know that he was angry with them without hurting himself, he smiled reflexively and got more interested in the therapeutic process.

Ignoring or Accepting Resistance Without Comment

At times, therapists may observe incidents of resistance and opt not to address them. Given the conceptualization of the client and concerns, it may be in the client's best interest to let some resistance go unexamined.

Transference and Countertransference

Experiences from past relationships affect subsequent encounters. A person that we meet in the present may remind us unconsciously of someone or a composite of others. We unwittingly may be influenced by the similarities in gauging our reactions toward the other person. If the current someone is an authority figure such as a teacher or physician, we may react as we have reacted to previous people holding such positions. Most of the time we are not aware that we "transfer" feelings and thoughts from past relationships onto current ones. These responses are part of "procedural memory," the memory for automatic sequences of behavior or procedures.

The human ability to construe the present in terms of the past is highly adaptive. We can predict the likely responses of the other person based on role similarities from the past. However, sometimes we incorrectly judge the similarities. Not uncommonly, couples transfer expectations from their parents onto their partners. One partner may emulate his father who took complete charge of finances and made all the major decisions. The other partner, having been raised by a deferential mother easily falls into the complementary role. Despite the familiarity, the deferential partner may notice a vague discomfort bordering on frustration and anger.

Transference and *countertransference* refer to interpersonal distortions that do not fit the present role expectations. The terminology can be confusing because there are actually two people in the relationship, both of whom are potentially distorting their relationships based on past experiences brought forward or on direct expectations from the other in the present. Both participants are subject to the effects of the other. Although the processes are parallel, the term *transference* is applied to the client and *countertransference* is applied to the therapist.

Clients transfer past interpersonal experiences onto their current relationships with therapists (transference), and therapists also transfer elements of their past relationships onto their clients (countertransference). These transferences and countertransferences are sometimes inappropriate and do not fit the current situation. They are distortions of the other person. If the interpersonal relationship could be "freeze framed" or paused, these transference and countertransference distortions could be seen as created by one person and applied to the other.

TABLE 8.5   Four Categories of Transference and Countertransference

1.	Client-originated transference (clients inaccurately apply their past to their therapist)
2.	Client-originated countertransference (clients induce a distorted response from their therapist)
3.	Therapist-originated countertransference (therapists inaccurately apply their past to clients)
4.	Therapist-originated transference (therapists induce a distorted response from clients)

But in real life interpersonal relationships are a continuing interchange, and the other person reacts to the transference or countertransference distortions. These reactions may include distorted responses that can also be considered transferences or countertransferences (depending on whether it is the client or the therapist who is responding). In other words, transferences and countertransferences can breed more transferences and countertransferences. There are four categories of transference and countertransference (Table 8.5).

As noted earlier, the terms *transference* and *countertransference* can be confusing. As Table 8.5 indicates, *transference* is when clients inaccurately apply their past to their therapist or respond in a distorted way to the therapist's countertransference. *Countertransference* is when therapists inaccurately apply their past to a client or respond in a distorted way to the client's transference.

Client-Originated Transference

Therapists are authority figures who may become targets of a client's transference. Clients may distort their views of therapists, sometimes seeing them as combinations of parents and lovers, depending on age. Older clients may see their younger therapists as children and bring them pastries, give them financial advice, or simply tell them what to do. These transferences clearly originate from the past experiences of the client.

Client-Originated Countertransference

As a therapist you may unwittingly fulfill the role expectation of your clients. You may begin to act like the authority figure clients expect you to be or the loving parent or friend they seek. You may find yourself becoming a dutiful child as the client expects. These responses are induced by the client's expectation of you; hence they are "client-originated."

> Transference occurs when clients inaccurately transfer thoughts and feelings from past experience to their relationship with their therapist. These distortions may interfere with therapy and/or provide a here-and-now focus for change.

Therapist-Originated Countertransference

Therapists are people too. We sometimes distort our relationships to clients. Some clients remind us of our parents, old friends, lovers, or enemies. Some become very attractive to us, and we wish to gain their approval and affection. Others we strongly dislike, less because of their actual qualities but rather because they remind us of some troublesome person from our past. They can also remind us of aspects of our own personality that we seek to disown (e.g., self-centeredness, neediness, resentfulness). Or they may fit some category of person whom we have found distasteful, difficult, or whom we have been taught to dislike by our cultural rules. We have reactions to clients that have little to do with how the client is acting with us and much more to do with our own needs and expectations. The distortion comes primarily from the therapist and hence is "therapist-originated."

Therapist-Originated Transference

The therapist's own distortions of the client may induce a distorted response in the client. If the therapist sees the client as a parent or lover, the client may wish to please the therapist and fall into the indirectly requested role. In these cases, the client's love, empathy, advice, or anger does not derive from the client's past but rather is a response to the implicit demands of the therapist (i.e, the therapist's countertransference distortions).

Of course, transference and countertransference responses are not confined to the therapy office. They are common interpersonal dynamics that can occur between any two people regardless of their relationship to each other. The following case involves a physician who had a countertransference response to a patient's transference.

A 35-year-old physician was treating a 62-year-old woman who had seen many other physicians in their small town. She had a chronic, debilitating disease, and she did not like to have doctors tell her what to do. The physician was about the same age as her son would have been had he not died in infancy. The patient acted toward the physician as if he were her son, bringing him cookies, commenting on his clothes, and complimenting him for his accomplishments. She was transferring feelings and thoughts about her son onto the physician. This transference originated in the patient's past, making it client-originated transference.

The physician knew the woman was resistant to medical advice. He saw himself as her last hope and was compliant with her wishes. She told him what to do and he agreed to prescribe as she requested. He was being the dutiful son. The patient was eliciting this response from him, making his response a client-originated countertransference.

Part of his response, however, was due to his own past relationship with his demanding mother. The physician felt a personal need to comply with the demands of the patient because they reminded him of those from his own mother. This part of his response, therefore, was physician-originated transference.

The physician's overcompliance with the patient's demands increasingly fueled her assertiveness. In other words, some of her behavior was created by the physician's countertransference. Thus, part of her behavior could be considered physician-originated transference.

This case illustrates that the physician was influenced both by the role that the patient wanted the physician to play, and by his own need to play it. Therapists will find similar dynamics occurring in their own practices.

Signs of Transference and Countertransference

There are many signs of transference and countertransference distortions (Table 8.6). The challenge for therapists is to answer the following question: How much of this distortion is contributed by the client and how much is contributed by me?

Dealing with Countertransference

Beginners often believe that countertransference is bad. However, countertransference offers signals of distortion that are very much worth examining. Self-observation and analysis will help you understand the client's effect on others as well as give you the opportunity to learn more about how you distort some of your relationships.

It is also important to note that countertransference is different from simply liking a client (just as transference is different from simply liking one's therapist). Therapists often like their clients and clients often like them. We must leave plenty of latitude for this most human reaction and not strive to feel strictly neutral about all our clients in our efforts to avoid countertransference.

Similarly, past positive experiences related to building trust with another person should be seen as separate from transference distortions. These past positive experiences can serve as templates for building the therapeutic alliance that is so vital to therapeutic progress.

Finally, transference and countertransference take place to some degree in most relationships. They are processes that can be envisioned not as exotic hothouse orchids but rather as common interpersonal roses and thorns. They should not be avoided or seen as signs of weakness or strangeness. They can help strengthen the working alliance and improve our understanding of how each participant systematically distorts primary relationships. They should be embraced as signals for the uncovering of new knowledge that may improve interpersonal relationships.

> While some therapists believe that countertransference should never occur, countertransference reactions can provide clues for therapists self-knowledge as well as a here-and-now understanding of how people in the client's life might be reacting to them.

TABLE 8.6 Signs of Transference and Countertransference

TRANSFERENCE	COUNTERTRANSFERENCE
Inappropriate or excessive:	Excessive deviations from your baseline feelings, behavior, or thinking as therapist:
Feelings, such as anger, hostility, hurt, envy, distrust, appreciation, concern, or erotic attraction.	*Feelings*, such as anger, irritation, anxiety, guilt, fear, sexual stimulation, disappointment, shame, helplessness, envy, boredom, awe, and excessive pride in the client's accomplishments. Also: high anticipation about seeing the client, resentment at having to see the client, or relief when the client does not come to a scheduled appointment.
Behaviors, such as calling the therapist at home, asking to see the therapist outside the office, asking the therapist for excessive personal information, writing a love letter to the therapist, excessively criticizing the therapist, or sending gifts.	*Behaviors*, such as arranging an opportunity to socialize with the client, criticizing or excessively reassuring the client, bragging to other therapists about the client's success, making fun of the client, asking favors of the client, trying to impress the client, keeping excessively silent, reducing or not charging the fee, avoiding discussion of the client's boundary violations (e.g., excessive phone calls), coming late for a session, or ending a session early.
Thoughts and fantasies, such as fantasizing about marrying and having children with the therapist, wanting to become a colleague of the therapist, or dreaming about the therapist.	*Thoughts and fantasies*, such as dreaming about the client or fantasizing about sexual involvement, romance, being best friends, or taking a trip together.
Resistances, any of which may suggest transference.	

Summary

Resistance, transference and countertransference are inevitable occurrences in counseling and psychotherapy. Clients sometimes do not meet therapists' expectations. Usually therapists believe the failure lies with the client, but the therapist's expectations may not fit the client's abilities, or the social network could be interfering in some way. Once identified, a resistance can be overcome in several ways, the most useful of which may be to consider it an inducing point for a treatment relevant pattern.

Transference and countertransference (which is most clearly defined as the therapist's transference to the client) result from the ordinary necessity for each person to use similarities between people known in the past to understand a person in the present. Past information is *transferred* from the past to the present. Both therapist and client can transfer such experience inappropriately, which once identified may lead to increased self-knowledge for the therapist and active in-the-office analysis of maladaptive interpersonal patterns also occurring in crucial outside-the-office relationships. Therapists can trigger transference reactions in their clients and clients can trigger countertransference reactions in them. *Do not be afraid of experiencing excessive emotion or thinking about a client. Instead, activate your self-awareness and examine the sources. Ask youself: "How much of this reaction is from me and how much is from my client?"* The answer will guide you toward your own introspection and perhaps consultation with a colleague, or toward clearly identifying an important interpersonal pattern worthy of scrutiny.

CHAPTER 9

Termination
Anticipating Challenges, Supporting Growth, Preventing Relapse, and Preparing Clients for Their Future

Parting is such sweet sorrow.
—WILLIAM SHAKESPEARE FROM *ROMEO AND JULIET*

The conclusion of counseling or therapy may provoke a variety of responses in the participants. When successful, termination can be a gratifying yet poignant moment for the participants—something like a graduation from school. At other times, the intensity of the therapeutic encounters may begin to taper off, with the participants realizing that the time is coming to end. On other occasions, termination may be a relief for both clients and therapists.

Less commonly, termination is wrenching and painful. The human distaste for change is rooted in anxiety about loss and ultimately death (Yalom, 1980). Termination often resonates with each person's awareness of that final change. When therapy ends, clients lose three interrelated relationships: the professional, the personal, and the transference-related. Sadness and grief typically accompany loss. Feelings of separation in the present may remind clients of previous losses and increase the likelihood that they (and perhaps the therapist) will repeat loss-response patterns of earlier days.

In terminating, therapists anticipate that clients will have sufficient momentum and skills to maintain their changes and continue to improve. Indeed, despite the therapeutic literature that emphasizes termination as a painful phase of treatment (Firestein, 1978; Mann, 1973), studies of social work therapists (Fortune, 1987), and staff at a university counseling center (Marx & Gelso, 1987) found that termination was more often a positive experience for clients than a negative one. That said, clients sometimes have negative reactions to termination, and therapists must be prepared to deal with them.

Varieties of Client Responses

Client responses to termination occur both outside and inside the therapeutic relationship. Table 9.1 (Beitman, 1987, pp. 274–276) lists common positive and negative responses that occur outside the therapy office. Table 9.2 (adapted in part from Kapoor, Matorin, & Ruiz, 2000) lists the positive and negative responses within it.

Client reactions to termination within the therapy relationship vary depending on the significance and length of therapy, clients' current experience of loss, the strength of their current social network, and the method of termination. Client loss encompasses the three aspects of the therapeutic relationship: transference, the relationship between two people who have come to like each other, and the professional relationship.

Marx and Gelso (1987) found that the two most powerful predictors of a need to discuss problems in termination were a history of interper-

---

TABLE 9.1   Client Responses to Termination Outside the Therapeutic Relationship

POSITIVE

- Strengthening of marriages and other friendships or relationships
- Separation from unhelpful or destructive relationships
- Increased functioning at work or school
- Initiation of employment advances
- Awareness of the excessive neediness of dependent people
- Realization that young children also need interpersonal distance

NEGATIVE

- Precipitous marriages or excessively fast intimacy
- Pregnancy
- Immediate entry into therapy with another therapist
- Sudden termination of a significant relationship

sonal loss and the extent to which loss was a theme of therapy. For those who have trouble with interpersonal loss, reactions to losing the therapist provide an opportunity to rework in a safe environment the meaning of previous losses.

They may encourage clients to discuss previous losses in some detail. They may also encourage clients to discuss a future without the therapist on a regular basis. Together therapists and clients can review their relationship and direct the here-and-now emotional expression of

---

TABLE 9.2   Client Responses to Termination Within the Therapy Relationship

- Happiness, relief, or satisfaction
- Neutral feelings
- Institutional transference (the client attaches to the institution rather than the therapist, such as a veteran attaching to a Veteran's Administration hospital; the client therefore experiences no problems with the loss because the institution is still there)
- Sadness and hurt
- Memories of previous losses (e.g., deaths of parents, siblings, close relatives, or friends; births of siblings; abortions; miscarriages; births of children)
- New symptoms
- Offering gifts to the therapist
- Dreaming of separation and loss
- Devaluing of the therapist
- Anger (manifested covertly) as:
  - cynical comments towards therapy
  - depreciation of the therapist
  - irritability during sessions
  - desire to terminate immediately
  - missed appointments
  - nonpayment of fees
- Recurrence of earlier problems or somatic symptoms
- Separation anxiety
- Feelings of rejection and abandonment by therapist
- Guilt (client attributes termination to personal flaws)
- Denial (concealing feelings of sadness and mourning with a nonchalant attitude)

> Processing the experience of separation during termination provides the opportunity for clients to learn to deal with endings, interpersonal losses, sadness, and grief in more productive ways that benefit them in the future.

the present meaning of the separation. At this time clients may interweave direct statements of appreciation and disappointment with regard to the therapy.

Therapists also have their own reactions to termination. Like client losses, therapist losses with regard to termination encompass the three aspects of the therapeutic relationship: transference, the mutual regard, and the professional. Table 9.3 (adapted in part from Kapoor et al., 2000, and Kleinke, 1993) lists common therapist responses to termination.

Though most termination problems are associated with client anxieties, they may actually represent therapists' difficulty with interpersonal loss. Boyer and Hoffman (1993) reported that therapists' past and present grief reactions predicted therapists' feelings of depression and anxiety around termination. Furthermore, therapists' perception of clients' sensitivity to loss correlated with therapist anxiety about termination. In support of this assertion, Fortune (1987) found that therapists who reported more loss in their lives tended to ascribe more negative client reactions to termination than did therapists who experienced fewer losses. Perhaps therapists tend to find the kinds of termination they are expecting.

Deciding When to Terminate

In some cases, the termination date is predetermined (when the therapist and client mutually agree in advance on a set number of sessions or a certain duration of treatment) or forced (by limitations imposed by insurance companies or by external factors such as therapist retirement or client relocation). But how do therapists decide when to end treatment when the termination is not predetermined or forced? Should termination be discussed when clients have reached their stated (or implied) goals? Or should termination take place when the client has *started* in the right direction, with the assumption that this new momentum will carry the person forward into the desired state? To date there are no certain answers to these questions. Table 9.4 lists signs indicating that clients are prepared to terminate therapy.

TABLE 9.3 Therapist Responses to Termination

- Fear of letting go (belief that the client cannot make it alone; feelings of inadequacy about one's professional or personal value)
- Avoiding discussion (minimization of one's importance to the client, or conversely, projection of one's own sadness about the loss onto the client and an overemphasis on the client's difficulty in separating)
- Relief (when therapy has been frustrating or the therapist was confused about how to help the client)
- Guilt (for not doing enough or for abandoning a client by having to leave)
- Feelings of therapeutic inadequacy or ineffectuality (In these cases, therapists sometimes seek reassurance from clients and attempt to offer advice, medication, or other "valuable" things.)
- Doubt about professional status or financial concerns (will the former client say negative things about me to others? Will I get fewer referrals?)
- Anger (belief that the client did not try hard enough)
- Sadness (when the therapist truly liked the client and enjoyed working with him or her)
- Denial (avoidance of recognizing one's importance to the client in order to avoid feelings of loss and sadness)
- Feelings of abandonment
- Separation anxiety (when therapists have unresolved interpersonal separation and individuation issues)
- Self-denigration (devaluing of one's importance by focusing on mistakes during therapy)

When therapists see signs that a client may be ready for termination, they can identify and describe to the client examples of the client's progress, patterns of change, and the client's acceptance of responsibility for change. Such a discussion prepares the client for the actual process of termination. In some cases, therapists may observe the recurrence of presenting symptoms during termination. What do these symptoms represent? As resistances, they are pleas to avoid separation and questions about whether the client can survive without the therapist. They can be viewed as evidence for how far the client has come by recognizing how strange and odd they now seem. In most instances, the symptoms are short-lived (Firestein, 1978; Langs, 1974).

TABLE 9.4   Signs of Client Readiness to Terminate

- *Clients have developed independence from their therapist.* Clients trust themselves to recognize problems, analyze costs and benefits, and formulate solutions or alternatives without the therapist. A client may say, "I wasn't able to stop myself from becoming overwhelmed and really listen to my thoughts until I found a solution that I was comfortable with."

- *Clients recognize their role in therapeutic change.* Instead of attributing positive change to therapists, clients accept their part in the positive outcomes of therapy. Therapy is a collaborative process, and change could not have occurred without the client's willingness to participate and take active steps toward desired goals.

- *Clients have developed a new trusting relationship.* Clients perceive the therapeutic alliance as a trusting relationship and generalize this trust to other relationships in their lives.

- *Patterns of change have occurred in the client's life.* Therapists recognize various instances during which the client has made the changes identified as therapy goals. These changes are consistent and integrated into the client's behavioral repertoire.

- *Clients have developed insight.* Clients can assess their own situation and arrive at an insightful conclusion. They go beyond the immediate emotional reaction to make meaningful connections between past and present experiences or to recognize the impact of future expectations.

- *Clients have accepted the limitations of their parents or caregivers.* Clients accept that their parents or caregivers are ordinary, fallible people with both positive and negative qualities. Clients can disagree with parental behavior or decisions without disliking the parent or caregiver as a person.

- *The appearance of latent content for termination of therapeutic relationship.* The ending of other commitments and relationships in the client's life maybe latent signs that the client is ready to say good-bye to the therapist. For example, a client may decide to end an unsatisfactory relationship around the same time therapy is ending.

- *Expression of appreciation.* Clients may recognize the positive outcomes of therapy, such as freedom from burdens, a new perspective, or removal of stumbling blocks, and express gratitude to the therapist.

Termination Approaches

There are two major styles of mutually-agreed termination: therapists and clients can decide upon an ending date, keep the frequency of sessions about the same, and then end on that date or, more commonly, therapists and clients can gradually lengthen the time between sessions, going from meeting weekly, to meeting every other week, to meeting monthly, and then to meeting every other month. Another option is to transition to a primary care model, leaving the door open for clients to return at

> Common events during smooth terminations include: a retrospective look at how therapy has proceeded, sharpening of client's future plans for life without the therapist, discussion of possible return appointments, and a statement of appreciation by both client and therapist.

some time in the future should the need arise. This "desensitization" to the loss also seems to suit many therapists and clients who do not wish to confront the sometimes painful emotional issues around separation and loss.

Types of Termination

The types of termination include: (1) mutually agreed, (2) client-initiated, (3) therapist-initiated, and (4) forced. Table 9.5 summarizes the four categories.

Mutually Agreed Termination

At some point during treatment, the therapist and client may begin to note a waning energy between them. Problems arise for the client but they get handled without much discussion, and are described as relatively unimportant events. Therapists looking for problems to solve become bored: Those searching for cognitive distortions or maladaptive

---

TABLE 9.5   Types of Termination

- *Mutually agreed:* Participants agree and decide on a date together
- *Client-initiated*: Client terminates before achieving what the therapist believes is a sufficient degree of change
- *Therapist-initiated*: Therapist sets a termination date with which the client disagrees
- *Forced*: External events dictate the end of therapy (e.g., session limit reached, the client moves, the therapist retires, client or therapist illness or death)

interpersonal schemas come up empty; those looking for maladaptive interpersonal patterns find that the client is already changing them before the therapist can comment on what to change. Both therapist and client agree that successful change has taken place and that little more needs to be done at this time. They might shake hands, thank each other, and make a quick exit. Or they may set a date for ending and thereby formally begin the termination process. As part of leaving, the client looks back, looks at the present, and looks to the future, reviewing the benefits and difficulties of therapy, acknowledging the therapist, and looking to a future without the therapist. The availability of returning if needed is typically discussed. At the time of actual departure, the client usually has a general plan or sense of how to maintain the changes made during therapy. The following report from an adult male who sought therapy for his longstanding dysthymia and recurrent major depressive episodes is an example of such a plan. Several years after mutually agreed termination from therapy, he described how he kept going:

I haven't had any depressive episodes. I keep doing my depression-management plan. If I feel depression coming, I check to make sure that I'm doing what I need to do to prevent it:

- Maintaining a positive social network (do something social that involves real conversation with a friend outside of work at least once per week).
- Regular cardiovascular exercise (at least 20 to 45 minutes two to three times a week).
- Not drinking too much alcohol (not more than one or two drinks and not more frequently than two to three times a week).
- Finding creative and worthwhile activities at work or outside of work
- Scanning my life for stressors that I've not been attending to
- Noticing what I'm feeling negative about, but not getting wrapped up in it. I monitor for negativity and then blow it away with the positive truth.
- Enjoying the company of my pets.

In the situation just described, the client had both changed enough and created sufficient positive coping mechanisms that he no longer needed the assistance of his therapist to function well.

Client-Initiated Termination

Clients often leave therapy before therapists think they are ready to go. In a survey of 173 therapists. Pekarik and Finney-Owen (1987) found that therapists preferred a longer duration of treatment than was desired by clients. When asked why clients prematurely terminated, the therapists cited dislike of the therapist or therapy less often than clients did. These findings suggest that therapists may incorrectly assess client estimates for therapy duration and their reactions to the therapist or the process of therapy. How much premature termination is related to therapist mismanagement and how much to conflicts about duration remains to be determined.

The average number of visits to a variety of therapists over a period of many years was five to eight sessions (Garfield, 1986). Some clients do improve in one session (Malan et al., 1975), but many more are probably treatment failures. Beginning therapists should not be discouraged when clients leave after a few sessions without seeming to have made much change because many clients do leave early. Clinics might do more to train clients in understanding their roles in psychotherapy (e.g., role induction), because research evidence suggests that clients who understand what is expected of them stay longer (Cartwright, Lloyd, & Wicklund, 1980; Lowe, Horne, & Taylor, 1983). At the same time, therapists and clinics should do all they can to provide an inviting and comfortable physical and interpersonal environment for their particular clients. Understanding clients' cultures is also key, and examining identity discrepancies between therapists and clients or the clinic's clientele and the clients (e.g., ethnic minorities, males) can be of great importance in getting and keeping clients in therapy. Once clients are committed to therapy, their average number of visits increases to almost 20 sessions (Beitman & Maxim, 1984).

There are many reasons why clients terminate therapy prematurely. Sometimes therapists drive their clients away through ineffective relationship management or poor technique. In one case, a therapist encouraged a client to tell his ex-spouse that he wanted to get back together. The client was unhappily surprised when the ex-spouse rejected the overture, and he did not return to treatment. In other cases clients quit when therapy becomes too threatening to their status quo; change may take more courage than they are willing to exert. Determining the precise reason for a client's premature termination may be difficult; however, there are some common predictors of premature termination that therapists are wise to keep in mind (Table 9.6).

Therapist-Initiated Termination

Therapists may initiate termination when the client appears to have made sufficient gains but seems reluctant to leave. Therapists also initiate termination when nothing seems to be happening—when the

---

TABLE 9.6   Client Predictors of Premature Termination

Lower socioeconomic class (Berrigan & Garfield, 1981; Hillis, Alexander, & Eagles, 1993; Weighill, Hodge, & Peck, 1983)

Lower occupational status, specifically in unskilled, partly skilled, or skilled manual occupations (Chiesa et al., 2000)

Less education (Blackburn, Bunce, Glenn, Whalley & Christie, 1981; Persons, Burns, & Perloff, 1988)

Ethnic/racial minority identity (Anderson & Myer, 1985; Greenspan & Kulish, 1985; Richmond, 1920)

Low anxiety (Jenkins, Fuqua, & Blum, 1986)

High initial depression (Persons, Burns, & Perloff, 1998)

Narcissistic, borderline, and schizoid personality disorders (Chiesa, Drahorad, & Longo, 2000; Persons, Burns & Perloff, 1988; Roback, 2000)

High level of psychopathology (Roback, 2000)

History of deliberate self-harm (Hillis et al., 1993)

Minimal previous contact with psychiatric services (Hoffman, 1985)

Poor understanding of how psychotherapy works (Cartwright et al., 1980; Lawe, Horne, & Taylor, 1983)

Unreadiness to change (Smith, Subich, & Kalodner, 1995)

Low perception of therapist as expert, likeable, and trustworthy (Kokotovic & Tracey, 1987; McNeill, May, & Lee, 1987)

Disagreement with therapist about the nature of the presenting problem (Epperson, Bushway, & Warman, 1983; Krauskopf, Baumgardner, & Mandracchia, 1981)

client and therapist seem to be wasting their time together. Either situation may be laden with potential therapist distortions. How does one decide when enough is enough? Just as clients may be correct in wanting to terminate badly conducted therapy, so they may be correct in wanting to gain more from an effective one.

When therapy appears to be going nowhere, bringing up the idea of termination can be either beneficial or harmful to change. In one instance, a therapist felt and expressed discomfort with a client's unwillingness to address interpersonal life changes. Having enjoying being listened to without pressure to change, the client reacted angrily and never returned. This therapist and client disagreed about the purpose of therapy: The client wanted a listening, supportive ear; the therapist wanted the client to change. Disagreement about purpose is a common reason for premature termination (Epperson et al., 1983 Krauskopf et al., 1981).

On the other hand, sometimes therapist-initiated termination can stimulate change. The following case, also involving a client reluctant to change, illustrated this.

Sarah, a young woman in her twenties, had been seeing her therapist for several months yet still seemed unwilling to examine problematic interpersonal patterns in her life. When her therapist suggested referral to another therapist, Sarah became indignant and declared that she had feared for some time that the therapist would make this suggestion and now could see that it was coming true. The therapist was giving up! Sarah stormed off and quickly selected a new therapist from the phonebook. After wasting time and money on three unproductive sessions, Sarah returned to the original therapist with an interesting insight: "I selected someone who was unlikely to help me, just as I usually asked my mother for help when she was the last person who was able to help me." The therapist quickly recognized this insight as the beginning of change for this client.

Freud (1963/1912) reported using a similar "blackmailing" device by setting a termination date for a young client spoiled by riches, who had stopped working on changing himself. Although Freud felt guilty for having employed this technique, he was impressed with its effectiveness in engaging the client with therapeutic change.

Therapist-initiated termination may also be caused by therapist discomfort with a client on an issue, as is illustrated by the following case. *Carol, a 60-year-old therapist, quietly wished that a 67-year-old client she was treating would leave and never return. The client was in the process of retiring, looking into volunteer work, and musing about the end of life. During a session in which the client reported that he had successfully resolved a minor interpersonal conflict, Carol quickly speculated aloud that perhaps the client was ready to end therapy.*

In this case, the client's life situation felt threatening to the aging therapist, who would soon be in a similar life stage. Another therapist grew irritated with a client who tended to cancel or arrive late for sessions. Preferring to play the "nice, helpful-person" role, the now-irritated therapist suggested that perhaps this wasn't a good time for the client to be in therapy. The client accepted the therapist's suggestion and terminated; his underlying alcohol abuse problem went unaddressed. Rather than force clients out in this way, therapists must examine their countertransference reactions first. Some clients may be beyond a therapist's competence or comfort level. For example, a therapist who was sexually abused as a child may recoil very strongly at hearing that a current client has sexually abused his or her own children.

Forced Termination

Forced termination is due to external factors, such as client or therapist relocation or agency- or insurance-based session limits. Trainee therapists often are required to terminate therapy with clients because their course or training is coming to an end. Those leaving town say good-bye to all their clients; others may be able to continue with some clients. But how do they decide whom to pick? There is no generally applicable good answer. Client welfare and therapist training needs are certainly considerations.

Consider the effects of forced termination on clients. Dewald (1965) studied the reactions of 11 clients when he relocated his practice to another city. He found that three responded negatively, four used the experience to promote therapeutic change, and four seemed neither to benefit nor suffer from the forced termination. The three described as responding negatively simply withdrew from therapy. Of those who were able to utilize the forced termination, one found the challenge of the set date to be a stimulus to work harder in therapy, two experienced the emotions of previous losses with which they became better able to deal, and one used the opportunity to express many deep and hidden emotions. This small sample suggests that for about a third of clients, forced termination may be useful. If so, how does one select such clients? And how does one assist the other two-thirds? Being alert to these alternative responses may help you predict which reaction your current clients might experience as you are forced to leave a certain setting.

Managed care organizations (MCOs) and health maintenance organizations (HMOs), which primarily manage costs (Beitman, 1998), have injected an additional uncertainty to the termination of therapy. Termination can be initiated not only by client or therapist, but also by sometimes uninformed "care coordinators" (expense reducers). Although some mature companies are becoming less intrusive upon therapeutic relationships, many still attempt to economize by arbitrarily deciding that the client has had enough therapy. Therapists and clients may feel helpless and powerless. What should therapists do when benefits are ending for clients who are still dependent upon the therapeutic relationship and will probably suffer without the support? The following case illustrates this type of predicament.

A 55-year-old married woman sought treatment for depression that she had struggled with much of her adult life. After stabilizing with a brief period of weekly therapy, she functioned reasonably well with monthly therapy sessions and antidepressant medication. If she missed sessions 2 months in a row, she started to become depressed again. Her MCO decided that she needed only medication despite her therapist recommending therapy. The client was irate, and the therapist was angry and uncertain of what to do—argue with the MCO, have the client call the MCO, or request that the client pay herself. They decided to have the client call the MCO, and after much assertive discussion they received authorization to continue in therapy.

Client suicide is sometimes the agent of premature therapy termination. Although it is considered infrequent, approximately one-third of therapists in practice experience this type of loss (DeAnglis, 2001; Hendin, Lipschitz, Maltsberger, Haas, & Wynecoop, 2000). Client suicide often creates deep emotional scars in therapists, striking to the core of their self-confidence and identity. Goldstein and Buongiorna (1984) reviewed the literature on therapist responses and surveyed 20 therapists, each of whom had experienced a client suicide. Disbelief, shame, anger, vulnerability, and loss of self-confidence were common responses. A sense of extreme loneliness enveloped most of the therapists, and this feeling was accompanied by obsessive questions about what could have been done differently. Although most wondered whose fault it was, only 8 of 20 respondents wanted a psychological autopsy (review of the case for examination of causes). The other 12 thought it might confound the problem. (However, if done correctly, these "critical-incident reviews" often reveal ideas that can be useful for all concerned with treating difficult clients.) Seventeen of the 20 reported that they subsequently became more active in exploring suicidal ideation. The feelings associated with the suicide were often reactivated by current clients' suicidal ideation.

A study by Hendin and colleagues (2000) of therapists' emotional reactions to client suicide found grief to be the most common response. Therapists' grief, which was often pervasive and persistent, included feelings of loss and sadness. In addition to experiencing anger, shame, disbelief, and loss of self-confidence, all widely described in the professional literature, therapists also responded with feelings of guilt, fear of blame and legal implications, inadequacy, and client betrayal. Nineteen of the 26 therapists studied interacted with the deceased client's relatives. In most cases, therapists were relieved by the noncritical and appreciative responses of relatives. Reassurance from colleagues that the suicide was inevitable did not relieve the therapist's sense of loss. Nevertheless, colleagues and supervisors can ease the emotional distress following client suicide by offering to share their own experiences with the suicide of one of their clients.

The unexpected death of a therapist causes an unplanned termination of therapy. The explosive news of a therapist's death may have a profound impact upon clients, particularly those who have become deeply dependent. One client, struggling with issues regarding his hostile and withdrawn mother, told his next therapist, "My mother has won" (Shwed, 1980). Shwed suggested that colleagues of the deceased should call the clients personally and arrange for immediate meetings with

Approximately one-third of therapists confront the suicide of their client during their professional life, sometimes leaving deep emotional scars. Feelings of shame, anger, disbelief and a loss of self-confidence are common. Support from colleagues and supervisors, especially those who have experienced similar losses, should be sought.

those who desire them. As with other traumatic events, the availability of prompt assistance and the opportunity to process reactions may be useful.

After Termination

Therapists may find it all too easy to stop thinking about clients they no longer see. Nevertheless, clients continue to face life's difficulties after they terminate. What happens to them? Do they continue to change on their own? Do they relapse? Do they seek professional help again? Do they join and stay with support and self-help groups like AA?

Therapists generally expect their clients to continue to improve after termination, but this belief remains a generally untested assumption (Steffen & Karoly, 1980). Evidence from the early 1980s suggests a consistent pattern of reduced therapeutic effect with the passage of time (Andrews & Harvey, 1981; Mash & Terdal, 1980; Smith, Glass, & Miller, 1980).

The National Institute of Mental Health undertook an intensive and extensive investigation of the treatment of depression through its Treatment of Depression Collaborative Research Program (TDCRP). The multisite collaborative study investigated the efficacy of cognitive-behavioral therapy and interpersonal therapy in comparison with imipramine (antidepressant medication) plus clinical management (CM) and a pill placebo plus CM. As part of this four-cell design, the group studied the course of depressive symptoms during an 18-month naturalistic follow-up. The treatment phase consisted of 16 weeks of randomly assigned treatment. Follow-up assessments were conducted at 6 months, 12 months, and 18 months after treatment. Of all the clients who had entered treatment and for whom follow-up data was available, the percentage who had recovered (8 weeks of minimal or no symptoms following the end of treatment) and remained well during follow-up did not radically differ among the four treatments: 30% for those in the cognitive-behavioral therapy group, 26% for those in the interpersonal therapy group, 19% for those in the imipramine plus CM group, and 20% for those in the placebo plus CM group. Among those clients who had recovered, rates of relapse were 36% for the cognitive-behavioral therapy group, 33% for those in the interpersonal therapy group, 50% for those in the imipramine group, and 33% for those in the placebo group. The authors concluded that 16 weeks of these specific forms of treatment was insufficient time for most clients to achieve full recovery and lasting remission (Shea et al. 1992).

Frank, Kupfer, Parel, Corns, Gerrit and Malinger (1990) compared interpersonal therapy and high-dose imipramine in various combinations and found that monthly interpersonal therapy sessions in combination with high doses of imipramine were no more effective in preventing recurrence of depression than imipramine alone across 3 years of maintenance treatment. Monthly interpersonal therapy sessions, either alone or with placebo, did provide some benefit when compared to the placebo condition. Interestingly, the preventative effects of interpersonal therapy were significantly stronger when the focus of therapy was on interpersonal problems (Spanier, Frank, McEachran, Grochocinski, & Kupfer, 1996) rather than on general nonspecific support. This suggests that keeping a therapeutic focus has beneficial protective effects. Although this study did not address the question of maintenance of change *after* treatment cessation, it is reasonable to hypothesize that factors preventing recurrence during treatment might also prevent recurrence after termination.

Barlow, Gorman, Sher, and Woods (2000) studied clients with panic disorder who were randomly assigned to receive imipramine, cognitive-behavioral therapy, placebo, cognitive-behavioral therapy plus imipramine, or cognitive-behavioral therapy plus placebo. Clients were treated weekly for 3 months (acute phase); responders were seen monthly for 6 months (maintenance phase) and then followed up for 6 months after treatment discontinuation. The researchers concluded that combining imipramine and cognitive-behavioral therapy appeared to confer limited advantage acutely but more substantial advantage by the end of the maintenance phase. Each of the treatment cells worked well immediately following treatment and during maintenance, but cognitive-behavioral therapy appeared to be the most durable in follow-up compared to imipramine or placebo. In other words, after their active treatments were concluded, clients receiving therapy did better than those who did not receive therapy. This finding supports the hypothesis that psychotherapy helps clients learn to make lasting changes, whereas receiving pharmacotherapy does not tend to produce changes that persist after clients stop taking the medication.

Butler and Beck (2000) conducted a review of studies examining cognitive therapy outcomes and concluded that cognitive-behavioral therapy is effective for adult depression, adolescent depression, generalized anxiety disorder, panic disorder, social phobia, and childhood depressive and anxiety disorders. Gloaguen, Cottraux, Cucherat, and Blackburn (1998) examined a subset of eight studies that com-pared relapse rates for cognitive-behavioral therapy versus antidepressants at least a year after discon-

> Therapy tends to help clients learn to make lasting changes, whereas changes produced by pharmacotherapy tend to diminish after stopping the medication.

tinuation of treatment. On average, only 30% of clients who received cognitive-behavioral therapy relapsed, compared to 60% of clients treated with antidepressants.

Although both cognitive-behavioral therapy and medications have been shown to be effective treatments for depression, clients who do not respond fully to one treatment or the other have been the focus of some study. Paykel and associates (1999) examined whether 16 ses-sions of cognitive-behavioral therapy would help prevent relapse among depressed clients who had responded partially to medications. They found that the cumulative relapse rate at 68 weeks was signifi-cantly lower for antidepressant plus cognitive-behavioral therapy clients (29%) than for clients who had only received continuation of antidepressants (47%). Shapiro and colleagues (1995) conducted a major study comparing the efficacy of cognitive-behavioral therapy and psychodynamic-interpersonal therapy for depression. This study also experimentally manipulated the duration of treatment (8 ses-sions versus 16 sessions). At the end of treatment, cognitive-behav-ioral therapy and psychodynamic-interpersonal therapy were equally effective. However, a year after completing treatment, clients who had received 8 sessions of psychodynamic-interpersonal therapy did worse on almost all measures compared with the other three treat-ment conditions (8-session cognitive-behavioral therapy, 16-session psychodynamic-interpersonal therapy, and 16-session cognitive-behavioral therapy). There was a trend for clients in the 16-session cognitive-behavioral therapy group to maintain their treatment gains better than the other three groups.

These data suggest that many clients do not fare well after therapy concludes. So what factors seem to influence the durability of change? The answer lies in part with the same variables that contribute to fos-tering and inhibiting change: diagnosis, symptom severity, social func-tioning, family and social support, and coping mechanisms.

In order to begin understanding what happens after termination, trainees might consider scheduling anniversary sessions with some clients, suggesting that they return a year after termination (or a briefer time if more manageable). The point being to provide some follow-up experience and to learn more about what clients perceive as making a difference in their lives. For clients, it is an opportunity to see how much they have or have not changed since termination.

Psychotherapy Without Termination

The duration of therapeutic contact ranges from a single session, to long-term, to interminable. Therapeutic contact that never terminates can take many forms, from frequent sessions throughout the client's lifetime to an initial period of frequent sessions that gradually tapers off to annual sessions or sessions on an as-needed basis. In the latter case, the therapist resembles a primary care physician: The client returns on the occasion of some kind of psychological difficulty. Our clinical experience suggests that clients who receive frequent sessions throughout their lifetime probably need a stable therapeutic relationship in order to function adequately. Our guess is that some of these clients need the continuing, reliable, validating attention of another to make up for the lack of this from their parent or caregiver early in their lives. Table 9.7 details many of the forms psychotherapy without termination may take.

In a questionnaire study about termination, 87% of psychoanalysts reported that they maintained phone or mail contact with some clients (an average of four per therapist). Most of these situations were related to cases in which the client or therapist moved before therapy was completed (Rosenbaum, 1977). Phone contact is useful as a way to help clients smooth the transition to new environments, keeping in mind the only way to bill is directly. Insurance rarely pays.

Among the more controversial forms of continuation are social contact and especially sexual contact. The easiest answer to the question of when social continuation is appropriate is never. Nevertheless, therapists and clients often do maintain social contact. What is wrong with coffee occasionally, especially when formal therapy has apparently ended? We have discussed the harmful effects of sexual contact, but what about other forms of nontherapy discourse? Because sexual or romantic involvement are wrong, can friendly social contact continue the relationship? No data are published on the question of how often relationships like this take place, but they do. Sometimes social contact cannot be avoided. For example, a client successfully treated for chronic

---

TABLE 9.7   Psychotherapy Without Termination

Ongoing regular sessions: Therapist and client keep meeting regularly and indefinitely, sometimes because the client's potential for relapse without therapeutic support is high and sometimes simply because the therapy is helpful and the client can afford this luxury.

Intermittent: Infrequent and irregular contacts.

Occasional "booster" sessions: When clients feel as if they are or may be about to slip backwards. For example, a client whose mother killed his father between Thanksgiving and New Year's became depressed annually at this time. Therapeutic support at this time helped prevent recurrence of this annual depressive response.

Annual follow-up: Checkup to see how the client is progressing (and to reinforce clients' more adaptive functioning).

Telephone therapy: Therapist and client separate geographically but maintain contact over the phone.

Letters or email: Some therapies end (and begin) on the Internet.

Fantasy: Clients consult an imagined image of their therapists, asking them for their opinion at a critical point or problematic time.

Therapist referral to another therapist: When the therapist or client is relocating, or when therapy with a particular therapist has run its course, or has been unsuccessful, transfer to another therapist can work well because the first therapist prepares the client to work effectively with the second. The first therapist may demonstrate how to build a therapeutic relationship; the second may help to initiate change. For example, clients with a history of trauma by a person of the opposite sex may first engage in therapy with a person of the same sex to do initial work on the trauma and their self-concept. They may then transfer to the same sex as their trauma perpetrator to experience a safe and supportive relationship with a person of that sex. Clients may be able to generalize these positive interpersonal experiences to their interpersonal relationships outside of therapy.

Self-referral to another therapist: Client decides to try again with someone new.

Social contact: This should be considered only with awareness of the potential dangers and professional consultation.

---

cannot be avoided. For example, a client successfully treated for chronic anxiety symptoms took a position in the hospital where the therapist worked. Their roles gradually brought them into closer contact. Although the former client occasionally made "jokes" about therapy in the therapist's presence, they developed an effective, respectful working relationship. Beginning therapists must be very careful to avoid or, at best, limit social contact. Experience may loosen these restrictions but even then care must be taken.

Summary

Termination may be the most predictable of the stages of counseling and psychotherapy since separation can take place in limited number of ways with a discrete number of possible responses from the participants. Clients often leave easily and satisfied but those who have had trouble separating from others may respond in numerous ways including missed appointments, the development of new symptoms, anger at the therapist, and guilt (due to perceived personal flaws). Therapists sometimes have greater difficulty letting go than do clients.

Ideally, client and therapist decide that they will say goodbye and pick a schedule for doing so. Unfortunately the termination process may take several other courses: client-initiated, therapist-initiated and termination forced by external events, each requiring special approaches. Research following up after termination suggests that, depending upon the length of therapy, many clients do not uphold their gains. For some clients more sessions may result in better outcomes. Some therapy relationships do not end at all, continuing by telephone, by email or simply through meeting regularly. For some clients on-going therapy provides an interpersonal life-line that maintains their ability to function. Continuing relationships as social rather than professional are potentially dangerous and require that therapists seek consultation from experienced colleagues.

Higher-Incidence
Concerns
& Effective Treatments

CHAPTER 10

Psychoeducational Interventions to Enhance Psychosocial Skills

Give people a fish and you feed them for a day.
Teach people to fish and you feed them for a lifetime.
—CHINESE PROVERB

onsider for a moment the massive number of psychosocial skills people are expected to use to function successfully in society. They must "self-regulate" their physical, nutritional, and sleep hygiene and substance use; self-motivate to complete aversive tasks (e.g., chores, school assignments, and work); resist "improper" pleasurable impulses; and manage their emotions and stress. They must discover what type of person they are, what type of relationships they want, what type of spiritual life they seek, and what type of life work they desire—and then go out and create them.

People are supposed to skillfully communicate with others both verbally and nonverbally, express their own individuality while also fitting in with various groups, be willing and able to resolve interpersonal conflicts, and interact acceptably about sexual matters. Given the complexity of life's psychosocial tasks and the dearth of corresponding skills instruction, it is surprising that most individuals are able to muddle along as well as they do.

Most therapists are aware that therapy may involve complex interpersonal dynamics in which skilled therapists must successfully negotiate clients' fears of intimacy, unresolved intense emotions, transference projections, and the like. However, in many instances, clients' primary problems

> Given the complexity of life's psychosocial tasks, it is surprising that most individuals are able to muddle along with as little effective guidance as they receive.

stem from simple skill deficits that can be successfully and efficiently resolved with proper psychoeducation. Table 10.1 lists basic assumptions underlying psychoeducational interventions.

TABLE 10.1 Assumptions Underling Psychoeducational Interventions
Psychosocial skills can be learned and improved upon.
Therapists can assist clients in acquiring and improving their skills.
Therapists can collaborate with clients to identify goals and offer psychoeducational activities designed to reach those goals.
Psychoeducational interventions can be tailored to individual clients' needs and sociocultural environments.
Enhancing psychosocial skills can improve clients' functioning at school or work and in interpersonal relationships.

Unlike the general public, mental health professionals are offered extensive educational and employment activities that focus specifically on improving their psychosocial knowledge and skills. We believe that therapists should apply the knowledge and skills that they use with their clients to their personal lives as well.

Therapeutic psychoeducational interventions differ in critical ways from advice clients typically receive from laypersons in their daily lives. First, therapists receive training and continue to expand their knowledge about which psychoeducational skill interventions tend to be effective for clients' specific concerns. Second, before offering interventions, mental health professionals seek to form a collaborative understanding of: (1) clients' views of their concerns, (2) clients' previous efforts to address their concerns, and (3) the types of activities clients are willing to undertake at this time. Third, therapists anticipate and assist clients in preparing for challenges and barriers they will probably encounter in the future. Fourth, therapists consult with clients' about their reactions, implementation, and subsequent refinements. In other words, skilled therapists tailor their interventions to clients and avoid delivering the same ineffective advice in the same ineffective way that other people in clients' lives already have.

People are exposed to a vast mix of myths, hype, facts, and advertising regarding psychosocial concerns and ways to resolve them. In seeking to join clients where they are, therapists should have some idea of the "pop" psychology ideas to which they have been exposed.

Therapists can then direct clients to appropriate psychoeducational resources specifically suited to their unique situations and concerns.

> Clients typically receive a variety of messages about their concerns from the media and society. Therapists can often assist clients in selecting psychoeducational resources appropriate to their issues and situations.

Psychoeducational Interventions

This chapter concentrates on those areas that therapists are likely to encounter frequently: relaxation and stress-management skills; problem solving; self-regulation; academic and career decision making; social skills (including initiating conversations with strangers, assertiveness, and anger management and conflict resolution); skills for coping with loss, grief, and bereavement; skills for coping with trauma, assault, and other intense emotional experiences; health promotion (including sleeping difficulties); parenting skills; and sexual enhancement. Suggested readings for clients (which you should consider reading too) are offered for those seeking more comprehensive descriptions of each of these important life skills.

Relaxation and Stress–Management Skills

Tension and stress are aspects of everyday life. Stress may be generally defined as any significant change that requires some sort of adaptive response, ranging from incredibly negative to very positive. Between these extremes lie the many day-to-day hassles that also require adaptation. Because stress is unavoidable, the real question is how people respond to stressors; it is the response that determines the impact that stress has on their lives.

Stress emerges from four general sources: (1) the environment, such as noise, temperature, traffic, and crowds; (2) social pressures, such as deadlines, financial concerns, tasks, disagreements, and requests from others; (3) physiological states, such as lack of sleep, lack of food, insufficient or excessive physical exercise, injury, and aging; and (4) one's thoughts, including how one interprets and ascribes meaning to the previous three sources (how our brains interpret these stimuli determines the neural circuits that are activated and the neurotransmitters that are released). Maladaptive reactions to stress include physiological responses such as headaches,

> Stress is an unavoidable aspect of being alive. Hence, how people respond to stress determines, to a large extent, the impact of stress upon their lives.

muscle tension, and stomach distress, as well as psychological responses such as obsessively anxious thoughts, panic, worry, and fear.

Stress researchers believe that individuals' appraisal of a situation (i.e., source #4) determines whether the situation actually becomes stressful. For example, standing on top of a steep mountain is exhilarating for some and terrifying for others. In looking at the situation, each individual assesses the danger, difficulty, and resources to cope. Anxious people are more likely to decide that the situation is dangerous, difficult, or painful, and that they lack the resources necessary to cope with it (Lazarus & Cohen, 1977).

When individuals perceive themselves as facing threats or danger, the brain and body may respond with *fight*, *flight*, or *freeze* responses. The biochemical changes associated with these responses were probably adaptive in earlier human times when threats were predominantly carnivorous predators, but these extreme responses are not useful in trying to successfully resolve most contemporary stressors. Chronic stress responses are associated with adverse health consequences (such as headaches, muscle tension, excessive adrenal gland secretion of corticoids, reduced resistance to infections, higher blood pressure, and gastric distress).

Just as a person's appraisal of a situation as overwhelmingly dangerous or difficult can trigger a stress response, people can also learn to initiate a *relaxation response* (Benson, 1975). Approximately 3 minutes after one's brain stops sending out danger messages, the body begins returning to normal levels.

Research indicates that optimal performance requires some anxiety. Performance actually improves as anxiety increases up to the point where the anxiety becomes so great that it interferes with performance. Effective stress management involves finding the right types and degrees of challenges for one's personality, priorities, social support, and current life situation so that performance and satisfaction are maximized.

Relaxation training is sometimes referred to as "behavioral aspirin" because it can be a beneficial component of intervention programs designed to address many concerns (e.g., stress, tension, anxiety, panic, trauma, headaches, pain, and difficulty tolerating unpleasant feelings). In general, relaxation training consists of three components: environment, body, and mind (Benson, 1975; Jacobson, 1938; Wolpe, 1982). The quieter the environment, the easier it is to

> Relaxation training is a generally beneficial component of interventions designed to address many anxiety and stress-related concerns.

achieve relaxation. As their relaxation skills increase, people are able to relax in less optimal environments. The body can increase anxiety responses because people tend to take quick, shallow breaths and tense their muscles when they are stressed. Relaxation involves slowing down one's body, breathing slowly and deeply, and consciously relaxing muscles. The mind plays a crucial role because its interpretations can activate either anxious or relaxed neural circuits and their associated neural transmitters.

A variety of mental activities are associated with the relaxation response. Suspending judgment ("observing" or "being mindful"), meditating, or repeating a neutral or positive word or phrase (e.g., a "mantra") can redirect one's attention and contribute to relaxation. Many clients find *The Relaxation and Stress Reduction Workbook* (Davis et al., 1995) to be an easily accessible, reassuring, and useful tool offering a variety of stress-reduction methods. Some clients find mindfulness-based stress-management techniques, such as those described in *Full Catastrophe Living: Using the Wisdom of Your Body and Mind to Face Stress, Pain, and Illness* (Kabat-Zinn, 1990), to be useful.

Following is an overview and sample script for progressive muscle relaxation, probably the most basic and widely accepted approach to relaxation training.

Progressive Muscle Relaxation

The aim of progressive muscle relaxation is to become practiced at relaxation and familiar with the feeling. As clients are better able to relax deliberately, they are able to relax more selectively and more quickly in stressful and competitive. Improving relaxation skills may also aid development of concentration skills and body awareness.

The following exercise is based on a progressive muscular relaxation (Benson, 1975; Jacobson, 1938). Muscle tensing is light tensing followed by relaxation that is synchronized with breathing for each part of the body.

Clients should be in a comfortable surrounding free from distractions. The exercise is performed in a sitting position such as an armchair. If an armchair is not available, have them sit comfortably with both hands in their lap. People tend to fall asleep if they lie down. The exercise takes about 15–20 minutes to complete. Clients should do the exercise about two to three times a week for several weeks. The following script is written for their therapist to deliver or audiotape for the client. Note that the ellipses refer to periods of silence while the client responds to the therapist's instructions.

Progressive Muscle Relaxation Script

Allow yourself to get comfortable. Feel free to adjust your position and get more comfortable. As you do so, notice the feel of the seat supporting your body . . . feel the weight of your feet against the floor . . . your arms resting on their supports . . . the comfortable balance of your head on your spine . . . the expansion and contraction of your chest as you breathe in . . . and out. . . . Allow any sounds in your environment to add to your relaxation.

Now ease your attention to your face . . . as you breathe in, frown slightly, feeling your forehead contract . . . experience the tension as you hold it. And as you breathe out, let go of the tension . . . breathe in . . . and again, let the tension flow away. . . .

Gently close your jaw, feeling your teeth connect . . . feel the tension in the muscles at the side of your face. And as you breathe out . . . let the tension go, and feel your face relax. . . .

And move on to your shoulders . . . tighten your shoulders and hold your shoulders tight. . . . And as you breathe out, let them relax . . . and feel the tension flow out. . . .

And move to your upper arms take on very little of the weight of your forearms, and as you breathe out evenly, let your arms' weight subside onto their supports . . . and again, feel the weight taken by the supports. . . .

And clench your fingers into your palms . . . hold the tension and feel it. . . . And now let the tension go as you breathe out . . . feeling the deep relaxation in your upper body . . . and your arms. . . .

And moving down to your buttocks, gradually tense the muscles in your buttocks, feel the tension. . . . And breathe out and let the tension melt away. . . .

And move your attention to your legs, tense the muscles in your legs as you breathe in . . . hold the tension and feel the tightness. . . . And relax again as you exhale . . . and feel the relaxation deepen and spread. . . .

Feel the deep relaxation through your body as you breathe . . . in . . . and out . . . in . . . and out. . . .

Move your attention back to your face, as you breathe out, let the last traces of tension slide away . . . and again. . . .

And down . . . to your shoulders and arms . . . feel the tension fading away as you breathe evenly and slowly. . . .

And so down to your legs, feeling the relaxation deepen and slow with your regular, even breathing. . . .

When you are ready, gradually allow your attention to come back to this room, becoming aware of the sounds around you . . . move your body . . . stretch and wake up . . . feeling more relaxed and refreshed, open your eyes when you are ready.

At the end of the exercise, encourage clients to take a few moments to pay attention to the feeling of being relaxed. Invite them to gradually "wake up" by moving and stretching their arms and legs to return normal circulation before standing up. Progressive muscle relaxation tends to produce lower heart rate and blood pressure that may cause dizziness or faintness if they stand up too quickly.

A couple of caveats to bear in mind when considering offering relaxation training: Clients who have experienced trauma may be reluctant to relax or close their eyes (i.e., to lessen their vigilance) and also may experience increased anxiety when they do allow themselves to relax (due to letting down their emotional-cognitive guard). Additionally, more concrete versions of relaxation training (such as that just presented) are preferable to fantasy-based relaxation techniques (e.g., guided imagery) for clients who are prone to disorganized cognitive functioning, thought disorders, or poor reality contact.

Problem-Solving Skills

Although approaching one's problems in a systematic way makes sense, people are not born knowing how to do this. Widely adopted by the medical and business professions, problem-solving models help individuals learn how to approach difficult situations to make better decisions. Table 10.2, adapted from D'Zurrilla and Goldfried (1971) and Goldfried and Davison (1976), illustrates six steps to effective problem solving. Clients may also benefit from Kleinke's (1998) presentation of the problem-solving model.

TABLE 10.2 Six Steps to Effective Problem Solving

1.	Define the Problem	Identify oneself as a problem solver and that a problem exists to be considered. Clearly identify the problem and one's goals.
2.	Generate Alternatives	Creatively and uncritically brainstorm potential solutions. Consider combining alternatives synergistically.
3.	Evaluate the Alternatives	Evaluate the pros and cons of the various options. Anticipate potential outcomes.
4.	Develop the Plan	Given the options, develop the specific plan that is most likely to reach the goal.
5.	Implement the Plan	Put the plan into action.
6.	Assess the Outcomes	Is the problem resolved? If yes, great! What can be learned from this success? If not, return to step #1 of the problem-solving process. With the additional information gained from the first attempt, consider each step keeping in mind that problem solving is an active process

Self-Regulation Skills

Self-regulation helps individuals manage themselves by maintaining a desired equilibrium (Baumesiter & Vohs, 2004). Individuals may make adjustments based on feedback received from internally generated information or from their environment. Difficulties associated with self-regulation may occur for a variety of reasons, including failing to detect an undesirable situation or from a lack of awareness regarding how to respond to an undesired situation. In some cases assisting clients in improving their self-regulation skills is relatively simple. Some potential examples might include suggesting that a client with mild hypoglycemia consider eating more frequent high-protein snacks, suggesting that a client who tends to procrastinate learn to break overwhelming tasks into smaller and more manageable "chunks," or suggesting that a forgetful and disorganized client consider keeping an appointment book and regularly update "to do" lists. Complex forms of self-regulation include helping people with severe borderline personality disorder learn to better regulate their fluctuating intense emotional states (Linehan, 1993; Marra, 2004; Spradlin, 2003).

Academic and Career Decision-Making Skills

People are not born knowing how to be good students, and U.S. society does a relatively poor job of educating people about the importance of education and career planning. Most students are not taught valuable academic skills, such as the empirically supported methods for taking notes, preparing papers, and excelling in examinations. Only the few students privileged to attend elite schools are systematically presented with this information. For most others, it is up to them (and those who care about them) to identify and assist the development of habits and study skills required for academic success. Hence, many individuals' potential talents and contributions are never fully realized.

For many students, learning is not an end in itself but rather a "means to an end" that they desire. Any student will be more likely to enjoy learning if he or she has the tools for success. Books like *How to Study in College* (Pauk, 2001) and *Becoming a Master Student* (Ellis, 2006) summarize research methods for improving the likelihood of success in academic settings. Behavioral and self-regulatory strategies can reinforce behaviors the individual desires to strengthen.

Although a few people seem to know from an early age "what they want to be" when they grow up, most people do not. The governments of some countries assign their citizens to educational tracks and subsequent jobs deemed to fit best perceived national needs. However, in North America, most people take rather serendipitous paths to finding their "life's work." Therapists are often consulted to assist individuals in identifying their academic major and career directions. The days of "test 'em and tell 'em" are long past. Although vocational psychology is a broad and deep specialty area, all therapists should have basic information to offer their clients with concerns in this area (see Gysbers, Heppner, & Johnston, 2003; Walsh & Heppner, 2006). Such interventions might include assessment and counseling regarding interests, values, abilities, personality, self-efficacy, and knowledge of career-search skills. Clients often find valuable *What Color Is Your Parachute: A Practical Manual for Job-Hunters and Career-Changers* (Bolles, 2005) and *Career Planning for the Twenty-First Century* (Blocher, Heppner, & Johnston, 2000).

Social-Skills Training

Interpersonal communication involves giving, receiving, and interpreting messages. Social skills are primarily developed through experiences in social settings (social learning). Influenced by the goals and messages people wish to convey, interactions also depend on the particular situation, the personalities of the individuals, their prior experiences, what they see in the other person, and the impressions they create. How the messages people wish to convey are experienced also depends upon the current situation, the personalities of the communicators, their prior experiences, what they see in the other person, and the general impressions they create.

Communication (described in greater detail in Chapter 3) includes verbal (semantic content of speech, the words and sentences) and nonverbal behavior (posture, use of eyes, tone of voice, and facial expressions). Conceptions of appropriate communication are defined by cultural background, familial expectations, and the particular social group and setting in which the communication is taking place. Communication tends to increase with social reinforcement from others. Social reinforcers include feeling praised, pleased, intrigued, calmed, or motivated in the presence of others. These reinforcers increase self-esteem and feelings of worth (Gottman, 1999).

For most people, relationships and communication with others provide some of the most rewarding and enjoyable aspects of their lives. Many types of relationships are encountered throughout each day and in a variety of circumstances. At school and work, people interact with their friends, classmates, coworkers, teachers, and bosses. In order to meet the needs of everyday living, we interact with cashiers, food servers, bank tellers, repair and maintenance workers, and healthcare personnel. Skills that facilitate developing and maintaining relationships are generally important. They are even more important with more intimate relationships with significant others, partners, friends, and family. In all of these areas, adequate social skills make life easier (Corey & Corey, 1997; Gambrill & Richey, 1985).

Social skills require appropriate timing and behavioral reciprocity. Additionally, social-skills requirements vary with environmental factors that include age, sex, and status of the other person. Although learning social skills can be difficult even when one is young and interacting with peers who are developing such skills at the same pace, they can be even more challenging to acquire after one's peers have already mastered them. Some general markers for social skill acquisition include:

- Learning to "play well with others" (sharing toys and taking turns) during preschool and early elementary school
- Learning to identify shared interests and activities and ways to relate with same-sex peers during elementary and middle school
- Learning to interact with the opposite sex and dating partners during middle school, high school, and early-adult years
- Learning to sustain committed romantic relationships by early adulthood
- Learning to set aside one's own wants and needs to prioritize the needs of children during parenthood

Developing appropriate social behavior may be impaired for various reasons, including:

- Lack of appropriate learning opportunities
- Inadequate support, encouragement, and feedback
- Inappropriate role models or lack of adequate role models
- Experiences of interpersonal trauma
- Periods of emotional disturbance or physical disability that interfere with or impair development of social skills

Failing to learn adequate social skills can lead to social isolation and feelings of loneliness, rejection, and poor self-esteem. Indeed, psychological problems such as depression, anxiety, sexual dysfunction, aggression, and suicide attempts can be both causes and effects of social-skill deficits. The severity of the social impairment varies more from person to person than from one situation to the next. For one person, the problem may be primarily poor eye contact. For another person, the deficit may include virtually every aspect of verbal and non-verbal behavior. Better later than never, typical social-skills training methods are described in Table 10.3.

Once clients are ready to apply their new social skills, therapists should acknowledge clients' willingness to take the risk and their effort to do the experiment. Therapists should also underscore the importance

238 COUNSELING AND PSYCHOTHERAPY ESSENTIALS

TABLE 10.3   Social–Skills Training Methods

Instruction: Providing an explanation and teaching different behaviors in detail so that clients learn the importance of their use in social situations.

Modeling: The therapist demonstrates the skill for the client.

Rehearsal and role playing: After receiving instruction, clients perform the skills they are seeking to acquire with the assistance and subsequent feedback of their therapist.

Reinforcement: Clients may receive reinforcement from the therapist and from themselves to help positively shape their behavior and to reinforce their efforts to change.

Homework: Assignments provide clients with opportunities to try out newly learned behavior in real-life situations that are likely to produce rewarding consequences (Corey & Corey, 1997; Gambrill & Richey, 1985).

of focusing on how well clients performed their part of the interaction (e.g., "How do they evaluate their proficiency with each step? What did they do particularly well? What challenges did they encounter? What modifications might they consider in the future?"). This focus is emphasized because clients typically want to focus on the outcome (e.g., "The person didn't respond favorably to my initiation; this proves I'm a social reject who will be alone forever"). Hence, when working with clients who are developing social skills, therapists stress the importance of concentrating on aspects of interpersonal interactions over which clients have control. Clients typically benefit from their therapists reassurance that with proper and sustained effort, they will improve their social interactions in the ways that they desire.

Initiating Conversations with Strangers

People often desire additional friends or to meet "that special person." These normal human desires are typically more intense for individuals who have recently moved, changed schools or jobs, ended a relationship or who find themselves socially isolated for any number of other reasons. The process of seeking to develop new friends is daunting for most people. It involves intentional effort by the initiator and the risk that others may react unfavorably. It can be particularly anxiety-provoking for people who have been experiencing depression (e.g., feel hopeless and powerless) or anxiety (e.g., fear that others will reject them). Like the aphorism "A journey of a thousand miles begins with a single step," creating new interpersonal relationships begins with an initial interaction with someone with whom we are not yet familiar. For many people, reducing the seemingly overwhelming task of creating new relationships down to the simple, masterable steps involved with initiating and enhancing conversations with strangers is both reassuring and empowering. Each of these basic steps can be explained and rehearsed in therapy (see Table 10.4).

TABLE 10.4   Six Steps for Initiating Conversations with Strangers

1. *Offer an opening line.* An opening line is a way of making initial contact with the other person. A common strategy is to comment upon something in your mutual environment (such as the weather or situation).

2. *Provide information about yourself.* Now that you have the other person's attention, provide a bit of information about yourself. By doing this, you provide the other person with information about you and give the person the opportunity to assess you and the situation.

3. *Ask the other person a question.* This shows your interest in the person and allows you to gather information about him or her.

4. *Ask follow-up questions* on the information the person provides, and *offer corresponding additional information about you.*

5. If this goes reasonably well, you can *tell the person that you enjoyed talking* with him or her and ask if the person would be interested in doing something again in the future (in general, asking someone to meet for coffee or lunch is a smaller step than suggesting a dinner date).

6. If the person expresses a willingness to meet again, *get his or her contact information and make plans to meet again.*

Assertiveness Training

Being assertive involves attempting to have one's needs met and rights acknowledged while also being respectful of the needs and rights of others. In contrast, people who are *aggressive* seek to have their needs met without adequate regard for the rights and preferences of others. People who are *acquiescent* or *passive* tend to allow others to have their way without adequately making their wants and needs known. More aggressive people tend to be viewed as self-centered, "pushy," or bullies, whereas excessively acquiescent people tend to be viewed as giving, timid, or weak. It should also be noted that acquiescent people are

> Assertiveness involves seeking to have one's rights acknowledged and needs met while also being respectful of the rights and needs of others.

prone to depression, because their wants and needs are less likely to be met. Hence, assertiveness training can be an essential aid for many depressed clients.

Although there are many types of assertive responses depending upon the situation, one basic assertion formula is: "I feel (*insert feeling*) when you (*describe undesired behavior*). I would prefer it if you would (*describe desired behavior*)." This assertion script has the advantage of being concise, direct, and specific. Individuals with features of borderline personality disorder tend to have difficulty managing their unpleasant emotions and maintaining harmonious relations with others. Hence, dialectical behavior therapy (DBT) offers a similar assertion formula: (1) state the observation, (2) state how you feel about it, (3) state what you need from the person, and (4) tell the person how he or she can fill that need for you (Linehan, 1993). Popular psychoeducational books addressing assertiveness include *Your Perfect Right* (Alberti & Emmons, 1974) and *The New Assertive Woman* (Bloom, 1980).

Caveats about assertiveness training are warranted. Clients should be cautioned that they may initially swing from one extreme of assertiveness to the other (e.g., from excessively acquiescent to excessively aggressive) before finding a reasonable middle ground in asserting their wants while also respecting the rights of others. Additionally, the social context in which clients exist warrants careful consideration. As conveyed in the Chinese expression "the nail that sticks up from the others will be hammered down," assertion occurs in broader social and cultural contexts. Gender and cultural expectations may severely sanction or punish individuals who deviate from gender or cultural roles. For example, assertive women may be labeled "bitches" or even be battered by their partners, assertive racial and sexual minorities may be targeted as "trouble makers" and be victims of hate crimes. Conversely, considerate or soft-spoken men may be denigrated or dismissed by others as "wimps." It is common for those emerging from subassertiveness to experience negative reactions from significant others to their newly found assertiveness. Indeed, significant others frequently react (perhaps subconsciously) in ways that seek to maintain the homeostasis of interpersonal dynamics.

Anger Management and Conflict Resolution

Anger is ubiquitous in society and contributes to many social ills, including child abuse, domestic violence, road rage, and murder. Beneath their anger, most people feel intense hurt and pain. Unfortunately, although anger often feels like a

> It is common for those emerging from subassertiveness to experience negative reactions from significant others to their newly found assertiveness.

release in the moment, it almost inevitably worsens the underlying pain. To a large extent, anger is a learned response, and this anger response can be altered with commitment and effort. Therapists are encouraged to read *Overcoming Situational and General Anger* (Therapist Protocol; Deffenbacher & McKay, 2000); recommended resources for clients include: *The Anger Control Workbook* (McKay & Rogers, 2000), *When Anger Hurts* (McKay, Rogers & McKay, 1987). *The Dance of Anger* (Lerner, 1985), and *Feeling Good: The New Mood Therapy* (Burns, 1980).

Skills for Coping With Loss, Grief, and Bereavement

The experiences of loss, grief, and bereavement are intensely emotional. Indeed, the loss of a loved one may be the most stressful event in people's lives. Therapists are often called upon to assist their clients in working through such experiences. Knowledge of the common psychosocial responses that individuals tend to have when dealing with such experiences can inform therapists, and allow them to in turn provide better guidance to their clients on their journeys. Because the stages of death and loss described in Kubler-Ross's (1969) *On Death and Dying* have permeated North American culture, we will first present them and then discuss loss in further detail.

Kubler-Ross (1969) observed individuals in the dying process, and her notions subsequently extended to how people deal with loss and grief in general. Although subsequent research has raised serious questions about the sequential nature of the stages and the degree of universality of her conclusions, many people find having a framework to consider in the midst of intense loss to be quite helpful.

1. *Denial and isolation*. There is often a temporary shock in response to bad news. Isolation can arise when people avoid the dying or bereaved person. People can slip back to this

stage when new developments occur or when people feel that they can't cope.

2. *Anger.* People have different ways of expressing their anger ("Why me?!"). They may project their anger on others in their environment or be angry with their God. They may experience envy of others who are not experiencing their loss, who are going about their regular lives, or who do not seem to care.

3. *Bargaining.* This is usually a brief stage in which individuals try to strike a deal: "I'll do (*good behavior*) if this loss will go away." Or they may attempt to postpone the loss: "If only I could live to see (*some desired future event*)."

4. *Depression.* This is the period when people mourn their losses. The depression can be both reactive (for losses already experienced) and preparatory (for anticipated losses yet to occur).

5. *Acceptance.* This is not a "happy" stage. Rather, it is characterized by a lack of intense feelings. It takes a while to reach, and people who opt to "fight 'til the end" will not reach it. It consists of essentially realizing that loss and death are inevitable.

Differing slightly from Kubler-Ross, the views of Bowlby (1961, 1969–1980) and Parkes (1987, 1988) have more research support and suggest that the process of bereavement involves the following four phases:

1. *Shock and numbness.* Initially, people are stunned and numb. They have difficulty processing the information regarding the loss.

2. *Yearning and searching.* People experience a combination of intense anxiety, denial, or disregard for the reality of their loss. They may search for ways to undo or alter the loss. Failure of these efforts leads to frustration, anger, or disappointment.

3. *Disorganization and despair.* People are easily distracted and have difficulty concentrating and focusing. They feel depressed and have difficulty planning future activities.

4. *Reorganization.* People begin to adjust to life after their loss.

As noted by Walsh and McGoldrick (2004) in *Living Beyond Loss*, there are no "right" or "wrong" ways to grieve. Indeed, there are great variations in cultural, social, spiritual, and personal issues that affect people's grief processes and reactions. Hence, the phases of grief suggested by Bowlby, Kubler-Ross, Parks, and others should not be viewed as prescriptions for appropriate grieving. Indeed, therapists can harm clients by misdirected efforts to guide clients into restrictive Western notions of "healthy" responses to loss.

The bereaved may be encouraged to seek out people who understand their loss, such as friends, family, clergy, therapists, and support groups. It may take a long time to move through the grieving process, so both social support and patience in allowing themselves to grieve are beneficial. Therapists seeking to assist clients with more extensive loss and bereavement should refer to resources addressing that subject (e.g., Worden, 1991).

Skills for Dealing With Trauma, Assault, and Other Intense Emotional Experiences

By definition, trauma is a painful emotional experience or shock, often producing lasting psychological effects. When people experience or witness emotionally overwhelming events, they are understandably susceptible to symptoms of shock and to developing posttraumatic stress disorder (PTSD). Traumatic and catastrophic events (such as childhood sexual or physical abuse, rape, assault, natural disasters, motor vehicle accidents, and war combat) are the cause of PTSD. These events may be sudden, overwhelming, and dangerous, either to one's self or significant others. The person affected may feel intense fear, helplessness, or horror either at the time or immediately afterwards. Because of their empathy and compassion for the survivor, close friends, family members, and professionals can also be affected by the trauma (i.e., vicarious traumatization). Common experiences of people who have experienced trauma include: persistent reexperiencing of the traumatic event (e.g., thoughts, dreams), avoidance of stimuli associated with the trauma (e.g., becoming "numb" and avoiding reminders of the trauma), and increased arousal (e.g., hypervigalence). However, people vary widely in how they respond to, cope with, and adapt to traumatic experiences. Depending upon the type of trauma the client has experienced, the following resources may be of value: *I Never Told Anyone: Writings by*

Women Survivors of Child Sexual Abuse (Bass & Thornton, 1983), *Courage to Heal* (Bass & Davis, 1994), *Victims No Longer* (Lew, 1988), *I Never Called It Rape* (Warshaw, 1998), *Abused Boys* (Hunter, 1990), and *Trauma and Recovery* (Herman, 1992). (PTSD and its treatments are also addressed in Chapter 12.)

Health Promotion

The psychosocial factors influencing biomedical health are extensive. Mental health professionals often assist individuals with exercise, diet, eating and weight concerns, hypertension, diabetes, pain, fibromyalgia, cardiac and pulmonary concerns, coping with acute and chronic diseases, and rehabilitating from injuries. Developing and participating in regular cardiovascular exercise helps reduce and prevent mild depression and anxiety-related concerns. Perhaps this relief begins with secretion of more endorphins (the brain chemicals that help reduce pain), which are associated with feelings of well-being ("endorphin high"). Additionally, exercise appears to be associated with increases in serotonin production, which tends to reduce depression and anxiety. When people engage in regular cardiovascular exercise, they generally feel better.

Sleeping Difficulties

Suggestions regarding sleep hygiene are often helpful in addressing client's difficulties with sleeping (Morin et al., 2004). The following suggestions are intended to make the bed the place to sleep and not a place for other problematic concerns.

- Spending no more than 2 nonsleeping hours per night in bed.
- Go to bed only when sleepy.
- Use the bedroom for sleep and sex only (no reading, television, or worrying in bed either during the daytime or at night)
- Get out of bed and go to another room if unable to fall asleep within 15 to 20 minutes.
- Arise at the same time every morning regardless of the amount of sleep that night

Parenting Skills

As new parents prepare to leave the hospital after the birth of their first child, they often wonder, "Are they going to let me just walk out of here with this baby? I don't know what I am doing. I'm not ready!" As humans we are not born being able to parent optimally. Given the degree of self-sacrifice and responsibility for a vulnerable human life that is involved with raising a child, it is indeed curious that society doesn't require parenting education and issue parenting licenses. Instead, parents turn to a variety of sources for guidance, including psychoeducational resources and therapists. Some recommended resources include: *What to Expect When You Are Expecting* (Murkoff, 2002), *The Parent's Handbook* (Dinkmeyer, McKay, & Dinkmeyer, 1997), and *How to Win as a Step-Family* (Visher & Visher, 1991).

Sexual Enhancement Skills

North Americans are known for being particularly predisposed to having "issues" with two aspects of their lives—anger and sexuality. Indeed, for a society that likes to view itself as sexually open, North Americans tend to have very limited exposure to the attitudes, knowledge, and skills associated with good sexual relationships. Rather than good, direct communication about sexual matters, innuendos, bad information, and myths are the norm.

Getting pregnant comes naturally for many; however, establishing and maintaining good sexual relationships are far more complex. Because sexual matters are rarely addressed directly, individuals are on their own to gather what information they can. Hence, magazines, TV shows, the Internet, peers, parents and religious institutions become sources that adolescents and adults consult as they try to understand their sexual urges and make sense of how these urges might be expressed with another person.

For men, many sexual myths have been identified, such as the belief that their penises should be "two feet long, hard as steel, and go all night" (Pridal, 2005; Zilbergeld, 1999). Most men have little idea about what their partners really enjoy sexually and have few skills in communicating candidly about sexual matters. Men are still prone to the "whore-madonna complex" in which they feel sexually attracted to "bad" women but want to marry "pure" women. This type of dualistic thinking contributes to difficulties sustaining lasting relationships with a woman who is both a "good" wife or mother and a sexual being. Men are also susceptible to fantasy sexual partners (particularly on the Internet and other pornographic sources) who are portrayed as physically striking, spontaneously receptive to new partners, quickly aroused, loud when they climax, and undemanding regarding a subsequent relationship. Hence, it is not surprising that many female partners demand that their porn-addicted male partners obtain therapy (Brooks, 1995; Good & Sherrod, 1997).

For many men with difficulties related to premature ejaculation, erections, or relationship sexuality issues, an initial component to successful problem amelioration can be obtaining accurate sexual information. The book *New Male Sexuality* by Zilbergeld (1999) provides facts, counters myths, and helps normalize men's expectations about sexual matters. *The Centerfold Syndrome* by Brooks (1995) offers suggestions for concerns associated with pornography use.

For women, learning to recognize and accept the sexual aspects of themselves is important. Barraged by unrealistic cultural messages, it is understandable that women might struggle with body image concerns or succumb to eating disorders (Kashubeck-West & Mintz, 2005). For women seeking to increase their enjoyment of sexual relations (e.g., greater interest, arousal, orgasm), obtaining accurate sexual information is a good first step. The book *For Yourself* (Barbach, 1975) provides facts, counters myths, and helps normalize women's expectations about sexual matters. Additionally, for many women, feeling emotionally close with their partner is an important aspect of their feeling connected and open to sexual relations. Indeed, for either partner, when irritation, anger, hurt, or resentment has built up, good sexual relations are typically more difficult to create and maintain.

Emotions and values also play interesting roles in people's sexual lives. Lust is obvious, but shame, guilt, dependence, vulnerability, fear, and anger are also common. Conservative religious beliefs lead many people to "split" their moral/religious selves from their unacceptable sexual selves and behaviors. Prior sexual trauma experiences are also relatively common, with sexual trauma survivors often finding that traumatic memories interfere with their sexual activities in the present. Normalizing their reactions, encouraging discussion with supportive others, and being patient can be beneficial.

What activities constitute "good sex" varies widely for different people. Good sex is defined mutually by the people having it—not by cultural myths, standards, or media portrayals. As long as no person is harmed or exploited, any type of sex couples desire to have can be good sex, and it will indeed be so if there is communication about likes and dislikes. It is preferable if a couple can learn to talk about sex before, during, and after—as well as at the dinner table with all their clothes on. For couples for whom sexual relations have gone astray, sensate focus can be helpful (see Chapter 14).

Summary

The psychoeducational interventions discussed in this chapter are intended to provide an introduction and basic skills to allow therapists to assist clients with improving their functioning in our increasingly complex society. We believe that clients have the right to expect that their therapists, as mental health professionals, be knowledgeable about an array of psychological issues and associated skills, and to provide informed guidance to them when such information exists. This chapter notes several important distinctions between effective psychoeducational interventions and advice that clients would typically receive from family and friends. For example, experienced therapists help clients anticipate and prepare for both internal experiences and reactions from others that they are likely to encounter given the nature of their current concerns (e.g., clients who have been subassertive typically encounter some individuals who react negatively to their increased assertion of their wants and needs). In general, therapists are encouraged to break down complex skills into smaller, more easily mastered steps. Additionally, therapists should encourage clients to focus on the aspects of skill acquisition and improvement under their control, rather than using others' reactions as the primary basis for their evaluations.

CHAPTER 11

Depression and Suicide

Although the world is full of suffering, it is also
full of the overcoming of it.
—HELEN KELLER

Everyone feels "down" or "blue" occasionally. Most people experience grief associated with upsetting life events such as the death of a family member, loss of a job, serious illness or loss of physical functioning, or the ending of a romantic relationship or marriage. These are normal human responses to upsetting life events. For most of us, feelings of sadness and grief diminish over time.

However, when feelings of sadness become more intense, interfere with one's performance of daily responsibilities, and last longer than 2 weeks, it is possible that something more serious than just transitory "feeling blue" is involved. People who are depressed tend to feel overwhelmed and exhausted and often withdraw from their routine activities and friends. They tend to feel hopeless and helpless and are prone to blaming themselves excessively. In some cases, depressed individuals have thoughts of suicide and may indeed end their lives. Clearly, depression engenders significant personal and family suffering, greatly adds to medical and social service costs, and generates major amounts of lost productivity due to absenteeism from work and school (Craighead, Craighead, & Llardi, 1998). This phenomenon is illustrated in the client situation described here.

Helen was a 29-year-old married mother of two young children. She sought therapy because she felt discouraged and overwhelmed. She reported having a hard time getting up in the morning and being generally despondent. Helen and her family had recently relocated to a new geographical region; her husband had been transferred by his employer. Before the move, she said that she felt a normal amount of being tired and hassled with the task of caring for her two children, but got along well enough with the support of her friends and family who lived in the area. Since the move, her husband had been working long hours to support his family, protect his job, and advance in the company. Helen reported feeling overwhelmed and like she was all alone. She was struggling to find the energy to do just the basic tasks of life.

Mood disorders are the most commonly diagnosed problem among adults. The National Institute of Health estimates that 17 million adults suffer from depression each year in the U.S. alone, and that up to 20% of the adult population experiences some depressive symptoms at any given time (Amenson & Lewinsohn, 1981; Antonuccio, Danton, & DeNelsky, 1995; Kessler et al., 1994; Oliver & Simmons, 1985). The lifetime prevalence rates range from 20–25% in women and 9–12% in men. At any one time (point prevalence) about 6% of women and 3% of men are depressed (Kessler et al., 1994). Women are consistently found to have rates of depression nearly twice that of men (American Psychiatric Association, 2000). Numerous factors contribute to women's greater rate of depression, including: adverse socio-cultural roles, abusive and traumatic experiences, and women's means of coping with these factors (Piccinelli & Wikinson, 2000; Worrell & Remer, 2003).

Theorists speculate that men may be more prone than women to express their distress externally in the form of irritability, anger, violence, and substance abuse (Cochran, 2005; Cochran & Rabinowitz, 2000). According to these scholars, symptoms of "male depression" are not included in current *DSM-IV-TR* diagnostic criteria, and hence would not be diagnosed as frequently as traditional depression which is characterized by turning against oneself. These theorists speculate that if externalized aspects of depression were included in diagnostic criteria, women and men would be found to have similar prevalence rates of depression (Cochran, 2005; Cochran & Rabinowitz, 2000). Terrance Real (1997) explores men's experience of depression in the book *I Don't Want to Talk About It: Overcoming the Secret Legacy of Male Depression*. Cultural factors are also related to how individuals experience, express, and seek assistance for depression (Patel, 2001; Sue & Sue, 2003)

> Depressive disorders are the most commonly diagnosed psychological problem among adults. The National Institute of Health estimates that, at any given point in time 20% of the adult population experiences some depressive symptoms, and 6% of women and 3% of men meet criteria for depression. Lifetime prevalence rates range from 20–25% in women and 9–12% in men. While women are consistently found to have rates of depression nearly twice that of men, theorists speculate that men may be more prone than women to express their distress externally in the form of irritability, anger, violence, and substance abuse.

The causes of mood disorders have been widely studied, with research identifying no single cause. For some individuals, their depression is associated with an underlying medical condition such as diabetes or thyroid disorder. Diabetics are more likely to have depression than the general population, sometimes preceding the diabetes diagnosis and sometimes subsequent to the diagnosis (Gavard, Lustman & Clouse, 1993). Depression is associated with changes in brain chemistry that influence mood and thought processes: The amygdales of depressed people are excessively active (Drevets, 2003). Genetics also influence sensitivity to depression-inducing effects of stressful life events.

The most powerful psychological stressors include assault, death of a close relative, and serious relationship concerns, breakup, or divorce with a significant other. Early life experiences of abuse, neglect, or separation may create sensitivities in the brain that, like genetic inheritances, may predispose individuals to react with depression to current stressors (Gabbard, 2000).

Depressed people often inadvertently create feedback loops in their interpersonal relationships with others that result in their feeling a lack social support and a sense of being criticized. Depression also tends to create a vicious cycle in which people feel down and therefore withdraw from activities, exercise, and social interactions, which in turn exacerbates their feelings of isolation, listlessness, and hopelessness, which further worsens their depression.

Psychotherapy of Depression

Therapy offers clients opportunities to identify factors that contribute to their depression and to effectively address the psychological, interpersonal, behavioral, and situational causes. More specifically, therapists can help clients identify the problems that contribute to their depression. They can then help clients identify aspects of their problems that are amenable to change and improvement. Therapists can further assist clients with developing appropriate goals and realistic plans to reach them. As depressed people tend to overgeneralize in the negative direction, therapists might encourage clients to identify problematic or distorted thinking patterns associated with feelings of hopelessness and helplessness, and then to develop and practice more adaptive ways of thinking (cognitive interventions). Therapists may also explore depressed clients' patterns of interacting with others, such as being excessively giving to others without adequately balancing this with assertion that one's own needs be met (interpersonal and relationship-oriented interventions). By assisting them in accomplishing new and difficult tasks, therapists help clients feel more empowered, thereby leading to a greater sense of control over the hassles and unpleasurable events in their lives.

Research on Treatments for Depression

Treatments of depression with therapy and medications have been studied more than any other problem. However, much more funding has gone into studying psychopharmacological approaches to depression than has into studying psychotherapeutic approaches. This is due to the fact that the majority of controlled clinical trials have been funded by pharmaceutical companies with the goal of obtaining approval for marketing their products. In contrast, most clinical trials for psychotherapies have been supported through research grants from National Institute for Mental Health.

Research in the treatment of major depressive disorder via therapy has been approached from three general perspectives: behavioral therapy, cognitive therapy, and interpersonal therapy, with all three receiving empirical support for their efficacy (Craighead et al., 1998; Frank, Karp, & Rush, 1993). Psychodynamic approaches have also shown some evidence of efficacy in clinical trials (Gabbard, 2000), as have couple therapy approaches (Friedman, 1975; Jacobson, Dobson, Fruzetti, Schmaling, & Salusky, 1991). Interestingly, as with antidepressants, the various therapeutic approaches to depression are about equally effective.

The relatively equal effects of different schools of therapy in the treatment of major depression might be due in part to: (1) common factors across the approaches, (2) adhering to a strict format, (3) staying with a focus, and (4) some clients in each treatment approach responding very well, and others responding less well. These relative responders may tend to even out the results.

> The integrative perspective taken in this book borrows systematically from each of the approaches within a disciplined integration using the stages of change as an organizing structure. Resistance, transference, counter-transference, and societal/cultural considerations are viewed as inevitable and often useful. The various strategies and techniques are viewed as more or less suitable for specific clients and concerns, varying in part with the degree of experience and predispositions of each therapist.

An Integrative Approach to Treatment of Depression

The integrative perspective borrows systematically from each of the approaches within a disciplined integration using the stages of psychotherapy as an organizing structure within societal/cultural considerations utilizing the concepts of resistance, transference and countertransference. The various strategies and techniques are tailored for specific clients and concerns, varying with the experience and predispositions of each therapist.

The following case study and accompanying discussion illustrate an integrated approach to the treatment of depression (adapted with permission from Good & Mintz, 2005).

Richard, a successful professional in his mid-forties, entered therapy after consulting with his employer's employee assistance program (EAP). Richard was becoming increasingly distracted, irritable, and distraught. He was married for a second time, had children, and was in the midst of an increasingly complicated extramarital affair. Although he was initially a bit cautious about therapy, he also recognized that he was in distress and wanted confidential assistance. He described feeling sad most of his life when he wasn't busy. Growing up, he felt valued by his parents but learned to conceal things that his parents would not have approved of. In the course of therapy, he described a pattern of wanting others to like him—and generally being quite successful at fulfilling this desire over the course of his adult life. However, in his marriages, his pattern of ignoring or concealing his wants and resentments from his spouse was causing him repeated problems. Because of his desire to be approved of—and concomitant desire to not risk rejection or shame by making his wants known in his primary relationship—Richard would seek approval from women who accepted him less conditionally than his spouse could. Over the course of therapy, Richard and his therapist identified this pattern and began referring to it as his "pleasing-others façade."

The therapist formed a therapeutic working alliance with Richard, engaged him in therapy, and identified one primary "client-specific pattern" (his "pleasing-others façade"). This specific pattern could be analyzed at two other more global levels of patterns. At the most general level, this pattern could be described as a "criticism-avoidant personality style." At the school-based level, both interpersonal and skills deficits can be seen (his difficulty expressing his needs, desires, and fears). Further, the issues Richard faced can also be traced back to the broader social environment that teaches men (and boys) to project strength and not to express vulnerability to others (his masculinity- and shame-based reluctance to directly attend to and express his wants, needs, hurt, and anger). The ability of therapists to recognize dysfunctional patterns and name them is important; effective gender-aware therapists will also be able to discern and understand patterns at several levels of specificity and tie them to the broader social environment when appropriate.

With his patterns identified, change processes were introduced. Richard kept a four-column thought record (see Figure 5.1). He identified situations in which he felt others might disapprove of him, identified dysfunctional cognitions ("It is awful if someone I care about is disappointed or mad at me"), and was able to create more adaptive cognitions ("It is generally better for me to know what I want and share it with others than to keep it to myself"). He also was able to trace his pattern back to his family of origin (psychodynamic and family therapy issues); his parents had criticized others severely for being "bad" and "sinful" for having normal human desires. He practiced responding to other's criticism in session via role plays. He explored his underlying fears of rejection and underlying negative self-concept. Gradually his longstanding depression lifted. He ended the affair, sought marital therapy, and remained vigilant about not slipping back into his old ways. In many ways, Richard learned to "activate his observing self" and "face his fears" (Beitman & Yue, 2004).

Resistance, transference, and countertransference were not major issues in this case. The therapist was conscientious about phrasing statements in ways that Richard would not find judgmental (i.e., not replicating the family dynamics that prompted development of his style). The therapist also directly invited and reassured Richard that he would like for him to express the views that he feared the therapist would disapprove of (corrective emotional experience). During termination, Richard opted to "leave the door open" to see his therapist on an as-needed basis (which ended up being approximately two to three times a year) when he found himself facing larger interpersonal challenges and desiring a safe place to clarify external demands and his inner experiences and to develop a plan that addressed them without shame, avoidance, or deception.

Summaries of Psychotherapeutic Approaches to Depression

The following sections summarize behavioral, cognitive, interpersonal, psychodynamic, couple, and integrative approaches to the treatment of depression.

Behavioral Interventions

Behavioral interventions for depression are built upon hypotheses generated by Lewinsohn (1974) and reviewed by McLean (1982). These hypotheses are summarized in Table 11.1 (from Frank, Karp, & Rush, 1993).

Craighead and colleagues (1998) summarized behavioral interventions for depression including techniques presented in Table 11.2. Client homework is an essential aspect of these interventions. Assignments include: monitoring daily activities, assessment of pleasure and mastery of activities, assignment of increasingly difficult activities, imagining behaviors to be performed, discussion of specific problems, and identification of behavioral solutions to these problems.

The case of Jackie illustrates behavioral interventions for depression.

TABLE 11.1 Behavioral Hypotheses About Depression

Depressed people elicit fewer behaviors from others than do nondepressed people.

Depressed people elicit a lower rate of positive reinforcement from others than nondepressed people do.

The number and kind of pleasant activities in which individuals participate affect their mood.

Those suffering from depression are more sensitive to aversive stimuli than are nondepressed people.

An increased rate of positive reinforcement occurs simultaneously with clinical improvement.

Jackie, a 26-year-old single graduate student, was accompanied to therapy by her mother. Her mother explained that Jackie had been rather reserved since puberty, when her family moved and she was the victim of emotional abuse inflicted by mean-spirited peers. Her depression and social withdrawal had recently grown much worse when her only real friend moved to another state. Jackie was now spending all of her time in her room alone and seriously considering suicide. Although interpersonal, cognitive, and psychodynamic interventions were attempted, Jackie discounted them and remained hopeless and highly critical of herself and others. She responded best to behavioral interventions in which she actually did the activities that she had avoided and been fearful of (speaking in class discussions, talking with strangers). It appeared that she could not as easily discount her strengths and skills when she successfully performed the tasks that she had been avoiding. Antidepressant medications also appeared to reduce the depth of her depression, allowing her a bit more energy with which to engage in therapy.

As the case of Jackie illustrates, helping clients to actually rehearse and perform the behaviors which they are avoiding may help to directly lift their depression.

Cognitive Interventions

Cognitive interventions for depression target depressed clients' negative tripartite view of the self, the world, and the future, and the subsequent emotions and behaviors that this view engenders (Beck, 1976). Cognitive therapy includes the use of behavioral interventions such as

TABLE 11.2   Behavioral Approaches to the Treatment of Depression

Self-monitoring of thoughts and behaviors
Improving social and communication skills
Increasing adaptive behaviors such as positive and negative assertion
Increasing response-contingent positive reinforcement for adaptive behaviors
Decreasing negative life experiences

activity scheduling and graded task assignment when the client's depressive symptoms warrant such intervention. Behavioral interventions can also serve as experiments that counter dysfunctional cognitions about activity and self-efficacy (e.g., "if I try and go out for a walk I'll just feel worse").

Clients are taught to recognize their automatic thoughts by asking themselves "What just went through my mind?" at the time of a significant mood shift. This shift to a more deliberate way of thinking, along with the help of the therapist via Socratic questioning, leads clients to evaluate their thoughts for logical errors including arbitrary inference, selective abstraction, overgeneralization, magnification and minimalization, personalization, and dichotomous thinking (Beck, 1976). An important aspect of the evaluation of automatic thoughts is that the therapist does not "tell the client what to think" but through a process of thoughtful questioning and behavioral experimentation helps the client draw alternative conclusions with the data at hand. If the client's automatic thoughts are accurate, then the therapist works with the client to identify whether they represent problems to be solved, or if they are problematic because they have a meaning to the client that reflects an underlying belief or assumption (e.g., if the automatic thought is "I'm alone" and that is true, the origin of the emotional disturbance may be the belief that "People who are alone are unlovable").

Clients' self-monitoring activities clarify their automatic thoughts. These automatic thoughts are then conceptualized by the therapist and client based on a comprehensive understanding of the client's life history, development and interpersonal environment as to how these thoughts relate to underlying cognitive schemas or beliefs (refer to the list of "common dysfunctional beliefs" in Chapter 1). These schemas are considered to be the source of the depressogenic (depression-causing) thoughts. Intermediate and core beliefs are also evaluated for accuracy and more functional and accurate belief systems developed with the client. This is important because more enduring improvement is related to the evaluation and modification of underlying beliefs (Sudak, 2006).

Therapists often encounter versions of the following dysfunctional thoughts in their work with depressed clients:

About the self:
- *I'm a loser and I'll always be a loser.*
- *There is no hope for me.*
- *I am nothing, no good.*
- *It's all my fault.*

About others and the world:
- *Everyone is happier than I am.*
- *No one likes me.*
- *I never can live up to other people's expectations.*
- *As hard as I try, I can't really help others.*
- *I've disappointed so many people.*
- *I'll always get a bad deal.*
- *Things never go my way.*

About the future:
- *There is no sense in trying.*
- *I'll never amount to anything.*
- *Whatever I do always comes out wrong.*
- *Things will never improve.*
- *There is no reason for me to be alive.*

Common dysfunctional thoughts with suggestions for overcoming them are described in *The Feeling Good Handbook* (Burns, 1999).

Cognitive processing errors are common in depression. One frequent processing error leading to dysfunctional automatic thoughts is *selective abstraction* (a single event means something terrible). *Selective abstraction* leads to *arbitrary inferences* (negative conclusions drawn from limited supporting evidence). Arbitrary inferences lead to:

- *Exaggerations* and *overgeneralizations* (general rules applied haphazardly)
- *Dichotomous thinking* (in which situations are either bad or good, black or white)

- *Personalization* (self-blame for problems of others and everyday occurrences)
- *Minimization* (of positive events and progress)
- *Magnification* (of negative events and setbacks)

By a collaborative process of examining evidence and designing behavioral experiments, clients are assisted in developing and incorporating more accurate and adaptive thoughts and schemas. The case of Susan illustrates some of these issues.

Susan, an 18-year-old female college student, was encouraged to seek counseling by her parents and primary care physician because she was having difficulties with her grades, mood, and social life. She was always a bit on the quiet side, but now that she was in college and living away from home for the first time, she had made few friends and was growing increasingly isolated and despondent. Also, although she was at a normal weight, she felt that she was too fat. Feeling bad about herself, she also had periods when she ate excessively (binged) and then purged by vomiting and abusing laxatives.

Susan was having a difficult time coping with the transition to college and the disruption of her old support system. Her tendency toward being interpersonally reserved exacerbated her negative self-concept as well as her ability to build new friendships. She did not see any way to improve her situation. She also experienced body image concerns and was developing an eating disorder. Susan responded well to the idea of keeping a thought record and was able to recognize the ways in which her thinking contributed to her depression, problematic eating, and compensatory behaviors. Assisting Susan in understanding the problematic messages that our culture gives women about unrealistically thin ideal body types helped provide a foundation for her understanding of her body image concerns and disturbed eating habits. With the support, practice, and encouragement of her therapist, Susan was able to recognize cues (such as when she was meeting new people) for dysfunctional thoughts ("I am fat, ugly, and nobody will ever like me!") and generate more adaptive and accurate statements ("I am attractive enough and people of quality will like me"). She began to change her thinking patterns and underlying cognitive schema. She also developed additional coping methods, such as planning her meals and being more effective socially, via role-playing social situations in therapy and gradually exposing herself to social encounters outside of session. This process resulted in thoughts about herself as effective and in control (exercise, initiating social activities with others, and talking on phone or via the Internet with friends).

Interpersonal Interventions

Interpersonal interventions are based upon the idea that clients' interpersonal relationships play a significant role in both the onset and maintenance of depression (Klerman et al., 1984). Therapists usually address current problems from four perspectives: unresolved grief, interpersonal disputes, role transitions, and interpersonal deficits (e.g., isolation, lack of assertiveness). The idea of interpersonal therapy is that depression can be treated by improving communication patterns and the ways people relate to others. Interpersonal interventions are illustrated in the following case.

Jackson, a large, 30-year-old ex-marine employed as a police officer, lifted weights, drank excessively, and became violent when drunk. He very reluctantly accompanied his wife to marital therapy. In the course of marital therapy, the emotions that he was feeling were identified. It became apparent that Jackson's angry "tough guy" façade was his attempt to cover up the deep hurt, insecurity, and despair that he felt about several central aspects of his life. At one point in therapy, Jackson's wife mentioned a particular aspect of his sexual behavior. Acutely embarrassed, Jackson became enraged. His jaw and fists clenched—he was ready to fight or flee the therapy situation and his marriage.

His therapist acknowledged the intensity of his feelings and asked Jackson to hang in there a little bit longer and explore what he was so angry about. Jackson realized that beyond being embarrassed that his wife would mention his sexual behavior, he was especially threatened by his wife's becoming successful and respected in her business. Beneath the surface, he feared that she would leave him for someone who made more money or was a better lover.

Now knowing that the most pertinent emotion was vulnerability rather than anger, therapy could progress. At a deeper level, Jackson had emotional baggage from his family of origin. His mother had had been distant and busy, and Jackson had intentionally chosen an attentive and nurturing spouse. With her growing business and the needs of their children, he was terrified that his wife would no longer be attentive to his emotional and sexual needs. His efforts to be tough and "in charge" of his emotions, his life, and his family members were ironically causing the exact outcome that he most feared—his wife was becoming more distant and less responsive to him (see Good & Mintz, 2005; Mahalik, 2005; Mahalik et al., 2003a).

Client characteristics that predict outcomes in response to behavioral, cognitive, and interpersonal approaches are listed in Table 11.3 (Craighead et al., 1998). This table, among other things, demonstrates the desirability of building upon clients' strengths (e.g., clients with few depressogenic cognitions responded well to cognitive therapy, clients with low levels of social dysfunction responded well to interpersonal therapy). These notions are consistent with the capitalization hypothesis that therapists should seek to build on clients' strengths

TABLE 11.3 Client Characteristics that Predict Outcomes with Three Different Psychotherapies*

BEHAVIORAL THERAPY

−Existential reasons for depression (e.g., life is meaningless)

COGNITIVE THERAPY

+Low on depressogenic cognitions

−High pretreatment depression

−Divorced

−Dysfunctional social relationships

−Low learned resourcefulness

−Failure to do homework (Burns & Nolen-Hoeksema, 1992)

INTERPERSONAL THERAPY

+Low levels of social dysfunction

−Personality disorders

−Trait neuroticism

−Cognitive dysfunction

* + predicts favorable outcome; − predicts poor outcome

(Cronbach & Snow, 1977; Good & Mintz, 2005; Nathan & Gorman, 1998; Sotskey et al., 1991).

Psychodynamic Interventions

Many psychodynamic approaches have been used as comparison therapies in the clinical trials of the previously mentioned treatments, and they tend to show less efficacy than the primary approach being evaluated. Perhaps some of the reason for this relative lack of strength was in the researchers' motivation to demonstrate the efficacy of their new targeted treatment protocol (Frank, Karp, & Rush, 1993).

Psychodynamic hypotheses suggest that there are two underlying types of depression: *anaclitic* and *introjective* (Gabbard, 2000). These types are summarized in Table 11.4.

Gabbard (2000) argued, with some research support, that the *introjective* type does not respond well to antidepressants perhaps because of obsessive-compulsive or narcissistic characterological traits and that long-term psychodynamic therapy might be the best treatment for such clients. In the treatment of depressed individuals, empathy by the therapist is a crucial correlate of outcome—at least with psychodynamic and cognitive-behavioral approaches (Burns & Nolen-Hoeksema, 1992).

TABLE 11.4   *Psychodynamic Hypotheses of Depression*

ANACLITIC

- Relationship-based: longing for a caring other who nurtures, protects and loves
- Fears of being abandoned and unprotected
- Feeling helpless, lonely, and weak
- Vulnerability to threats of lost relationships

INTROJECTIVE

- Accomplishment-based: requires self to perform maximally in the world, to be better than everyone else, to change the world in a significant way
- High tendency to be self-critical, perfectionistic, and fear criticism or disapproval from others
- Feeling unworthy, inferior, guilty, and like a failure
- Vulnerability to loss of autonomy and threat to an effective sense of self

Psychodynamic approaches to depression are illustrated in the case of Greg.

Greg was a lawyer in his forties who had experienced depression most of his life. His father was a dominant and well-respected professional in the community. His mother was well-intentioned but always yielded to his father. Greg felt that his parents were always highly critical of him and that he and his accomplishments were never good enough. Additionally, when his parents viewed him as having made a mistake, they withdrew their love and approval. Through psychodynamic exploration, Greg gradually became aware of the degree to which he hungered for a special caring person who valued and loved him, yet he felt unworthy of such love. In the course of therapy, his sense of being helpless, weak, and lonely lessened, and his fears of abandonment became less terrifying. He reduced his drinking. He gradually came to be able to incorporate a sense of his consistent and caring therapist into his psyche, and he was thus able to "be my own good parent" in ways that gradually ameliorated his depression.

The case of Greg illustrates how one's need for approval through accomplishment and the desire to feel very special to someone may lead to depression, and how understanding these desires may help to alleviate it.

Couple and Marital Interventions

Depression often occurs in the context of a significant relationship and tends to increase the degree of friction between the couple (see Frank, Karp, & Rush, 1993). Relationship discord itself can be a trigger for a depressive episode. In addition, relationship distress often continues after the depressive episode is over—suggesting that couple therapy might prevent recurrence. Indeed, one of the best single predictors of relapse is depressed clients' perception that their partner is highly critical (Hooley & Teasdale, 1989). Depressed clients tend to provoke much hostility from their family members, and therapists may need to help family members overcome their guilty feelings about such reactions so that they can recognize and

> A strong predictor of relapse in depressed clients is their perception that their partner is highly critical.

address them as common responses to depressed people (Gabbard, 2000).

Integration

The models of therapy described by these five approaches are not mutually exclusive. Behavioral therapy emphasizes finding ways to increase positive reinforcement. Couple therapy and interpersonal therapy help to increase interpersonal positive reinforcement. Cognitive therapy addresses negative mindsets challenging dysfunctional patterns of thinking and developing adaptive thought patterns. When couple therapists address the tendency of one spouse to criticize the other, they are also addressing the cognitions that lead to criticism. If therapists using cognitive techniques examine the underlying schemas that create excessively high expectations of self and others, they are also examining the sources of anaclitic and introjective psychodynamic types. Positively reinforcing interpersonal responses can help to dissolve rigid self-other expectations. In essence, therapists help clients better understand and subsequently address the emotions, cognitions, behaviors, interpersonal relationships, systemic dynamics, and ultimately the neural circuits that are related to their depression.

Pharmacotherapy and Depression

Both psychotherapy and pharmacotherapy can effectively alter neural circuits and ameliorate depression. As antidepressant medications have demonstrated efficacy in the treatment of depression, Table 11.5 lists the conditions under which such medications should be considered.

The pharmaceutical industry has generated several classes of antidepressants (e.g., tricyclics, monoamine oxidase inhibitors, selective serotonin reuptake inhibitors, "atypical antidepressants"). Nevertheless only 50–60% of clients seem to respond to antidepressant treatment. Of these responders, perhaps only 30% achieve complete remission. Evidence is accumulating to suggest that without complete remission, clients are likely to relapse (Nemeroff & Shatzberg, 1998). Some clients respond within a week of beginning treatment. If clients have not responded within 4 weeks, they may be quite unlikely to respond (Schatzberg & Nemeroff, 1998). Many different

> Therapists help clients better understand and subsequently address the emotions, cognitions, behaviors, interpersonal relationships, systemic dynamics, and neural circuits related to their depression.

TABLE 11.5   Indicators for Pharmacotherapy

Psychotherapy by a competent therapist is not available (e.g., some in rural locations).
The client prefers medication.
The depression is severe.
The client had a favorable response to medication for a similar concern in the past.
There are melancholic features (disturbances of appetite and sleep as well as feeling much worse in the morning and better in the evening) or atypical features (excessive sleep and excessive eating with great sensitivity to interpersonal rejection). In these cases MAOIs have been found to be especially effective.
There are psychotic features (loss of touch with reality). In these cases antipsychotic medication is required for maximum efficacy.
Prophylactic (preventative) medication is indicated when clients have had two previous episodes of major depression. Also, individuals over age 55 who have a first episode of major depression are very likely to have another one. Frank and Gunderson (1990) found that maintenance medication prevents recurrence, whereas monthly maintenance therapy delays recurrence but does not prevent it (see Frank, Karp, & Rush, 1993).

strategies are being developed for non-responsive clients, including switching to another medication or augmenting treatment responsiveness by adding lithium, thyroid medication, buspirone, another antidepressant, or olanzapine.

Selection of antidepressant is guided by family history and side effect profile. If a family member has responded well to a particular medication, that medication should be tried on the current client. If a client will be troubled by the sexual side effects typical of the SRIs (serotonin reuptake inhibitors), another class of medications should be considered. If weight gain and dry mouth would be disturbing to the client, then tricyclics should be avoided. If sedation is desired, the tricyclics, imipramine and amitrytiline, should be considered. It should be noted that the term *antidepressant* misrepresents the range of effectiveness of the medications included within this category. Many medications in this class are useful for most of the anxiety disorders, bulimia, pain reduction (e.g., amitriptyline), insomnia (e.g., trazodone), and night terrors (e.g., imipramine). These medications might more accurately be called "antineurotic" medications, as they primarily target the "worry, obsessive, ruminative" circuits of the brain.

How long should clients remain on antidepressants? Generally, after a single episode of major depression, clients should be treated for 6 months. If the client has a very strong family history of depression, has suffered more than one episode, or suffered an episode that was quite severe (e.g., with a serious suicide attempt) or was particularly difficult to treat, long-term treatment should be considered (Nemeroff & Schatzberg, 1998).

Suicide

Therapists are obligated to know their competencies and the limitations of their competencies, including those associated with suicidal clients. A *suicide risk assessment* includes a multiaxial differential diagnosis and accompanying estimation of whether the suicide risk is low, moderate, or high. Information can also be gathered from family, friends, and other healthcare providers. Documentation of assessment is essential for risk-management and for tracking changes in clients' status over time.

Direct questions about suicide are essential. Therapists should inquire about suicidal thoughts, plans, and behaviors. Inconsistencies between clients' verbal responses, their symptoms, and their nonverbal behaviors suggest a need for further inquiry or soliciting information from other sources. If clients report suicidal ideation, therapists should inquire about specific suicide plans. Clients who have already taken steps to enact their plans (such as obtaining a gun or pills, or tying a noose) or rehearsed the act are at increased risk. Further indicators of serious intent include making preparations for one's death, such as giving away prized possessions, making a will, and saying goodbye to loved ones. Suicidal clients with access to firearms pose further complications, as decisions must be made about whether and how restriction to firearms should be accomplished. Past suicide attempts and aborted attempts (e.g., putting a gun in one's mouth) are major risk factors for future suicide. Alcohol and substance use similarly increases suicide risk. In general, the clearer the intent, the higher the risk of suicide (Jacobs & Brewer, 2004).

The American Psychiatric Association's *Practice Guideline for the Assessment and Treatment of Patients with Suicidal Behaviors* states that "Suicide cannot be predicted and in some cases cannot be prevented, but an individual's suicide risk can be assessed and a treatment plan can be designed with the goal of reducing that risk" (2003, p. 380). Table 11.6 presents characteristics that therapists should use to evaluate clients who may be suicidal (American Psychiatric Association, 2003, p. 374).

Evaluation of suicidal risk includes assessment of both short-term and long-term risk factors as listed in Table 11.7 (Clark & Fawcett, 1992).

Following a thorough assessment of risk factors, intervention focuses on the suicidal client's immediate safety. Overall, research indicates that a combination of therapy and pharmacotherapy provides the best strategy for reducing suicidal behaviors. Therapy should be provided in the least restrictive environment that still protects clients' safety. As with therapy in general, the essential element in therapy with suicidal clients is a positive and sustaining therapeutic relationship. Therapy should focus on modifiable risk factors, such as removing access to lethal weapons, and on enhancing protecting factors like clients' social support systems. Therapy can help clients manage feelings of hopelessness, anxiety, and despair. It can also help counter clients' denial and foster insight into maladaptive patterns. No-harm contracts, though widely used, have not been found to reduce the risk of suicide. Therapists should not allow establishing a no-harm contract to reduce their vigilance. Additionally, such contracts are particularly likely to have limited utility with psychotic, impulsive, or new clients for whom little relationship has been established, or with clients in hospital emergency rooms.

Therapists occasionally try to leap to the rescue (often as an attempt to avoid the fear that they will be criticized if the client commits suicide) rather than recognizing that there is often little we can do to prevent a person intending to die from committing suicide. Unless the person is declaring immediate suicidal intent, hospitalization is usually not an option. Family members and significant others need to help reduce substance abuse and remove firearms. Some therapists try to meet the client's fantasy of being rescued by a powerful other by accepting phone calls at all hours or by seeing the client every day including weekends. Therapists are more useful to clients when they try to understand the intended effects of the completed suicide, which may include relief from unendurable

> For suicidal clients, a thorough suicide risk assessment that includes direct questions about suicide is essential. Initial interventions focus on the suicidal client's immediate safety and modifiable risk factors.

TABLE 11.6 Characteristics Evaluated in the Assessment of Clients With Suicidal Behavior

---

CURRENT PRESENTATION OF SUICIDALITY

- Suicidal or self-harming thoughts, plans, behaviors, and intent
- Specific methods considered for suicide, including their lethality and the client's expectation about lethality, as well as whether firearms are accessible
- Evidence of hopelessness, impulsiveness, anhedonia, panic attacks, or anxiety
- Reasons for living and plans for the future
- Alcohol or other substance use associated with the current presentation
- Thoughts, plans, or intentions of violence toward others

PSYCHIATRIC ILLNESSES

- Current signs and symptoms of psychiatric disorders with particular attention to mood disorders (primarily major depressive disorder or mixed episodes), schizophrenia, substance use disorders, anxiety disorders, and personality disorders (primarily borderline and antisocial personality disorders)
- Previous psychiatric diagnoses and treatments, including illness onset and course and psychiatric hospitalizations, as well as treatment for substance use disorders

HISTORY

- Previous suicide attempts, aborted suicide attempts, or other self-harming behaviors
- Previous or current medical diagnoses and treatments, including surgeries or hospitalizations
- Family history of suicide or suicide attempts or a family history of mental illness, including substance abuse

PSYCHOSOCIAL SITUATION

- Acute psychosocial crises and chronic psychosocial stressors, which may include actual or perceived interpersonal losses, financial difficulties or changes in socioeconomic status, family discord, domestic violence, and past or current sexual or physical abuse or neglect
- Employment status, living situation (including whether there are infants or children in the home), and presence or absence of external supports
- Family constellation and quality of family relationships
- Cultural or religious beliefs about death or suicide
- Individual strengths and vulnerabilities

TABLE 11.6 (continued)

COPING SKILLS

- Personality traits
- Past responses to stress
- Capacity for reality-testing
- Ability to tolerate psychological pain and satisfy psychological needs

pain, retaliation against a current significant other, or the desire to join a dead relative (Gabbard, 2000). Countertransference irritation and resentment tend to develop in therapists of suicidal clients, which contribute to therapists making ill-advised interventions, offering critical verbal or non-verbal responses, and ignoring clients' basic therapeutic needs. Some clients hold the threat of suicide over the therapist like a sword ready to be dropped if their therapist makes one false move.

TABLE 11.7 Short- and Long-Term Risk Factors for Suicide

SHORT-TERM

- Panic attacks
- Psychic anxiety
- Severe loss of pleasure and interests
- Depressive turmoil involving rapid switching of mood from anxiety to depression to anger or vice versa, alcohol abuse, diminished concentration, and global insomnia
- Substance abuse
- Recent adverse events
- Financial problems or unemployment
- Living alone
- Being widowed or divorced
- Male
- Age 60 or older

LONG-TERM

- Hopelessness
- Suicidal ideation
- Suicide intent
- Previous suicide attempts

Mental health trainees have between an 11 to 54 percent likelihood of losing a client to suicide during their training (Courtenay & Stephens, 2001; Dewar, Eagles, Klein, Gray, & Alexander, 2000; Kleespies, Penk, & Forsyth, 1993; McAdams & Foster, 2000). Practicing psychologists have approximately a 25 percent chance of this over the course of their entire careers (Chemtob, Hamada, Bauer, Torigoe, & Kinney, 1988; Pope & Tabachnick, 1995). Because it is not a rare event, client suicide is an occupational hazard for all mental health professionals. Indeed, mental health professionals rank suicidal clients as the most stressful aspect of their work (Deutsch, 1984). Therapists who lose a client to suicide respond in a manner similar to that of the death of a family member, with additional stressors including possible loss of professional esteem, malpractice lawsuits, and complaints to licensure boards (Chemtob et al., 1988).

Summary

Mood disorders (dysthymia and depression) are the most commonly diagnosed psychological problems among adults. Hence, specific knowledge and skills for working with depressed clients are essential for mental health professionals. Cognitive, behavioral, interpersonal, psychodynamic, and couple/relational techniques have displayed evidence for effectiveness with some clients experiencing depression. Cultural and gender-related beliefs should be considered. Assisting clients in altering their depressogenic patterns, potentially including depression-related neural circuits, appears central to the therapeutic endeavors.

For suicidal clients, a thorough suicide risk assessment that includes direct questions about suicide is essential. Initial interventions focus on the suicidal client's immediate safety and modifiable risk factors. Approximately 50–60% of depressed individuals have a favorable response to antidepressant medications. Overall, the central element in therapy with depressed and suicidal clients is a positive and sustaining therapeutic relationship.

CHAPTER 12

Anxiety and Panic Concerns

*You gain strength, courage, and confidence by every experience in which you
really stop to look fear in the face. . . . The danger lies in refusing to face the
fear, in not daring to come to grips with it. . . . You must make yourself
succeed every time. You must do the thing you think you cannot do.*
—ELEANOR ROOSEVELT

Everybody feels anxious and stressed from time to time. Situations like speaking in public, racing to meet deadlines, competing for limited opportunities, and meeting new people are often accompanied by feelings of anxiety. These feelings of unease are normal human responses to threatening or stressful situations.

Mild anxiety can improve people's performance by prompting them to be more alert and focused on challenging or threatening situations. For example, anxiety about performing poorly can prompt us to focus our attention and engage in additional preparation so that we avoid shame and embarrassment when performing the activity in front of others. Anxiety can be channeled into valuable creativity and productivity. Worries about one's worth help drive some people to contribute to the world. In contrast, however, more severe forms of anxiety can cause debilitating distress and major disruption of life activities. When anxiety becomes prolonged or severe, when it occurs in the absence of stressful triggers, or when it interferes with important aspects of everyday life, it is probably a problem worthy of professional attention.

There are six major anxiety disorders: specific phobia, social anxiety disorder (SAD), panic disorder (PD), posttramatic stress disorder (PTSD), obsessive-compulsive disorder (OCD), and generalized anxiety disorder (GAD). These anxiety disorders and the methods individuals use to avoid phobic stimuli are listed in Table 12.1.

TABLE 12.1   Phobic Stimuli and Forms of Avoidance in the Anxiety Disorders

DIAGNOSIS	PHOBIC STIMULI	AVOIDANCE STRATEGIES
Specific phobia	Animals, natural environment, blood, injection, injury	Avoidance of all situations containing phobic stimulus
SAD	Critical thoughts projected into the minds of others	Avoidance ranging from specific social activities to avoidance of all social contact
Panic Disorder	Places, body sensations, anger, separation	Avoidance of places, exercise, anger triggers, threats of separation
PTSD	Memories of traumatic events	Avoidance of reminders of the trauma, emotional numbness
OCD	Dirt, incomplete tasks, lack of symmetry, blasphemous thoughts	Rituals such as handwashing, checking, counting, ordering, prayer
GAD	Lack of money, job loss, school failure, poor health	Exhaustive worry, seeking of reassurance

The six major anxiety disorders have several components in common including: physical and cognitive experiences, catastrophic thinking (believing the worst will happen), a specific set of phobic stimuli (ideas or images that trigger the physical experiences and anxious thoughts), and methods of avoiding the phobic stimulus. The physical and cognitive experiences of anxiety are listed in Table 12.2.

Most clients who suffer from anxiety know they are exaggerating the risks but cannot stop themselves. They are able to self-reflect on the problem sufficiently to know that their worries are excessive but are unable to reduce those worries to a "normal" level. Catastrophic thinking, which involves imagining a low-probability event so vividly that the likelihood of its occurring seems to rise to 100%, is a common component of anxiety disorders. The thought of the feared event becomes a "ticking time bomb" in the head of the client—ready to go off at any moment and increasing the client's distress.

TABLE 12.2 Symptoms of Anxiety

Palpitations, rapid heart rate	Shortness of breath
Chest pain or discomfort	Hot or cold flashes
Nausea or diarrhea	Fear of dying, losing control, or going crazy
Abdominal distress	Depersonalization or derealization
Dizziness	Excessive worry
Sweating	Hypervigilance
Choking sensation	Irritability
Trembling or shaking	

Avoidance of the feared stimuli may be narrowly focused or broad. For example, some people with SAD experience performance anxiety in a limited number of situations whereas others fear almost any human contact. Some people experiencing agoraphobia fear only specific locations, like shopping malls or sporting events, whereas others cannot leave their houses without a "safe" other person. Anxious individuals' avoidance behaviors are maintained by the reduction of anticipatory anxiety about entering the feared situation, as well as the avoidance of fear by not encountering the phobic stimulus. In essence, the anxious person's inner dialogue about avoidance goes something like: "I successfully avoided the situation, thought, or feeling and did not become too anxious. Therefore, I'm going to avoid it again in the future!"

However, some clients with anxiety-related issues are not able to step back from their beliefs and instead firmly believe that what they think is true. One subset of such clients is convinced that they are deeply psychologically flawed (e.g., due to some nonmodifiable inner defect, others will reject or harm them if allowed the opportunity). A second subset of clients is certain that they have an undetected medical ailment (such as cancer, lead poisoning, or heart disease) despite the lack of supporting biomedical evidence. A third subset of clients "knows" that something terrible will happen if they do not perform certain rituals. These people are best described as delusional. Individuals who firmly believe in (and are unwilling to reconsider) their catastrophic expectations generally cannot be helped with psychotherapy alone, because they are unable to consider their beliefs as possibly false.

Therapy helps clients suffering from any type of problem change their neural circuitry. In the case of anxiety and panic, therapy helps clients gain greater cerebral control (self-reflective ability) over their limbic system's (primarily the amygdala) fear response.

Worry Circuits

A mind-brain approach to anxiety-related concerns utilizes the reasonable hypothesis that a *worry circuit* (or set of worry circuits) in the brain is hyperactive. Research on OCD implicates several brain structures including the orbitofrontal cortex, thalamus, and caudate. Mental health professionals, whether using therapy or pharmacotherapy, seek to help clients reduce the intensity of the worry circuit activity (Baxter et al., 1992; Rauch, Shin, & Wright, 2003). By helping clients with anxiety target their worry circuits, therapists provide clients with a more specific view of brain dysfunction than that afforded by the vague description "abnormal brain chemistry." This can be a more constructive way of viewing and addressing the problem (Schwartz, 1996). Therapy helps suffering clients change their abnormal circuitry. In the case of anxiety and panic, therapy helps clients gain greater cerebral control (self-reflective ability) over their limbic system's (primarily the amygdala) fear response (Viamontes, Beitman, Viamontes & Viamontes, 2005).

Worry circuits can be activated via the increasingly vicious spirals common to most of the anxiety disorders (especially to social phobia, panic attacks, OCD, and GAD). This type of anxiety spiral is illustrated in the following example. When a socially anxious person begins to talk, the listeners' eyebrows might elevate (in a show of attentiveness). However, the anxious person interprets this eyebrow movement (or other nonverbal behavior) as criticism. This causes the socially anxious individual to become distracted and wander off the topic. The listener might cough, which the socially anxious person interprets as a clear indicator of growing criticism (after all, he or she wandered off the topic). The listener may look concerned, which the speaker takes to mean yet greater criticism. The anxious person's heart begins to race and voice begins to tremble. The listener may glance away, leading the speaker to become convinced that he or she is being rejected. As the panic escalates, the socially anxious person may faint, freeze, or flee, and subsequently increase their efforts to avoid such horrible and doomed situations in the future.

Therapy helps clients gain greater cortical control (self-reflective and planning ability) over their limbic system's (primarily the amygdala) fear responses.

Panic attacks involve similar spirals. In this case, a physical sensation rather than a raised eyebrow may be the trigger. The trigger might be chest pain, a headache, or an odd feeling in the abdomen. The odd sensation spurs catastrophic thinking, which increases firing of the fear-responsive amygdalas that increase many different bodily sensations like chest discomfort. The resulting increase in bodily sensation is interpreted as catastrophic, building quickly to a crescendo of panic attack. The hypervigilant brain then seeks out such sensations. After a few episodes, the brain is trained to respond to minor shifts in body states—it has learned to be afraid.

The Meaning of Anxiety

Anxiety symptoms can be viewed from two sometimes contradictory perspectives: as "bad things" to be eliminated, or as signals of psychological concerns to be attended to. Perceiving anxiety as "a message from yourself to you" can turn stumbling blocks into potential stepping stones. More specifically, anxiety can be reframed from a negative experience to be avoided or eliminated into a valuable message that should be attended to and that can increase self-awareness. Among the underlying messages of anxiety are fear of not living up to one's standard of moral behavior, fear of one's anger, fear of separation, and fear of loss, annihilation, and death.

Predispositions

Genetics and life experience both contribute to the development of anxiety concerns. For example, specific phobias may have been evolutionarily adaptive by helping early humans avoid snakes, spiders, and other potentially dangerous animals. Social anxiety involving sensitivity to anger, criticism, and other forms of social disapproval may have protected early humans from expulsion.

For specific individuals, a mix of physiological predispositions and environmental events seem to create the anxiety syndromes. For example, some children show a tendency early in their lives toward "behavioral inhibition to the unfamiliar" (Kagan, Reznick, & Snidman, 1988). Such children are easily frightened by strange things in

> To view anxiety as a "message from yourself to you" can be helpful. Clients can reframe their anxiety as the opportunity to discover specific fears with which they need to come to terms.

their environment. Compared to children without anxiety concerns, they are significantly more likely to have parents with two or more anxiety disorders (Rosenbaum, et al. 1992). In addition to passing their genetic inheritance, these parents probably teach their already anxiety-susceptible children that the world is a dangerous place in which to live. Most anxiety symptoms worsen under stress and abate in calm circumstances.

General Considerations in Treating Anxiety

Researchers and practitioners have identified numerous general considerations when treating people with anxiety-related concerns. In particular various methods of exposing clients to their fears, family therapy, and medications are discussed.

Exposure

Exposure, also called *facing the fear* or *desensitization*, is central to successful therapy for anxiety-related concerns. The actual process of confronting the feared stimulus may not require self-reflection beyond awareness of the degree of anxiety generated by the exposure. Sometimes during the process of exposure, memories of related anxieties, new understandings of distortions associated with the fear, and other insights may emerge for self-reflective processing. Many variations in exposure treatments are required for each category of anxiety disorder due to differences in the qualities of the feared stimulus and variations in individuals' forms of avoidance. General forms of exposure include the following:

Systematic Desensitization
Systematic desensitization can be either *in vivo* (live) or imagined. It involves slowly approaching the feared idea, situation, or image in little steps. Therapists use subjective units of distress (SUD) by having clients rate themselves on a scale from 1 (no anxiety) to 10 (or 100; extreme anxiety). If clients are reexperiencing a traumatic memory or imagining a future frightening event, they

> Identifying the phobic stimulus and associated cognitions, and encouraging exposure, are fundamental to the treatment of anxiety-related disorders.

can limit their exposure if their SUD ratings get too high. They can also report their SUD ratings afterward as a way to measure success or failure of their exposure efforts. Whether real or imagined, the stimuli used depend on the disorder being addressed. In agoraphobia, for example, research suggests that real-life exposure works much better than imagination (Barlow, Esler, & Vitali, 1998). For traumatic memories, imagining alone can be effective because the traumatic event cannot be recreated. Phobic images can be practiced as if they are happening now. They can also be rehearsed for the future possibility of repetition.

Mass Practice, Implosion, or Flooding

This involves remaining in the feared situation (*in vivo* or imagined) for a long time until the very intense anxiety dissipates. Some research suggests that this method may be more cost-effective than slower and more gradual approaches; however, clients may be less likely to accept it because of the intense anxiety that accompanies it (Barlow, Esler, & Vitali, 1998). As an extreme example, a busload of individuals with agoraphobia could be driven downtown, dropped off, and instructed to use the support of their colleagues for 4 hours until their intense anxiety dissipates. For most, the anxiety would be heightened initially but would then gradually recede.

Cognitive Interventions

Cognitive interventions assist clients in better understanding their thoughts as they pertain to their worries and fears. What do they fear is going to happen? What are they saying to themselves about this situation? What is the basis for this concern? Is it reasonable? Therapists help clients develop more adaptive cognitions for their current situation and learn to engage in this process with future concerns. Building additional psychosocial skills also increases the likelihood of success with tasks involving their fears in the future.

Turn Stumbling Blocks Into Stepping Stones

Reframing helps clients understand the advantages in the process of facing their fears. What can be learned from the process of exposure? For example, individuals afraid of rejection by strangers can view this as an opportunity to initiate conversations in which they can practice

their rejection management skills if rejection should occur. People terrified of losing their jobs can be encouraged to examine the advantages of
job loss. Individuals with fear of anger can examine the value of anger
as well as its frightening qualities during exposure. In crisis there is
opportunity.

Paradox

This involves directing clients to intentionally experience the symptoms of anxiety freely, frequently, and to an extreme (ultimately laugh-
able or absurd) degree. Essentially, clients are directed to do or to wish
to have happen whatever it is that they most fear (Frankl, 1966). For
example, clients afraid to urinate in public restrooms could be
instructed to go into the restroom and do everything associated with the
act—but under no circumstances are they to urinate. Clients who
always try to be "nice" and please others due to their fear of rejection
can be instructed to make sure that none of their wants get met in their
interpersonal interactions. Individuals fearful of not pleasing their
partner in sexual interactions may be instructed not to have an orgasm.
In each case, the prescription of the symptom may unburden the
symptom bearers by allowing them to face their fears and to find that
nothing terrible has happened. In some cases the exaggeration of the
symptoms can be humorous. For example, a client who was uncomfortable with others looking at her was invited to rent an outrageous cos-
tume and parade down a street. She had a great time! This can be
beneficial: By shifting the context from serious to funny, clients' problematic patterns may become less rigid and oppressive. (See Seltzer,
1986, for an extensive review of paradoxical approaches.)

Mindfulness Meditation

Increasing evidence and popular use of mindfulness meditation are
leading therapists to incorporate the practice into their treatment plans
(Kabat-Zinn, 1990). Whereas most therapies essentially attempt to take
apart, analyze, confront, or otherwise directly eliminate problematic
anxious thoughts, the mindfulness meditation approach allows clients
to accept their thoughts and "let them go." The relatively simple
description of this process ("accept your thoughts and let them go") is
deceptive. In practice, mindfulness meditation requires training of the
brain that is generally not taught in Western approaches to the mind. A
neurobiology of mindfulness is being developed with research evidence

supporting its effectiveness (Davidson et al., 2003; Reibel, Greeson, Brainard, & Rosenzweig, 2001).

Family Therapy

Anxiety, like depression, usually occurs in an interpersonal context—clients' anxiety may be triggered by disturbed relationships with important others. Anxiety disorders can have a tremendous impact on family systems. For example, family members of clients with OCD sometimes allow themselves to give in to the client's excessive demands for orderliness, cleanliness, or following of specific rituals (Gabbard, 2000). Some families, for instance, continue to buy new clothes instead of waiting for the individual with OCD to complete excessively detailed clothes-washing rituals. In such situations, the hidden familial resentments can be quite intense. It should also be noted that treatment of anxiety disorders can threaten homeostasis. For example, the partners of some agoraphobic and socially phobic clients may be secretly comforted by the fact that they know exactly where their partners are (i.e., always at home). Successful therapy may create anxiety in the client's partner because the client starts developing a wider social network—perhaps threatening the partner with loss of control and fear of abandonment.

Help from supportive family members in facing fears generally benefits individuals with OCD (Mehta, 1990) and agoraphobia (Barlow, O'Brien, & Last, 1984). Having significant others understand these disorders and how they may be treated can be invaluable in overcoming interpersonal barriers to change. Friends and family members can also be encouraged to help resolve the difficulties caused by the disorder.

Pharmacotherapy

Clients with anxiety disorders are often also depressed or abusing substances. The decision of whether to use therapy, medications, or both depends on several factors including clients' preferences, the intensity of their symptoms (more intense symptoms indicate greater appropriateness of medications), and therapists' abilities and beliefs.

Medications may be used as the major treatment modality or as an adjunct to therapy. As an adjunct to therapy, pharmacotherapy may allow clients to pursue their exposure treatment as well as treat cooccurring concerns like depression. Some people assert that medications directly relieve the symptoms of the disorder. These individuals tend to believe that medications exclusively should be used to treat anxiety-related concerns, as neurobiological changes seem to accompany anxiety disorders. This perspective ignores that fact that therapy techniques also are associated with corrective changes in brain function (Baxter et al., 1992).

Table 12.3 presents an overview of antianxiety medications. Medications for the anxiety disorders include most of the antidepressants and the benzodiazepines. The first choice is usually one of the newer antidepressants, including the SSRIs like paroxetine (Paxil). Conversly, no current medication has demonstrated effectiveness in the treatment of simple phobias. For obsessive-compulsive disorder, serotonin reuptake inhibitor medications are particularly valuable. Benzodiazepines should be used for only the most acutely anxious clients because of their high potential for abuse and long-term dependence. Serotonin reuptake medications can be problematic because they frequently cause sexual side effects, including decreased sexual drive and inability to achieve orgasm. Buspirone appears effective primarily in GAD. Gabapentin may be useful in several disorders including SAD, panic disorder, and GAD. Many clients do not respond to a single medication, leaving their provider to try untested combinations of medications.

Because most medication clinical trials have been short-term, it is difficult to make generalizations about the long-term effectiveness of medications. It is likely that after treatment discontinuation, therapy has more favorable results because clients likely have "learned something" useful in preventing relapse. In contrast, clients treated with

TABLE 12.3   Medications for the Anxiety Disorders

ANXIETY CONCERN	ANTIDEPRESSANTS	BENZODIAZEPINES	OTHERS
Specific Phobia	–	–	–
Social Phobia	++	+	Beta blockers
Panic	++	+	Ondansetron
PTSD	++	Not recommended	Anticonvulsants
OCD	*++	+	Neurosurgery
GAD	++	+	Buspirone

++ denotes first choice; + denotes second choice; * indicates that serotonin-enhancing medications are required.

medications alone have relied solely on the effect of the medication. Individuals most likely to relapse after therapy are likely to have had incomplete remission of symptoms, to have comorbid psychiatric disorders, or to have experienced a stressful life event. An interesting future challenge will be to develop ways to teach clients to maintain their medication-induced brain state after medications are discontinued following successful remission of symptoms.

The Six Major Anxiety Disorders

This section address each of the six major anxiety disorders in detail, first describing the disorder and then suggesting psychotherapeutic approaches.

Specific Phobias

Five subtypes of specific phobias are included in DSM-IV-TR: animal (e.g., snakes, spiders), natural environmental (e.g., water, heights), blood/injection/injury (e.g., needles, dentists), situational (e.g., bridges, elevators, flying), and other. The "other" category includes fears that do not fit into the first four, including fears of choking, vomiting, or contracting an illness. Approximately 7–11% of the general population experiences a specific phobia at some time in their lives. The specific phobias differ along several dimensions, including age of onset and gender. For example, the mean age of onset for animal, blood, storm, and water phobias tends to be early childhood, while the mean age of onset for height phobia is adolescence. Women are at least twice as likely to have animal phobias compared to men, whereas height and blood/injection phobias are more evenly distributed (Barlow, Esler, & Vitali, 1998).

Treatment Approaches

In vivo exposure is generally accepted as the most powerful treatment for specific phobias. Although the principle of exposure may be simple to describe, many subtleties emerge. Therapists must first gather information about the client's specific feelings, thoughts, and behaviors concerning the feared object or situation. Clients are informed that *in vivo* exposure works and that all exposures will be predictable and under their control. Clients can be taught to challenge cognitive distortions that arise during exposure and use relax-ation responses to reduce anxiety. Research has demonstrated that intense, prolonged exposure yields the best and quickest results for animal, injection, and blood phobias, although many clients are reluctant to take this option. In addition, research findings suggest that the presence of the therapist in one session of *in vivo* exposure dramatically increases the likelihood of a positive outcome for spider and snake phobias compared to self-directed exposure. Certain pho-bias may require additional refinement. For example, people with injection phobias commonly faint upon exposure. In order to prevent fainting, clients can be taught *applied tension*—tensing and relaxing all large muscle groups of the body including arms, torso, and legs for five cycles of 15 seconds each before exposure to an injection. Applied tension counteracts the drop in blood pressure and pulse (vasovagal syncope). The specific phobias are not simple to treat; each class may require different variations on the exposure theme (Barlow, Esler, Vitali, 1998). Also note that pharmacotherapy is not useful for the specific phobias.

Social Anxiety Disorder

SAD involves fear of embarrassment or humiliation in social situations. Fear of public speaking is the most common of all social phobias. The anxiety associated with social phobia can be so intense that people avoid social situations completely.

SAD is the most common anxiety disorder, with a lifetime preva-lence of about 13% and a 12-month prevalence of 8% (Kessler et al., 1994). It is the third most common mental disorder after major depres-sive disorder and alcohol dependence. Onset often occurs around age 13 and rarely begins after age 25. Approximately half of individuals with social anxiety report specific phobias, as well as substance abuse, major depression or OCD (Barlow, Esser, & Vitali, 1998).

Unlike the specific phobias, the phobic stimulus is not perceivable by anyone other than the client. With SAD, the phobic stimulus is clients' perception of critical, rejecting, humiliating, or embarrassing thoughts in the minds of other people. For example, people with SAD are likely to be concerned that others will judge them as stupid, crazy, inadequate, weak, or anxious. The avoidance of social contact can be situation-specific, such as speaking in front of a group (narrow band avoidance) to complete withdrawal from human contact (avoidant personality disorder). Such individuals typically recognize that their fear is out of proportion to the threat involved in the situation.

Treatment Approaches

The exposure requires the client to repeatedly confront the feared situation until the anxiety response diminishes. Exposure is best conducted *in vivo* with the stimulus encountered in the natural environment (Barlow, Esser, & Vitali, 1998). Role playing with the therapist and group therapy can also be very useful by exposing clients to other people in a safer environment. Individuals are most likely to benefit if they remain in the anxiety-provoking situation until they experience at least a 50% reduction in self-reported anxiety. The SUD scale can be useful in monitoring the degree of anxiety experienced. Therapists may need to encourage clients to be fully engaged in the exposure rather than being distracted by background noise, speaking quickly, or avoiding eye contact. Because they fear their anxiety, clients often fail to perform agreed-upon homework assignments because the initial assignment proves too difficult (raises their anxiety).

As mentioned earlier, socially phobic people perceive others as being critical of them. In reality the critical thoughts in the minds of others are rarely as intense or pervasive as socially phobic people believe they are. So where does the idea of the critical thought arise? It must arise from the mind of the socially phobic person, who projects the critical thought onto the mind of the others. Therapists attempt to correct this cognitive distortion by more accurately defining the source of the phobic stimulus. For some clients, looking into the historical antecedents for this belief is helpful. For example, highly critical parents or painful peer-rejection experiences sensitize some people to social anxiety. These clients seem to have internalized the views of parents, caretakers, siblings, or peers who have shamed, criticized, ridiculed, humiliated, abandoned, or embarrassed them. These internalized views are probably established early in life and then repeatedly projected onto persons in the environment (Gabbard, 2000). A review of these forces and their manifestation in the transference relationship may also be useful.

Therapists treating socially phobic clients must ensure that the feared situation is carefully defined. The following case studies illustrate the importance of defining the feared situation.

Melissa, a bright female in her mid-twenties, avoided most all social inter-actions. She was especially fearful of interacting with strangers and of talking in groups. She had both a highly critical, opinionated parent and traumatic peer-rejection experiences during adolescence. Melissa's non-verbal communication included rolling her shoulders forward, looking down, avoiding eye contact, and not smiling. In interpersonal situations that she could not avoid, she spoke haltingly, as little as possible, and in a very soft voice. She was highly critical of herself (and of others), depressed, pes-simistic about ever being "normal," and said she "just wanted to die." She had coped with her highly critical parent and with rejection during adoles-cence by avoiding interpersonal interactions in general.

Melissa's social anxiety was generalized. The client in the following case experienced a very different form of social anxiety.

Van, a single man in his late twenties, was able to initiate and maintain con-versations with other men and older women with relative comfort, but he was quite fearful of talking to young women whom he found attractive. Growing up, Van had limited, predominantly unsuccessful experiences with attempting to talk with girls to whom he was attracted. He had subse-quently directed his efforts toward school and work and avoided contact with potential romantic partners.

Van's social anxiety was more restricted. Therapy in both cases sought to reduce anxiety associated with each client's specific feared stimulus, to provide graded exposure to the specific feared stimulus, and to address their specific underlying cognitions. Salient social skills deficits were also addressed.

Social-skills training may be a particularly useful supplement to exposure for individuals with SAD (see Chapter 10). When clients improve their social skills, they are likely to improve their real-world performance and are thus likely to receive more favorable responses from others. Common content for social-skills instruction with SAD includes: nonverbal attending skills (e.g., holding one's head up, shoul-ders back, making eye contact, smiling, and managing extraneous body movements), self-management skills (positive self-talk, slow deep breathing, keeping body posture flexible and relaxed), conversation skills (how to initiate, sustain, and conclude informal conversations), and friendship and relationship skills (where and how to meet and develop friendships and romantic partners). These skills can be discussed, demonstrated, rehearsed in session, and then practiced in the real world. In the case examples mentioned earlier, both clients benefited from social skills enhancement directed to their specific needs. Melissa's interpersonal encounters improved when she lifted her head and looked at people with whom she was communicating. Van's social interactions improved when he cognitively reframed his task as that of helping put the other person at ease.

Generalized Anxiety Disorder

GAD is characterized by chronic anxiety that lasts for at least 6 months and is not accompanied by phobias, obsessions, or panic attacks. The phobic stimuli for generalized anxiety disorder consist of common human concerns brought to the brink of continuing terror. Typically these feared stimuli include: imagined catastrophes related to work, school, health, relationships, and finance. Symptoms of GAD include restlessness or feeling on edge, fatigue, concentration difficulties, irritability, and sleep disturbance.

The lifetime prevalence of GAD is about 5% with a 12-month prevalence of 3% (Kessler, et al., 1994). Clients with GAD usually report being worriers most of their lives. GAD may be more frequent among women, African-Americans, young adults, and persons with low income or low occupational status; environmental contextual factors may contribute to the baseline worries of individuals within these groups. It may be among the most common anxiety disorders—although only approximately 10% actually seek treatment (Borkovec & Roemer, 1996). The overlap with major depression (concentration difficulties, irritability, and sleep disturbance) indicates that the two disorders may be difficult to distinguish and that clients with GAD often have depression as well.

The anxiety-related thoughts associated with GAD spiral like those of OCD, SAD, and panic attacks, but they also differ in an important way. GAD anxiety spirals are cued by a wider variety of stimuli that interact with each other to propel the spiral into increasing intensity. Because the early phase of the cycles are easier to slow down, the earlier in the sequence the growing spiral is identified, the easier it is to stop it.

Treatment Approaches

Clients can equip themselves with increased ability to self-reflect, a list of the cues, and the willingness to consider their scary thoughts and images as hypotheses about themselves and others rather than as truth. Anxiety moves into spirals not because people with GAD are actually threatened, but rather because they react with anxiety to their anxious reactions. It is theorized that GAD is sustained by "basic fears" such as fear of losing control, fear of not being able to cope, fear of failure, fear of rejection or abandonment, and fear of death and disease (Beck & Emory, 1985). The individual elements of worry spirals include catastrophic images, scary thoughts, physical reactions like rapid heart rate and sweating, anxious and depressed emotions, and common behavioral reactions like subtle avoidance or procrastination. Each of these elements can act as a cue that something is indeed wrong. The longer a person engages in worrying, the more ideas and images can be incorporated in the chain of associations (Borkovec & Roemer, 1996). GAD can be aggravated by a variety of situations that elicit stress and fear—relationship conflicts, demands for increased performance, and so on.

GAD treatment approaches help clients develop more flexible responses to their anxiety cues. Clients are encouraged to keep diaries listing the cues, to develop corrective thoughts, and to learn relaxation exercises or meditation. This helps clients become more aware of incipient spirals triggered by a cue ("my house will be repossessed by the bank") and follow those cues with an alternative image or thought ("I have enough savings to survive for 6 months if I lose my job"). Clients can learn to "let go" of these frightening images and thoughts (Borkovec & Roemer, 1996). Many also find bibliotherapy (the use of assigned psychoeducational readings on the subject) useful (e.g., Burne, 2000).

Clearly examining the feared ideas and images helps to bring the worry process itself under control. Using the "anxiety equation" (Table 12.4), clients can challenge the probability of the negative consequences and work on increasing their resources to cope with the negative consequences should they begin to happen.

Overestimation of threat or danger can be addressed by defining the probability that the feared consequence will take place. For example, a

---

TABLE 12.4   Anxiety Equation

$$\text{Excessive Anxiety} = \frac{\text{Overestimation of threat or danger}}{\text{Underestimation of coping resources}}$$

---

man in his thirties was fearful that his house would catch fire and his mother would burn to death while he was at work. Using the anxiety equation, he examined how likely it was that his house would catch fire while he worked and, if the house did catch fire, how likely was it that his mother would not escape. (His mother was a 55-year-old woman in good health.)

Underestimation of coping resources can be addressed by listing various ways of helping oneself, including internal resources like problem-solving ability, recalling past successes in similar situations, external resources like supportive friends and family, professional help, and spiritual assistance. For many clients, it is easier to increase awareness and use of coping resources than it is to reduce the overestimation of threat and danger.

Excessive worry can also be viewed as a distraction from more disturbing underlying concerns, unwanted emotions (e.g., anger, grief, sadness, resentment), unwanted memories (e.g., sexual abuse), or unwanted physical sensations. Problems in family, work, and other relationships may trigger anxiety about health and money when disturbing problems in key interpersonal relationships arise (Gabbard, 2000).

Posttraumatic Stress Disorder

PTSD is characterized by intense anxiety-related symptoms following a traumatic event. With PTSD, the phobic stimulus is not the traumatic event itself, but rather the *memory* of the event. Aspects of the memory sometime involuntarily intrude on conscious awareness, creating uncontrolled triggers for anxiety. Individuals with PTSD feel compelled to be constantly vigilant due to the unremitting risk of intrusive, highly unpleasant thoughts and images. Avoiding memory activation requires numbing of responsiveness to oneself as well as avoiding potential reminders.

The distinctive symptom clusters of PTSD are:

- *Intrusive symptoms* including unexpected thoughts of the trauma, nightmares, unanticipated reliving of aspects of the trauma event (flashbacks), preoccupation with the event, and hyperresponsiveness both physiologically and psychologically to cues of the trauma.
- *Avoidance* of reminders of the trauma (thoughts, people, and places), emotional numbing to many emotional situations, and dampening of most positive and negative human emotions (as a way to avoid feeling anxiety associated with the traumatic memory)
- *Hyperarousal* involving being easily startled, sleeping difficulties, difficulties paying attention, hypervigilance, irritability and excessive anger or rage.

The quality of the trauma plays a primary role in determining whether or not PTSD emerges. People who have experienced torture, such as concentration camp survivors and prisoners of war, have prevalence rates of approximately 50–75%. The prevalence rate among combat veterans is about 30%. Among people who have been exposed to natural disasters such as earthquakes, hurricanes, volcanic eruptions, and fires, the rate is approximately 4–16%. The most frequently studied traumatic events are rape, assault, and combat, but the most common precipitating event among persons with PTSD could be the sudden, unexpected loss of a loved one (Breslau, Kessler, & Chilcoat, 1998).

People's interpretation of the event may play a crucial role in whether or not PTSD symptoms follow. For this reason the DSM-IV-TR includes the following criterion: "the person's response involved intense fear, helplessness, or horror. (Note: In children, it may be expressed instead by disorganized or agitated behavior")" (APA, 2000, p. 468; Gabbard, 2000). In recovery, the ability to self-reflect may play a crucial role in helping survivors of trauma to rework their significantly distorted cognitive-emotional map of current reality.

The PTSD syndrome abates within 2 to 3 years for the majority of trauma survivors. Unfortunately, for the minority of individuals who remain symptomatic, symptoms tend to increase in severity, and these individuals also tend to develop depression, other anxiety disorders, and substance abuse (Yehuda et al., 1994). Additional factors associated with increased risk for developing chronic PTSD include: the severity of the trauma; a prior history of trauma, abuse, and stress; a history of psychiatric problems; genetic predispositions including a family history of psychopathology; subsequent exposure to reactivating situations; and current coping strategies (Yehuda, Marshall, & Giller, 1998). Much more research is required to define differential treatments for different types of traumatic events such as domestic violence, robbery, hostage situations, automobile accidents, natural disasters, traumatic deaths of loved ones, sexual abuse, rape, and torture. More research on client compounding factors (comorbidities) and historical predispositions is also needed.

Most of the therapeutic and psychopharmacological treatment trials have involved Americans returning from Vietnam (usually men) and victims of rape and sexual assault (usually women). How well the results of these research treatment trials generalize to other categories of trauma is unclear. Men report higher frequency of exposure to traumatic events whereas women report greater frequencies of PTSD. This difference may be due to the quality of the stimulus (rape versus other forms of violence) as well as gender differences as seen in higher rates of reported and diagnosed depression in women (Egan, 1998).

Treatment Approaches

All therapeutic approaches for PTSD include exposure to the phobic memory. This does not mean talking *about* what happened but rather *reliving* the experience as thoroughly as possible. The reliving requires immersion in all physical sensations, emotions, and thoughts associated with the traumatic event, as well as experiences (e.g., helplessness, severe isolation) and guilty thoughts about how the trauma could have been avoided or was deserved ("If only I had done . . ." or "I really deserved it then and deserve to suffer now"). Unfortunately clients who have had serial traumas may never be able to go through all the details of multiple terrifying experiences adequately. Exposure generally involves incremental increase in duration and intensity within the limits of clients' ability to tolerate the exposure and feel in control. For some clients reexposure further traumatizes them so that they must learn stronger inhibitors of anxiety activation.

Clients vary in their ability to tolerate the tremendous waves of emotion engendered in reliving their memories. The use of SUD ratings to moderate their experiences helps tailor the exposure to the tolerance of

> Severe trauma affects brain functioning involving the hippocampus (the memory server) and the amygdala (the judge of emotional intensity). Trauma creates a hyper-intense response by the amygdala preventing ordinary storage of memory in the cerebral cortex through the hippocampus. Exposure appears to activate aspects of the prefrontal cortex that can diminish the hyper-response to trauma cues.

each client. Therapists should consider helping clients change the thoughts generated during and after the traumatic events (e.g., "I'll never get over this"; "I wish I were dead"; or "No one ever really cared about me"). Review of reminders of previous but less intense traumatic events and clients' attributed reasons for them may help maintain recovery.

Research indicates that severe trauma affects brain functioning involving the hippocampus (the memory server) and the amygdala (the judge of emotional intensity). A simple brain model of PTSD and its treatment involves the activation of a hyper-intense response during the trauma by the amygdala. This response prevents ordinary storage of memory in the cerebral cortex through the hippocampus. Exposure appears to activate aspects of the prefrontal cortex that can diminish the hyperresponse to trauma cues (Viamontes et al., 2005).

Eye movement desensitization and reprocessing (EMDR) has gained preliminary research and clinical support in the treatment of PTSD (Shapiro, 1995). Detailed in Table 12.5, Keane (1998) noted that its first 5 components have much in common with the exposure approaches mentioned earlier.

Like the standard cognitive-behavioral approaches, the theoretical basis of EMDR effectiveness is related to integration of fragmented aspects of the traumatic experience (behavior, affect, sensation, and cognitions) by steadily increasing the "dose" of exposure. Clients are assisted in repeatedly recreating and dismissing their traumatic memories. This gives them a sense of mastery regarding their ability to manipulate mentally disturbing psychological events. However, the eye movement aspect that separates EMDR from other approaches is also supported by weak reference to unknown neurobiological actions that may be related to the rapid eye movement (REM) of dreaming sleep. Shapiro (1995) stated that there is a special neurobiological mechanism but could not articulate it (Allen & Lewis, 1996). The eye processing component of EMDR may be useful as a point of distraction, allowing clients to avoid hyperarousal by partially attending to their trauma memories while also directing part of their attention elsewhere.

Reprocessing of memories by exposure does not eliminate memories but rather aids development of "conditioned inhibition" via cre-

TABLE 12.5   The Six Components of EMDR Trauma Treatment

1.	Evocation of trauma-relevant images and memories
2.	Psychological evaluation of the painful qualities of these images/memories
3.	Identification (with or without therapist assistance) of an alternative cognitive evaluation of the image/memory
4.	Examination of physiological reactions to the image/memory
5.	Focus on individually determined positive appraisals of the image/memory
6.	Repeated sets of conscious lateral eye movements (like those sleep) (Keane, 1998).

ation of new memory associations. There are a variety of associative pathways that will activate a memory. New associations allow clients to avoid becoming immersed in a fixed, reverberating, and escalating circuit. Desensitization takes place through four primary domains:

- Temporal: Learning to distinguish the past from the present.
- Cognitive: Elaborating new meanings that are incompatible with the traumatic memory.
- Behavioral: Learning new behaviors while reliving the experience. For example, instead of cringing while remembering, clients can learn to hold their heads up.
- Interpersonal: Experiencing secure attachment to the therapist in conjunction with talking about and remembering the traumatic experience to counteract the loss of trust engendered by the terrifying event (Allen & Lewis, 1996)

Treatment of individuals who have endured prolonged and repeated trauma is often complex and difficult. Understandably, these individuals may be very reluctant or unwilling to relive their traumatic events. Similarly, therapists may be so appalled by the horror of extensive torture or repeated sexual abuse that they involuntarily withdraw from listening or experience vicarious (secondary) traumatization themselves. For most clients, trauma loosens their belief in the "just world" and "goodness of the people." They trust others with much greater difficulty and may blame themselves for what happened rather than believe they live in a world where violence is random (Gabbard, 2000).

Panic Disorder

Panic disorder is characterized by recurrent, sudden, unexpected attacks of extreme anxiety or intense fear. Panic disorder may also involve persistent anxiety about having another attack and avoidance of situations that the individual believes might trigger an attack, like shopping malls and crowds (agoraphobia). Fears of major medical illnesses are also common. As noted earlier, panic attacks can be accompanied by physical or cognitive symptoms such as palpitations, chest pain or discomfort, shortness of breath, dizziness, sweating, numbness or tingling, hot or cold flashes, abdominal discomfort, nausea or diarrhea, depersonalization or derealization, and fear of dying, going crazy, or losing control. Panic episodes can last from a few minutes to several hours. The usual length of time is less than 10 minutes, with many lasting less than a minute. They come in ranges of intensity from mild and brief to intense and long. Long, intense attacks can be very exhausting.

Approximately one-third to one-half of the population will or has experienced a panic attack at some time in their lives. The lifetime prevalence of panic disorder is about 3–5%, and the 1-month prevalence about 1.5%. Twice as many women as men report having panic disorder, with the usual age of onset being late teens and early twenties. Panic disorder often runs in families, and stressful life events often occur before the onset of the disorder (Roy-Byrne & Cowley, 1998). These events tend to be connected to alterations in the level of expectations placed on clients, including changes in job responsibilities and losses of central figures in their lives. Clients with panic disorder often perceive their parents as threatening, temperamental, critical, controlling, demanding, and unsupportive. A theme of "feeling trapped" also emerges (Cooper, & Klerman, 1991).

The phobic stimuli include: fear of being someplace that might cause a panic attack, amplified bodily sensations (Barlow & Craske, 1994), and fear of intense anger and imagined separation from an important other (Milrod, Busch, Cooper, & Shapiro, 1997). Intense anger and separation fears may also create a vicious spiral: The client's anger threatens the connection with a significant other, which increases the client's fear of separation, which increases the client's anger at the potentially deserting other (see Figure 12.1). Panic clients seem to have difficulty modulating the normal oscillation between separation and attachment because they fear the loss of their freedom and fear the loss of interpersonal safety and protection. They may then try to operate within a narrow interpersonal band, trying to avoid too much separation and too much attachment. Their parents, lovers, and spouses may experience them as very controlling (Gabbard, 2000).

In addition, the out-of-awareness triggering of a traumatic memory or unresolved grief can also induce panic attacks. Interestingly, except for panic in response to some physical sensations, clients are not aware of these phobic stimuli, which makes the panic seem to come "out of the blue" or be spontaneous. However, a trigger for panic attacks can often be found. The panic attack itself can serve as an avoidance of awareness of hidden, frightening images and memories.

Treatment Approaches

Therapy requires exposure to the feared stimuli once they are identified. In the treatment of agoraphobia, clients usually construct a list of situations that are increasingly anxiety-provoking and then gradually and persistently proceed through them. For example, fear of driving outside the city limits can be approached by first driving 100 yards, then

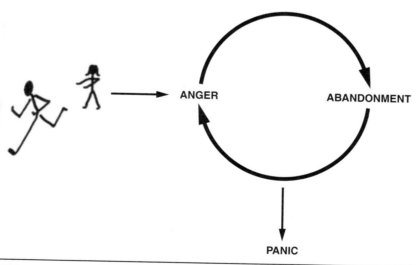

FIGURE 12.1   Abandonment–Anger Spiral

200 yards, then 300 yards past the city limits. This "baby steps" process makes many clients feel foolish, but in conjunction with encouragement from a partner and therapist it can effectively dissolve clients' fears over time. There is no substitute for doing the exposure *in vivo*. There is some evidence that for clients with agoraphobia so severe that they have difficulty leaving the house, therapist contacts by phone can be quite useful. For milder forms, pamphlets describing how to go about gradually desensitizing oneself to feared situations can be effective (Barlow, Esler, & Vitali, 1998).

For many clients, amplified bodily sensations trigger a vicious spiral of terror: "I feel chest pain; maybe I am having a heart attack!" This frightening idea leads to increased heart rate. The increased heart rate leads to greater chest discomfort. The greater chest discomfort confirms the belief that a heart attack is coming. Panic control therapy includes three components: (1) exposure to interoceptive (physical) sensations similar to ones that trigger panic attacks (e.g., clients who fear heart attacks are asked to run up stairs to increase heart rate), (2) addressing the thoughts that interpret the sensations as catastrophic, and (3) breathing retraining to correct hyperventilation as well as to incorporate the calm that comes from breathing-focused meditation (Barlow & Craske, 1994). Direct focus on cognitions has also been shown to be beneficial (Beck & Emery, 1985)

When the phobic stimuli are rage and separation, clients may need to examine the manner in which they avoid these experiences and ideas. Panic attacks themselves may be viewed as ways to avoid anger, as can a focus on somatic sensations and catastrophic illness. Fears of separation as well as bursts of anger may also appear in relationship to the therapist, providing an immediate opportunity for facing these fears in an interpersonal context.

Obsessive-Compulsive Disorder

OCD is characterized by recurring, persistent, uncontrollable, and unwanted thoughts or feelings (obsessions) and rituals or routines via which people seek to prevent or rid themselves of those thoughts (compulsions). People naturally vary in the extent to which they are neat, tidy, and orderly, with some degree of these characteristics being helpful in life. However, with OCD, these tendencies are executed to an extreme and disruptive degree.

Common obsessions include: images of violence, fear of germs, worry that the stove is on, or concern that a door is unlocked. Common compulsions include the "three Cs": *cleaning* (e.g., to remove germs), *checking* (to correct dangerous errors and oversights), and *counting* (to prevent harm that would come to oneself or others if the ritual was not performed). Hence, common rituals include repeated hand washing, house cleaning, checking of stoves and doorknobs, and unusual counting behaviors. The lifetime prevalence rate for OCD is approximately 1–2.5% of the population, with a 50/50 distribution between men and women (APA, 2000). It overlaps with Tourette's syndrome (characterized by intrusive sensations and urges, as well as a drive to perform motor and vocal tics like barking or cursing). Both disorders seem to involve malfunctions of circuits through the basal ganglia, with OCD symptoms associated with caudate dysfunction and Tourette's syndrome with putamen dysfunction (Rauch & Jenike, 1998; see Figures 15.1–15.3).

The phobic stimuli common to OCD include dirt, fear of failure to complete a task ("Did I lock the doors?"), and fear of having done something terrible ("Did I hit someone with the car?"). Each of these leads to pathological doubt ("Is someone lying dead in the road?"). Other stimuli include: lack of symmetry, images of violence and sex, religious blasphemy, as well as a sense that something bad will happen if a certain ritual is not performed correctly. Most clients have multiple compulsions as well as multiple obsessions (Rauch & Jenike, 1994).

OCD may be precipitated by environmental stressors including pregnancy and childbirth. Symptoms seem to wax and wane in response to the presence or absence of environmental stressors and depression severity. Improvement tends to occur when stressors and depression are reduced (Gabbard, 2000).

Treatment Approaches

Therapy centers on exposure and response prevention (ERP). Adequately planned systematic exposure involves confrontation of the obsession-evoking stimuli (e.g., dirt) usually for 90 minutes or longer once per week (or more frequently) for a period of 15 to 20 sessions. Adequate ritual prevention includes clients' voluntary compliance with the instructions to refrain from doing the ritual (e.g., hand washing). Clients should also expose themselves to the stimulus and restrain themselves from doing the rituals in between therapist-aided exposures.

Focus on themes of self-responsibility and guilt may increase thera-peutic outcomes (Franklin & Foa, 1998). Twenty-five percent of clients either refuse behavior therapy or drop out early. Of those remaining in therapy, 25% do not improve and 20% of the improved clients require subsequent "booster sessions" due to reemergence of symptoms over time (Cottraux, 1989).

Cognitive therapy interventions may focus on common OCD-related cognitions including:

- Belief that imagining an action is synonymous with per-forming it (e.g., thoughts of killing a baby are akin to actu-ally killing the baby)
- Belief that failing to prevent (or failing to try to prevent) harm to self or others is morally equivalent to causing harm (accidentally hitting someone with a car is akin to intention-ally hitting someone with a car)
- Belief that responsibility for harm is not diminished by extenuating circumstances (fear of contaminating family members)
- Belief that failing to engage in a ritual response to an unac-ceptable idea constitutes the intention to perform the unac-ceptable idea (not counting squares in response to the thought of harming someone is akin to actually intending to harm the person)
- Belief that one should exercise control over one's thoughts. (Salkovskis, 1985, p. 579).

Adapting Buddhist mindfulness procedures, Schwartz (1996) offered four "R" techniques for treatment of OCD:

- *Relabeling.* Recognize obsessive thoughts and compulsive urges through activating your observing self. Assertively label these thoughts and impulses as "obsessions" and "com-pulsions."
- *Reattributing.* Recognize that the cause is not you, it is your brain. You are not your thoughts. The problem is not you; it is OCD.
- *Refocusing.* When you experience an OCD thought or behavior, choose to do something else. Pick a hobby, a con-

versation, or a pleasant task to do. Do that activity for at least 15 minutes before giving in to the OCD ritual.
- *Revaluing.* Instead of being taken by surprise by an OCD thought or urge, expect it. And then accept it for what it is—a brain malfunction. There is no need to criticize yourself.

Summary

Anxiety disorders are common, disabling, and for the most part treatable. Defining the phobic stimulus and encouraging exposure remain fundamental to any therapeutic approach. Pharmacotherapy, particularly SSRIs, may also be very useful. The increasing popularity of mindfulness meditation suggests that this approach to a variety of disorders involving "hot cognitions" may be an effective adjunct to therapy. Perhaps therapists should also learn this method to help reduce their own stress and exercise their own self-observational powers.

CHAPTER 13

Substance Use, Abuse, and Dependence

That's all drugs and alcohol do, they cut off your emotions in the end.
—RINGO STARR

Drug and alcohol abuse and addiction have an impact upon a large percentage of the population, both directly and indirectly. Addiction can be defined as the repetitive and compulsive use of a substance that continues in spite of negative consequences resulting from the use of that substance. A study prepared for the National Institute on Drug Abuse (National Institute of Drug Abuse, 2005a) found that in 1992, the overall cost of alcohol and drug abuse in the U.S. was estimated to be $246 billion. This included the costs of reduced job productivity, crime and social welfare costs, treatment costs, costs of prevention, and healthcare costs.

The use of substances in and of itself is not problematic for the majority of the population. However, for many individuals, the substance use compounds or creates life problems that would not be evident without the substance use. Drug use begins with the initial, conscious choice to use a substance. The pleasurable feelings associated with the substance use increase the chance of further use. When drug dependence develops, the individual is no longer making conscious, rational choices to continue to use. There is a great deal of evidence that drugs disrupt normal brain functioning, creating short- and long-term changes in physiology that prevent individuals from quitting on their own (National Institute on Drug Abuse, 2004c). Chronic use essentially

This chapter was co-written with Chris Lawrence.

hijacks the brain. The drugs interfere with naturally occurring chemicals in the brain, resulting in a compulsive desire to continue drug use to maintain the chemical changes. There is also evidence that exposure to cues associated with drug use, such as friends who use, drug paraphernalia, or even receiving a paycheck, causes a surge in dopamine that mimics the drug effects. These chemical surges can trigger intense desires to use, even after months of sobriety (National Institute on Drug Abuse, 2004c).

Despite these immense challenges, many people enter recovery every day. With or without treatment, many people change their destructive patterns and learn to live free of alcohol and drugs. The path to recovery is different for every individual, but rarely does anyone recover without the help of someone—family members, friends, religious/spiritual leaders, or support groups. Mental health professionals are in a unique position to work with clients affected by their own or someone else's substance abuse. It is important for therapists to understand addictive behaviors and be able to intervene when they have the opportunity.

Substance Dependence and Abuse Diagnoses

The *DSM-IV-TR* differentiates between dependence and abuse of all classes of substances. In making a diagnosis, it should first be determined whether the individual meets criteria for dependence, which is the more stringent diagnosis. If individuals do not meet a dependence diagnosis, it should be determined whether they meet criteria for abuse (American Psychiatric Association, 2000).

Substance Dependence

Once clients meet criteria for dependence on a substance, they will *always* have a dependence diagnosis, with relevant qualifiers to indicate when their dependence is in remission. It is important to note that withdrawal and tolerance are two potential criteria for dependence but they are *not* required to diagnose substance dependence. Dependence can be diagnosed based solely on behavioral indicators such as giving up activities that do not support substance use or unsuccessful attempts to limit use (American Psychiatric Association, 2000).

Tolerance and Withdrawal

Tolerance occurs in response to the physical adaptation of the body to the presence of the substance. As a result of this physical adaptation, the amount of the substance that produced a given effect at one time no longer produces that given effect. Tolerance results in changes in drug-use patterns in order to achieve the same effect. Higher doses of the drug may be needed; the drug may be used more frequently; or the means by which the drug is taken may change. For example, individuals who use methamphetamines frequently begin by inhaling the drug into the nose (snorting). Once tolerance begins to develop, they may switch to smoking it, and then eventually inject it intravenously. Alcoholics who initially drink two to three beers per night may eventually progress to drinking more than six and then switch to harder alcohol as their addiction progresses. *Withdrawal* is the result of the body's physiological dependence on the substance.

Substance Abuse

If it is determined that dependence is not evident, a determination about abuse should be made. For a diagnosis of abuse, the substance use must have become maladaptive and have led to significant impairment in the areas of work, school, home, judgment, and legal, social, or interpersonal relations. Only one area needs to have been affected in order to meet criteria for substance abuse.

Co-Occurring Disorders

Co-occurring disorders (or dual diagnosis) refers to the existence of both substance abuse/dependence and one or more psychiatric disorders within the same individual. Those who struggle with other mental health issues are at increased risk to abuse substances. Many individuals use drugs and alcohol to self-medicate the symptoms of mood and other psychological problems (Dixon, Haas, Weiden, Sweeney, & Frances, 1990; Gafoor & Rassool, 1998; Schneider & Siris, 1987). One study found that for those with a mental disorder, there was a lifetime prevalence of addictive disorders of 29%. For those with an alcohol disorder, 37% had a comorbid mental disorder; 53% of those with substance disorders involving drugs other than alcohol had a mental disorder (Regier et al., 1990). Women who use substances are particularly prone to have dual diagnoses, with rates of depression, anxiety, eating disorders, and PTSD very high in this population (Pelisser & Jones, 2005; Peters, Strozier, Murrin, & Keanrs, 1997).

It is generally believed that each disorder is a separate, chronic disorder with its own separate course of illness. However, it is also generally accepted that treating co-occurring disorders at the same time is the most successful course of action (Gafoor & Rassool, 1998). Because the different disorders interact in a variety of ways, attempting to treat one in isolation can cause a relapse in the other. In addition, treatment for addiction can result in the development of psychiatric symptoms, such as extreme anxiety in those recovering from alcohol abuse; it is important for providers to address these issues simultaneously.

Additionally, the use of a particular drug can produce serious problems that would not have normally surfaced. For example, the use of methamphetamine is associated with the development of paranoia, delusions, and hallucinations. In many individuals, these symptoms continue for a period of time after abstaining from the use of the drug. If left untreated, they can cause a return to use of the drug. For a minority of users of methamphetamines, the psychotic symptoms become permanent. Treatment with antipsychotic medications can significantly improve the chances of recovery from the addiction. The chronic use of cocaine, especially crack cocaine, has been found to result in neurochemical changes that result in affective changes such as dysphoria, anhedonia and anxiety. These changes can last for months after individuals stop using the drug. Stress exacerbates this situation and can set up individuals for relapse in order to deal with these affective changes. Short-term treatment with antidepressants can alleviate this situation.

Substances of Abuse

The following classes of substances of abuse are described in this section: sedative hypnotics, stimulants, opioid pain relievers, and marijuana/psychedelics.

Sedative Hypnotics (Depressants)

This class of drugs includes alcohol, benzodiazepines such as diazepam (Valium) and alprazolam (Xanax), and barbiturates such as pentobarbital sodium (Nembutal). Taken in small doses, they cause a euphoric feeling and disinhibition (lowered anxiety and fear), along with increased sociability. Higher doses cause motor impairment, dysphoria, impaired gait, and emotional lability; very high doses can cause unconsciousness and death (Smith & Seymour, 2003). Blackouts are a hallmark of sedative hypnotics. A blackout is the experience of having no memory of activities while under the influence of these substances, although individuals were conscious during the whole episode. Blackouts are caused by the effects of these drugs on short-term memory and are a significant indicator of addiction. All sedative hypnotics are cross-tolerant, which means that tolerance to one translates into tolerance for all others, even if they have never been used. When two or more sedative hypnotics are used, there can be a multiplication of effects, which is the cause of most overdoses. This effect is typically seen when individuals drink alcohol while also taking benzodiazepines or barbiturates.

Stimulants

This class includes a wide variety of drugs including cocaine, methylphenidate (Ritalin), methamphetamine, and amphetamines. Effects include increased alertness and energy, improved concentration, performance enhancement, and feelings of invincibility. Toxic effects include restlessness, irritability, and anxiety. Longer-term use exacerbates these feelings and can also lead to extreme feelings of paranoia, often in the context of drug use (e.g., a belief that the police are currently staking out the house). Eventually the user can experience paranoid psychosis, with loss of touch with reality and auditory and visual hallucinations. Heart attack and strokes are associated with the use of stimulants even in small amounts (National Institute on Drug Abuse, 2005g).

Opioid Pain Relievers

Opioids are prescribed for their beneficial use in the treatment of pain. Commonly prescribed opioids include oxycodone (OxyContin), propoxyphene (Darvon), hydrocodone (Vicodin), hydromorphone (Dilaudid), codeine, and meperidine (Demerol). Opium and heroin are illicit categories of opioids. Prescription opioids are abused because of their ability to eliminate pain and, in some cases, create extreme euphoria. Tolerance and physical dependency are highly likely for those who use heroin, due to the rapid onset of action and short duration of effects on the brain. Withdrawal symptoms with opioid use are extremely unpleasant and include muscle and bone pain, insomnia, diarrhea and vomiting, cold flashes, restlessness, and extreme drug cravings (National Institute on Drug Abuse, 2005e). Chronic use creates a situation where the drug must be used simply to avoid the pain of withdrawal. The abuse of prescription pain killers has increased significantly in all segments of the population, especially among adolescents between 12 and 18 years (National Institute on Drug Abuse, 2004b). The elderly are particularly susceptible to the abuse of pain medications due to their tendency to be taking multiple medications and differences in how the body metabolizes medications with aging.

Marijuana/Psychedelics

This drug class includes the most commonly abused illicit drug, marijuana. It also includes such substances as hashish, LSD, psilocybin-containing mushrooms, and ecstasy (MDMA). Typical effects of all hallucinogens include an altered state of consciousness that affects perceptions and thinking.

Marijuana is the most commonly used cannabis derivative and is most generally used by smoking or eating the dried leaves and flower clusters of the plant. More Americans meet criteria for cannabis abuse or dependence and seek treatment for cannabis use than for all other illicit substances combined, with adolescents and young adults particularly affected (Epstein, 2002). Marijuana has been found to be the most common illegal drug to be used during pregnancy (Feng, 1993). In the short term, marijuana can cause problems with memory and learning, distorted perception, difficulty with thinking and problem solving, and loss of coordination, all of which can affect job and school performance (Bray, Zarkin, Dennis, & French, 2000; Lynskey & Hall, 2000; National Institute on Drug Abuse, 2005d). Chronic marijuana users often adamantly argue that marijuana is not addictive. However, withdrawal symptoms such as irritability, sleeplessness, and anxiety have been reported (Kouri, Pope, & Lukas, 1999). Tolerance has been docu-

> More Americans meet criteria for cannabis abuse or dependence than all other illicit substances combined, with adolescents and young adults particularly affected.

mented in many chronic users. Further, with the exception of alcohol, more people seek treatment for their inability to stop marijuana use that has resulted in legal and other consequences than for any other drug (Epstein, 2000).

Barriers to Treatment for Women

Although all addicts face barriers to accessing treatment (such as denial, lack of insurance, or lack of family support), women experience unique barriers due to their gender. Women's role as primary caretakers impedes their ability to seek outside help, both due to pressures from family members and internal pressures to be able to "handle" whatever is going on *and* continue to take care of the family. Women who abuse alcohol and drugs deal with social stigma resulting from the expectation that they be dependable mothers, wives, and caretakers. These expectations compound the shame and embarrassment that are so familiar to substance abusers (Conte, Plutchik, Picard, Galanter, & Jacoby, 1989).

Many women fear that the act of seeking treatment will cause social services to become involved with their family, and this fear is multiplied greatly when the woman is pregnant. If a woman does not have a support system or access to a treatment program where she can bring her children, she may choose not to go to treatment out of fear about what will happen to her children while she is away. This fear is significant and needs to be addressed in as many different ways as possible. Informed consent, which includes clearly explaining what does and does not constitute child abuse and what does and does not require reporting, is particularly important. It is also important to ask female clients directly if they have had these fears so that they can be discussed openly and honestly, particularly with those considering entering a treatment program. Additionally, women who abuse substances tend to be involved in relationships with other substance abusers, making it even more difficult to make the changes they need to stay clean (Peters et al., 1997).

Assessment

A thorough assessment is necessary to identify problems associated with substance use. The therapist's attitude during the assessment process can set the stage for current and future conversations about the use of substances. Questions about drug and alcohol use should be a natural part of the assessment process. The following suggestions can help in this process:

- Avoid yes or no questions. More information can be obtained by asking "When was the last time you used alcohol?" or "How often do you drink alcohol?" than by asking "Do you drink alcohol?"
- Ask questions about all substances. Do not skip substances under the assumption that this client could not have possibly used it.
- Assess the method, amount, and frequency of all substances used.
- Ask questions about the circumstances, context, and setting where the substance use occurs.
- Ask about any consequences of use—legal, social, sexual, medical, familial, and psychiatric.
- Assess for family history of substance use.
- Gather information about prior attempts to stop or curtail use—both informal and formal (i.e., treatment). Assess what was successful or unsuccessful.

A number of studies have demonstrated that women who use substances experienced greater incidences of physical and sexual abuse as children as compared to men (Boyd, Blow, & Orgain, 1993; Pelisser & Jones, 2005; Peters et al., 1997). Among women who experience co-occuring disorders such as substance abuse and depression, anxiety, or PTSD, the rate of childhood violence and victimization is extremely high (Alexander, 1996). The combination of childhood victimization and ongoing substance abuse in women also contributes to the fact that the experiences of trauma continue throughout their adulthood (Goodman, Dutton, & Harris, 1995). Watkins and colleagues concluded that "the high levels of both childhood abuse and adult victimization suggest that victimization and violence are normative experiences for many dually diagnosed women" (1999, p. 116). Women with histories of substance abuse should be assessed for a history of trauma. Similarly, therapists working with women with a history of trauma should continually assess for use of chemicals as a means to self-medicate trauma symptoms.

Assessing for misuse of prescription medications is important but particularly difficult. What can start as legitimate prescription drug use can easily become misuse, abuse, and dependence. For the most part, it is impossible to predict when someone may become dependent upon a prescribed drug. However, individuals with a history of chemical abuse are at great risk of becoming dependent on prescription medications. Identifying and treating prescription medication abuse is often difficult and frustrating. The fact that the medications were prescribed serves to legitimize their use, which leads to rationalizations about their use. Physicians may not inform clients of the potential for abuse, may not be adept at identifying signs of abuse, and may not discuss the dangers inherent in taking these medications along with other medications or alcohol. Failure to inform patients about drug interactions can have serious or even life-threatening consequences. For example, the combination of sedative hypnotics and alcohol is highly dangerous as they belong to the same class of drugs and taking them together potentiates their effects, making overdose a very real possibility. Because these medications are legal, arrests related to their use (when they are legally prescribed) are uncommon. However, addiction to these medications can lead to illegal behavior such as "doctor shopping," buying the drugs illegally, and forging prescriptions.

If therapists suspect that clients may be misusing or abusing their prescription medications, the following questions can help clarify the need for concern:

- Are there times you use an extra dose to get through a tough situation?
- Do you need an extra dose now and then to calm down?
- Has your dosage increased over time?
- When you miss taking your usual dose do you become depressed, shaky, or nervous?
- Do you now take your prescription to help with problems that are different from the one you originally needed it for?
- Did you get your prescription for occasional use but now use it regularly?
- Has your doctor suggested that you reduce the amount that you are taking?
- Are you receiving prescriptions from more than one doctor or at more than one pharmacy?

- Do you tell your family, friends, or doctor that you are taking less of the drug than you actually are?
- Do you find yourself drinking when you are out of medication?
- Have you tried to quit or cut down on your own and found it difficult?

If clients answer yes to any of these questions, this can be used for further exploration to determine what their patterns of use are and to provide education about the appropriate use of these medications, including the short-term nature of most of them. Collaboration with a physician in this process is essential, as any decision clients make about wanting to stop or cut down on drug use must be negotiated with the prescribing physician. Addressing the underlying reasons for misuse of medications is also important, particularly when the prescription use began as a way of treating pain (Grinstead & Gorski, 1997).

Modes of Treatment

There are a number of different modes of treatment for substance abuse problems, ranging from least restrictive (individual therapy and 12-step meetings) to most restrictive (detoxification and residential programs). Many individuals who are treated for substance-related problems do not formally seek treatment initially. Instead, they are experiencing mental or emotional problems that are manifested in mood disorders, relationship problems, or anxiety symptoms. When a client has identified substance use as a problem, the decision to seek formal treatment can be difficult. It is generally considered important to refer clients to the least restrictive level of treatment that can reasonably address their substance use and its physical and emotional consequences.

Although there are a variety of treatment options of differing intensities, one research finding is clear. The longer an individual is engaged in formal treatment and the more intensive the treatment, the more successful the outcome (Condelli & Hubbard, 1994; Fiorentine, Anglin, Gil-Rivas, & Taylor, 1997). Therapists should research the treatment options available in their communities so that they can effectively refer clients when necessary. In addition, it is impor-

> Therapists need to be prepared to assess for substance use and abuse in any setting, with the understanding that a client's concerns about substance abuse may not be expressed until well into the treatment process.

tant to have materials about 12-step meetings available so that clients can access meetings should they choose to do so.

The following sections go into more detail on different modes of treatment, including 12-step programs, aftercare, intensive outpatient programs, residential and day treatment programs, therapeutic communities, detoxification, and pharmacotherapy. Individual or family therapy may be used in conjunction with these treatment modes, many of which incorporate varied psychotherapeutic approaches.

12-Step Meetings

In the 1930s, Bill W. convened the first meeting of Alcoholics Anonymous (AA). AA meetings flourished a decade later. Narcotics Anonymous (NA) meetings were established in 1953 for those who were recovering from substances other than alcohol. Since that time, AA and NA meetings have become the cornerstone of many treatment centers. Cocaine Anonymous was developed for individuals who are addicted to cocaine and Dual Recovery Anonymous for those who are recovering from addictive diseases as well as mental health diseases.

Twelve-step meetings provide several very important functions for those in recovery. They provide an established support system that can begin to replace the unhealthy support system that encourages continued use. Identifying a sponsor who attends a 12-step fellowship can be essential for individuals in recovery, as this person serves as a support, role model, and surrogate parent for clients struggling through the steps they need to take to get and stay clean. Secondly, meetings offer a message of hope for those who are struggling to stay clean. One of the tenants of 12-step fellowships is sharing your experience, strength, and hope in order to help others who are struggling. Hearing other addicts speak about the lengths they went to in order to continue to use, followed by their message about how they are recovering, can provide inspiration and hope to others. Finally, through the 12-steps, these fellowships provide a blueprint for how to "live life on life's terms," by accepting that one lost control when one was using, by asking for help from others, by looking honestly at oneself and the things one has done to hurt others, and by taking responsibility for one's choices.

In order to effectively refer clients to meetings, it is important for clinicians to familiarize themselves with the 12-Steps by attending a few meetings and reading relevant literature (Gorski, 1989). Meetings are identified as either closed or open. Open meetings are available to anyone who is interested in attending, whereas closed meetings are only for those who struggle with addiction. On-line support groups can provide a means to connect to others in recovery if 12-step meetings are limited or unavailable. The following sites are available:

Websites
- Alcoholics Anonymous: www.alcoholics-anonymous.org
- Al-anon/Alateen: www.al-anon.alateen.org
- Cocaine anonymous: www.ca.org
- Narcotics Anonymous: www.na.org
- Heroin addiction: www.notinmyhouse.org

On-line Support Groups
- www.alcoholicsanonymous.org
- www.soberrecovery.com
- www.12steps.org
- www.aalivechat.com
- Dual Recovery Anonymous (for individuals with substance abuse and other mental health disorders): www.draonline.org
- Sex Addicts Anonymous: www.sexaa.org
- www.gamblersanonymous.org

Aftercare

Aftercare programs usually consist of individual therapy and occasionally group therapy once per week. Aftercare is designed to be utilized by those individuals who have successfully completed a residential or intensive outpatient program. The goal of aftercare programs is to assist the individual in maintaining abstinence beyond the initial stages of recovery. Integration back into the community following a residential treatment stay can be a particularly high risk time. Stress associated with resumption of responsibilities such as employment and family duties can cause urges to use. Aftercare programs can provide assistance in dealing with daily stressors, as well as other drug using cues through relapse prevention work and encouragement of ongoing 12-Step involvement. Clearly explaining the benefits of regularly attending an aftercare program has been found to increase length and frequency of attendance (Lash, 1998). Due to their relative cost-effectiveness, aftercare programs can be longer in duration than intensive outpatient programs.

Intensive Outpatient Programs

Intensive outpatient programs (IOP) generally consist of a combination of individual therapy, group therapy, and psychoeducational groups. These programs may also be referred to as *partial hospitalization* by some insurance companies. Clients meet several times per week in these various modalities. IOP programs are time-limited, with a focus on becoming engaged in an ongoing support system through church, 12-step meetings, or other methods. These programs frequently provide cognitive behavioral relapse prevention interventions as well as strategies to manage stress. Achieving initial sobriety while attending an IOP program is an important criterion before moving to a less intensive treatment, since this demonstrates an addict's ability to cope with various stressors while continuing to live and work in his or her own environment. In addition, involvement in another supportive system, such as a spiritual program or a 12-Step program, is an indication that an individual is ready to end involvement in an IOP program. Many treatment centers, especially those that are publicly funded, do not offer IOP programs.

Residential and Day Treatment Programs

Residential programs can be located either in a hospital setting (typically referred to as *inpatient treatment*) or in a stand-alone facility (often referred to as *residential treatment* or *rehab*). These programs usually range from 5 to 30 days, with a few providing longer-term residential treatment. Activities within these programs tend to be highly structured, with a variety of rules that apply to the client's activities. Structure and rules in residential programs serve two purposes: (1) They provide safety for individuals who have great difficulty staying clean if left to their own devices; and (2) they provide a model for how to live life without drugs. A large majority of residential programs provide exposure to 12-step meetings, along with individual, group, and family therapy. Education about topics relevant to recovery, building life planning skills, and relapse prevention strategies are also addressed. Day treatment (DT) programs are offered as an alternative to residential treatment. DT programs are appropriate only when the client has a stable, drug-free place to return to at the end of the day.

Therapeutic Communities

Treatment in a therapeutic community (TC) setting consists of relatively long-term treatment (15 months to 2 years) that focuses on assisting individuals in changing many different facets of their lifestyle, thinking, and personality, with the optimal goal of returning to the mainstream community and remaining drug-free. The programs are highly structured and use peer support as well as significant relationships with staff members to achieve change. Contingency management is often a significant aspect of TCs and consists of rewards and consequences for behavioral change. Individuals who participate in TCs are often taught basic life skills that they were not able to learn prior to the development of their addiction. TC programs are often found in incarceration settings, where inmates can attend the programs until their release (National Institute on Drug Abuse, 2005c).

Detoxification

Detoxification is the process of medically assisting an individual who is going through withdrawal due to physical dependence on a substance. It is generally conducted in a medical setting or in a special area of a residential program. For some substances, detoxification is necessary to prevent life-threatening complications from withdrawal. This is especially important with central nervous system depressants such as benzodiazepines, opioids, and alcohol. Withdrawal from other substances, although not life-threatening, can also be extremely difficult and uncomfortable. Methamphetamine is one example, with withdrawal causing extreme fatigue, aches, and nausea. In these situations, detoxification can be an important process in keeping the individual engaged in treatment.

Psychotherapeutic Approaches

There are a variety of therapeutic interventions used to treat substance abuse problems. Many programs provide a variety of methods and services designed to meet the individual needs of their clients. This section focuses on the engagement process, motivational interviewing (MI), stages of change, cognitive-behavioral interventions, family therapy and psychopharmacological interventions.

Engagement

As with other mental health issues, treatment of substance abuse begins with the process of engaging the individual in the treatment process. The engagement phase has been described as the process by which "clients . . . develop comfortable and trusting relationships with treatment providers in either a mental health or substance abuse setting" (Watkins et al., 1999, p. 117). The engagement process is essential for successful treatment, as motivation and early engagement have been found to be associated with better retention in treatment (Simpson, Joe, & Rowan-Szal, 1997). Because of their chronic ambivalence, engaging and retaining substance abusers in treatment can be difficult and individuals with dual diagnoses are especially difficult to engage in treatment (Peters et al., 1997). Engagement can be fostered through use of motivation-enhancing techniques. The motivational interviewing style of interacting (see next section) allows clients to identify and explore their own goals, thereby reducing any feelings of threat or resistance they may have initially brought into treatment. Motivational techniques have been found to be particularly useful with male substance abusers who tend to have issues with authority (Watkins et al., 1999). Demonstrating concern and interest is also essential with this clientele. Concern can be demonstrated by following up absences with phone calls and by increasing the frequency of initial sessions. The provision of concrete advice and assistance has been identified as important to engaging dually diagnosed clients. These clients return to see helpers whom they feel can benefit them (Watkins et al., 1999). Assisting clients in meeting their immediate goals, such as helping them make a phone call to get food stamps, can help further engagement.

For women, engagement and retention is related to the provision of supports that address their gender-specific needs. Childcare, transportation, employment training, parenting advice, mental health treatment, medical care, and trauma services are examples of supports that, when provided along with substance abuse treatment, help to keep women engaged in treatment (Howell, Heiser, & Harrington, 1999). Additionally, providing services within a context that is safe, nurturing, empowering, and non-threatening is essential given the extremely high rates of victimization in women with addictive disorders (Pelisser & Jones, 2005; Watkins et al., 1999).

Motivational Interviewing

In the past, motivation has been defined as a dichotomous concept—the client was either motivated for treatment and recovery or was unmotivated. However, more recent contributions in the literature regarding stages of change and motivational enhancement have described motivation as a dynamic, fluid process (Miller & Rollnick, 1991, 2002). In fact, every client who walks into a therapist's office or treatment center is motivated by something. The problem lies in the fact that what the client is motivated to achieve may not match the therapist's ideas of what the client *should* want to achieve. This can be the case with any client, with any presenting problem, and with any theoretical orientation. A mismatch between the clients' goals and the treatment providers' goals can result in therapeutic "failures." However, this mismatch is especially prevalent when substance abuse is an issue. Most substance abusers who first enter treatment or therapy do *not* want to stop using drugs or alcohol; rather, they seek to decrease the stress and emotional pain that they are currently experiencing.

Redefining the therapist's goals of "treatment" is an essential part of successfully engaging clients so that the work can be done. A key step in this process is identifying goals that are acceptable to the client and represent a change in the status quo. For example, a client presents for individual therapy with dependence on both marijuana and cocaine. While the therapist may want to address both addictions, the client may recognize only the problems associated with cocaine use. Initially addressing the goals with which clients present may provide opportunities to address additional goals in the future.

The use of motivational interviewing (MI) techniques has been found to improve engagement and to maintain a positive, rather than punitive, relationship between the therapist and client (Steinberg et al., 2002). Developed out of the work of Prochaska and colleagues (1992, 2003) who identified various stages that individuals go through when attempting to change behaviors, MI advocates the use of a client-centered, reflective, and empathic stance with substance users. This stance allows clients to fully explore the positive and negative aspects of their use and to make fully informed choices about what they want to do about it.

> The central strategies of motivational interviewing include: expressing empathy, developing discrepancy, avoiding argumentation, rolling with resistance and supporting clients' self-efficacy.

Expressing empathy, developing discrepancy, avoiding argumentation, rolling with resistance, and supporting client self-efficacy are central strategies of MI (Miller & Rollnick, 1991, 2002). Miller and Rollnick articulated these strategies as follows:

Expressing Empathy

A cornerstone of most therapeutic styles, expressing empathy is key to MI. In many traditional treatment programs, empathy was not seen as an important ingredient for change. Instead, the focus was on a challenging and confrontational style that directly addressed clients' denial. In MI, empathy is used to bypass resistance in the therapeutic process. Active listening is essential and allows therapists to fully understand the client's point of view—something often overlooked when dealing with substance abusers.

Developing Discrepancy

Empathy and active listening allow therapists to help clients clarify their actual goals. Often clients come in complaining that other people have goals for them, and they then spend a great deal of time and energy negating those goals. However, if clients are encouraged to openly explore what they would like to be different in their life or what goals they have for their future, it is possible to help them begin to recognize the discrepancy between where they are and where they want to be and consider the role of substance use in that discrepancy.

Avoiding Argumentation

Working with substance abusers is frequently frustrating. However, the work can be much less frustrating if therapists do not feel pressured to convince clients to see things a certain way. Arguing for a particular point (i.e., whether a client should attend AA meetings) often only evokes more resistance and arguing, particularly if the client is in the early stages of change.

Rolling with Resistance

This strategy provides alternatives to arguing in favor of change. It involves turning arguments into reframes that allow clients to make a change that they are willing to make, even if it is not the change that the therapist would like to see them make. For example, suppose a client refuses to attend AA. The therapist could verbally agree that AA may not be right for the client, but also emphasize that identifying a support system is important to recovery. The therapist could challenge the client to identify other ways of creating a support system without attending AA (such as activity, support, or religious/spiritual groups). The therapist might also help the client identify ways of recognizing whether those alternative support systems are working or not. If the alternative support system is not working, the client may need to reconsider the value of attending AA. The focus here should always be on free choice.

Supporting Client Self-Efficacy

Clients' belief that they are able to make changes is essential to committing to and following through with change. Therefore, therapists should regularly review progress with clients, focusing on the changes that they are successfully making and encouraging continued growth and change.

Stages of Change

Research by Prochaska and colleagues (1992) identified common characteristics found in individuals and situations where change was successfully sought. More specifically, they identified four stages of change that offer a basis for MI interventions. These stages, and the interventions associated with them, can be successfully applied to all situations in which change is needed or desired. However, they are particularly useful in the area of substance abuse, when initial motivation to make changes often appears to be limited or nonexistent (Valasquez, Maurer, Crouch, & DiClemente, 2001).

Precontemplation

Knapp succinctly and forcefully summed up the precontemplation stage: "So on it goes. You lie and you deflect blame and you rationalize and the hole you dig yourself gets deeper and deeper. Denial—first of drinking, then of self—stretches to include more and more bits of reality; after a while you literally cannot see the truth, cannot see your own role in the disaster you've made of your life. Cannot see who you are or what you need or what choices you have" (1996, p. 206).

Precontemplators are completely unaware that they have a substance abuse problem. They do not have abstinence as their primary goal and seek treatment for other life problems that they believe are unrelated to their substance use—problems with their boss, spouse, finances, or the law (Watkins et al., 1996). These clients usually fail to see the connection between their substance use and their life problems or make inaccurate assumptions about the causes of their problems. They often believe that their use is in *response* to their problems rather than seeing that the problems are the *result* of their use. These clients can be mildly to extremely defensive when the issue of their substance use is addressed. The defensiveness allows them to maintain their belief that the substance use is a noncontributing issue.

The primary therapeutic goal when working with clients at this stage is to create a climate where clients do not have to defend their use of substances or the choices they have made. Therapists should adapt a very supportive, curious, learning stance. The focus should be on learning as much as possible about what brought the client in and about the client's view of what the real problem is. A curious, nonjudgmental stance allows therapists to learn a great deal not only about what the client thinks the problem is, but also about possible alternative reasons for the problem (which the client may have considered and rejected) and about how other people in the client's life have viewed the problem. Such a stance also helps therapists understand what clients are willing to do to resolve the problem as *they* see it.

If so many clients do not initially have the goal of halting their use of drugs and alcohol, what *are* their goals? For many, the goals involve addressing the concerns that others may have. Clients who are referred by external sources such as probation/parole or child protective services have a desire to appease these referral sources. They may seek to appease an employer who has expressed concerns or lessen the concerns of a spouse or other family member. These are all valid and workable motivations that are unfortunately often ignored in treatment. If therapists fully address these concerns without trying to convince clients that their *real* problem is the use of chemicals, they leave room for full exploration of the multiple complexities of the problem. Furthermore, aligning with the client often significantly reduces defensiveness and fosters the establishment of a working alliance. Therapists should particularly avoid labeling, diagnosing, and confronting at this stage. Strategies such as asking open-ended questions and allowing clients to talk about their concerns while using reflective listening are particularly helpful (Miller & Rollnick, 1997, 2002).

For example, consider the following statement from a therapist to a client who is precontemplative: "As you have described the situation so far, it seems as if your wife spends a good deal of time telling you how much she dislikes your drinking. But you think that if she didn't nag so much about this, you wouldn't need to leave every night with your friends. Thus, the nagging is a real problem. If coming to see me every week would reduce the nagging, would you be willing to make a commitment to doing that?" By maintaining the focus on the client's perception of the problem, the therapist can gain a commitment from the client to engage in weekly sessions, which will increase the likelihood of success in future interventions with regard to the substance use as well as possibly reduce some of the marital tension.

Another helpful intervention during this stage is to negotiate an "experiment" with the client. This is best done once a strong alliance has been established. The experiment consists of establishing a "rule" for substance use that would require a change in the pattern of use, typically a decrease in frequency or amount of use. For example, a client may agree not to drink for a week or agree to use marijuana only after 9 P.M. Most precontemplative clients will insist that they are able to control their use. With a client's permission, this experiment allows them to learn about their true ability to control their use. The therapist approaches this experiment from a curious stance, describing it as an opportunity for clients to learn more about themselves. It is important to make it clear to clients that this is not a test to be passed or failed but rather an opportunity to observe their responses to a change in the rules. Normalizing an inability to follow the rules is also important. Asking clients to journal their thoughts and experiences during this assignment can be helpful for the next session. If clients are successful in making the change, then the impact of reducing the substance use on work, relationships and health can be explored. If clients are unsuccessful in making the change, this may open the door to exploring the possibility that they are not as in control as they might think.

Contemplation

"Sometimes you see, but you're not ready to act" (Knapp, 1996, p. 190). Unlike precontemplators, contemplators recognize that there may be a problem with the substance use itself. However, they maintain that the problem is not nearly as concerning as others would believe and are ambivalent about the amount of commitment that they would need to make in order to change. These clients are known for their use of the words "yes, but." For every argument that is presented to them in favor of changing their behavior, they present an argument in favor of not changing. Ambivalence is the key characteristic of this stage and allows them to continue to use (Miller & Rollnick, 1991, 2002). Whereas it may be important to the people who care about them to convince them of the need for change, it is just as important to clients that they convince themselves that they do not really need to change as much as everyone thinks they do. When others suggest reasons why these clients should change, they are met with a "yes, but"—followed by a reason why clients do not need to change or an explanation of how their use is not really as bad as everyone says.

Those addicted to alcohol and drugs frequently use defense mechanisms to maintain their substance use. Denial, minimization, and projection are all very familiar to therapists who work with these clients. Knapp illustrated this when he described the typical contemplator's mindset: "Bad things didn't happen every time I drank, but every time something bad did happen, drinking was involved. If you're an active alcoholic, you focus in on the times when bad things *didn't* happen, when you went out drinking and had a good time, got home safely, woke up in your own bed. And when those more destructive or embarrassing episodes occur . . . well, you make excuses, find someone or something to blame" (Knapp, 1996, p. 166).

It is also important to remember that early on, substance use served a worthwhile purpose. For some, drinking eased social anxiety and allowed them to enjoy social functions. For others, the use of pain medications allowed them to work and function despite chronic pain. Using cocaine may have allowed trauma survivors to avoid painful memories. The

"Bad things didn't happen every time I drank, but every time something bad did happen, drinking was involved. If you're an active alcoholic, you focus in on the times when bad things didn't happen, when you went out drinking and had a good time, got home safely, woke up in your own bed. And when those more destructive or embarrassing episodes occur . . . well, you make excuses, find someone or something to blame" (Knapp, 1996, p. 166).

paired association between the use of the drug and the numbing of feelings or easing of pain and anxiety is very powerful. In most situations, negative consequences do not start to occur until well after the substance use began. In addition, bad things do not happen every time an individual uses, so the association between bad events and substance use is often weak.

However, eventually negative events begin to add up. Often the consequences of the substance use (e.g., relationship problems) eventually become the reason for the continued use ("If she would just stop nagging me, I wouldn't need to drink so much"). In order to maintain the illusion that the alcohol or drug use is still serving the same, helpful function that it once did, the individual now begins to employ cognitive distortions. Many individuals believe that the substance use is helping them to survive. Because of chemical changes that occur in their brain, abusers and addicts receive the message that if they do not use the chemical when they are anxious, stressed, or scared, their very survival is at risk. No wonder they minimize, project, and blame to distance the substance use from the bad things that are happening in their life.

Miller and Rollnick (1997) described the importance of ambivalence in the treatment of addictive disorders. Ambivalence is the result of both wanting and not wanting a particular behavior. This ambivalence can be extremely anxiety-provoking for clients, especially as the negative aspects of their substance use increase. Denial is a very effective tool to deal with ambivalence. It effectively eliminates one side of the ambivalent equation by removing the negative aspects of using from clients' awareness. As previously described, MI can be especially helpful in working with clients who have developed strong defenses about their use of drugs and alcohol.

When formulating therapeutic goals with clients at the contemplation stage, there is one vital requirement: patience, patience, and more patience. Clients at this stage are known for their tendency to vacillate between the idea that they need to change and the idea that change is not needed. As with clients who are precontemplative, the therapeutic environment is critical to helping contemplators move along the path of change. These clients need to be able to openly explore all sides of the problem. This should include the negative consequences of using as well as the positive consequences of using. Therapists cannot help clients resolve their ambivalence and explore ways of replacing the positive consequences of drug use if they also haven't allowed them to talk about the positive consequences.

It is especially helpful in this stage to assist individuals in assessing the pros and cons of their behaviors. A *decisional balance* (a balanced view of the pros and cons of changing or not changing a given behavior) can be instrumental in helping clients consider all their options. When asking clients to complete a decisional balance, it is important to start with the pros of the current behavior and the cons of changing the behavior. By focusing on the reasons they have for using, you can reduce resistance when it comes time to consider the cons of continuing to use (Miller & Rollnick, 1991).

After identifying the pros and cons of using, therapists can assign tasks to evaluate how effective using is in achieving the positive benefits that the client has identified. Therapists can explore this issue by asking questions such as:

- The last time you used, what benefits were you expecting?
- Were you able to get that benefit?
- How well did it work for you?
- Were you disappointed?
- Did you feel better or worse afterwards?

Therapists can also ask clients to evaluate why they are going to use before it happens by asking themselves: "Why am I choosing to use right now? What am I expecting?"

An overall goal of the therapeutic work at this stage is to elicit *self-motivational statements* from clients. These statements are indications that the client is considering a change. Self-motivational ("change talk") statements can indicate problem recognition, concern about the problem, desire to make changes, and optimism about change (Miller & Rollnick, 1997). Every self-motivational statement a client makes moves the client along the path from ambivalence to commitment to change. Therapists can help elicit self-motivational statements by using evocative questions that invite clients to consider the need for change:

> Therapists help to identify the pros and cons of substance use by asking questions such as, "The last time you used, what benefits were you expecting? Were you able to get that benefit? How well did it work for you? Were you disappointed? Did you feel better or worse afterwards?"

- If you could change anything about your life, what would you change?

- What worries you about your drug use?
- On a scale of 1 to 10, how satisfied are you with your life? (*after the client answers, ask the following*) Why didn't you say 10? What could be different?
- If you woke up tomorrow and your life was different, what would have happened?
- What negative things have happened in your life that you would like to go back and change?

The goal at this stage is to recognize even small indications of a desire to change or recognition of a problem and then encourage more exploration of that statement through encouragement and openness to considering both the reasons to change and the reasons not to change (Shaffer & Robbins, 1995).

There are often wide variations in clients' point of view during the contemplation stage. They may vacillate in this stage for quite some time. For example, some clients may enter treatment after a crisis such as being arrested for a DWI. Immediately after the arrest they may be able to talk extensively about the negative effects of drinking, openly discussing how it has affected their relationships, work, and legal status. However, after the immediate crisis has passed, the benefits that they received from drinking may begin to resurface. If drinking allowed them to unwind at the end of a difficult day at work, this benefit will resurface and affect them the next time they have a difficult day. As the fear and shock from the DWI arrest dissipate, the benefits of drinking may take more precedence, leading the client to again focus on the positive aspects of using.

In sum, during the early stages of precontemplation and contemplation, the focus of therapy should be on understanding the clients' internal representation of the situation. During these stages, treatment should not focus on the need to make changes; premature focus on action and change often causes premature termination of treatment due to the mismatch between the therapist's and client's expectations. Instead, the focus should be on increasing awareness of positive and negative effects of the use of substances, evaluating future goals as well as past goals that have not been met, clarifying reasons for using and not using, exploring how using and its consequences fit with the client's values, and opening up options for change should that become a goal.

Action

"There are moments as an active alcoholic where you *do* know, where in a flash of clarity you grasp that alcohol is the central problem, a kind of liquid glue that gums up all the internal gears and keeps you stuck" (Knapp, 1996, p. 3). In the action stage, the decisional balance has tipped in the direction of making change and individuals are ready to commit to a plan of action. Often the action stage is entered after a significant event such as an arrest, a car accident, or a medical complication resulting from use. Other times it is the result of a subtle, brief shift in point of view that allows the client to fully consider the consequences of the substance use. Generally, movement into the action stage is limited—a "window of opportunity" that if not taken advantage of can close just as quickly. This is the time when individuals often begin attending AA or enter treatment.

The first therapeutic goal at this stage is to recognize the client's readiness to make changes. Indicators that a client is moving into the action stage include decreased resistance, increased self-motivational statements, and questions about what changes could be undertaken (Miller & Rollnick, 1997). The next step is to assist clients in developing a plan for change. It is important to avoid plans that are too ambitious, keeping the focus on identifying the areas that need changing and the small steps the client is willing to take to work toward those changes. It is also important at this stage to avoid becoming a strong advocate for change.

As in other stages, the focus must remain on the client's control of the process rather than on the therapist's desire for the client to change. Therapists should remain neutral about changes—encouraging clients to make choices for themselves but also remaining open to the very real possibility that the changes will not work or that the client will return to the contemplative stage. If therapists become "cheerleaders" for change, clients may not return to therapy if they change their mind. Therapists can maintain neutrality by making comments such as: "You've really made up your mind that you are going to stop drinking after work every day. What made you decide this? How do you think you'll respond?" At this stage, clients may not be aware of specific changes they can make. If this is the case, therapists can say: "You seem at a loss as to how to proceed. Would it help if I gave you some

> The action stage may be triggered by a traumatic event such as an arrest, a car accident or a medical complication resulting from substance use.

ideas about changes other clients have made in this situation?" If clients indicate that they would like suggestions, provide them with a wide range of options. Allowing clients to choose the option that suits them best increases their feeling of being in control of the situation.

Maintenance

This stage is difficult to achieve and maintain. Taking action in the previous stage is not difficult once clients have achieved the appropriate mindset. However, in the maintenance stage, significant life changes must be made in order to maintain the steps taken in the action stage. Many individuals enter treatment believing that beginning treatment is the biggest step they will need to take. Although beginning treatment is significant, the changes that need to be made to maintain a substance-free lifestyle are life-altering and often take years to establish.

The therapist's role at this stage is helping clients remain consistent with changes they have made, resolve any ambivalence that arises, and address emotional, behavioral, or spiritual issues that threaten their sobriety. Use of cognitive-behavioral therapy to address triggers and increase coping skills is essential at this stage. Undiagnosed mental health issues also must be addressed and treated. Family therapy can be utilized to reinforce the positive changes made and address the family dynamics that maintained the addiction. It is fairly common for clients to make initial changes, achieve a period of sobriety, and then begin to back off of the changes they made. This often leads to a *lapse*, or brief period of substance use. In order to prevent a full blown *relapse*, an extended period of substance use, it is helpful in this stage to develop a plan for how to respond should this occur.

In sum, the later stages of change—action and maintenance—should focus on setting specific, concrete goals that include taking steps to significantly change areas of clients' lives in ways that will eliminate substance use. Interventions used during these stages are behavioral in nature and include: stimulus control to eliminate or avoid the internal and external cues that contribute to using, positive reinforcement for behavior changes, learning alternative responses in stressful situations, increasing self-efficacy, and making positive connections to supportive others (Valasquez et al., 2001).

Clients may move back and forth through the stages. Although this can be discouraging

> Many individuals enter treatment believing that beginning treatment is the biggest step that they will need to take. They gradually come to learn that the changes necessary to maintain a substance free life often take years.

for therapists, it should be kept in mind that once clients' awareness of the negative impact of their substance abuse has been raised, it becomes harder and harder for them to ignore this insight. If clients move from precontemplation to action and then slip back to precontemplation, they are more likely to be successful the next time they move to the action stage because they have already begun the work (Valasquez et al., 2001). Many individuals who go through formal treatment more than once note that treatment "messed up my high"—meaning that they simply could not forget the things they learned in treatment when they were using again. If individuals who are in treatment (or in therapy prior to going into treatment) are treated with respect and encouraged to explore their thoughts and feelings about their drug use and its impact on themselves and others, the therapist will have the opportunity to plant many seeds that will not be easily forgotten.

Cognitive-Behavioral Interventions

Cognitive-behavioral interventions are the mainstay of the many treatment manuals for clients who abuse substances (Gorski, 1992). These interventions address the thinking patterns and behaviors that have maintained substance use and seek to replace maladaptive patterns with more positive, healthy thoughts and behaviors. Cognitive-behavioral strategies include: identifying triggers, dealing with cravings and urges, identifying relapse warning signs, analyzing relapses, changing lifestyle, and resisting invitations to use.

Identifying Triggers

Clients are taught to identify triggers that lead to the desire to use drugs or alcohol. Triggers are very individualized and are associated with the particular drug of choice, the method of use, the context of use, and the particular factors that maintained the use. Clients should identify both internal and external triggers. External triggers include environmental factors associated with substance use, including bars, friends who use, advertisements, social or leisure activities, and anything associated with getting, preparing, or using a substance. Internal triggers are thoughts or emotional states that can lead to drug use. Emotional states that have led to drug use in the past are particularly dangerous in early recovery. These can include stress, anxiety, boredom, fatigue, or depression, as well as positive emotional states such as excitement and relief.

External triggers for substance use include bars, friends who use drugs, advertisements, social or leisure activities, as well as anything associated with getting, preparing or using a substance. *Internal triggers* include stress responses, anxiety, boredom, fatigue, or depression, as well as positive emotional states such as excitement, celebration and relief.

Thoughts that are triggers include cognitions that minimize the danger or maximize the benefits of using, such as "One drink will not cause a problem for me."

Triggers are dealt with primarily through education, thought avoidance, and response-prevention techniques (Gorski, 1992). Clients benefit greatly from education about what triggers are, how they affect individuals in recovery, and how to best respond to them. Describing and normalizing the experience of "being triggered" can eliminate guilt and shame associated with experiencing triggers. In addition, explaining how associations are developed between drug use and external and internal triggers helps clients understand why they respond in certain ways to these triggers.

Many external triggers are best avoided due to their threat to a recovering individual. Clients are taught to "avoid people, places, and things" that are associated with their use in order to reduce feeling triggered by these things. However, many internal triggers, as well as some external triggers, are unavoidable. Clients in recovery will experience strong emotions and times of stress that will lead to thoughts about using and strong desires to use. However, clients can be taught to minimize strong emotions through stress management, anger management, relaxation training, and lifestyle changes. Making lifestyle changes is particularly important in the process of avoiding internal triggers. Twelve-step programs stress the avoidance of HALT: becoming too hungry, angry, lonely, or tired.

Dealing With Cravings and Urges

Exposure to triggers can lead to cravings in which the person experiences a strong, sometimes urgent desire to use a substance. This experience is sometimes accompanied by feeling as if they can taste or smell the substance. They may experience extreme anxiety as well as irritability. Response prevention is the primary way to deal effectively with cravings. Clients are encouraged to develop a detailed, specific plan to deal with cravings. They can be taught to rate the craving on a scale of 1 to 10, with different responses depending on the rating. Lower-rated cravings can be dealt with by using distraction, by engaging the intellect through reading or journaling, by mindful observation of the craving, or by positive self-talk ("This craving is just a 2. It's a very low-level craving and I know it will pass soon"). Visualization and mental imagery are also helpful with lower-rated cravings. Clients can be taught to "ride out" the craving by visualizing themselves riding waves on a boat, with smooth water just ahead when the craving passes (Daley & Lis, 1995). For higher-rated cravings, responses should focus on reducing isolation and gaining support. Clients are encouraged to make lists of individuals they can call for support when they experience a craving. It is best if these individuals are in recovery themselves or have a good understanding of how to respond when the client calls them. It is important to have support people who will encourage clients, remind them that "this too shall pass," and offer to be with them in a safe environment until the crisis passes. Twelve-step support groups are an important part of dealing with cravings and urges to use, as the fellowship involved in these meetings provides a built-in support system to utilize in times of crisis. The plan clients develop for how to respond to cravings should include as many helpful details as possible and be portable enough that the clients can have the plan with them at all times. Due to the physiological nature of cravings, it is very difficult for individuals to think about and remember their prevention plan while experiencing a craving. If they have a written plan, the only thing they have to remember is to take the plan out and read it.

Identifying Relapse Warning Signs

Relapse after a period of sobriety is not a discrete event but rather a process that begins long before actual use of the substance. It is important for clients to develop a comprehensive list of "warning signs" that could indicate that they have begun heading toward a relapse. Warning signs consist of behaviors, thoughts, attitudes, and emotions that are not conducive to recovery (see Table 13.1).

Analyzing Relapses

When clients experience a relapse, conducting an analysis of the factors that led to the return to substance use provides a blueprint for how to prevent future relapses. Relapse analysis allows individuals to recognize the changes they were reluctant to make and to understand how that reluctance led to using again (Daley & Lis, 1995). These changes are called *reservations*; they are specific changes that may have been

TABLE 13.1   Common Warning Signs of Relapse

TYPE OF WARNING SIGN	EXAMPLES
Behaviors	Hanging out with friends who use
	Over or under sleeping
	Irregular eating
	Lack of daily structure
	Lying
	Increased use of over-the-counter medications
	Dropping out or suspending attendance of treatment or 12-step programs
	Increased cross-addictions such as gambling, shopping, eating, working, or sexual activities
	Isolation
	Major life changes
Thoughts	Believing that one is cured
	Denial of fears
	Viewing problems as unsolvable
	Wishful thinking
	Overanalyzing of self
	Fantasizing about using
	Questioning whether one has an addiction
Attitudes	Overconfidence
	"Not caring"
	Blaming others
	Excessive pride
	Overreacting to stress
	Rejecting help
	Negativity toward authority figures
Emotions	Depression
	Irritability
	Listlessness
	Resentments
	Self-pity
	Aches and pains

recommended by others and were resisted by the client. It is important to help clients trace their behaviors, thoughts and emotions prior to their relapse as far back as possible.

Often clients will indicate that the relapse "just suddenly happened" without warning signs. However, review of a comprehensive list of relapse warning signs usually helps clients identify issues that were occurring outside their awareness. Another important part of processing a relapse is identifying "seemingly inconsequential decisions" that occurred prior to the relapse. These are minor decisions that clients make long before a relapse. They can be very small decisions such as deciding to skip treatment sporadically, accepting a job in a restaurant that has a bar, having dinner with an old using friend, or driving by a favorite restaurant or bar.

Several studies have found that negative affect is a reliable predictor of substance use for women (Griffin, Weiss, Mirin, & Lange, 1989; McKay, Cacciola, Kabasakalian-McKay, & Alterman, 1996; Pelissier & Jones, 2005; Peters et al., 1997). Studies have found that females with substance abuse issues report more depression, anxiety, and suicidal behavior than men, whereas men present with more antisocial tendencies (Pelissier & Jones, 2005; Peters et al., 1997). As mentioned earlier in the chapter on depression, women may be more likely to internalize their distress as depression, whereas men may be more likely to externalize their distress as irritability and antisocial behaviors. McKay and colleagues (1996) found that women reported more unpleasant affect and more interpersonal problems prior to a relapse as compared to men. Men were more likely to have been paid and to have been experiencing positive affect prior to a relapse. Men also reported more thoughts that included self-justification and minimization following a relapse as compared to women (McKay et al., 1996). In addition, men are more likely to report that they use for peer acceptance (Pelissier & Jones, 2005).

Changing Lifestyle

One of the most significant areas that should be addressed for clients attempting sobriety is the area of lifestyle changes. When individuals are using drugs or alcohol to the degree that it is interfering with their functioning, it is likely that they have developed a lifestyle that supports using. Their leisure activities, relaxation strategies and social outlets often involve using. They seek out friends who use drugs and alcohol and avoid friends and family who do not use. If they stop using but continue with the same lifestyle, it is unlikely that they will be able to refrain from using for long. In part, this is due to the pressure that they will receive from others that are using with them. In addition, their lifestyle will include many triggers, with exposure to a large number of triggers usually leading to relapse. To facilitate lifestyle changes, it is helpful to have clients create a *time analysis* that details their daily activities during a typical week when they were using. This provides an opportunity to identify the social cues and antecedents associated with use. Clients can then create an alternative time analysis for a typical week in recovery and begin changing and replacing things in their life associated with using. The issue of balance is particularly important for those in recovery. One of the hallmarks of addiction is the tendency to do things in excess. This not only applies to drug and alcohol use but also to sexual relationships, eating, shopping, exercise, working, and recovery activities. For example, individuals attending 15 recovery meetings per week may be applying their tendency toward compulsive behaviors to meeting attendance. It is generally impossible to remain in recovery when acting compulsively in other life areas. Therefore, therapists must help clients work toward balance in all areas of their life. This is usually a work in progress, with small steps toward the ultimate goal of maintaining a balanced, healthy lifestyle.

Resisting Invitations to Use

A nearly universal struggle for people in recovery is the pressure that they experience from others to use. For some, their addiction has progressed to the latter stages where they use solely in isolation and have no using relationships. However, most people entering recovery have a network of friends and family who have helped them to maintain their relation with their substance of choice. One of the most challenging and difficult tasks in recovery is deciding what to do about these relationships. In some situations, conducting family therapy to help clients educate their partners, friends, or family members about addiction and assisting the client in setting boundaries can be extremely helpful. Additionally, some clients have relationships that they need to avoid or end. However, it is important to help clients determine how they will deal with pressure when they have contact with old relationships. Role playing can be an extremely helpful way of giving clients the language, skills, and practice that they will need to disengage themselves from these situations. It can be helpful to make a list of refusal strategies that clients can keep with them. Therapists may also role play with clients about how to get a moment to themselves to review these strategies when they need them. The most difficult decisions involve close friends and family members who continue to use and with whom it is dangerous for clients to be in a relationship. This can be a painful process, with failure to take action leading to relapse.

Family Therapy

The disease of addiction is well-known for its ability to tear families apart. The dishonesty and denial that maintain addiction create pain, hurt, and anger in affected individuals. Addiction is an isolating disease and individuals who use find themselves spending decreasing time with their family members. Families who are affected by addiction generally have no avenue for communicating and exploring what is happening in their family. In many situations, the family members have no idea why things are happening—they do not recognize the disease for what it is—and they typically benefit from education in much the same way that clients do. In addition, parents who use substances model how to function (or not function) as an adult for their children. Family therapy can repair the damage done by addiction and, more importantly, can prevent further damage for families and children.

Research on the use of family therapy with substance abusers has generally found positive results (Center of Substance Abuse Treatment, 2004). One study examined parents who were attending a methadone program that included long-term family therapy. They found significant improvements in both abstinence from drugs and family functioning (Catalano, Gainey, Fleming, Haggerty, & Johnson, 1999). Many programs advocate the inclusion of family members in treatment with substance abusers. One program designed to treat marijuana abusers had structured educational sessions with family members to provide information about the abuse of marijuana and treatment goals, allowed family members to discuss the impact of the substance use on their relationship with clients, and identified ways family members could directly support abstinence (Steinberg et al., 2002).

Although family therapy can be an important part of working with substance abusers, the focus and purpose of the family therapy differs depending on where the abuser is in the process of recovery. In the initial stages of change (precontemplative and contemplative), family therapy can be utilized to help therapists understand the impact of the substance use on the family, which may be explored further in later individual sessions. Family therapy can also help family members become "unstuck" from their traditional roles in the family. For example, enablers often find themselves protecting substance abusers from the consequences of their use. Family members who are enablers can benefit greatly from education that demonstrates how their behaviors help the client use successfully. Once they understand this concept, they may choose an alternative strategy the next time they are called upon to cover for the substance abuser.

When clients are preparing to make changes to support sobriety, family therapy can support this process as well. Family members may inadvertently undermine changes that clients are trying to make. If they are not involved in the process, they may resent changes that interfere with the family's schedule or that take the person away from the home. Involving family members in the decision-making process reduces the likelihood that they will sabotage the changes. For example, family members can help plan the best time for the client to attend meetings. Educating family members about triggers and coping skills is also helpful at this stage.

During the maintenance phase, family therapy can focus on longer-term goals. It is important at this stage to address family member roles that may need to be adjusted once clients are abstinent. For example, a wife may have assumed the role of budgeter because her husband was irresponsible with money when he was using. Now that he is clean, he may automatically want to make more financial decisions. This can lead to resentment by the wife, who had been doing just fine managing their money. Another very common issue is the parentification of children. During active substance abuse, much of the family's time and energy goes toward dealing with the substance user. As a result, children are often left to their own devices, such as lacking enforcement of curfews and bedtimes or monitoring of homework and chores. Once a parent stops using, these rules frequently change, and children have difficulty adjusting to the increase in structure, expectations, and limits. Many times, as described earlier, family homeostatic dynamics result in a strong, unconscious push for the substance abuser to begin using again, if only to allow the family system to return to its old familiar patterns. It is important to address and predict this phenomenon with the family before it happens.

Pharmacotherapy

Pharmacotherapy with substance use disorders serves different functions. Some medications block the substance's effects, while others reduce cravings. Still other medications allow for safe withdrawal as individuals go through the process of detoxification. Although pharmacological interventions are often imbedded within established treatment programs, many treatment programs do not have the resources to offer this type of treatment. Research has demonstrated that pharmacological interventions are most effective when combined with other supportive therapy services (National Institute on Drug Abuse, 2005b). Table 13.2 lists common medical interventions used with substance-abusing clients.

Withdrawal from alcohol and sedatives can be life-threatening. Medical evaluations are essential components of treatment for addiction to these substances. Clients should never stop using these substances without meeting with a medical professional first. Often they are placed on a comparable medication and then slowly taper off this medication to prevent seizures and other complications associated with withdrawal. At times this occurs on an outpatient basis, but it is much safer in a hospital or detoxification unit.

Post-Acute Withdrawal

Regardless of the treatment mode used, recovering addicts and treatment providers must deal with post-acute withdrawal (PAW), which is the constellation of symptoms that occur after the obvious, physiological process of acute withdrawal. PAW is the effect of the long-term process of damage to the central nervous system that is the result of chronic drug or alcohol use as well as the result of stressful events that are inherent in the recovery process. Typically, PAW symptoms begin 6 to 8 weeks after abstinence, peak between 3 and 6 months, and resolve between 6 and 24 months after the onset of abstinence.

TABLE 13.2   Pharmacological Interventions for Substance Abuse

PRESCRIBED DRUG	SUBSTANCE USED FOR	PURPOSE	PROS	CONS
Buprenorphine	Opiates	Blocks the effects of opiates when they are ingested; prevents cravings	Safe in case of overdose; can be discontinued easily; less likely to be abused; can be dispensed in a doctor's office	Can be prescribed by a physician, so there may not be supportive therapy services available in physician's office
Disulfiram (Antabuse)	Alcohol	Prevents ingestion of alcohol by causing extreme illness when used with alcohol	Immediate response when alcohol is ingested	Clients must be highly motivated to take it; must be taken prior to drinking; response can be avoided by not taking it
Naltrexone	Alcohol; opiates	Blocks the effects of alcohol and opiates	Prevents binging if there is a lapse	Does not affect craving for opiates or alcohol
Methadone	Opiates	Blocks the effects of opiates when they are ingested; prevents cravings; facilitates withdrawal from opiates	Successfully prevents cravings; clients can be maintained for long periods of time; prevents binging due to slower onset	Can be addictive; clients need to be withdrawn from it; can be expensive to maintain
Benzodiazapines	Alcohol	Treats alcohol withdrawal by allowing a taper dose of the medication	Prevents medical complications from withdrawal from alcohol; reduces cravings	Can be addictive; can be life-threatening if used with alcohol

The most obvious symptoms of PAW include the inability to manage responses to stress and difficulty problem solving. Specific symptoms include:

- *Inability to think clearly*: difficulty concentrating, poor abstract reasoning, rigid thinking
- *Memory problems*: primarily short-term; resulting in difficulty with learning new tasks

- *Emotional over reactivity or numbness*: generally fluctuating between overreaction and numbness
- *Sleep problems*: disturbing dreams, difficulty falling or staying asleep, abnormal sleep patterns
- *Physical coordination problems*: dizziness, balance problems, poor coordination that often results in accident proneness
- *Stress sensitivity*: difficulty distinguishing between low- and high-stress situations, inappropriate responses to stress; complicated by the fact that all previous symptoms worsen during times of high stress or when the response to stress is high

These symptoms fluctuate over the short and long term. Some people may never experience all of them, but many people struggle with some symptoms after a period of abuse of substances. In part, these symptoms result from using a substance to deal with stress. If clients have used drugs or alcohol to cope with stress, stressful situations without the numbing effects of substances seem overwhelming. Physiologically, clients respond to the stress as if their survival is under attack. This is a high-risk time, as everything in their body tells them to use drugs to reduce the symptoms of stress. Explaining this process to clients and normalizing the stress response and the strong desire to use can be very comforting, as clients often believe they are going crazy when they experience these reactions to stress.

The single best treatment of PAW symptoms is prevention of stress. Lifestyle changes that support daily structure and self-care help minimize the symptoms of PAW. It stands to reason that if individuals in recovery get enough sleep, exercise regularly, eat well, and minimize stress, the symptoms of PAW, which are worsened by stress, will be minimized. Some suggestions for managing symptoms of PAW are as follows:

- Eat well-balanced meals regularly
- Limit the use of caffeine, sugar, and nicotine, all of which can aggravate symptoms
- Get plenty of rest
- Practice meditation or other relaxation techniques daily
- Engage in regular aerobic exercise
- Talk about symptoms with others regularly

- Develop techniques to help with short-term memory loss to reduce frustration
- Learn stress-management techniques
- Read about PAW symptoms to learn as much as possible about what you are experiencing

Therapists must remain vigilant with their post-acute withdrawal clients for the on-going difficulties involved with maintaining sobriety. Their brains and bodies are vulnerable to stress so they are urgently need to develop and strengthen a healthy lifestyle to help prevent relapse.

Summary

Therapists have more tools to work with when helping substance abusers than they might realize. While working with someone who abuses substances can be overwhelming and frustrating, many of the same skills used for other problems are beneficial when working with these clients. Because of the intense issues typically involved in working with substance abusers, intense countertransference responses are common. Supervision and peer consultation are essential for maintaining open minds and utilizing our therapeutic skills in helpful and nonjudgmental ways.

The skills learned in graduate school and practiced over the years are the same skills that are helpful when working with those who abuse substances. Empathy is a key ingredient tied to outcome with problem drinkers (Miller, Taylor, & West, 1980). In order to develop empathy with any client, reflective listening can find the story behind the story. What is it that this client stands to gain or lose by giving up substance use? Once empathy is established, a message of hope and choices, presented in a caring, nonjudgmental manner, can have a significant impact. By utilizing MI techniques, therapists give their clients the message that change is their choice, that no one can force them to change, and that they have the ability to look at their life and make good choices for themselves. Even if clients choose not to make these changes at a particular time, therapists can rest assured that these messages will stay with them and can help them to make changes in the future.

CHAPTER 14

Couple, Marital, and Family Therapy

The course of true love never did run smooth.
—WILLIAM SHAKESPEARE, FROM *A MIDSUMMER NIGHT'S DREAM*

Maintaining relationships and marriages can be very challenging. Half of all individuals seeking therapy report problems with their primary relationships. Often compounding relationship problems is the fact that couples wait an average of 6 years from the time that they detect serious problems to the time that they seek help. Further, less than 1% of couples who divorce receive marital counseling during the year prior to their divorce. For these reasons and others, it is not surprising that in the U.S. almost half of all first marriages and more than half of all second marriages currently end in divorce (Johnson & LeBow, 2000).

Couple and family therapy (CFT) has been growing rapidly, both as a profession (e.g., licensed marriage and family therapists, licensed professional counselors) and in public recognition of need. Mental health professionals at all levels are often expected to work effectively with couples and families who are experiencing a wide variety of issues and problems. The CFT field has grown through various stages. Initially, theories and techniques from individual therapy were applied to couples and families. Subsequently, family and systemic theories were developed to address specific weaknesses of traditional individual psychodynamic approaches, such as family influences on major mental illnesses such as schizophrenia (e.g., Mental Research Institute group and

Theories and techniques associated with couple, family, and sex therapies build upon those associated with individual therapy, and include additional features designed to address the complexity of systemic functioning.

Bowen) and assisting people living under conditions of poverty and disenfranchisement (e.g., Aponte, 1976; Ho, 1987; Minuchin, 1974). Currently, all of these perspectives are being incorporated with research offering therapists greater evidence-based guidance than was previously available (Johnson & LeBow, 2000; Lebow, 1997). This chapter provides an overview of the theory, concepts, and techniques associated with couple, marital, and family therapy.

Theory and Concepts

As noted earlier, therapists' views of couple and family processes initially emerged from extrapolations of theories of therapy for individuals. The subsequent development of systemic perspectives brought about greater focus on understanding couple and family processes as distinct entities. In essence, therapists need additional concepts and techniques when working with more than one individual in therapy or when treating problems based in couple or family systems.

Systemic Perspectives

Couples and families are more than just the sum of the individual family members: They have a life of their own. Hence, skillful family therapists can often accomplish more doing therapy with a family than by having each individual family member receive individual therapy—the family itself is receiving assistance. Family members are *interconnected* (affect one another). Family members have varying *boundaries* between one another (characteristic ways in which they interact, control, and influence one another). The appropriateness of boundaries (e.g., how much children should be separate from their parents) is a controversial subject and varies widely by culture. Families also have *homeostatic* self-monitoring mechanisms that resist change in individual members (Jackson, 1957). *Positive and negative feedback mechanisms* are the operative concepts behind interconnectedness and homeostasis (e.g., "I anticipate criticism and so adopt a defensive or hostile stance, which gets me criticized, which causes me to adopt a defensive or hostile stance, and so on").

Family systems theorists posit that family *rules* are inferred patterns of interaction that maintain the homeostasis (Jackson, 1965a). Similarly, *quid pro quo patterns* ("you do this and in turn I'll do that") are metaphorical statements of the couple relationship bargain (i.e., how the couple has agreed to define themselves within the relationship) (Jackson, 1965b, p. 12). The *"quid pro quo* pattern becomes an unwritten (usually not consciously recognized) set of ground rules" that allow partners to

> Couples and families are more than just the sum of the individual family members: They have a life of their own. Their homeostatic self-monitoring mechanisms resist change. Family members are interconnected and influence each other through the varying boundaries among and between them.

assure themselves that they are equals and thereby preserve their dignity and self-esteem (Lederer & Jackson, 1968, p. 179).

Systemic views of therapy focus on reciprocal causation rather than on linear notions of causality. These views are also based on the belief that behaviors cannot be understood apart from their context. Primary aspects of systemic views of communication are delineated in Watzlawick, Beavin, and Jackson's (1967) five axioms of communication which follow in Table 14.1.

The concept of the *double bind* arose from studies of communications among troubled families, particularly those with schizophrenia (Bateson, Jackson, Haley, & Weakland, 1956). In essence, a double bind is a psychological impasse resulting from contradictory demands made of an individual; no matter which directive is followed, the response can be construed as incorrect. A simple example is the directive: "Be spontaneous!" (No matter how one responds, one is not being spontaneous because one was instructed to do it). However, double binds can be far more complex and insidious (see Watzlawick et al., 1967). They may involve conflicting levels of communication and an injunction against commenting upon the discrepancy. The classic double bind example is that of a young man recovering from a schizophrenic episode who is visited by his parent at the hospital. He was glad to see the parent and put his arms around the parent's shoulders. The parent stiffened, the young man pulled his arm back, and the parent said, "Don't you love me any more?" The young man blushed and the parent said, "Dear, you must not be so easily embarrassed and afraid of your feelings." The young man was only able to handle being with his parent a few more minutes before he assaulted an aide and was restrained (Watzlawick et al., 1967). In this situation, the parent was giving the son conflicting nonverbal and verbal messages, and he was unable to comment upon the discrepancy.

TABLE 14.1	Five Axioms Regarding Family Communication
1.	One cannot not communicate (for example, not responding is a response).
2.	Each communication has both a report (content) and a command (process or relationship-defining) aspect. The command may serve as a comment on the content. For example, the statement "I am hungry" conveys factual content but also may include an unstated relationship-defining message such as "Our relationship is such that I expect you to prepare or buy a meal for me."
3.	The nature of a relationship depends on the punctuation of a repetitive series of events (who does what to whom, in response to what). Sources of dysfunction may arise from failure to recognize the repetitive quality of certain communication patterns, alternative ways of punctuating the events, and the possibility of breaking the chain of certain communications. For example, one person may view fights as starting when the other partner raises his or her voice, whereas the other person views fights as starting when the partner rolls their eyes, looks away, and uses a sarcastic tone. These patterns tend to repeat, with each person pointing to different points in their circular interaction pattern as the "cause" of subsequent conflict.
4.	Humans communicate both verbally and nonverbally (for example, through gestures and facial expressions). Nonverbal communications often yield ambiguous messages open to misinterpretation.
5.	Communications are either complimentary (based upon inequality of power and status) or symmetrical (based upon relative equality of power and status and minimization of differences). Examples of complimentary communication include a parent telling a child what to do, and a boss ordering an underling to do something, with the subordinate person acquiescing to the dominant person's demand. An example of symmetrical communication reflecting equality and minimization of differences include a balanced conversation among peers.

Strategic and Structural Family Therapy

The patterns of interaction in the family influence the behavior of each family member. *Patterns of interaction* are defined as the sequential behaviors among family members that become habitual and repeated over time (Minuchin 1974; Minuchin, Montalvo, Guerney, Rosman, & Schumer, 1967). Thus, in the strategic view, symptoms are viewed as associated with one family member's attempts to change or modify problems that he or she has identified in another family member. The very actions taken by family members to improve difficulties often only make them worse. Vicious circles of deterioration and rigid, unproductive efforts on the part of the family to stimulate change are the object of family intervention in the strategic approach. Hence, strategic approaches seek to create changes in the family interaction patterns.

One common pattern is that of the family *symptom bearer* (Bowen called this person the "identified patient"). Other family members (and often this person as well) view this person as having or being the problem, and seek therapy to get this person straightened out. Family members might say, "Our family is fine except for Mary who is really a mess." However, in some family systems, Mary, the identified patient, may be the main symptom bearer for problems elsewhere in the family system. For example, Mary may be an adolescent who seeks attention when her parents have a serious fight. In extreme cases, Mary may initiate a drug overdose, engage in cutting, risk suicide, or get arrested to attract attention. The role of the therapist in strategic therapy is to identify the family interaction patterns associated with the symptom bearer's behavior problems. For example, caregivers who are arguing about establishing rules and consequences for a problem adolescent may never reach agreement because the adolescent disrupts their arguments with self-destructive attempts to get attention. Hence, strategic interventions carefully target the problematic behavior and provide practical ways to change the patterns of interaction (e.g., the way in which caregivers attempt but fail to establish rules and consequences) that are directly linked to the adolescent's problem behaviors (adapted from National Institute on Drug Abuse, 2005h).

Bowenian Family Therapy

Murray Bowen (1978) noted that as tensions and anxieties develop in interpersonal relationships, some dyads involve a third person in their relationship to deflect attention, reduce anxiety, and increase stability. This process, called *triangulation*, may lessen tensions between the original dyad temporarily, but does not address the underlying issue.

Bowen emphasized individuals' *differentiation of self*, which involves both the psychological separation of intellect and emotion as well as independence of self from others. He viewed individuals' capacity to be ruled by reason as an index of their differentiation. In Bowen's view, healthy people have both a sense of belonging to their family as well as a sense of separateness and individuality. Snarch (1998) extended Bowen's approaches to emphasize authenticity and differentiation. It should be noted that Bowen's concepts of differentiation, individuality, and emphasis on reason have been criticized by feminist and multicultural scholars for being biased against women and those from collectivist cultures (e.g., African and Asian), as well as against those in which filial piety is emphasized (e.g., Asian and Asian-American).

Narrative Therapy

White and Epston (1990) emphasized a collaborative therapeutic stance with interventions arising from social constructivist approaches to therapy. Central tenants of narrative therapy are that people's lives and relationships are shaped by the knowledge and stories that communities create together and then engage in to give meaning to their experiences. Individuals develop certain practices of self-in-relationship that constitute ways of living associated with this knowledge and these stories. Narrative therapy examines the ways in which these stories frame interactions and both foster and preclude possibilities. The basic premise of narrative therapy is the idea that the person is never the problem: The problem is the problem. Two key techniques are deconstruction and externalization of the problem (discussed later in this chapter). In essence, narrative therapy assists clients in resolving problems by: (1) enabling them to separate their lives and relationships from knowledge and stories that they judge to be impoverishing; (2) helping them to challenge the ways of life that they find subjugating; and (3) encouraging them to re-author their lives according to alternative, preferred stories of identity and according to preferred ways of life.

Emotion-Focused Couple Therapy

Emotion-focused therapy (EFT) emphasizes the centrality of emotions in couple distress therapy (Johnson, 1996, 1999; Johnson, Hunsley, Greenberg, & Schindler, 1999). Based on attachment theory (described earlier in this book), EFT views distressed relationships as "insecure bonds in which essential healthy attachment needs are unable to be met due to rigid interaction patterns that block emotional engagement" (Johnson & Greenberg, 1995, p. 121). In the context of couple therapy, EFT assists partners in exploring and communicating their emotional experiences regarding issues including affiliation, closeness and control, and dependence within the context of the current relationship. EFT theorizes that once these valid attachment needs are clarified, people will understand themselves and their partners more clearly and sympathetically. This new understanding leads to new and less defensive interaction patterns.

> In the context of couple therapy, EFT assists partners in exploring and communicating emotional experiences regarding issues including affiliation, closeness and control, and dependence within the context of the current relationship.

Insight-Oriented Marital Therapy

Insight-oriented marital therapy (IOMT) emphasizes "the resolution of conflictual emotional processes that exist either within one or both spouses separately, between the spouses interactively, or within the broader family system. This approach attempts to integrate individual, couple, and family functioning by addressing developmental issues, collusive interactions, incongruent contractual expectations, irrational role assignments, and maladaptive relationship rules" (Snyder & Wills, 1989, p. 41). The IOMT approach emphasizes "probes, clarifications, and interpretation in uncovering and explicating those feelings, beliefs, and expectations which spouses had toward themselves, their partners, and their marriage, which were either totally or partially beyond awareness, so that these could be restructured, or renegotiated at a conscious level" (Snynder & Wills, 1989, p. 41).

Although IOMT places greater emphasis on psychodynamic issues that are partially or fully at an unconscious level, both IOMT and EFT ask clients to explore the feelings, thoughts, and needs believed to underlie the couple's current distress. Both approaches view sharing these more vulnerable aspects of oneself as central to the partner's gaining greater empathy and understanding of the other. This frees the couple to interact in healthier ways. Thus, both EFT and IOMT focus on the couple's current situation, with their interaction patterns becoming alterable when individuals' needs and reasons for acting negatively are made explicit within the context of emotional expression and insight.

Behavioral Marital Therapy

Behavioral marital therapy (BMT) is a skills-oriented approach based on social learning principles. BMT assists couples in gaining skills and understanding of relationship interactions to improve their marriages (Baucom, & Epstein, 1990; Jacobson & Margolin, 1979; Stuart, 1980). Treatment focuses primarily on teaching couples how to communicate with each other and to solve problems more effectively. Therapists typically assist clients in planning behavioral changes designed to increase the frequency of pleasing interactions and to minimize destructive, negative interactions. Although there are differences among behavioral interventions, most focus on the present, address behaviors and interaction patterns that are in the couple's awareness, involve specific behavioral changes designed to promote more adaptive functioning, and incorporate application of behavioral principles outside of the session via homework activities (Baucom, Shoham, Muesser, Daiuto, & Stickle, 1998).

Cognitive-Behavioral Marital Therapy

Cognitive-behavioral marital therapy (CBMT) seeks to enhance the effectiveness of BMT by supplementing it with cognitive interventions. Hence, in addition to employing behavioral techniques, CBMT assists partners in thinking about and understanding their relationship and each partner's behavior in less destructive ways. Partners might be helped to consider alternative, more adaptive explanations or attributions for the other partner's undesired behaviors. Similarly, partners might be encouraged to examine and revise their unrealistic expectations about their partner or their relationships.

Gottman and Associates

The CFT field has benefited from research on relationship satisfaction and distress and from the development of models of couple relationship development and communication patterns (Gottman, 1994; Heavey, Christensen, & Malamuth, 1995). Perhaps not surprisingly, these researchers found that couples in satisfying relationships have far more positive exchanges and communicate better than those in troubled relationships. In general, these studies find that *emotional engagement* and *mutual soothing* are of crucial importance to maintaining and healing relationships (Johnson & LeBow, 2000).

Following are suggestions for preserving strong relationships (adapted from Gottman, 2005):

- *Seek help early.* As noted earlier, the average couple waits 6 years before seeking help for relationship problems (half of all marriages that end do so in the first 7 years). This means the average couple lives with unhappiness for far too long.

- *Edit yourself.* Couples who avoid saying every critical thought when discussing touchy topics are consistently the happiest.

- *Soften your "startup."* Arguments may "start up" because a partner quickly escalates the conflict by making a critical or contemptuous remark in a confrontational tone. Bring up problems gently and without blame.

- *Accept influence.* Relationships succeed when partners accept influence from each other. Based on Gottman's findings, the most common problem in this area is the need for male partners to accept greater influence from the female partner. If a woman says, "Do you have to work Thursday night? My mother is coming that weekend, and I need your help getting ready," and her husband replies, "My plans are set, and I'm not changing them," this guy is likely to be in a shaky relationship. A man's ability to be influenced by his partner is crucial because women are generally more practiced at accepting influence from men. A true partnership only occurs when men can do so as well.

- *Have high standards.* Happy couples have high standards for each other even as newlyweds. The most successful couples are those who, even as newlyweds, refuse to accept hurtful behavior from each other. The lower the level of tolerance for bad behavior in the beginning of a relationship, the happier the couple is down the road.

- *Learn to repair and exit the argument.* Successful couples know how to exit an argument. Happy couples know how to repair the situation before an argument gets completely out of control. Successful repair attempts include: changing the topic to something completely unrelated, using humor, stroking your partner with a caring remark ("I understand that this is hard for you"), making it clear you are on common ground ("This is our problem"), backing down (in a relationship, as in the martial art Aikido, you sometimes have to yield to win), and, in general, offering signs of appreciation for your partner and his or her feelings along the way ("I really appreciate and want to thank you for. . . ."). If an argument gets too heated, take a 20-minute break and agree to approach the topic again when you are both calm.

- *Focus on the bright side.* In happy relationships, while discussing problems, couples make at least five times as many positive statements to and about each other and their relationship as negative ones. Good relationships benefit from a rich climate of positivity.

In contrast, *negative emotions* and specific *negative interaction patterns* (such as criticism and contempt expressed by one partner responded to with distancing and stonewalling by the other partner) are associated with unfavorable relationship satisfaction. Indeed, "the four horsemen" associated with relationship breakdown and divorce were identified as: (1) escalation of criticism, (2) defensiveness, (3) contempt, and (4) stonewalling (an unresponsive attitude toward one's partner). When these types of patterns become pervasive in the relationship, emotional engagement becomes difficult to sustain, with polarization and distancing accelerating the process of relationship dissolution.

Additionally, many people are emotionally illiterate; they fail to notice or are unaware of what their partner is saying and are unable to read a facial expression or voice (Declaire & Gottman, 2002; Good, 1998; Lebow, 2000). Healthy people have access to the full spectrum of human emotions. When individuals cut off awareness or expression of certain emotions (such as anger, sadness, grief, and vulnerability), problems often arise. Further, rigid roles and expectations, including stereotypical gender roles (beliefs that "girls or women should . . . and boys and men should . . ."), are typically unhealthy for relationships and tend to cause problems (Philpot, 2005).

Gottman suggested that therapists teach couples how to communicate and resolve conflicts. Couples are encouraged to remember to treat their partners with the courtesy and respect that they would show people if they were guests in their home. Focusing on transactions, Gottman observes that partners' initial offerings and responses are critical, as these small moments serve as the building blocks to intimacy and trust. In examining the overall results of his studies, Gottman concluded that:

> Emotional engagement and mutual soothing are critically important to maintaining and healing relationships (Johnson & Lebow, 2000). The "four horsemen" associated with relationship breakdown are: escalation of criticism, defensiveness, contempt, and stonewalling.

Part of the marital bond is the global or perceptual filter couples have of the relationship. If you have a strong marital bond, you give your partner a break when times are tough. With a strong bond, even if a couple doesn't agree on something they find ways of avoiding destructive arguments because they really like each other and appreciate the differences. With a weak bond, you don't give respect and kindness to your partner. There is a lot more disagreement and a lot less friendship. . . . A lot of couples neglect the friendship in marriage and it erodes over time because of such things as career demands and having children. . . . When you neglect friendship, the positive perceptual filter you have about your partner begins to fail. People need to make time to nurture their marriage, just like they take time to work out, for the health of the relationship. (Schwartz, 2000)

[The happiest couples] know the value of their partner in their life and know they are not out to get them. It is really beautiful music. With the unhappiest couples there is no symmetry. There is no respect for each other. Individuals are really nasty with each other and they struggle to find positive things to say about each other or the relationship. . . . Couples who do well have realistic expectations of one another and their marriage, communicate well, use conflict resolution skills, and are compatible with one another. (Gottman, as quoted by Schwartz, 2001)

Couple therapy researchers have discovered unexpected findings. First, despite therapists' widespread view that clients' accurate communication of feelings is the foundation of effective couple therapy, such communication is actually *contraindicated* when clients feel great contempt for their partner (Lebow, 2000). In other words, if the couple wants to stay together, it may hurt their cause if one partner expresses how much disrespect he or she feels for the other partner. Second,

> Despite therapists' widespread view that clients' accurate communication of feelings is the foundation of effective couple therapy, such communication is actually contraindicated when clients feel great contempt for their partner.

couple's angry interactions *per se* are not as poisonous to close relationships as often thought. Some couples have high levels of conflict and remain satisfied with their relationship as long as they also maintain positive sentiments about the relationship (Gottman & Krokoff, 1989). In other words, while perhaps not most therapists' view of an optimal relationship, some couples seem to enjoy intense conflict as part of their overall satisfying relationship.

Other researchers have added to our knowledge of couples, families, and therapy. For example, simple overarching notions of relationship satisfaction have been expanded to allow for partners' potentially highly differentiated positive and negative components. Thus mental health practitioners should not assume that just because an individual has many complaints about his or her partner that there is automatically a corresponding lack of positive relating. Similarly, individuals with relatively few complaints do not automatically have a high degree of positive relating with their partners. Therapists looking for additional practical professionally-oriented resources in couple and family therapy may want to consider the following: Donovan (1999) *Short-Term Couple Therapy*; Heitler (1995) *The Angry Couple: Conflict-Focused Treatment* [video]; Horne (1999) *Family Counseling and Therapy*; and Johnson (1993) *Emotion-Focused Couple Therapy: Healing Broken Bonds* [video].

Multicultural Perspectives

Families, peers, and neighborhoods exist within a wider cultural context that influences the family and its individual members (see Figure 2.2). Extensive research on culture and the family has demonstrated that the family and the child are influenced by their cultural contexts (Szapocznik & Kurtines, 1993). Multicultural approaches emphasize race and culture and how these concepts apply to therapeutic work. Multicultural, postmodern, and solution-focused practices also emphasize nonpathological approaches to clients. These perspectives assist therapists in learning to respect diversity and recognize the strengths in the families they

> Multicultural perspectives emphasize that families and their individual members exist within wider cultural contexts. Therapists are encouraged to respect diversity and are challenged to increase their awareness of cultural and gender-related issues in their work.

serve. All therapists are challenged to become culture- and gender-sensitive. Therapists are also expected to develop interventions that are responsive to social justice issues.

Research on CFT Effectiveness

As mentioned earlier, CFT approaches were developed to address concerns that responded poorly to individual therapies. It was initially thought that family interaction patterns, such as the double bind (Mental Research Institute) or poor differentiation (Bowen), caused schizophrenia. Although this turned out to not be the case, family interaction patterns certainly do influence the course of schizophrenia, and family therapy is helpful in ways that analysis of transference is not. Likewise, environmental factors such as poverty exert powerful influences that often require strong and direct interventions.

Evaluations of the empirical support for CFT interventions concluded that EFT and BMT met criteria as efficacious, with EFT being particularly beneficial for mildly to moderately distressed couples (Baucom et al., 1998). Additionally, IOMT, CBT, cognitive therapy for couples, and couple systemic therapy all met criteria as possibly efficacious treatments. All the previously mentioned interventions were superior to wait list controls (Baucom et al., 1998). The common efficacy of these various approaches is probably due less to specific techniques than it is to contextual factors associated with therapy, such as an effective therapeutic working alliance and expectations for change (Wampold, 2001).

Developmental Aspects of Relationships and Family Life

Romantic relationships and families tend to progress through several stages. Therapists providing services to couples or individual clients whose primary concern has to do with their long-term romantic relationship or families may assess how the concerns are potentially related to developmental issues.

Stages of Romantic Relationships/Marriage

Prosky (1991) provided a potentially useful three-phase model for understanding different challenges that romantic relationships/marriages tend to encounter over time.

1. *Awareness of similarities ("fusion")*. This phase is theorized to last from about 6 months to 1 year. Fusion is characterized by intense awareness of partners' shared similarities and compatibility. Individuals at this stage might say "We are so alike! We always like to do the same things!" This is the "honeymoon" phase romanticized by media. In this phase, the other person fills one's void and completes the other. Some people understandably think this is what relationships should always be like. Thus, people may end relationships when the work part begins ("If this relationship takes this much work, this must not be the right relationship for me!").

2. *Awareness of differences ("intense pulling")*. During this phase, individuals become more aware of their differences with their partner. They might ask, "Where is the partner I married?" and "What happened to our romance?" Individuals may try to change the other person to be more similar to them (e.g., values, habits, preferences, default assumptions). The underlying messages may be "Do it my way!" and "Your way is bad!" Indeed, everyone has their own, usually unquestioned, views of how they believe relationships should work (e.g., how frequently to interact with relatives, how fights should be conducted and resolved, what topics and feelings are best left unsaid). These implicit beliefs about relationships typically emerge from experiences in one's family of origin. Individuals may seek to replicate (or at times react in strong opposition to) implicit rules, understandings, and ways of doing things that they experienced growing up ("Of course this is the way that towels should be hung on the rack!" or "Of course this is the way that conflicts should be resolved!"). The intense pulling phase may resolve in various ways:
   - *Separation*. Separation may occur before partners acknowledge their differences and gain mutual understanding. Such separations tend to involve significant blaming and anger. Alternatively, separations occurring after mutual understanding is achieved typically have a "sadder but wiser" emotional tone. Partners recognize their contributions to the breakup, with both partners

learning something and reaching closure in ways that may benefit them in future relationships.

- *Institutionalization of differences.* Holding frozen anger and resentments, couples may lock into *not* relating: "You won't meet my needs, so I won't meet your needs!" They may continue sharing a household but not connect in their interpersonal worlds. Their differences and dynamics may become exaggerated, rigid, and repetitive, with each being dependent upon the other. The children and friends of these couples tend to say, "I don't know why they are together. They don't seem to even like one another!"

3. *Emergence of clarity ("I & thou").* Couples entering this phase recognize that the other person is different. The other person is not better or worse, but rather has different strengths and weaknesses. Disagreements are more about the true issues. For the first time there is clarity about the relationship and the difficulties it encounters. Individuals at this phase might say, "We share these interests, but not others" and "It is okay to do some things together and do other things with others." These couples realize that their partners have differing gifts, and that their lives and relationship are improved by the strengths that their partner brings to the relationship. As poetically stated by Octavio Paz, "The ultimate test of a relationship is to disagree but to hold hands."

Common Glitches in the Couple-to-Family Transition

There are common challenges as people enter into long-term relationships or marriages and again when they have children.

From Single to Couple

Many individuals find it challenging to learn to attend to one's partner without losing oneself ("we" and "me"). Growing up, healthy individuals learn to balance the various aspects of themselves. They learn to seek to get their needs met and also to deny seeking gratification of desires that would probably cause them problems. They learn to regulate their emotions and interpersonal relations and to maintain their health. Thus, when individuals enter into a relationship, they must negotiate "how we are going to be together" with varying degrees of accommodation to their individual patterns being made to fit with the preferences of their partner.

Some individuals may be prone to being very focused on getting their own needs met and therefore be relatively less focused on what is good for their partner and their relationship. Individuals who display insufficient accommodation toward their partner and the relationship may be viewed as self-centered, narcissistic, aggressive, inflexible, rigid, or controlling. Conversely, others may be prone to excessive accommodation to the desires (or their perception of the desires) of their partner. These individuals are sometimes viewed as considerate, giving, thoughtful, acquiescent, meek, or subassertive. These individuals are at increased risk for depression, anxiety, and passive-aggressiveness, as their personal wants and needs are insufficiently addressed.

Couples need to negotiate various aspects of cohabitation—such as differences in spending/saving habits, messy/cleanliness, scheduled/spontaneousness, and punctual/tardiness, as well as differences in preferred conflict-resolution styles, preferred social activities and with whom to do them, preferred sexual frequency/activities, and religious/spiritual involvement. Couples who do well at this phase understand that their preferred way (or the way that it was done in their family of origin) is not automatically the "right" way. They respect their partner and appreciate their differences, recognizing that good solutions can often be identified through working together.

Having Children

Couples often have children with relatively little forethought. Indeed, it is rather difficult (if not downright impossible) to describe in words what people have in store when they have children. How does one tell individuals who have developed patterns and expectations in which their lives revolve around fulfilling their own needs that such times have come to an end? Effective childrearing necessarily involves giving up not only avocations and hobbies, but also more basic needs like time for sleep, personal hygiene, and uninterrupted conversations.

This is a very challenging period for most couples. Adults are often seeking to establish their careers at the very time that their young children demand tremendous time and energy. Hence, it is not surprising that couples often experience a great deal of stress. Partners with primary childcare duties are often sleep-deprived and stressed by the high demands of young children. Partners who work are often stressed with the pressures of seeking to launch and advance their careers. When the two individuals get together, it is not surprising that both want their partner to provide appreciation, attention, and generally help in meeting their needs. Not surprisingly, when two tired and stressed people get together expecting to have their needs attended to, somebody's needs are not going to be attended to. This is further compounded by the ongoing need to care for the child (or children), prepare the meals, do household tasks, and perhaps attend to additional work.

In practice, therapists often hear complaints that one partner comes home and assumes that his or her work is done for the day, while the other partner has been doing childcare, meal preparation, and housework, which does not stop with the end of the workday. Therapists may also hear from the working partner that the other partner is tired, nagging, and uninterested in sex. This is a time when adults are faced with the task of realizing that life isn't about what *they* want anymore. There are now young people whose lives literally depend on their caretakers' putting the children's needs ahead of their own.

This is a time of major transition for "grown-up kids" who are used to indulging themselves. They must learn to redirect and sublimate their energies to meet the needs of their family. Individuals who are accustomed to looking out for themselves and who do not recognize the sacrifices that are associated with being effective parents may either be very unhappy about the sacrifices that they feel obligated to make or opt not to curtail their self-centered ways and be less effective partners and parents. This is often a time when expectations and discussions about roles, tasks, and equality of task allocation produce conflict.

As children enter the picture, couples must negotiate who will care for the children and how much of the time. Also, time now allocated for childcare is no longer available for household chores (e.g., cooking, cleaning, laundry, shopping, maintenance, or bill paying). Historically, women moved toward children and domestic responsibilities and men remained in the workforce. In more recent generations, women have continued to assume primary childcare responsibilities while also remaining in the workforce (perhaps in a reduced capacity) and men have continued in their role as workers but have assumed more responsibility in childcare and household duties. Nonetheless, a common exasperated response from partners at this phase is that their partner must not be doing their fair share because the other person is working so hard and there is always so much more to do!

This is often a difficult time for relationships. Couples should know this going into this life phase, try to appreciate what their partner is doing, reduce their expectations of their partner, seek to get some of their needs met via interactions with others, and be direct in expressing their essential wants/needs to their partner. Therapists can help defuse escalating spirals of hurt, anger, and resentment, as well as help couples understand their developmental situation and learn to work more collaboratively. The goal for this phase of life is: *Do no lasting harm to the relationship. Hang in there, things will improve!* Typically, partner relations improve slightly as the children enter school and need less constant and intensive care. Families with school-aged children are busy; there are many needs to balance.

Should We Stay Together?

Couples often ask therapists to render their opinion on whether the relationship or marriage is worth saving. In general, we believe that therapists should be relatively neutral, as it is really up to clients to determine if their relationship is worth it to them. Indeed, it may well be presumptuous of therapists to believe that they know what is best for their clients in terms of their romantic relationships. We do believe that good relationships experience challenges and tears, and that mending and repairing reasonably functional relationships is generally better for children. When angry couples wonder if they should stay together, it is sometimes helpful for them to realize that the opposite of love is not hate, but rather apathy. More specifically, love and hate both involve intense feelings for the partner. In contrast *apathy* reflects an absence of feeling or interest in the partner.

Essential Aspects of CFT

Effective counselors and therapists for couple and family concerns follow the general aspects of counseling and therapy described earlier: communicating therapeutically; forming effective therapeutic working alliances; identifying clients' goals and patterns to be changed; planning how to accomplish this; anticipating likely sources of support and resistance to change, as well as interpersonal reactions that may assist and prevent change; and assisting clients in recognizing and preparing for challenges they will probably encounter in the future, including helping them prepare for successful functioning without direct support from the therapist after termination. The remainder of this chapter is dedicated to a more extensive discussion of identifying patterns and techniques for facilitating change.

> Couples often ask therapists to tell them whether their relationship or marriage is worth saving. In general, we believe that therapists should be relatively neutral, as it is up to clients to determine the value of their relationship to them.

Identifying Patterns

Couples and families typically enter therapy with a stated "problem." This is typically the *content* of their concern (*"what* they talk about"). Chores, sex, money, parenting, and children are among the most common topics. People successfully resolve issues all the time—so what is it about this particular problem that creates greater or more lasting tension for the clients? At this point therapists should attend to and reflect their understanding of clients' concerns about this content, as well as offer tangible ideas about what they might do to resolve their conflicts when possible. Couples are often surprised that chores and household tasks become the source of so much conflict and ill feelings. Indeed, household responsibilities often take on symbolic meanings in terms of individuals' perceptions of privilege, fairness, appreciation, and respect. In a related vein, new fathers commonly complain about their wives ' lack of interest in sexual relations. In our experience, one of the best aphrodisiacs for new mothers is having their partner take on increased responsibility for the exhausting demands of household chores and childcare. When fathers contribute to household chores and childcare, mothers tend to feel a bit *less* exhausted and resentful, fathers get a bit *more* tired and appreciative, and their respective libidos come into closer harmony.

Although the content of clients' problems is important to address, their *process and patterns* for dealing with those problems (*how* they interact) are almost always more important. For example, how does each person tend to communicate with the other? How does each prefer to resolve conflict? What type of interpersonal stance does each tend to assume (e.g., dominant, aggressive, controlling, punishing, appeasing, confused, withdrawn, resistant, helpless, submissive)? What is each person's underlying assumption about themselves, others, and the relationship? Do they listen to each other? Do they demonstrate their understanding of the other person's perspective? Does one person escalate while the other shuts down? To what extent is the "identified patient" showing symptoms of the system or family? How does each partner show respect and caring for the other partner? Do they enter into destructive communication patterns?

An example of a common dysfunctional communication pattern is asking questions when one really has an underlying criticism or statement. Suppose one partner comes home after work in the evening, finds the other person watching TV (or doing any other potential form of relaxation), and asks, "What are you doing?" Is this really a neutral question? Quite often an indirect criticism underlies (or is perceived by the other to underlie) the question. The recipient of the question tends to respond defensively ("I just sat down a minute ago!"), and relations deteriorate from there. In couples in which a pattern of criticism has developed, partners become conditioned to mistrust the other's intent and to react negatively, even in situations where the questioner really is purely seeking information. Thus, when seeking to help defuse conflictual relationships, therapists should consider encouraging couples to make their intentions known via direct "I statements" (e.g., "I am hungry and would like to discuss our plans for dinner"). Powerful changes in the couple or family system can be made when therapists help couples and families: (1) address problematic interactional patterns, (2) learn to recognize, comment upon (metacommunicate), and alter dysfunctional patterns, and subsequently (3) interact more effectively.

Techniques

Effective CFT approaches have much in common. They tend to explore the thoughts and feelings of each person, assist clients in listening to each other, improve communication, elicit the underlying dynamics, analyze how the dynamics connect to each person's vulnerabilities and boundaries, and offer appropriate strategies for altering these dynamics. The following techniques and strategies are used in working with couples and families to facilitate change and gain greater information about the system (adapted from Smith & Stevens-Smith, 1992). Strategies should be judiciously applied and viewed as not a cure but rather as methods to help mobilize the family. The when, where, and how of each intervention rests with the therapist's professional judgment and personal skills.

Tracking

Structural family therapists view tracking as an essential part of the therapist's joining process with the family (Minuchin & Fishman, 1981). During the tracking process, the therapist listens intently to family stories and carefully records events and their sequence. Through tracking, the therapist identifies the sequence of events operating in a system to maintain homeostasis. Knowing what happens between point A and point B or C to create D can be helpful when designing interventions. For example, when (A) the parents are too preoccupied to parent effectively and attend to their child's needs, (B) the child acts out and draws (negative) attention, causing (C) one parent to become excessively angry and the other to become excessively anxious and protective, which leads to (D) the parents' fighting and failing to develop or implement a reasonable parenting plan, and then back to (B) the child's acting out again.

> Effective couple and family therapy approaches have much in common. They tend to explore the thoughts and feelings of each client, assist them in listening to each other, improve communication, elicit the underlying dynamics, analyze how the dynamics connect to each client's vulnerabilities and boundaries, and offer appropriate strategies for altering these dynamics.

Reinforcement and Practice

With reinforcement and practice, the therapist assists the family in identifying new skills, behaviors, or dynamics will that create desired change in the family. This might mean that individuals who previously have been neglecting some aspect of their family obligations are specifically recognized and reinforced when they engage in the desired behavior (e.g., children doing homework or chores after school; parents making clear requests for what they want).

Maintaining New Functional Interaction Patterns to Create a Virtuous Cycle

When problematic interactional patterns have developed, therapists can assist families in creating new patterns that create virtuous cycles. For example, when previous disagreements tended to spiral into vicious fights, new communication patterns can be developed, practiced, and reinforced so that disagreements are effectively and respectfully resolved.

Altering Rigid or Enmeshed Boundaries

When relations become too *enmeshed* between some family members, boundaries can be altered so that better relations are created. For example, when one caregiver is becoming ineffective in his or her interactions with a surly adolescent (enmeshed), the other less involved (detached) caregiver can be enlisted in ways that help address the adolescent's problematic behavior and that give the initial caregiver a chance to step back and gain greater perspective on the situation and the adolescent's phase of life. Additionally, issues or imbalances in the couple's relationship should be considered when their children display problematic behavior.

Reframing

Reframing is a method to both join with the family and to offer a different perspective on presenting problems. Reframing involves taking something out of its logical class and placing it in another category (Herman & Fredman, 1986). For example, a parent's repeated grilling of his or her child's behavior after a date can be seen as genuine caring and concern rather than as intrusive or distrustful. Through reframing, a negative activity or intention may be reframed into a positive. This reduces resistance to subsequent changes within the couple or family system.

Genograms

As described earlier, family genograms are graphic depictions of individuals' three-generational family history that reveal the family's basic structure and demographics (McGoldrick & Gerson, 1985). As an informational and diagnostic tool, the genogram is developed by the therapist in conjunction with the family. It can provide data that aid both clients and therapists in better understanding critical events in families' emotional processes. Genograms typically note dates of births, deaths, marriages, and divorces. Additionally, it is often helpful to delineate information about cultural or ethnic origins, SES, the nature of relations among family members, spiritual beliefs and practices, as well as psychological issues such as anxiety, depression, suicide, mental illness, substance abuse, incarcerations, and violence. From a family systems perspective, it is particularly important to note themes (e.g., emotional cut-offs, relationship boundary violations) that are carried through generations via repetition and reactions. Genograms may also help decrease shame and blame, as problems can be observed within their generational family context.

Deconstructing the Problem

Deconstructing the problem refers to breaking problems down into their component assumptions, analyzing these "texts," observing what is being assumed as well as what is missing from these current texts, and helping clients create healthier and more empowering narratives for their lives (White & Epston, 1990). For example, a child with tantrum problems might be asked "What did the tantrums have you doing?" instead of "I hear that you had a tantrum today; tell me more about it." Follow up questions might include: "Did that surprise you?" and "Is that something that you want more of in your life?" (White, 2000).

Externalizing the Problem

Arising from the notion that the person is not the problem, externalization of the problem involves viewing the problem as separate from the client or the family. It also involves the client's perception of "what is the problem?" The problem could be a certain attitude, behavior, interaction style, or compensatory method. Rather than viewing the problem as something inherent in the person and unavoidable, clients are encouraged to see the problem as something separate that can be controlled by the client and family. Externalization of the problem allows people to discuss it more openly and cooperatively, as well as see possible alternatives. Examining their effect on the problem may also allow clients to recognize their contributions to the survival of the problem, which may help them in gaining control over it (White & Epston, 1990).

The Empty Chair

The empty chair technique can also be used in CFT (Perls, Hefferline, & Goodman, 1985). For example, a client may be invited to engage in a dialogue with absent or deceased parents, family members, or children, then play the role of the other person, and carry on the dialogue. In this way, clients can articulate and potentially resolve intense thoughts and feelings that they may hold toward otherswho are not present ("unfinished business"). For example, a husband may engage in a dialogue with his deceased mother while his wife observes, with the result being that they both better appreciate how his issues with his mother tend to get played out in their current relationship.

Strategic Alliance

This technique involves meeting with one member of the family as a supportive means of helping that person change. The individual is asked to behave or respond in a different manner, with this individual change being expected to affect the entire family system. For example, the therapist may invite an excessively dominant, aggressive, and controlling person to consider the notion that individuals who are truly powerful are not afraid to share their power and decision making with others. The therapist may then invite this person to interact with family members in more collaborative ways in the future. This technique attempts to disrupt a circular system of behavior pattern.

Paradoxical Directives

Paradoxical directives seek to create changes in dynamics. The therapist may recommend, for example, the continuation of a symptom, such as indecision, anxiety or worry. Specific directives may be given as to when, where, with whom, and for what amount of time one should do these things. As clients follow this directive, a sense of control over the symptom may develop, resulting in subsequent change. For example, when therapists prescribe indecision, the indecisive behavior may be framed as taking appropriate time on important matters affecting the family. A directive is given to not rush into anything nor make any hasty decisions, which may subsequently free their decision-making processes.

However, as discussed earlier, paradoxical interventions can be viewed by clients as cruel ("I came in for help with my problem and you are telling me to continue it!") and may have unintended effects (e.g., self-injurious behavior). Hence, paradoxical directives should be used only after more collaborative and straightforward interventions have been unsuccessful and only when the prescription will not endanger the client or others.

Family Sculptures and Choreography

Family sculpting allows clients to represent relationships among family members. Therapists invite family members to physically arrange the family to reflect their perception of relationships. For example, an adolescent may view him or herself as unvalued and disconnected from other family members. When sculpting the family, this person may put his or her sibling together with the parents in a joyous group hug, while positioning him or herself as crouching alone on the other side of the room. Adolescents often benefit from the opportunity that family sculpting provides to nonverbally communicate their thoughts and feelings about the family. In addition to its diagnostic uses, family sculpting also fosters insight and empathy among family members (Duhl, Kantor, & Duhl, 1973).

Family choreography arrangements go beyond initial sculpting. Family members may position themselves according to how they see the family and then depict how they would like the family situation to be. Family members may be invited to reenact a family scene and to possibly resculpt it to a preferred scenario. This technique can create lively interactions and create greater openness to change.

Family Photographs

The family photographs technique has the potential to provide information about past and present functioning. One use of family photographs is to view the family album together; clients' verbal and nonverbal responses to pictures and events are often quite revealing. An adaptation of this method is to request family members to bring in significant family photographs and discuss their personal significance. These discussions help therapists and family members more clearly see family relationships, rituals, structure, roles, and communication patterns.

Family Council Meetings

Family council meetings provide specific times for the family to meet and interact with one another. The therapist might prescribe council meetings as homework, set a specific time for the family to meet, and specify rules for the meeting. The council should include the entire family; any absent members have to abide by decisions made during the meeting. The agenda may include concerns of any family member. Attacking others during this time is not acceptable. Family council meetings help provide structure for the family, encourage full family participation, and facilitate communication. Having specific times for family council meetings allow family members to be more relaxed between meetings because they know there is a designated time for addressing difficult issues.

Caring Days

Couples and families that are stuck frequently exhibit predictable behavior cycles. Boredom and fixed patterns are present, and family members pay little real attention to one another. In such cases, family members feel unappreciated and taken for granted. "Caring days" can be set aside when couples or families make special effort to connect and show caring for one another. Specific times for caring can be arranged with certain actions in mind (Stuart, 1980) and to help increase the frequency of positive exchanges (Gottman & Silver, 1999).

Improving Communication Skills

Communication patterns and processes are often major factors in preventing healthy family functioning. Many techniques focus on building communication skills. Listening techniques including restatement of content, reflection of feelings, taking turns expressing feelings, and nonjudgmental brainstorming are some of the methods utilized in communication skill building. Conflict resolution techniques assist couples in learning how to fight fairly, to listen, to paraphrase, and to assert themselves. They may instruct adolescents on how to express themselves with adults. Therapists look for ways to instill new communication patterns that will improve the functioning of the couple or family system.

Marriage Skills Programs

Marriage education is based on the premise that couples can learn how to increase the behaviors that make a marriage successful and decrease those associated with marital distress and divorce. The National Institute of Mental Health concluded that destructive parental conflict is one of the generic risk factors for child and adult mental health problems, with mismanaged conflict predicting both marital distress and negative effects for children. Marriage skills programs emphasize that an important difference between couples who survive and thrive in marriage and those who do not lies primarily in how couples understand and accept the fact that at times they will disagree and how they handle their inevitable differences. Behaviors and attitudes that predict success are taught to couples. Along with teaching couples how to communicate more effectively, manage conflict, and work together as a team, programs may also teach the benefits of marriage for couples and their children and what to expect in the course of marriage. Some programs have been adapted for specific populations (e.g., teenagers). Program length ranges from several hours to semester-long courses, with most being 8 to 20 hours long. These programs have been growing in popularity in the U.S. in part due to a large infusion of federal funds (Adapted from the U.S. Department of Health and Human Services, 2005).

Psychoeducational Resources

Bookstores typically contain multiple rows of self-help books for improving couple, marital, and family functioning. Some of the more widely recommended psychoeducational resources include: *The Relationship Cure: A 5-Step Guide to Strengthening Your Marriage, Family, and Friendships* (DeClaire & Gottman, 2002); *The Seven Principles for Making Marriage Work* (Gottman & Silver, 1999); *The Power of Two: Secrets to a Strong and Loving Marriage* (Heitler, 1997); *Getting the Love You Want: A Guide for Couples* (Hendrix, 1988); *Too Good to Leave, Too Bad to Stay* (Visher & Visher, 1991); *How to Win as a Stepfamily* (Kirshenbaum, 1996); *We Love Each Other But . . . Simple Secrets to Strengthen Your Relationship and Make Love Last* (Wachtel, 1999).

Sex Therapy

Individuals and couples often seek therapy regarding concerns with their sexual relationships. While acknowledging that all couples are different and warrant tailored solutions, Jack Annon (1976) suggests a 4-level PLISSIT model of sex therapy. In this model, many clients seek *P*ermission from their therapist (i.e. reassurance about their activities). Others respond to *L*imited *I*nformation or *S*pecific *S*uggestions, while a smaller proportion require *I*ntensive *T*herapy (and treatment by a specialist). As sexual relations are an important aspect of most couples' relationships, it is critical that therapists learn to discuss sexual matters openly, directly, and comfortably. In this process, clients may find psychoeducational books such as Barbach's (1975) *For Yourself: The Fulfillment of Female Sexuality* and Zilbergeld's (1999) *The New Male Sexuality* to be useful in providing information, dispelling myths, and normalizing clients' concerns.

When clients raise sexual concerns, therapists typically inquire about the problem, about clients' upbringing and family background, about what they learned about sex, about their past sexual experiences (including abuse, assault, or trauma), and about their past and present relationships. Therapists then typically share their perception of the likely causes of the problem(s), as well as of how therapy may help them. In general, clients frequently learn things they were not aware that they did not know. Clients tend to realize that sexual relations are pleasing ways to communicate and share with their partner. Sex therapy often begins with exercises called *sensate focus* done at home (Kaplan, 1988; Masters & Johnson, 1970).

It is important to establish ground rules for sensate focus exercises. Ground rules help partners come together in greater safety, mutuality, and likelihood of success. Table 14.2 lists ground rules for sensate focus, which may be adapted according to clients' specific needs.

Sensate focus starts with touching in a nonsexual manner. Clients then progress to sensuous touching, and then to gentle sexual touching. People are often surprised by changes in how they feel about their bodies and their sexual abilities. The stages of sensate focus are detailed in Table 14.3

Caveats About Sex Therapy

Therapists need to be aware that some clients' sexual concerns or relationship dynamics can be very intense, complex, or resistant to change. In such cases, referral to sex therapists with specific knowledge, attitudes, skills, training, and supervision is warranted. Additionally, sexual relations between therapists and their current or recent clients are *always* unethical and cause for licensing discipline and lawsuits.

Summary

Theories and techniques associated with couple, family, and sex therapies build upon those associated with individual therapy, and include additional features designed to address the complexity of systemic functioning. Fortunately, therapists serving couples and families have extensive theory and research to help guide their practice. In addition to reviewing theories, this chapter described numerous couple and family problematic phenomenon and patterns (such as "symptom bearer," "triangulation," and "enmeshed boundaries") and techniques and resources for promoting adaptive change. Nonetheless, therapists need to be sensitive to adapt CFT theories and techniques according to their clients' specific needs, concerns, interpersonal contexts, developmental stages, and cultural beliefs. With the focus on fostering healthy couple and

---

TABLE 14.2   Ground Rules for Sensate Focus

- Create an inviting environment by deciding where the activity will occur, determining a comfortable temperature, and preventing interruptions. Gentle music, candles, and soft lighting may add to the experience. As this is a learning exercise, seek to make it enjoyable and special.

- Agree on a moratorium on intercourse and touching of the breasts, nipples, and genitals.

- Pay attention to what you are experiencing rather than focusing on trying to please your partner.

- Share information about your likes and dislikes before or after the session. Talking during the session tends to reduce concentration, so talk only if the touch of your partner is uncomfortable or painful. Otherwise assume that what is being done is acceptable.

- Engage in twice-weekly sensate focus exercises. These sessions should begin with about 20 minutes and increase to up to 50 minutes over 4 weeks. For many busy people, this involves scheduling in their appointment books.

TABLE 14.3   Stages of Sensate Focus

1. Taking plenty of time, one person explores the other's body, avoiding sexual areas and with a ban on intercourse. It is typically optimal to start with wearing underwear. Partners are instructed to not try to give pleasure, but rather to focus on the physical and emotional feelings from both doing and receiving. If going well after 2 weeks of twice weekly practice, move to touching that includes the chest and breasts. Different ways of touching, including the use of massage oil may be tried. If this is going well, individuals may tell their partner what they like, including guiding their partner's hand.

2. Maintaining the ban on intercourse, gradually include light touching of sexual areas as part of the whole body, without focusing on genitalia. Individuals can touch sexual areas to give pleasure but not with the aim of orgasm.

3. Retaining the ban on intercourse, decide how to approach penetration in a gradual way. The first step is allowing shallow entry of about an inch or less, without movement. Try a little gentle movement once this is managed comfortably. Clients should start very gently and become aware of what they both want. Return to earlier stages if things feel uncomfortable or difficult at any time, and return to this stage more gradually later.

family functioning, therapists cannot be limited to a restricted set of hypotheses, a rigid set of techniques, or prescribed operational procedures. Therefore, consideration of theory and research, creative judgment, and personalization of application are appropriate.

This chapter also noted the importance of therapists being both knowledgeable about and comfortable with discussing clients' sexual concerns. A four-level **PLISSIT** model of sex therapy interventions was noted, with the basic considerations and procedures of sensate focus exercises being described.

CHAPTER 15

Medications, Therapy, and the Neural Circuitry of the Brain

The highest activities of consciousness have their origins in physical occurrences of the brain just as the loveliest melodies are not too sublime to be expressed by notes.
—SOMERSET MAUGHAM

Psychotherapy targets the brain and mind. Accumulating evidence from multiple research efforts demonstrates that the mind changes when the brain changes and that the brain changes when the mind changes (Beitman et al., 2003). Therapists help clients to change the neural circuits of their brains through their minds, whereas psychopharmacologists (providers who prescribe) help clients change their minds through the effects of medications on many of the same neural circuits. This chapter first reviews the research comparing medications with psychotherapy. In many studies of anxiety and depression, therapy and medications show equivalent results. The combination is often better than either one alone. One of the key variables for choosing medications, psychotherapy, or the combination relates to what the client prefers. Belief in the efficacy of a treatment correlates highly with outcome no matter what the form of treatment (Wampold, 2001).

Following this review of research is a comprehensive tabulation of the common classes of psychiatric medication and their diagnostic indications, some of which have already been described. Therapists must be familiar with these medications because many of their clients and their clients' family members have, are, or will be taking them.

How medications can play a role in each of the stages of psychotherapy is discussed next. This portion of the chapter also focuses on the relationship between medication and transference and counter-transference issues.

The chapter ends with a look toward the future: How does psychotherapy work on the brain? Using basic neuranatomical information, this section outlines some of the brain changes that occur during engagement, pattern search, and change.

Medications or Psychotherapy?

Research studies comparing medication and psychotherapy in the treatment of depression and anxiety consistently show equal efficacy in the short term. About 50% of clients respond well (Westen et al., 2004). In fact, psychotherapy is often slightly superior, especially in the treatment of bulimia nervosa. Although drug company advertising has attempted to convey a very rosy outcome picture, particularly in the treatment of depression, research shows a less than optimal 50% of people continuing to have symptoms in varying degrees. The highly touted empirically-supported therapies (ESTs) have also fallen considerably short in the long term. Follow-up studies show that approximately 50% of those who appeared to do well at the end of the study relapse and seek further treatment (Westen et al., 2004). Generally speaking, the combination of medications and psychotherapy outperforms either modality alone, but there are many exceptions (Beitman et al., 2003). Panic disorder, for example, seems to respond better to psychotherapy than to medications (Barlow et al., 2000).

Your expectations of medications should be cautiously optimistic. Some clients will experience dramatic and long-lasting positive responses, whereas the majority will experience both some positive and some negative effects. Some will have only negative effects. Some clients will need multiple medications rather than just one.

For the more severe diagnoses like recurrent major depression, bipolar disorder, and schizophrenia, medications provide an essential platform for psychosocial and psychotherapeutic interventions. Medications for alcoholism and drug abuse remain promising but relatively ineffective. Antabuse (disulfiram) induces nausea when alcohol is ingested whereas Revia (naltrexone) reduces the intensity of the alcoholic craving. Campral (acamprosate) may be the best aid yet for absti-

> When comparing medication and psychotherapy in the treatment of depression and anxiety, research studies consistently show equal efficacy in the short term.

nent alcoholics in reducing the pleasurable response to the drug. All alcohol-related pharmacotherapies need to be accompanied by psychosocial interventions.

Under what conditions should a therapist suggest a psychoactive medication to a client? Table 15.1 lists factors to consider when deciding whether to suggest that a client pursue pharmacotherapy several of which have been described earlier.

To which physicians should therapists make referrals for prescribing purposes? Approximately 70% of all antidepressant drugs are prescribed by primary care physicians. Clients can be encouraged to return to their primary care physicians or to seek one out. However, primary care physicians generally spend little time with their patients. If the case is complex, your client might be better served by a psychiatrist who will be able to spend more time in the initial interview and would likely draw from a wider range of medications. The field of psychopharmacology is changing constantly. Primary care physicians must keep up with new developments across many different categories of medications (e.g., antibiotics, nonsteroidal anti-inflammatories, antihypertensives). Thus primary care physicians typically have less knowledge regarding difficult-to-treat psychological disorders than do psychiatrists.

TABLE 15.1   Factors Influencing the Consideration of Pharmacotherapy

- *Severity of the disorder and social support.* The more severe the problem (including high symptom severity) and the more diminished the psychosocial support, the more medications should be recommended (Beutler et al., 2002).

- *Chronicity.* The longer the problem has existed, the more likely it is that medications will be useful. Clients who are in their third episode of major depression should be advised to consider medications because the likelihood of relapse increases with each subsequent episode.

- *Family history.* If a biologically related family member has the same problem and has responded well to medications, the same medication should be considered.

- *Client willingness.* Some clients are very much against medications, which is why they are seeing a therapist instead of their primary care physician or psychiatrist. If they are not ready to use medications, they are less likely to take them and to facilitate their effectiveness. Treatment compliance is enhanced when clients are matched to treatments they prefer compared to clients randomly assigned to either medications or psychotherapy (Chilvers, Dewey, & Fielding, 2001).

Commonly Prescribed Medications

Table 15.2 lists the most commonly prescribed medications.

A basic knowledge of medications and their side effects helps therapists engage clients in therapy by offering additional help and expertise. A close working relationship with a psychiatrist or primary care physician will provide practical information that can benefit any client considering a medication intervention in addition to psychotherapy.

Diagnosis and Medications

Many medications are used not only for the diagnosis indicated but also for crossover to other diagnoses. For example, antidepressants are used for many anxiety disorders, and mood stablizers may be used for aggressiveness and impulsiveness as well as for bipolar disorder.

Depression

The medications with which to become most familiar are the ones most often used: the selective serotonin re-uptake inhibitors (SSRIs). The worldwide annual sales for this class of medications exceeded 8 billion dollars in 2003. They have become so commonly prescribed because they are not lethal in overdose the way earlier generations of antidepressants such as imipramine (Tofranil) and amitriptyline (Elavil) were. Weight gain and sexual side effects (reduced sexual desire, impotence, and difficulty with orgasm) may become significant problems with SSRIs. Many depressed clients already feel bad enough about themselves; weight gain becomes another reason to be self-critical. For these reasons many clients refuse to take SSRIs. Buproprion (Wellbutrin) has made its market niche with its minimal weight gain and minimal sexual side effects.

Mood Stabilizers

Bipolar disorder is characterized by mood swings lasting several weeks or months. Manic episodes usually involve less need for sleep, great talkativeness, spending sprees, hypersexuality, and impulsive decision making. The restraint of the right prefrontal cortex is, for some reason, diminished while other parts of the

> Weight gain and sexual side effects (reduced sexual desire, impotence, and difficulty with orgasm) are common problems with SSRIs.

TABLE 15.2   Psychiatric Medications

GENERIC NAME	TRADE NAME
Antidepressants	
Amitriptyline*	Elavil
Bupropion***	Wellbutrin
Citalopram**	Celexa
Clomipramine*	Anafranil
Desipramine*	Norpramin and others
Doxepin*	Sinequan and others
Escitalopram**	Lexapro
Fluoxetine**	Prozac, Sarafem
Imipramine*	Tofranil and others
Mirtazapine***	Remeron
Nortriptyline*	Pamelor
Paroxetine**	Paxil
Sertraline**	Zoloft
Venlafaxine***	Effexor
Mood Stabilizing Agents	
Carbamazepine	Tegretol, Carbatrol
Lamotrigine	Lamictal
Lithium Carbonate	Lithobid, Eskalith
Valproate	Depakote, Depakene
Psychostimulants	
Amphetamine salts	Adderall
Atomoxetine	Straterra
Dextroamphetamine	Dexedrine and others
Methylphenidate	Ritalin, Concerta, others
Anti–Anxiety/Hypnotic Agents	
Alprazolam	Xanax
Buspirone	Buspar
Chlordiazepoxide	Librium
Clonazepam	Klonopin
Diazepam	Valium
Gabapentin	Neurontin
Lorazepam	Ativan
Tiagabine	Gabitril
Zolpidem	Ambien

(continued)

TABLE 15.2   (continued)

GENERIC NAME	TRADE NAME
Antipsychotics	
Aripiprazole*****	Abilify
Chlorpromazine****	Thorazine
Haloperidol****	Haldol
Olanzapine*****	Zyprexa
Quetiapine*****	Seroquel
Risperidone*****	Risperdal
Ziprasidone*****	Geodon

*Older antidepressants

**SSRIs

***Newer non-SSRI antidepressants

****Older antipsychotic

*****Newer antipsychotics

brain run wild. Drugs used for the treatment of seizures (carbamazepine, valproate) help calm the brains of clients with mania but are generally not very useful for the depressed phase (with the exception of lamotrigine, which can help to reduce the recurrence of depression). Lithium, mined from the earth rather than made in laboratories, has been the mainstay of bipolar treatment for decades. It too is primarily useful for preventing manic episodes rather than preventing depression.

Physicians have tended to ignore the value of psychotherapy for bipolar clients (Basco & Rush, 1996, 2005; Scott, 2004). Manic episodes often disrupt families. Depressive episodes make clients exquisitely sensitive to mood changes; for example, fearing that another episode will take place when they are actually reacting to normal losses. This was the case with Joan, a 44-year-old woman with a history of several manic and depressive episodes.

Joan came into her therapist's office worried that she was heading into a deep depression. Her mother had promised to finally leave her abusive stepfather and move in with her, but then her mother changed her mind. Joan had been looking forward to movies, shopping trips, and talking with her mother. After assessing the client for symptoms of depression, the therapist suggested that Joan was not experiencing another depressive episode—she was simply mourning the loss of her new life with her mother. As Joan realized this trigger, she cried her way through the loss and did not enter her feared depression.

Attention Enhancers

ADHD can be treated quite well with stimulants like Adderall and Ritalin. Controversy continues over the value of medicating young children, but parents who see behavioral and grade improvements after medication celebrate the treatment effectiveness. Increasing evidence demonstrates that ADHD kids grow up to be ADHD adults, opening up a new area for diagnostic consideration. Atomoxetine (Straterra) is a nonaddictive, nonstimulant medication that was first tested in the treatment of depression. For those reluctant to use controlled substances, atomoxetine is worth considering. Buproprion, although somewhat less likely to be effective, may also have fewer side effects. Psychotherapy for ADHD adults often involves enhancing clients' planning skills and addressing compensatory maladaptive coping mechanisms they have developed to mask their difficulties. These compensatory mechanisms often include substance abuse and avoidance of difficult tasks such as those requiring reading, organizing, or sequential skills.

Anti-anxiety Drugs

Anti-anxiety drugs are widely used. Benzodiazepines (alprazolam, chlordiazepoxide, clonazepam, and lorazepam) have high addiction potential and thus "street value." They are quickly effective in calming hyperactive amygdalas (see the last section of this chapter) and reducing anxiety. They are so effective that many people become afraid to be without them. Cognitive therapy has proved useful in helping clients withdraw from these drugs (Morin et al., 2004). Buspirone has very few side effects and may be useful in treating GAD. Gabapentin (Neurontin) and tiagabine (Gabitril) were first used as antiseizure drugs but have been increasingly used as substitutes for benzodiazepines because clients have little difficulty in withdrawing from them. Zolpidem (Ambien), used as a sleeping pill, is related to benzodiazepines but has a slightly different mechanism of action. It also generates dependence—it is very effective in the short term but difficult to stop. As mentioned earlier, SSRIs are often used for anxiety as well as depression.

Antipsychotics

Counselors and therapists in general practice see clients taking antipsychotic drugs relatively infrequently. Primarily used in the treatment of schizophrenia, these drugs help to control delusions, racing thoughts, and hearing voices. The older generation of drugs (thorazine, haldol) cause movement disorders (trembling, involuntary muscle movements) whereas several of the newer ones cause excessive weight gain and perhaps diabetes (e.g., olanzapine and quietiapine) without causing movement problems. These drugs are also effectively used for mania. Quietiapine is more often used as a sleeping pill than an antipsychotic, working very much like over-the-counter diphenhydramine (Benadryl). The prefrontal cortex of schizophrenics is usually under-functioning. The new antipsychotics (e.g., aripiprizole) may help strengthen prefrontal activity and its associated ability to execute plans. In addition, therapies focused on practical decision making and planning appear to be much more effective with schizophrenics than had generally been considered (Turkington, Dudley, Warman, & Beck, 2004).

The Interactions Between Medications and Therapy During the Stages of Psychotherapy

Medications can and do affect the course of psychotherapy—usually in positive ways but sometimes in negative ways. Psychotherapists must also remember that medications not only directly change brain biochemistry but also have symbolic meaning to clients that can help clarify maladaptive patterns. Medications can influence the development of the therapeutic alliance, can be useful in defining maladaptive patterns, can influence the process of change, may free up the potential for self-awareness, and can create transference, countertransference, and resistance. For example, clients who have problems accepting medications when they are indicated may also have trouble accepting useful ideas (Beitman et al., 2003).

Engagement

Like relaxation training or suggesting relevant psychoeducational books, successful referral for medications can strengthen the working alliance. Clients learn that their therapists can be helpful and are doing what they can to be of assistance to them.

Many factors influence the decision to suggest medications. Therapists will want to try psychotherapy first without medications simply because that is what they know and do best. Research and clinical experience strongly suggest that they will be successful sometimes. But when psychotherapy alone is insufficient (see Table 15.1), early referral to pharmacotherapy is appropriate for clients with severe symptoms and poor social support, as they seem to require medications. Clients with OCD who refuse exposure techniques and response prevention are unlikely to respond to other psychotherapeutic approaches and thus also should be referred to pharmacotherapy.

There is some legal precedent for considering medications in addition to psychotherapy. A depressed man treated in a long-term inpatient facility with psychotherapy alone brought suit against the facility for not having started him on antidepressants (Klerman, 1989). The therapy persisted for many months before medications were finally added. Clearly, therapists should consider medications after some period of little or poor response to therapy alone.

Referral for medications should not be considered a psychotherapeutic failure but rather another way to help. Sometimes the successful referral helps strengthen the therapeutic alliance, as is illustrated by the following case.

Lynn, a 22-year-old graduate student with intense anxiety, was referred to a therapist by a friend. In evaluating the new client, the therapist began to feel very anxious. She looked more carefully at Lynn and noticed her bitten nails, her trembling hands, and her shaking voice and began to attribute some of her own anxiety to being in the same room with a very anxious person. Lynn's anxiety was contagious! When Lynn reported having been this way since the sixth grade, the therapist concluded that medications seemed necessary if there was to be any chance of helping her control her anxiety psychotherapeutically. The psychiatrist treated Lynn with a benzodiazepine (clonazepam) and an atypical antipsychotic (quetiapine). Lynn quickly experienced a reduction in anxiety. When she returned to therapy, she expressed even stronger confidence in her therapist's ability to help because of the effective referral.

> Clients tend to react to the prescription of medications in much the same way they characteristically react to other emotionally laden stimuli. Clients' idiosyncratic reactions to medications may therefore be an indicator of maladaptive patterns.

Occasionally medications are so effective that clients terminate therapy. This should not be seen as a psychotherapeutic failure but rather one of those fortunate instances in which a medication quickly accomplishes the client's desired intention. The therapist can be available should therapeutic assistance be desired in the future.

Pattern Search

Odd events around the process of offering, prescribing, and ingesting medications can provide inducing points for defining dysfunctional patterns. Clients react to medications in much the same way that they react to other emotionally laden stimuli. For example, overly compliant people who wish to please but do not want to take a pill may accept a medication referral but refuse to keep the appointment. Or they might accept a prescription but refuse to fill it. Perfectionistic clients may expect the medication to take away every symptom and make them feel happy most of the time. The following case illustrates one of the many ways reactions to medication can be used as inducing points to better understand clients' patterns.

Alan, a guilt-ridden, highly self-critical man, believed that he should suffer because of his many transgressions. At the insistence of his wife, he grudgingly saw a therapist whom he liked and to whom he described his many failures. The therapist thought Alan's depressive symptoms were severe enough to refer to a psychiatrist. Alan accepted the referral, accepted a prescription for paroxetine, filled the prescription, took the pills for a week, and then stopped. When asked why he stopped, he responded: "I just don't deserve to feel better."

This client was applying his general view of himself to medications. Therapy then focused directly and very productively on his unwillingness to allow himself not to suffer.

Change

The pharmacotherapeutic process—usually in combination with therapy—can be used to help clients give up old patterns and initiate and maintain new ones. The following case adapted from Beitman and colleagues (2003, p. 21) illustrates this.

Chandra, a 20-year-old depressed college student was deeply attached to her mother. All major decisions required consultation with her mother. Her therapist thought an antidepressant would bolster her spirits and assist with the process of change. Chandra dutifully asked her mother's opinion. Her mother replied: "I don't want a drug addict for my daughter!" Chandra subsequently refused the referral. After several more sessions, both client and therapist became convinced that the deep enmeshment with her mother was a central aspect of her depression and that the client desired greater independence from mother. Because Chandra continued to experience symptoms of moderate depression, she agreed that medications were worth trying. She also decided not to share her decision with her mother. With SSRI medication, her depression lifted; however, neither she nor her therapist were certain how much of the change was due to the pharmacotherapeutic effects of the SSRIs and how much was due to her increasing autonomy and gradual separation from her mother.

Medications can also be helpful for clients just beginning to change, as was the case with Roberto.

A 32-year-old father of two young children, Roberto came to therapy because he was distressed by his wife's repeated affairs with other men. He wanted to stay with her because of the children, but her abusive language, volatile temper, and unwillingness to change frustrated him. After being in therapy for several months, Roberto decided to tell his wife that if she did not join him in couple therapy he would initiate divorce proceedings. She refused and he reluctantly contacted a lawyer. Partway through the long and painful divorce proceedings, he fell into a moderate depression: low energy, excessive guilt, suicidal thinking, and poor sleep. The therapist referred him

> for an SSRI. He gratefully accepted the suggestion. After experiencing sig-
> nificant side effects to fluoxetine (Prozac), Roberto was switched to bupro-
> prion (Wellbutrin) and began to feel moderately better. He could then carry
> though with the difficult steps to separate and divorce.

Transference and Countertransference

The suggestion to consider medications can trigger strong interpersonal responses in some clients. They may think the therapist is trying to transfer them to someone else because they do not deserve to be listened to and understood. Some may think that they are being rejected or abandoned, or assume that the therapist has given up. Certain clients may feel narcissistically injured by this apparent assault on their autonomy—on their ability to master themselves without chemical help. To others, the medication offers potential salvation from the distress of self-examination and self-change—an effortless way to feel better. Each of these responses is usually a distortion and requires some discussion.

Therapists who strongly believe in the power of their scientific art may feel ashamed when they suggest referral, much like therapists who feel humiliation after a client's suicide attempt. These therapists see referral for medications as an indication of the limitations their psychotherapeutic ability. This is a dangerous mindset to fall into. A significant portion of the problems clients experience are beyond the scope of psychotherapy alone, and these clients are best served by referral.

Some clients are so difficult that referral for medication comes with a hidden hope of a miracle cure—that pills will somehow work a magical transformation with a client who is becoming increasingly problematic. Therapists may implicitly hope for some kind of consultation or supervision. They may also unconsciously (or consciously, if the client has been difficult!) hope that the client and psychiatrist connect so well that the client transfers to the new provider. On the other hand, therapists may be *afraid* of just that—that their client will do so well on medication or that they will engage with the psychiatrist so well that they lose the client. While this does happen occasionally, for most clients it is worth the risk. The vast majority appreciate therapists' willingness to explore all potentially useful avenues of assistance.

Once the "split treatment" arrangement has been established, some clients will play one clinician off against the other. Beware! The client may be describing the physician in negative terms. ("He is so cold; he hardly ever looks at me. He's nothing like you.") The devaluation of one and the idealization of the other are likely to reflect character problems that potentially are central to the psychotherapeutic focus. For example, people diagnosed with borderline

In "split treatment" arrangements in which one clinician prescribes medication and the other does therapy, beware! Some clients will devalue one and idealize the other. The truth lies somewhere between.

personality disorder often tend to "split" people into "all-good" or "all-bad" categories. Sooner or later, the therapist would likely become part of the bad categories.

Toward a Neural Circuitry of Psychotherapy

As our knowledge of brain function continues to accelerate, we more clearly learn how mental activities correlate with patterns of brain activation. Although the debate continues about which is primary—the mind or brain—we have come to believe that the brain is probably the primary organ of the mind just as the heart is the organ for circulation. This new perspective means that psychotherapists can no longer theorize about how psychotherapy works without also hypothesizing about how psychotherapeutic processes are mapped onto the brain. Knowledge of how the brain works can help sharpen our ideas about therapy just as knowledge of therapy can help sharpen our ideas about brain function (see Beitman, Blinder, Thase, Riba & Safter, 2003; Beitman & Nair, 2004).

Brain imaging studies demonstrate an important commonality among the anxiety disorders and depression. The amygdalas, almond shaped organs buried deeply in the lower front part of each cerebral hemisphere, are excessively active in anxiety and depression (Drevets, 2003; Rauch, 2003). SSRIs can slow down amygdala firing, which may partially explain why they are effective in the treatment of both anxiety and depression. Interestingly, cognitive therapy has been shown to be useful for both depression and anxiety disorders, perhaps through effects on the amygdalas from a different angle—the prefrontal cortex.

Beginning counselors and therapists may believe that learning the brain will have little relevance in their clinical practice. We argue to the contrary. The brains of our clients are the target of our efforts—we are helping our clients retrain the way their brains process information. As therapists become increasingly familiar with the parts of the brain they are attempting to affect, they will develop sharper ideas about how their

> When amygdalas are excessively active, people feel frightened. Amygdalas can be calmed down (dampened) by activation of the prefrontal cortex or by serotonin increases from the *dorsal raphe nuclei*.

responses to clients may aid (or hinder) the accomplishment of their therapeutic intentions.

When amygdalas are excessively active, people feel frightened. They may want to fight, flee, or freeze. Amygdalas are located next to the lateral hypothalamus that controls sympathetic arousal like heart rate, blood pressure, and respiration rate. Amygdalas can be calmed down (dampened) by activation of the prefrontal cortex or by serotonin increases from the *dorsal raphe nuclei*. The amygdalas also influence facial muscles, so people look frightened as well. The pupils will be constricted. People with social phobias have amygdalas that are hyperreactive to normal faces (Rauch et al., 2003). If you found that every time you looked at a neutral face (no anger, sadness, or anxiety) your amygdalas were triggered and you felt anxious, you would quickly learn to avoid looking at people. This becomes a way to understand the mechanism of some social anxiety and the experiences of those suffering with it.

Figure 15.1 illustrates the brain structures that control emotions. The brain is viewed from the left side with the face looking to the left. The dorsolateral prefrontal cortex appears to be activated during psychotherapy to help reduce emotional intensity.

Figure 15.2 illustrates the brain structures that generate emotions. The lower view represents a slice from ear to ear through the middle of the brain. Amygdalas generate anxiety and fear while activation of the nucleus accumbens is associated with drug abuse and sex.

These figures demonstrate a very simple model of the effects of psychotherapy and pharmacotherapy on the amygdalas. Psychotherapy activates self-awareness in order to change views of the future. The ability to project ourselves into the future lies with the dorsolateral prefrontal cortex. (*Dorsal* refers to top, *lateral* to side, and *prefrontal* to the front part of the cortex.) Focused activation of this area can help to diminish amygdala firing. Psychotherapy is considered a "top down" process because the dorsolateral prefrontal context is located above the amygdalas.

SSRIs increase serotonin in the synapses (the spaces between nerve cells). Serotonin is one of many neurotransmitters that help pass information from one nerve to another. Increases in serotonin tend to diminish nerve firing; the nerves are calmed down. The greatest serotonin-containing area of the brain is the *dorsal raphe nuclei*. Nerves from the dorsal raphe nuclei project all over the brain like a lawn sprin-

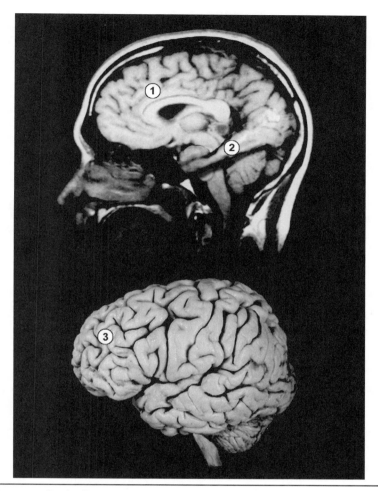

FIGURE 15.1   Brain Structures that Control Emotions. The top half of the figure contains a composited MRI (magnetic resonance imaging). Key components of the dorsal emotional system include the following regions: (1) dorsal anterior cingulate gyrus, (2) hippocampus, (3) dorsolateral prefrontal cortex. The dorsal emotional system functions in the regulation of emotional responses. (As described by Phillips, Drevets, Rauch, & Lane, 2003).

kler system. One of the places the serotonin nerves project into are the amygdalas. Increases in serotonin created by SSRIs help calm down the amygdalas. Thus, SSRI medication is considered a "bottom up" approach, as the dorsal raphe is located below the amygdalas.

Our clinical experience suggests that many clients appreciate this model for their anxiety or depression because it gives them an anatomical explanation for their distress and a target for their psychotherapeutic treatment efforts. This was the case with Martha, a client who sought therapy for her excessive fear of death.

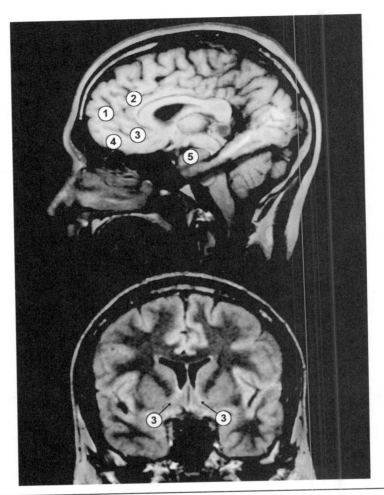

FIGURE 15.2   Brain Structures that Generate Emotions. The top half of the figure contains a composited MRI that includes a mid–sagittal view of the brain as well as a more lateral portion that shows the hippocampus and amygdala. The bottom half is a coronal view. Key components of the ventral emotional system include the following regions: (1) ventromedial prefrontal cortex, (2) anterior cingulate gyrus, (3) nucleus accumbens (the accumbens, or recumbent nucleus, forms the ventral striatum, and is clearly visible in the coronal section), (4) orbitofrontal cortex, and (5) amygdala. The ventral emotional system functions in the generation of the physical and psychological components of the emotional responses. (As described by Phillips, Drevets, Rauch, & Lane, 2003).

Martha described herself as having been a very sensitive child raised by a mother who only saw the negative. As an adult, each time Martha saw a child she had not seen in several years she marveled at how much the child had changed and then dropped into a sad anxiety. The child's growth marked the passage of time, which harbingered her own death.

When Martha's therapist explained the role of the amygdalas in brain functioning, Martha's face lit up. She began to consider that both genetically and environmentally, her amygdalas had become too easily triggered by anything that suggested the passage of time. After considering the amygdala hypothesis, Martha was able to imagine how stimuli such as the growth of children triggered more activity in her amygdalas. Once she understood this, she could also understand how self-talk could be effective in calming down her amygdalas.

David, an adult professional seeking assistance for a lifelong history of depression and anxiety, also found a neural circuitry explanation very helpful.

A bright and sensitive child, David had been raised by parents who had significant psychological issues (depression, emotional trauma, and workaholism). David grew up feeling (probably accurately) that he could not trust others to consistently be there for him. He had tried numerous antidepressant and anxiolytic (anxiety reducing) medications, and had sought individual, group, and marital therapy throughout his life. Gaining an understanding of the likely neural circuitry involved in his chronic depression and anxiety proved an invaluable explanation (or perhaps metaphor) supporting the importance of his consciously and consistently observing his emotions and thoughts for his habitual (amygdala) responses. When he detected that either his old neural circuitry patterns were getting activated or he anticipated situations in which this would likely occur, he then consciously redirected (prefrontal cortex) his attention to more adaptive responses (alternate neural circuits). With this new awareness, David subsequently improved his interpersonal relationships and was able to prevent recurrence of anything more significant than mild hints of depression or anxiety.

Our brains are constructed out of several highly interconnected structures. For therapists, the most important structures include the amygdalas (fear), hippocampus (memory), nucleus accumbens (pleasure), anterior cingulate (generating as well as organizing thought and emotion), and prefrontal cortex (planning, restraint). These structures are interconnected and reciprocally affect one another. These

The brain structures most important for therapists to know include the amygdalas (fear), hippocampus (memory), nucleus accumbens (pleasure), anterior cingulate (generating as well as organizing thought and emotion), and the prefrontal cortex (planning and restraint).

structures are also part of five discrete loops or circuits that connect limbic (emotional brain) areas with cortical (thinking brain) areas (Figure 15.3). These loops share pathways through the caudate-putamen (known as the *striatum* because when cut they are striated or striped), the thalamus receives inputs and distributes outputs in an automatic way), and the cortex. Thus, they are called the thalamocorticostriatal circuits (Mega & Cummings, 2001). Psychotherapy appears to work in part by affecting how these circuits activate (Viamontes et al., 2005).

The top ellipse refers to the cortical part of each loop and identifies its main functions: (A) visually scanning the environment, (B) executing movement, (C) emotion generation, (D) social restraint, and (E) planning.

For our psychotherapeutic purposes, we are concerned with loops C, D, and E illustrated in Figure 15.3: the anterior cingulate (emotion), the lateral orbitofrontal (social restraint), and the dorsolateral prefrontal (planning). Three loops, three very different functions: Loop C is limbically driven, activated by emotion from the amygdalas, hippocampus, and nucleus accumbens; loop D restrains emotional impulses by social rules; and loop E helps to plan for desired outcomes while balancing the intents of the others and other environmental influences.

During engagement, therapists are confronted with anxious people whose amygdalas are excessively active. Through empathic reception, warm positive regard, the establishment of trust, and the instillation of hope, therapists help calm (decrease) clients' fear (amygdalas) and increase activation of the pleasure centers (the nucleus accumbens). The therapist's face becomes associated with positive feelings in much the same way a child's face activates the nucleus accumbens of a loving parent. The therapeutic situation takes on the properties of reward, replacing the properties of fear.

The search for maladaptive patterns often reveals a conflict between what is socially acceptable and how emotions are driving behavior. For example, a nonassertive person may be overusing the social restraint loop (lateral orbitofrontal) and underusing the emotion (anterior cingulate) loop. The therapist's task during the change stage of therapy is to

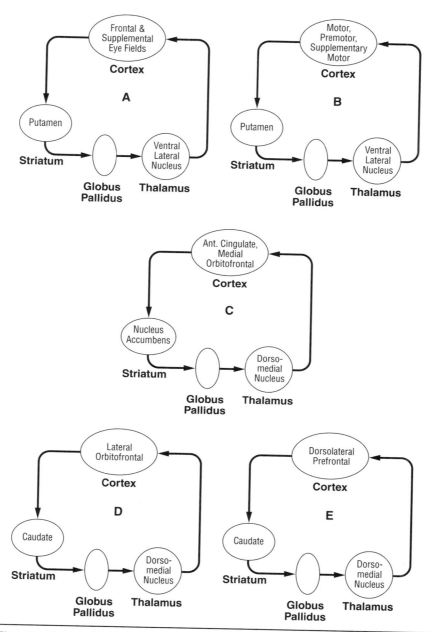

FIGURE 15.3 Five Cortico-thalamic-striatal Loops. In general, these loops function in the processes of attention and action selection. The globus pallidus inhibits the thalamus, and establishes a baseline for the intensity of stimuli that have not been identified as noteworthy. The striatum, globus pallidus, thalamus, and cortical regions involved in the loops contain a large array of separate tracts, or "channels," that can represent individual objects or events as distinguished from competing stimuli. The representation of a particular object or event can therefore be selectively enhanced or suppressed. (A) oculomotor circuit, (b) motor circuit, (c) anterior cingulate circuit, (d) lateral orbitofrontal circuit, (e) dorsal prefrontal circuit. See Viamontes (in press) for more information.

During engagement, therapists are confronted with anxious people whose amygdalas are excessively active. Through empathic reception, warm positive regard, the establishment of trust, and the instillation of hope, therapists help calm client fear (amygdalas) and increase activation of the pleasure centers (the nucleus accumbens).

help the client activate the anterior cingulate (emotion) loop until it exceeds the activation of the lateral orbitofrontal (social restraint) loop. Note that many therapy models usually include descriptions of separate selves. The three loops approximate several of these theoretically different selves: id-ego-superego, child-adult-parent, and critical self versus experiencing self.

Some surprises are emerging from brain-imaging findings regarding changes that occur in the brain when someone faces a fear and "overcomes" it. Gradual or rapid exposure to a feared object seems to "dissolve" the fear. Indeed, therapists have long thought that their encouragement for clients to face fears helps the fear to go away. As described earlier, this cherished notion appears to be incorrect. More precisely, once a set of responses is built into the brain, the response set appears to remain in the brain. It may become less active, but it does not disappear. Thus, once a fear response is established, it does not, upon exposure, disappear. Instead, exposure helps to develop a "memory" (or alternative neural circuit) to not be afraid. This memory is located in the cortex between the eyes—the medial prefrontal cortex. When the now less fearful client confronts the phobic stimulus, the medial prefrontal cortex circuit activates to calm the overly excited amydalas (Charney, 2004).

A more comforting discovery for therapists involves "mirror neurons" (Gallese, Keysers, & Rizzolatti, 2004). Researchers studied the brain activity of monkeys as the monkeys picked up a raisin. During a break in the research action, one of the researchers picked up a raisin while a monkey was still hooked up to the brain imaging apparatus. The same parts of the monkey's brain lit up while the monkey watched the researcher pick up the raisin! In other words, the monkey's brain mirrored the researcher's activity. Based on these findings, we can speculate that in good therapy, therapists' brain activity (hence their mental experiences) will mirror those of their clients, and clients' brain activities may come to mirror those of their therapists. Hence, therapists may opt to directly discuss and rehearse engaging in clients' feared activities with them—first from the client's brain per-

The three neural circuits approximate the functions of the id-ego-superego, child-adult-parent, and critical versus observing selves.

spective and then later from the therapist's brain perspective. This would mean that, in a sense, therapists could go to where their clients are (adapt their brain activities to those of their clients), and then clients could learn to mirror the mental processes of their therapist.

Human brains are social brains—developed to hunt and build houses and create cities and nations all as a group. We must be able to "tune into" the minds and experiences of others like us. Many highly empathic people have sensed that sometimes when they are feeling something (a pain or emotion), that feeling is not their own but rather the mental state of another person, which the empathizer is "picking up on." When we are aware of the fact that we are picking up on another person's mental state, we call it empathy; when the therapist feels something but is not sure about the source, we may call it countertransference. Mirror neurons help explain this once mysterious process.

Summary

The mind relies upon the brain for its survival, at least as far as science can tell us. Brain-imaging research demonstrates how counseling and therapy help clients change the ways in which their brains function. On the other hand, psychoactive medications change clients' brains in ways that change their minds. These medications are highly indicated for the more severe and chronic disorders, family histories of the disorder and, of course, clients willing to take them. The ways clients respond to psychoactive medications may provide inducing points for identification of patterns appearing through the stages of therapy or illustrated in transference and countertransference reactions.

The amygdalas, located deep in the temporal lobes of the brain, generate fear. The amygdalas are excessively active in most anxiety disorders and most depressive disorders. They may be calmed with medications working through the serotonin containing nuclei of the dorsal raphe nuclei and by psychotherapeutic activation of the dorsolateral prefrontal cortex. Increasing knowledge of brain structure and function, particularly knowledge of thalamororticostriatal circuits will sharpen therapeutic model building to provide increasingly better education and more finally honed targets for the efforts of counselors and therapists.

References

Addis, M. E., & Mahalik, J. R. (2003) Men, masculinity, and the contexts of help seeking. *American Psychologist, 58,* 5–14

Adler, A. (1917). *Study of organ inferiority and its physical compensation.* New York: Nervous and Mental Diseases Publishing.

Adler, A. (1964a). *Social interest: A challenge to mankind.* New York: Capricorn. (Original work published 1929.)

Adler, A. (1964b). *Problems of neurosis.* New York: Harper. (Original work published 1929).

Ahn, H., & Wampold, B. E. (2001). Where oh where are the specific ingredients? A meta-analysis of component studies in counseling and psychotherapy. *Journal of Counseling Psychology, 48,* 251–257.

Alberti, R. E., & Emmons, M. L. (2001). *Your perfect right: Assertiveness and equality in your life and relationships.* Atascadero, CA: Impact.

Alexander, F., & French, T. M. (1946). *Psychoanalytic therapy.* New York: Ronald.

Alexander, M. J. (1996). Women with co-occurring addictive and mental disorders: An emerging profile of vulnerability. *American Journal of Orthopsychiatry, 66*(1), 61–70.

Allen, N. B. (1996). Cognitive psychotherapy. In S. Bloch (Ed.), *An introduction to the psychotherapies* (3rd ed., pp. 173–174). New York: Oxford University Press.

Amenson, C., & Lewinsohn, P. M. (1981). An investigation into the observed sex difference in prevalence of unipolar depression. *Journal of Abnormal Psychology, 90,* 1–13.

American Psychiatric Association (1994). *Diagnostic and statistical manual of mental disorders* (4th ed.). Washington, DC: Author.

American Psychiatric Association (2000). *Diagnostic and statistical manual of mental disorders* (4th ed., text rev). Washington, DC: Author.

American Psychiatric Association (2003). Practice guideline for the assessment and treatment of patients with suicidal behaviors. Arlington, VA: Author.

American Psychological Association (1979). Principles concerning the counseling and therapy of women. *The Counseling Psychologist, 8,* 21.

American Psychological Association (1991). *Guidelines for psychological practice with ethnic and culturally diverse populations.* Washington, DC: Author.

American Psychological Association (1993). *Guidelines for providers of psychological services to ethnic, linguistic, and culturally diverse populations.* Washington, DC: Author.

American Psychological Association (2002). *Ethical principles of psychologists and code of conduct.* Washington, DC: Author.

American Psychological Association Division 44/Committee on Lesbian, Gay, and Bisexual Concerns, Task Force on Guidelines for Psychotherapy with Lesbian, Gay, and Bisexual Clients (2000). Guidelines for psychotherapy with lesbian, gay, and bisexual clients. *American Psychologist, 55,* 1440–1451.

Anderson, T. R., & Myer, T. E. (1985). Presenting problems, counselor contacts, and "no shows": International and American college students. *Journal of College Student Personnel, 26,* 500–503.

Andrews, G., & Harvey, R. (1981). Does psychotherapy benefit neurotic patients? *Archives of General Psychiatry, 38,* 1203–1208.

Annon, J. S. (1976). The PLISSIT model: A proposed conceptual scheme for the behavioral treatment of sexual problems. *Journal of Sex Education and Therapy, 2,* 1–15.

Ansbacher, H. L., & Ansbacher, R. (Eds.) (1964). *The individual psychology of Alfred Adler.* New York: Harper Torchbooks.

Antonuccio, D. O., Danton, W. G., & DeNelsky, G. Y. (1995). Psychotherapy versus medication for depression: Challenging the conventional wisdom with data, *Professional Psychology: Research and Practice, 26,* 574–585.

Antony, M. M., & Swinson, R. P. (2000). *The shyness and social anxiety workbook.* Oakland, CA: New Harbinger.

Aponte, H. J. (1976). Underorganization in the poor family. In P. J. Guerin, Jr. (Ed.), *Family therapy: Theory and practice* (pp. 432–448). New York: Gardner.

Arieti, S. (1977). Psychotherapy for severe depression. *American Journal of Psychiatry, 134,* 864–868.

Barbach, L. G. (1975). *For yourself: The fulfillment of female sexuality.* New York: Doubleday.

Bargad, A., & Hyde, J. S. (1991). Women's studies: A study of feminist identity development in women. *Psychology of Women Quarterly, 15,* 181–202.

Barlow, D. H. (1990). Long-term outcome for patients with panic disorder treated with cognitive-behavioral therapy: *Journal of Clinical Psychiatry, 51*(Suppl. A), 17–23.

Barlow, D. H., Esler, J. L., & Vitali, A. E. (1998). Psychosocial treatments for panic disorders, phobias, and generalized anxiety disorder. In P. E. Nathan & J. M. Gorman (Eds.), *A guide to treatments that work* (pp. 288–319). New York: Oxford University Press.

Barlow, D. H., Gorman, J. M., Sher, M. K., & Woods, S. W. (2000). Cognitive-behavioral therapy, imipramine, or their combination for panic disorder: A randomized controlled trial. *Journal of the American Medical Association, 283,* 2529–2536.

Barlow, D. H., O'Brien, G. T., & Last, C. G. (1984). Couples treatment of agoraphobia. *Behaviour Research & Therapy, 19,* 245–255.

Basco, R., & Rush, A. J. (1996). *Cognitive therapy for bipolar disorder.* New York: Guilford.

Bass, E., & Davis, L. (1988). *The courage to heal: A guide to women survivors of childhood sexual abuse.* New York: Harper & Row.

Bateson, G. (1972). *Steps to an ecology of mind.* New York: Ballantine.

Bateson, G., Jackson, D. D., Haley, J., & Weakland, J. (1956). Toward a theory of schizophrenia. *Behavior Science, 1,* 251–256.

Baucom, D. H. & Epstein, N. (1990). *Cognitive behavioral marital therapy.* New York: Brunner-Mazel.

Baucom, D. H., Shoham, V., Muesser, K. T., Daiuto, A. D., & Stickle, T. R. (1998). Empirically supported couple and family interventions for marital distress and adult mental health problems. *Journal of Consulting and Clinical Psychology, 66*, 53–88.

Baumeister, R. F., & Vohs, K. D. (2004). *Handbook of self-regulation: Research, theory, and applications.* New York: Guilford.

Baxter, L. R., Schwartz, J. M., Bergman, K. S., Szuba, M. P., Guze, B. H., Mazziotta, J. C., Alazraki, A., Selin, C. E., Ferng, H-K, Munford, P., & Phelps, M. E. (1992). Caudate glucose metabolic rate changes with both drug and behavior therapy for obsessive-compulsive disorder. *Archives of General Psychiatry, 49*, 681–689.

Bechtoldt, H., Norcross, J. C., Wyckoff, L. A., Pokrywa, M. L., & Campbell, L. F. (2001). Theoretical orientations and employment settings of clinical and counseling psychologists: A comparative study. *The Clinical Psychologist, 54*(1), 3–6.

Beck, A. (1995). An interview with a depressed and suicidal patient. In D. Wedding & R. Corsini (Eds.), *Case studies in psychotherapy* (2nd ed., pp. 116–134). Itasca, IL: Peacock.

Beck, A. T. (1976). *Cognitive therapy and the emotional disorders.* New York: International Universities Press.

Beck, A. T., & Emory, G. (1985). *Anxiety disorders and phobias: A cognitive perspective.* New York: Basic.

Beck, A., Rush, A., Shaw, B., & Emery, G. (1979). *Cognitive therapy of depression.* New York: Guilford.

Beck, A., & Weishaar, M. (1989). Cognitive therapy. In A. Freeman, K. Simon, L. Beutler, & H. Arkowitz (Eds.), *Comprehensive handbook of cognitive therapy* (pp. 21–36). New York: Plenum.

Bedi, A., & Matthews, B. (2003). *Retire your family karma.* York Beach, ME: Nicholas-Hays.

Beitman, B. D. (1987). *The structure of individual psychotherapy.* New York: Guilford.

Beitman, B. D. (1998). *The psychotherapist's guide to cost containment.* Thousand Oaks, CA: Sage.

Beitman, B. D., Blinder, B. J., Thase, M. E., Riba, M., & Safter, D. L. (2003). *Integrating psychotherapy and pharmacotherapy: Dissolving the mind-brain barrier.* New York: Norton.

Beitman, B. D., & Maxim, P. E. (1984). A survey of psychiatric practice: Implications for residency training. *Journal of Psychiatric Education, 8*, 149–153.

Beitman, B. D., & Nair, J. (Eds.). (2004). *Self-awareness deficits in psychiatric patients.* New York: Norton.

Beitman, B. D., & Soth, A. M. (In press). Activation of self-observation: A core process among the psychotherapies. *Journal of Psychotherapy Integration*.

Beitman, B. D., Soth, A. M., & Bumby, N. A. (2005). The future as an integrating force through the schools of psychotherapy. In J. C. Norcross & M. R. Goldfried (Eds.), *Handbook of psychotherapy integration* (2nd ed., pp. 65–83). Oxford, UK: Oxford University Press.

Beitman, B. D., & Yue, D. (1999a). *Learning psychotherapy* [video]. New York: Norton.

Beitman, B., & Yue, D. (1999b). *Learning psychotherapy: A time-efficient, research-based, and outcome-measured training program*. New York: Norton.

Beitman, B., & Yue, D. (2004). *Learning psychotherapy: A time-efficient, research-based, and outcome-measured training program* (2nd ed.). New York: Norton.

Bem, S. L. (1993). *The lenses of gender*. Yale University Press: New Haven.

Benson, H. (1975). *The relaxation response*. New York: Morrow.

Berrigan, L. P., & Garfield, S. L. (1981). Relationship of missed psychotherapy appointments to premature termination and social class. *The British Journal of Clinical Psychology, 20*, 239–242.

Beutler, L. E. (2004). The empirically supported treatments movement: A scientist-practitioner's response. *Clinical Psychology: Science and Practice, 11*, 225–229.

Beutler, L. E., Harwood, T. M., Alimohamed, S., & Malik, M. (2002). Functional impairment and coping style. In J. C. Norcross (Ed.), *Psychotherapy relationships that work* (pp. 145–170). Oxford: Oxford University Press.

Beutler, L. E., Mohr, D. C., Grawe, K., Engle, D., & MacDonald, R. (1991). Looking for differential psychotherapy efficacy. *Journal of Psychotherapy Integration, 1*, 121–142.

Blagys, M. D., & Hilsenroth, M. J. (2000). Distinctive features of short-term psychodynamic-interpersonal psychotherapy: A review of the comparative psychotherapy process literature. *Clinical Psychology: Science and Practice, 7*, 167–188.

Blagys, M. D., & Hilsenroth, M. J. (2002). Distinctive activities of cognitive-behavioral therapy: A review of the comparative psychotherapy process literature. *Clinical Psychology Review, 22*, 671–706.

Blocher, D. H., Heppner, M. J., & Johnston, J. A. (2000). *Career planning for the twenty-first century*. Denver, CO: Love.

Bloom, L. Z. (1980). *The new assertive woman*. New York: Dell.

Bodin, A. M. (1981). The interactional view: Family therapy approaches of the Mental Research Institute. In A. Gurman & D. Kniskern (Eds.), *Handbook of family therapy* (pp. 267–309). New York: Brunner/Mazel.

Bohart, A. C. (1995). The person-centered psychotherapies. In A. S. Gurman & S. B. Messer (Eds.), *Essential psychotherapies* (pp. 85–127). New York: Guilford.

Bordin, E. S. (1979). The generalizability of the psychoanalytic concept of the working alliance. *Psychotherapy: Theory, Research and Practice, 16*, 252–259.

Borkovec, T. D., & Roemer, L. (1996). Generalized anxiety disorder. In C. Lindeman (Ed.), *Handbook of the treatment of anxiety disorders*. Northvale, NJ: Jason Aronson.

Boscolo, L., Cecchin, G., Hoffman, L., & Penn, P. (1987). *Milan system family therapy*. New York: Basic.

Bourne, E. J. (2000). *The anxiety and phobia workbook* (3rd ed.). Oakland, CA: New Harbinger.

Bowen, M. (1978). *Family therapy in clinical practice*. New York: Aronson.

Bowlby, J. (1961). Processes of mourning. *International Journal of Psychoanalysis, 42*, 317–340.

Bowlby, J. (1969). *Attachment and loss*. (Vols. 1–3). New York: Basic.

Bowlby, J. (1988). *A secure base: Parent-child attachment and health human development*. New York: Basic.

Boyd, C. J., Blow, F., & Orgain, L. S. (1993). Gender differences among African-American substance abusers. *Journal of Psychoactive Drugs, 25*(4), 301–305.

Boyer, S. P., & Hoffman, M. A. (1993). Counselor affective reactions to termination: Impact of counselor loss history and perceived client sensitivity to loss. *Journal of Counseling Psychology, 40*, 272–277.

Brach, T. (2003). *Radical acceptance: Embracing your life with the heart of a Buddha*. New York: Bantam.

Brammer, L. M., & McDonald, G. (1996). *The helping relationship: Process and skills* (6th ed.). Boston: Allyn & Bacon.

Bray, J., Zarkin, G., Dennis, M., & French, M. (2000). Symptoms of dependence, multiple substance use and labor market outcomes. *American Journal of Drug and Alcohol Abuse, 26*, 77–95.

Brooks, G. B. (1995). *The centerfold syndrome*. San Francisco: Jossy-Bass.

Bronfenbrenner, U. (1979). *The ecology of human development*. Cambridge, MA: Harvard University Press

Bronfenbrenner, U. (1986). Ecology of the family as a context for human development. *Developmental Psychology, 22*, 723–42.

Bronfenbrenner, U. (1989). Ecological systems theory. In R. Vasta (Ed.). *Annals of Child Development, 6* (pp. 187–251). Greenwich, CT: JAI.

Bronfenbrenner, U., & Ceci , S. J. (1994). Nature-nurture reconceptualized: A bio-ecological model. *Psychological Review, 101*, 568–586.

Brown, H. N. (1987) Patient suicide during residency training (1): incidence, implications and program response. *Journal of Psychiatric Education, 11*, 201–216.

Burns, D. (1999). *The feeling good handbook*. New York: Plume.

Burns, D. D., & Nolen-Hoeksema, S. (1992). Therapeutic empathy and recovery from depression in cognitive behavioral therapy: A structural equation model. *Journal of Consulting & Clinical Psychology, 60*, 441–449.

Burns, D. D., & Spangler, D. L. (2000). Does psychotherapy homework lead to improvements in depression in cognitive-behavioral therapy or does improvement lead to increased homework compliance? *Journal of Consulting and Clinical Psychology, 59*, 305–311.

Butler, A. C., & Beck J. S. (2000). Cognitive therapy outcomes: A review of meta-analyses. *Journal of the Norwegian Psychological Association, 37*, 1–9.

Campbell, J. (1971). *The portable Jung*. New York: Penguin.

Caplan, P. (1991). Delusional dominating personality disorder (PDPD). *Feminism and Psychology, 1*, 171–174.

Carkhuff, R. R., & Berenson, B. G. (1967). *Beyond counseling and psychotherapy*. New York: Holt, Rinehart, & Winston.

Carson, R. C. (1969). *Interaction concepts of personality*. Chicago: Aldine.

Cartwright, R., Lloyd, S., & Wicklund, J. (1980). Identifying early dropouts from psychotherapy. *Psychotherapy: Theory, Research, and Practice, 17*, 263–267.

Cashdan, S. (1973). *Interactional psychotherapy*. New York: Grune and Stratton.

Cass, V. C. (1984). Homosexual identity formation: Testing a theoretical model. *The Journal of Sex Research, 20*, 143–167.

Catalano, R. F., Gainey, R. R., Fleming, C. B., Haggerty, K. P., & Johnson, N. O. (1999). An experimental intervention with families of substance abusers: One-year follow-up of the Focus on Families Project. *Addiction, 94,* 241–254.

Center of Substance Abuse Treatment (2004). *Substance Abuse Treatment and Family Therapy.* Treatment Improvement Protocol (TIP) Series, No. 39. DHHS Publication No. (SMA) 05–4006. Rockville, MD: Substance Abuse and Mental Health Services Administration.

Charney, D. S. (2004). Psychobiological mechanisms of resilience and vulnerability: Implications for successful adaptation to extreme stress. *American Journal of Psychiatry, 161,* 195–216.

Chemtob, C. M., Hamada, R. S., Bauer, G., Torigoe, R. Y., & Kinney, B. (1988). Patient suicide: Frequency and impact on psychologists. *Professional Psychology: Research and Practice, 19,* 416–420

Clark, A. J. (1995). An examination of the technique of interpretation in counseling. *Journal of Counseling and Development, 73,* 231–236.

Chiesa, M., Drahorad, C., & Longo, S. (2000). Early termination of treatment in personality disorders treated in a psychotherapy hospital. *British Journal of Psychiatry, 177,* 107–111.

Chilvers, C., Dewey, M., & Fielding, K. (2001). Antidepressant drugs and generic counseling for treatment of major depression in primary care: Randomized trial with patient preference arms. *British Medical Journal, 322,* 772–775.

Clark, D. C., & Fawcett, J. (1992). An empirically based model of suicide risk assessment for clients with affective disorder. In D. Jacobs (Ed.), *Suicide and clinical practice* (pp. 55–73). Washington, DC: American Psychiatric Press.

Cochran, S. (2005). *Men and depression: New findings, new questions.* Symposium presented at the 113th Annual convention of the American Psychological Association. Washington, DC.

Cochran, S., & Rabinowitz, F. (2000). *Men and depression.* San Diego: Academic Press.

Collier, H. V. (1982). *Counseling women.* New York: Free Press.

Condelli, W. S., & Hubbard, R. I. (1994). Relationship between time spent in treatment and client outcomes from therapeutic communities. *Journal of Substance Abuse Treatment, 11*(1), 25–33.

Conte, H. R., Plutchik, R., Picard, S., Galanter, M., & Jacoby, J. (1989). Sex differences in personality traits and coping styles of hospitalized alcoholics. *Journal of Studies on Alcohol, 52*(1), 26–32.

Coppersmith, E. (1980). The family floor plan: A tool of training, assessment, and intervention in family therapy. *Journal of Marital & Family Therapy, 6*, 141–145.

Corey, G. (1996). *Theory and practice of counseling and psychotherapy*. Pacific Grove, CA: Brooks/Cole.

Corey, G., & Corey, M. S. (1997). *I never knew I had a choice*. Pacific Grove, CA: Brooks/Cole.

Cormier, W., & Cormier, S. (1991). *Interviewing strategies for helpers* (3rd ed.). Pacific Grove, CA: Brooks/Cole.

Cottraux, J. (1989). Behavioral psychotherapy for obsessive-compulsive disorder. *International Review of Psychiatry, 1*, 227–234.

Courtenay, K. P., & Stephens, J. P. (2001). The experience of patient suicide among trainees in psychiatry. *Psychiatric Bulletin, 25*, 51–52

Craighead, W. E., Craighead, L. W., & Llardi, S. S. (1998). *Psychosocial treatments for major depressive disorder*. In P. E. Nathan & J. M. Gorman (Eds.), *A guide to treatments that work* (pp. 226–239). New York: Oxford.

Craske, M. G., Barlow, D. H., & Meadows, E. (2000). Mastery of your anxiety and panic (3rd ed.): *Therapist guide for anxiety, panic, and agoraphobia*. San Antonio, TX: Psychological Corporation

Cross, W. E. (1971) The Negro to Black conversion experience: Towards the psychology of Black liberation. *Black World, 20*, 13–27.

Daley, D. C., & Lis, J. A. (1995). Relapse prevention: Intervention strategies for mental health clients with comorbid addictive disorders. In A. M. Washton (Ed.), *Psychotherapy and substance abuse: A practitioner's handbook* (pp. 243–263.). New York: Guilford.

Davidson, R. J., Kabat-Zinn, J., Schumacher, J., Rosenkrantz, M., Muller, D., Santorelli, S. F., et al. (2003). Alterations in brain and immune function produced by mindfulness meditation. *Psychosomatic Medicine, 65*, 564–570.

Davidson, R. J., & Parker, K. C. H. (2001). Eye movement desensitization and reprocessing (EMDR): A meta-analysis. *Journal of Consulting and Clinical Psychology, 69*, 305–316.

Davis, M., Eshelman, E. R., & McKay, M. (1995). *The relaxation and stress reduction workbook*. Oakland, CA: New Harbinger.

Dawes, R. (1996). *House of cards: Psychology and psychotherapy built on myth*. New York: Free Press.

DeAnglis, T. (2001). Surviving a patient's suicide. *Monitor on Psychology, 32*(10), 70–73.

DeClaire, J., & Gottman, J. (2002). *The relationship cure: A 5 step guide to strengthening your marriage, family, and friendships*. New York: Crown.

de Shazer, S. (1985). *Keys to solution in brief therapy*. New York: Norton.

de Shazer, S., & Berg, I. K. (1988). Constructing solutions. *Family Therapy Networker*, September/October, 42–43.

Deutsch, C. J. (1984). Self-reported sources of stress among psychotherapists. *Professional Psychology*, 15, 833–845.

Dewald, P. A. (1965). Reactions to forced termination of therapy. *Psychiatric Quarterly*, 39, 102–126.

Dewar, I., Eagles, J., Klein, S., Gray, N., & Alexander, D. (2000). Psychiatric trainees' experiences of, and reactions to, patient suicide. *Psychiatric Bulletin*, 24, 20–23.

Dinkmeyer, D. C., Dinkmeyer, D. C., Jr., & Sperry, L. (1990). *Adlerian counseling and psychotherapy* (2nd ed.). Englewood Cliffs, NJ: Prentice Hall.

Dinkmeyer, D. C., McKay, G. D., & Dinkmeyer, D. C., Jr. (1997). *The parent's handbook*. Atascadero, CA: Impact.

Dixon, L., Haas, J., Weiden, P., Sweeney, H., & Frances, A. (1990). Acute effects of drug abuse in schizophrenic patients: Clinical observation and patients' self reports. *Schizophrenic Bulletin*, 16(1), 69–79.

Drevets, W. (2003). Prefrontal cortical-amygdalar metabolism in major depression. *Annals New York Academy of Sciences*, 877, 614–637.

D'Zurrilla, T. J., & Goldfried, M. R. (1971). Problem solving and behavior modification. *Journal of Abnormal Psychology*, 78, 107–126.

Egan, G. (2002). *The skilled helper: A problem-management and opportunity-development approach to helping* (7th ed.). Pacific Grove, CA: Brooks/Cole/Thomson Learning.

Ekman, P., Friesen, W. V., & Ellsworth, P. (1972). *Emotion in the human face: Guidelines for research and an integration of the findings*. New York: Pergamon.

Ellis, A. & Harper, R. A. (1997). *A guide to rational living*. North Hollywood CA: Melvin Powers.

Ellis, D. (2006). *Becoming a master student*. Boston: Houghton Mifflin.

Elkin, I., Shea, T., Watkins, J. T., Imber, S. D., Sotsky, S. M., Collins, J. F., Glass, D. R., Pilkonis, P. A., Leber, W. R., Docherty, J. P., Fiester, S. J., & Parloff, M. B. (1989). National Institute of Mental Health Treatment of Depression Collaborative Research Program: General effectiveness of treatments. *Archives of General Psychiatry, 46,* 971–982.

Epperson, D., Bushway, D., & Warman, R. (1983). Client self terminations after one counseling session: Effects of problem recognition, counselor gender, and counselor experience. *Journal of Counseling Psychology, 30,* 307–315.

Epstein, J. F. (2002). Substance dependence, abuse and treatment: Findings from the 2000 National Household Survey on Drug Abuse. NHSDA Series A-16. DHHS Publication no. SMA 02–3642. Rockville, MD: Substance Abuse and Mental Health Services Administration, Office of Applied Studies. Available at: http://www.DrugAbuseStatistics.SAMHSA.gov.

Epstein, R. S., & Simon, R. I. (1990). The exploitation index: An early warning indication of boundary violations in psychotherapy. *Bulletin of Menninger Clinic, 54,* 450–465.

Erikson, E. (1950). *Childhood and society.* New York: W. W. Norton.

Evans, D. R., Hearn, M. T., Uhlemann, M. R., & Ivey, A. E. (2003). *Essential interviewing: A programmed approach to effective communication* (6th ed.). Monterey, CA: Wadsworth.

Eysenk, H. H. (1959). Learning theory and behavior therapy. *British Journal of Medical Science, 105,* 61–75.

Fabrega, H. (1992). Diagnosis interminable: Toward a culturally sensitive DSM-IV (1994). *The Journal of Nervous and Mental Disease, 180,* 5–7.

Feng, T. (1993). Substance abuse in pregnancy. *Current Opinions in Obstetric Gynecology, 5*(1), 16–23.

Fenichel, O. (1945). *Psychoanalytic theory of neurosis.* New York: Norton.

Fiorentine, R., Anglin, M., Gil-Rivas, V., & Taylor, E. (1997). Drug treatment: Explaining the gender paradox. *Substance Use and Misuse, 32,* 653–678.

Firestein, S. K. (1978). *Termination in psychoanalysis.* New York: International Universities Press.

Fischer, A. R., Tokar, D. M., Mergl, M. M., Good, G. E., Hill, M. S., & Blum, S. A. (2000). Assessing women's feminist identity development: Studies of convergent, discriminant, and structural validity. *Psychology of Women Quarterly, 24,* 15–29.

Foa, E., & Meadows, E. (1997). Psychosocial treatments for posttraumatic disorder: A critical review. *Annual Review of Psychology, 48,* 449–480.

Fonagy, P., Steele, M., Steele, H., Higgitt, A., & Target, M. (1994). The theory and practice of resilience. *Journal of Child Psychology and Psychiatry, 35,* 231–257.

Foreman, S. A., & Marmar, C. R. (1985). Therapist actions that address initially poor therapeutic alliance in psychotherapy. *American Journal of Psychiatry, 142,* 922–926.

Fortune, A. E. (1987). Grief only? Client and social worker reactions to termination. *Clinical Social Work Journal, 15,* 159–171.

Frank, A. F., & Gunderson, J. G. (1990). The role of the therapeutic alliance in the treatment of schizophrenia. *Archives of General Psychiatry, 47,* 228–236.

Frank, E., Karp, J. F., and Rush, A. J. (1993). Efficacy of treatments for major depression. *Psychopharmacology Bulletin, 29,* 457–475.

Frank, E., Kupfer, D. J., Perel, J. M., Cornes, C., Jarrett, D. B., Mallinger, A. G., Thase, M. E. McEachran, A. B., & Grochocinkski, V. J. (1990). Three-year outcomes of maintenance therapies in recurrent depression. *Archives of General Psychiatry, 47,* 1093–1099.

Frank, J. D., & Frank, J. B. (1991). *Persuasion and healing: A comparative study of psychotherapy* (3rd ed.). Baltimore: Johns Hopkins.

Frank, J. D., Hoen-Saric, R., Imber, S. D., Liberman, B. L., & Stone, A. R. (1978). *Effective ingredients of successful psychotherapy.* New York: Brunner/Mazel.

Frankl, V. E. (1966). Logotherapy and existential analysis: A review. *American Journal of Psychotherapy, 20,* 252–261.

Franklin, M. E., & Foa, E. B. (1998). Cognitive-behavioral treatments for obsessive-compulsive disorder. In P. E. Nathan & J. M. Gorman (Eds.), *A guide to treatments that work* (pp. 339–358). New York: Oxford University Press.

Freeman, A., Simon, K. M., Beutler, L. E., & Ackowitz, H. (1989). *Comprehensive handbook of cognitive therapy.* New York: Plenum.

Freeman, A., & White, D. (1989). The treatment of suicidal behavior. In A. Freeman, K. Simon, L. Beutler, & H. Arkowitz (Eds.), *Comprehensive handbook of cognitive therapy* (pp. 321–346). New York: Plenum.

Freud, S. (1953). The interpretation of dreams. In J. Strachey (Ed. & Trans.), *The standard edition of the complete works of Sigmund Freud* (Vol. 4 & 5). London: Hogarth. (Original work published 1900.)

Freud, S. (1953). Fragment of an analysis of a case of hysteria. In J. Strachey (Ed. & Trans.), *The standard edition of the complete psychological works of Sigmund Freud* (Vol. 7, pp. 15–122). London: Hogarth. (Original work published 1905.)

Freud, S. (1961). The infantile genital organization: An interpolation into the theory of sexuality. In J. Strachey (Ed. & Trans.), *The standard edition of the complete psychological works of Sigmund Freud* (Vol. 19, pp. 141–149). London: Hogarth. (Original work published 1924.)

Freud, S. (1963). Recommendations for physicians on the psychoanalytic method of treatment. In P. Rieff (Ed.), *Therapy and technique* (pp. 117–126). New York: Collier. (Original work published 1912.)

Friedman, A. S. (1975). Interaction of drug therapy with marital therapy in depressed clients. *Archives of General psychiatry, 32*, 619–637.

Fuller, F., & Hill, C. E. (1985). Counselor and helpee perceptions of counselor intentions in relation to outcome in a single counseling session. *Journal of Counseling Psychology, 32*, 329–338.

Gabbard, G., & Wilkinson, S. (1994). *Management of countertransference with borderline patients*. Washington, DC: American Psychiatric Press.

Gabbard, G. O. (2000). *Psychodynamic psychiatry in clinical practice* (3rd ed.). Washington, DC: American Psychiatry Press.

Gafoor, M., & Rassool, H. (1998). The co-existence of psychiatric disorders and substance misuse: Working with dual diagnosis patients. *Journal of Advanced Nursing, 27*, 497–502.

Gallese, V., Keysers, C., & Rizzolatti, G. (2004). A unifying view of the basis of social cognition. *Trends in Cognitive Sciences, 8*, 396–403.

Gambrill, E., & Richey, C. (1985). *Taking charge of your social life*. Belmont, CA: Wadsworth.

Garfield, S. (1986). Research on client variables in psychotherapy. In S. Garfield & Y. A. Bergin (Eds.), *Handbook of psychotherapy and behavior change* (3rd ed., pp. 213–256). New York: Wiley.

Garfield, S. L. (1995). *Psychotherapy: An eclectic-integrative approach* (2nd ed.). New York: Wiley.

Garfield, S. L., & Bergin, A. E. (1986). *Handbook of psychotherapy and behavior change* (3rd ed.). New York: Wiley.

Gavard, J. A., Lustman, P. J., & Clouse, R. E. (1993). Prevalence of depression in adults with diabetes: An epidemiological evaluation. *Diabetes Care, 16*, 1167–1178.

Gelso, C., & Carter, J. A. (1985). The relationship in counseling and psychotherapy: Components, consequences, and theoretical antecedents. *Counseling Psychologist, 13,* 155–243.

Girnstead, S. F. & Gorski, T. T. (1997). *Addiction-free pain management: Relapse prevention counseling workbook.* Independence, MO: Herald House/Independence.

Gitlin, M. J. (1999). A psychiatrist's reaction to a client's suicide. *American Journal of Psychiatry, 156,* 1630–1634.

Gloaguen, V., Cottraus, J., Cucherat, M., & Blackburn, I. M. (1998). A meta-analysis of the effects of cognitive therapy in a depressed patient. *Journal of Affective Disorders, 49,* 59–72.

Goldfried, M. R., & Davison, G. C. (1976). *Clinical behavior therapy.* New York: Holt, Rinehart and Winston.

Goldfried, M. R., & Padawer, W. (1982). Current status and future directions in psychotherapy. In M. R. Goldfried (Ed.), *Converging themes in psychotherapy: Trends in psychodynamic, humanistic, and behavioral practice* (pp. 3–49). New York: Springer.

Goldstein, L. S. & Buongiorna, P. A. (1984). Psychotherapists as suicide survivors. *American Journal of Psychotherapy, 38,* 392–398.

Gomes-Schwartz, B. (1978). Effective ingredients in psychotherapy: Prediction of outcome from process variables. *Journal of Consulting and Clinical Psychology, 46,* 1023–1035.

Good, G. E. (1998). Missing and underrepresented aspects of men's lives. *Society for the Psychological Study of Men and Masculinity Bulletin, 3*(2), 1–2.

Good, G. E. & Brooks, G. R. (Eds.) (2005). *The new handbook of psychotherapy and counseling with men: A comprehensive guide to settings, problems, and treatment approaches* (Rev. ed.). San Francisco: Jossey-Bass.

Good, G. E., Gilbert, L. A., & Scher, M. (1990). Gender aware therapy: A synthesis of feminist therapy and knowledge about gender. *Journal of Counseling and Development, 68,* 376–380.

Good, G. E., & Mintz, L. B. (2005). Integrative therapy for men. In G. Good & G. Brooks (Eds.), *The new handbook of psychotherapy and counseling with men: A comprehensive guide to settings, problems, and treatment approaches* (Rev. ed., pp. 248–263). San Francisco: Jossey-Bass.

Good, G. E., Robertson, J. M., O'Neil, J. M., Fitzgerald, L. F., Stevens, M., DeBord, K. A., Bartels, K. M., & Braverman, D. G. (1995). Male gender role conflict: Psychometric issues and relations to psychological distress. *Journal of Counseling Psychology, 42*, 3–10.

Good, G. E., & Sherrod, N. (1997). Men's resolution of non-relational sex across the lifespan. In R. Levant & G. Brooks (Eds.), *Men and sex: New psychological perspectives* (pp. 182–204). New York: Wiley.

Good, G. E., & Sherrod, N. (2001). The psychology of men and masculinity: Research status and future directions. In R. K. Unger (Ed.), *Handbook of the psychology of women and gender* (pp. 201–214). New York: Wiley.

Good, G. E., Wallace, D. L., & Borst, T. S. (1994). Masculinity research: A review and critique. *Applied and Preventive Psychology, 3*, 3–14.

Good, G. E., & Wood, P. K. (1995). Male gender role conflict, depression, and help-seeking: Do college men face double jeopardy? *Journal of Counseling and Development, 74*, 70–75.

Goodman, L. A., Dutton, M. A., & Harris, M. (1995). Episodically homeless women with serious mental illness: Prevalence of physical and sexual assault. *American Journal of Orthopsychiatry, 65*, 468–478.

Gorski, T. (1989). *Understanding the twelve-steps: A guide for counselors, therapists and recovering people*. Independence, MO: Herald House/Independence.

Gorski, T. (1992). *The staying sober workbook*. Independence, MO: Herald House/Independence Press.

Gottman, J. M. (1994). *Why marriages succeed or fail*. New York: Simon & Schuster.

Gottman, J. M. (2005). *Gottman's "Marriage Tips 101."* Retrieved June 17, 2005 from http://www.gottman.com/marriage/self_help/.

Gottman, J. M., & Krokoff, L. J. (1989). Marital interaction and satisfaction: A longitudinal view. *Journal of Consulting and Clinical Psychology, 57*, 47–52.

Gottman, J. M., & Silver, N. (1999). *The seven principles for making marriage work*. New York: Crown.

Greenberg, L. S., & Johnson, S. M. (1988). *Emotionally focused couples therapy*. New York: Guilford.

Greenberg, L. S., Rice, L. N., & Elliott, R. (1993). *The moment by moment process: Facilitating emotional change*. New York: Guilford Press.

Greenberg, L. S., & Webster, M. C. (1982). Resolving decisional conflict by Gestalt two-chair dialogue: Relating process to outcome. *Journal of Counseling Psychology, 29*, 468–477.

Greenson, R. R. (1967). *The technique and practice of psychoanalysis* (Vol. I). New York: International Universities Press.

Greenspan, M., & Kulish, N. M. (1985). Factors in premature termination in long-term psychotherapy. *Psychotherapy, 22*, 75–82.

Griffin, M. L., Weiss, R. D., Mirin, S. M., & Lange, U. (1989). A comparison of male and female cocaine abusers. *Archives of General Psychiatry, 46*, 122–126.

Griffin, W. A. (1993). *Family therapy*. New York: Brunner/Mazel.

Grinstead, S. F., & Gorski, T. T. (1997). *Addiction-free pain management: Relapse prevention counseling workbook*. Independence, MO: Herald House/Independence Press.

Growe, M. (1996). Couple therapy. In S. Bloch (Ed.), *An introduction to the psychotherapies* (pp. 193–211). New York: Oxford University Press.

Gurtman, M. B. (1997, February 1). *The interpersonal circumplex* [Online]. Available: www.uwp.edu/academic/psychology/faculty/netcirc.htm

Gutheil, T. G., & Appelbaum, P. S. (2000). *Clinical handbook of psychiatry and the law* (3rd ed.). Baltimore: Lippincott, Williams & Wilkins.

Gysbers, N. C., Heppner, M. J., & Johnston, J. A. (2003). *Career counseling: Process, issues, and techniques* (2nd ed.). Boston, MA: Allyn & Bacon.

Haley, J. (1963). *Strategies of psychotherapy*. New York: Grune & Stratton.

Haley, J. (1973). *Uncommon therapy: The psychiatric techniques of Milton H. Erickson*. New York: Norton

Haley, J. (1987). *Problem-solving therapy* (2nd ed.). San Francisco: Jossey-Bass

Hall, E. T. (1968). Proxemics. *Current Anthropology, 9*, 83–108.

Hall, R. C., Popkin, M. K., Devaul, R. A., Faillace L. A., & Stickney, S. K. (1978). Physical illness presenting as psychiatric disease. *Archives of General Psychiatry, 35*, 1315–1320.

Harper, J. A., Wiens, A. N., & Matarazzo, J. D. (1978). *Nonverbal communication: The state of the art*. New York: Wiley.

Heavey, C., Christensen, A., & Malamuth, N. (1995). The longitudinal impact of demand and withdraw during marital conflict. *Journal of Consulting and Clinical Psychology, 63*, 797–801.

Hedges, L. E. (1983). *Listening perspectives in psychotherapy.* New York: Jason Aronson.

Heitler, S. (1997). *The power of two: Secrets to a strong and loving marriage.* Oakland, CA: New Harbinger.

Helms, J. (1985). Toward a theoretical explanation of the effects of race on counseling: A Black and White model. *The Counseling Psychologist, 12,* 153–165.

Helms, J. (1990). Toward a model of white racial identity development. In J. Helms (Ed.), *Black and white racial identity* (pp. 49–66). Westport, CT: Greenwood Press.

Hendin, H., Lipschitz, A., Maltsberger, J. T., Haas, A. P., & Wynecoop, S. (2000). Therapists' reactions to patients' suicides. *American Journal of Psychiatry, 157,* 2022–2027.

Hendrix, H. (1988). *Getting the love you want: A guide for couples.* New York: Henry Holt.

Henry, W. P, Strupp, H. H, Schacht, T. E., & Gaston, L. (1994). Psychodynamic approaches. In A. E. Bergin & S. Garfield (Eds.), *Handbook of psychotherapy and behavior change* (4th ed., pp. 467–508). Oxford: John Wiley & Sons.

Hepworth, D., Rooney, R., & Larsen, J. (1997). *Direct social work practice: Theory and skills* (5th ed.). Pacific Grove, CA: Brooks/Cole.

Herman, J. L. (1992). *Trauma and recovery.* New York: Basic.

Highlen, P. S., & Hill, C. E. (1984). Factors affecting client change in individual counseling: Current status and theoretical speculations. In S. D. Brown & R. W. Lent (Eds.), *The handbook of counseling psychology* (pp. 334–397). New York: Wiley.

Hill, C. E. (1982). Counseling process research: Methodological and philosophical issues. *Counseling Psychologist, 10,* 7–19.

Hill, C. E., Carter, J. A., & O'Farrell, M. K. (1983). A case study of the process and outcome of time-limited counseling. *Journal of Counseling Psychology, 30,* 3–18.

Hill, C. E., Helm, J. E., Tichenor, V., O'Grady, K. E., & Perry, E. S. (1988). Effect of therapist response modes in brief psychotherapy. *Journal of Counseling Psychology, 35,* 222–233.

Hill, C. E., & O'Brien, K. M. (1999). *Helping skills: Facilitating exploration, insight, and action.* Washington, DC: American Psychological Association.

Hill, C. E. & O'Brien, K. M. (2004). *Helping skills: Facilitating exploration, insight, and action* (2nd ed.) Washington, DC: American Psychological Association.

Hill, C. E., & O'Grady, K. E. (1985). List of therapist intentions illustrated in a case study and with therapists of varying theoretical orientations. *Journal of Counseling Psychology, 32,* 3–22.

Hillis, G., Alexander, D. A., & Eagles, J. M. (1993). Premature termination of psychiatric contact. *International Journal of Social Psychiatry, 39,* 100–107.

Ho, M. K. (1987). Family therapy with ethnic minorities: Similarities and differences. In M. K. Ho, *Family therapy with ethnic minorities* (pp. 230–272). Newbury Park, CA: Sage.

Hoffman, J. J. (1985). Client factors related to premature termination of psychotherapy. *Psychotherapy, 22,* 83–85.

Hooley, J. M., & Teasdale, J. D. (1989). Predictors of relapse in unipolar depressives: Expressed emotion, marital distress, and perceived criticism. *Journal of Abnormal Psychology, 98,* 229–235.

Horowitz, M. J., Marmar, C., Weiss, D., Dewitt, K. N., & Rosenbaum, R. (1984). Brief psychotherapy of bereavement reactions: The relationship of process to outcome. *Archives of General Psychiatry, 41,* 438–448.

Horvath, A. O. (1981). *An exploratory study of the working alliance: Its measurement and relationship to outcome.* Unpublished doctoral dissertation, University of British Columbia, Vancouver, Canada.

Horvath, A. O. (1995). The therapeutic relationship: From transference to alliance. *Psychotherapy in Practice, 1,* 7–17.

Horvath, A. O., & Symonds, B. D. (1991). Relationship between working alliance and outcome in psychotherapy: A metanalysis. *Journal of Counseling Psychology, 38,* 139–149.

Howell, E. M., Heiser, N., & Harrington, M. (1999). A review of recent findings on substance abuse treatment for pregnant women. *Journal of Substance Abuse Treatment, 16*(3), 195–219.

Hull, C. (1943). *Principles of behavior.* New York: Appleton-Century-Crofts.

Hunter, M. (1990). *Abused boys: The neglected victims of sexual abuse.* Lexington, MA: D. C. Heath.

Ivey, A. E. (1994). *Intentional interviewing and counseling: Facilitating client development in a multicultural society* (3rd ed.). Pacific Grove, CA: Brooks/Cole.

Ivey, A. E., Gluckstern, M., & Ivey, M. (1997). *Basic attending skills* (3rd ed.). North Amherst, MA: Microtraining Associates.

Ivey, A. E., & Ivey, M. B. (2002). *Intentional interviewing and counseling: Facilitating client development in a multicultural society* (4th ed.). New York: Brooks/Cole.

Jackson, B. (1975). Black identity development. In L. Golubschick and B. Persky (Eds), *Urban social and education issues*, (pp. 158–164). Dubuque, IA: Kendall-Hall.

Jackson, B. W., & Hardiman, R. (1983). Racial identity development: Implications for managing the multiracial work force. In R. A. Ritvo & A. G. Sargent (Eds.), *NTL manager's handbook* (pp. 107–119). Arlington, VA: NTL Institute.

Jackson, D. (1957). The question of family homeostasis. *The Psychiatric Quarterly Supplement, 31*(part 1), 79–90.

Jackson, D. D. (1965a). The study of the family. *Family Process 4*(1), 1–20.

Jackson, D. D. (1965b). Family rules: Marital quid pro quo. *Archives of General Psychiatry*, 12, 589–594.

Jacobs, D., & Brewer, M. (2004). APA practice guideline provides recommendations for assessing and treating patients with suicidal behaviors. *Psychiatric Annals, 34*, 5.

Jacobson, E. (1938). *Progressive relaxation*. Chicago: University of Chicago.

Jacobson, N. S., Dobson, K. S., Fruzetti, A. E., Schmaling, K. B., & Salusky, S. (1991). Marital therapy as a treatment for depression. *Journal of Consulting and Clinical Psychology, 59*, 547–557.

Jacobson, N. S., & Margolin, G. (1979). *Marital therapy: Strategies based on social learning and behavior exchange principles*. New York: Brunner/Mazel.

Janowsky, D. S. (1999). *Psychotherapy indications and outcomes*. Washington, DC: American Psychiatric Press.

Jenkins, S. J., Fuqua, D. R., & Blum, C. R. (1986). Factors related to duration of counseling in a university counseling center. *Psychological Reports, 58*, 467–472.

Johnson, S. M. (1996). *The practice of emotion-focused couple therapy: Creating connection*. New York: Brunner/Mazel.

Johnson, S. (1999). Emotion focused couples therapy: Straight to the heart. In J. Donovan (Ed.), *Short-term couple therapy* (pp. 13–42). New York: Guilford.

Johnson, S., & Greenberg, L. (Eds.). (1994). *The heart of the matter: Emotion in marriage and marital therapy.* New York: Bruner Mazel.

Johnson, S. M., & Greenberg, L. S. (1995). The emotionally focused approach to problems in adult attachment. In N. S. Jacobson & A. S. Gurman (Eds.), *The clinical handbook of marital therapy* (pp. 121–141). New York: Guilford.

Johnson, S. M., Hunsley, J., Greenberg, L., & Schindler, D. (1999). Emotionally focused couples therapy: Status and challenges. *Clinical Psychology: Science and Practice, 6,* 67–79.

Johnson, S., & LeBow, J. (2000). The "coming of age" of couple therapy: A decade review. *Journal of Marital and Family Therapy, 26,* 23–38.

Kabat-Zinn, J. (1990). *Full catastrophe living: Using the wisdom of your body and mind to face stress, pain, and illness.* New York: Delta.

Kadushin, A., & Kadushin, G. (1997). *The social work interview* (4th ed.). New York: Columbia University Press.

Kagan, J., Reznick, J. S., & Snidman, N. (1988). Biological bases of childhood shyness. *Science, 240,* 167–171.

Kaplan, H. S. (1998). *Illustrated manual of sex therapy.* New York: Brunner/Mazel.

Kaplan, M. (1983a). The issue of sex bias in DSM III. *American Psychologist, 38,* 802–803.

Kaplan, M. (1983b). A woman's view of the DSM-III. *American Psychologist, 38,* 786–792.

Kapoor, V., Matorin, A. A., & Ruiz, P. (2000). Termination of psychotherapy: A training perspective. *Journal of Psychiatric Practice, 6,* 334–340.

Kashubeck-West, S. K., & Mintz, L. B. (2005). Separating the effects of gender and weight loss desire on body satisfaction and disordered eating behavior. *Sex Roles, 53,* 505–518.

Keane, T. M. (1998). Psychological and behavioral treatments of post-traumatic stress disorder. In P. E. Nathan & J. M. Gorman (Eds.), *A guide to treatments that work* (pp. 398–408). New York: Oxford University Press.

Keats, D. (1993). *Skilled interviewing.* Australia: Acer.

Kernberg, O. (1975). *Borderline conditions and pathological narcissism.* New York: Jason Aronson.

Kernberg, O. (1976). *Object-relations theory and clinical psychoanalysis.* New York: Jason Aronson.

Kessler, R. C., McGonagle, K. A., Zhao, S., Nelson, C. B., Hughes, M., Eshleman, S., Wittchen, H. U., & Kendler, K. S. (1994). Lifetime and 12-month prevalence of DSM-IIIR psychiatric disorders in the United States: Results from a national comorbidity survey. *Archives of General Psychiatry, 51*, 8–19.

Kiesler, D. J. (1983). The 1982 interpersonal circle: A taxonomy for complementarity in human transactions. *Psychological Review, 90*, 185–214.

Kivlighan, D. M. (1990). Relationship between counselor use of intentions and clients' perception of working alliance. *Journal of Counseling Psychology*, 37, 27–32.

Kivlighan, D. M., & Schmitz, P. J. (1992). Counselor technical activity in cases with improving working alliances and continuing poor working alliance. *Journal of Counseling Psychology, 39*, 32–38.

Kleespies, P. M., Penk, W. E., & Forsyth, J. P. (1993). The stress of patient suicidal behavior during clinical training: Incidence, impact, and recovery. *Professional Psychology: Research and Practice, 24*, 293–303.

Klein, M. (1975). *Envy and gratitude and other works, 1946–1963*. New York: Free Press.

Kleinke, C. L. (1993). *Common principles of psychotherapy*. Pacific Grove, CA: Brooks/Cole.

Klerman, G. L. (1989). The responsibility of the psychiatric profession [Abstract]. *Proceedings of the American Psychiatric Association* (p. 137). San Francisco, CA.

Klerman G. L., & Weissman, M. M. (1993). *New applications in interpersonal psychotherapy*. Washington, DC: American Psychiatric Press.

Klerman, G. L., Weissman, M., Rounsaville, B., & Chevron, E. (1984). *Interpersonal psychotherapy of depression*. New York: Basic.

Knapp, C. (1996). *Drinking: A love story*. New York: Dell.

Kohut, H. (1971). *The analysis of the self. New York: International Universities.

Kohut, H. (1977). *The restoration of self*. New York: International Universities.

Kohut, H., (1984). *How does analysis cure?* Chicago: University of Chicago.

Kokotovic, A. M., & Tracey, T. J. (1987). Premature termination at a university counseling center. *Journal of Counseling Psychology, 34*, 80–82.

Kokotovic, A. M., & Tracey, T. J. (1990). Working alliance in the early phase of counseling. *Journal of Counseling Psychology, 37,* 16–21.

Kouri, E., Pope, H., & Lukas, S. (1999). Changes in aggressive behavior during withdrawal from long-term marijuana use. *Psychopharmacology, 143,* 302–308.

Kramer, J. R. (1985). *Family interfaces: Transgenerational patterns.* New York: Brunner/Mazel.

Krauskopf, C., Baumgardner, A., & Mandracchia, S. (1981). Return rate following intake revisited. *Journal of Counseling Psychology, 28,* 519–521.

Lambert, M. J., & Ogles, B. M. (2003). The efficacy and effectiveness of psychotherapy. In M. J. Lambert (Ed.), *Bergin and Garfield's handbook of psychotherapy and behavior change* (5th ed., pp. 139–193). New York: Wiley.

Langs, R. (1974). *The technique of psychoanalytic psychotherapy* (Vol. 2). New York: Jason Aronson.

Lash, S. J. (1998). Increasing participation in substance abuse aftercare treatment. *American Journal of Drug and Alcohol Abuse, 24,* 31–36.

Lawe, C., Horne, A., & Taylor, S. (1983). Effects of pretraining procedure for clients in counseling. *Psychological Reports, 53,* 327–334.

Lazarus, A. A. (1971). *Behavior therapy and beyond.* New York: McGraw Hill.

Lazarus, A. A. (1996). The utility and futility of combining treatments in psychotherapy. *Clinical Psychology—Science & Practice, 31,* 59–68.

Lazarus, R. S., & Cohen, J. B. (1977). Environmental stress. In I. Altman & J. Wohlwill (Eds.), *Human behavior and environment* (Vol. 2). New York: Plenum.

Leahy, R. L. (2001). *Overcoming resistance in cognitive therapy.* New York: Guilford.

Leahy, R. L. (Ed.). (2003). *Roadblocks in cognitive behavioral therapy: Transforming challenges into opportunities for change.* New York: Guilford.

Leary, T. (1957). *Interpersonal diagnosis of personality.* New York: Ronald.

Lebow, J. (1997). Why integration is so important in couple and family therapy. *Family Process, 36,* 23–24.

Lebow, J. (2000). What does the research tell us about couple and family therapies? *Journal of Clinical Psychology/In Session: Psychotherapy in Practice, 56,* 1083–1094.

Lederer, W., & Jackson, D. (1968). *Mirages of marriage*. New York: Norton.

Lerner, H. G., (1985). *The dance of anger*. New York: Harper & Row.

Levant, R. (2004). The empirically-validated treatments movement: A practitioner/educator perspective. *Clinical Psychology: Science and Practice, 11*, 219–224.

Levant, R. (2005). Evidence-based practice in psychology. *Monitor on Psychology, 36*(2), 5.

Levant, R. F., & Pollack, W. S. (Eds.). (1995). *A new psychology of men*. New York: Basic.

Levitsky, A. & Perls, F. (1970). The rules and games of gestalt therapy. In Fagan, J. & Shepherd, 1. *Gestalt therapy now* (pp. 140–149). Middlesex, England: Penguin.

Levy, S. (1990). *Principles of interpretation*. Northvale, NJ: Aronson.

Lew, M. (1988). *Victims no longer: Men recovering from incest and other sexual abuse*. New York: Harper & Row.

Lewin, K. (1951). *Field theory in social science: Selected theoretical papers*. Westport, CT: Greenwood.

Lewinsohn, P. M. (1974). A behavioral approach to depression. In R. J. Friedman & M. M. Katz (Eds.), *The psychology of depression: Contemporary theory and research*. Washington, DC: Winston.

Linehan, M. M. (1993). *Cognitive-behavioral treatment of borderline personality disorder*. New York: Guilford.

Logue, A. W. (1995). *Self-control: Waiting until tomorrow for what you want today*. Englewood Cliffs, NJ: Prentice Hall.

Luborsky, L. (1976). Helping alliances in psychotherapy. In J. L. Cleghorn (Ed.), *Successful psychotherapy* (pp. 92–116). New York: Brunner/Mazel.

Luborsky, L., & Crits-Christoph, P. C. (1990). *Understanding transference*. New York: Basic.

Luborsky, L., McLellan, A. T., Woody, G. E., O'Brien, C. P., & Auerbach, A. (1985). Therapist success and its determinants. *Archives of General Psychiatry, 42*, 602–611.

Lynskey, M., & Hall, W. (2000). The effects of adolescent cannabis on educational attainment: A review. *Addiction, 95*, 1621–1630.

Mahalik, J. R. (2005). Interpersonal therapy for men. In G. Good & G. Brooks (Eds.), *The handbook of counseling and psychotherapy approaches for men* (pp. 234–247). San Francisco: Jossey-Bass.

Mahalik, J. R., Good, G. E., & Englar-Carlson, M. (2003a). Masculinity scripts, presenting concerns and help seeking: Implications for practice and training. *Professional Psychology: Research and Practice, 34*, 123–131.

Mahalik J. R., Locke B. D., Ludlow, L. H., et al. (2003b). Development of the Conformity to Masculine Norms Inventory. *Psychology of Men & Masculinity, 4*, 3–25.

Mahler, M. S. (1968). *On human symbiosis and the vicissitudes of individuation*. New York: International Universities Press.

Malan, D. H., Heath, E. S., Balal, H. A., & Baltour, F. H. G. (1975). Psychodynamic changes in untreated neurotic patients. *Archives of General Psychiatry, 32*, 110–126.

Mann, J. (1973). *Time-limited psychotherapy*. Cambridge, MA: Harvard University Press.

Marlo, H., & Kline, J. S. (1998). Synchronicity and psychotherapy: Unconscious communication in the psychotherapeutic relationship. *Psychotherapy: Theory, Research, Practice, and Training, 35*, 13–22.

Marra, T. (2004). *Depressed and anxious: The dialectical behavior therapy workbook for overcoming depression & anxiety*. Oakland, CA: New Harbinger.

Martin, J. R. (1997). Mindfulness: A proposed common factor. *Journal of Psychotherapy Integration, 7*, 291–312.

Marx, J. A., & Gelso, C. J. (1987). Termination of individual counseling in a university counseling center. *Journal of Counseling Psychology, 34*, 3–9.

Marziali, E. (1984). Predictions of outcome of brief psychotherapy from therapist interpretative interventions. *Archives of General Psychiatry, 41*, 301–305.

Mash, E. S., & Terdal, L. S. (1980). Follow-up assessment in behavior therapy. In P. Karoly & J. Steffen (Eds.), *Improving the long-term effects of psychotherapy* (pp. 82–96). New York: Gardner.

Masters, W. H., & Johnson, V. E. (1970). *Human sexual inadequacy*. London, Churchill.

May, R. (1977). *The meaning of anxiety* (Rev. ed.). New York: Norton.

Mbiti, J. 1970. *African religions and philosophy*. Garden City, NJ: Anchor.

McAdams, C. R., & Foster, V. A. (2000). Client suicide: Its frequency and impact on counselors. *Journal of Mental Health Counseling, 22*, 107–122.

McGoldrick, M., & Gerson, R. (1985). *Genograms in family assessment*. New York: Norton.

McKay, J. R., Rutherford, M. J., Cacciola, J. S., Kabasakalian-McKay, R., & Alterman, A. (1996). Gender differences in the relapse experiences of cocaine patients. *Journal of Nervous & Mental Disease, 184*(10), 616–622.

McKay, M., Davis, M., & Fanning, P. (1997). *Thoughts and feelings: Taking control of your moods and life*. Oakland, CA: New Harbinger.

McNeill, B. W., May, R. J., & Lee, V. E. (1987). Perceptions of counselor source characteristics by premature and successful terminators. *Journal of Counseling Psychology, 34,* 86–89.

Mead, G. H. (1934). *Mind, self, and society*. Chicago: University of Chicago.

Mead, M. (1974). On Freud's view of female psychology. In J. Strouse (Ed.), *Women and analysis* (pp. 95–106). New York: Grossman.

Meehl, P. (1954). *Clinical vs. statistical prediction*. Minneapolis: University of Minnesota Press.

Mega, M. S., & Cummings, J. L. (2001). Frontal subcortical circuits: Anatomy and function. In S. P. Salloway, P. F. Malloy, & J. D. Duffy (Eds.), *The frontal lobes and neuropsychiatric illness* (pp. 15–32). Washington, DC: American Psychiatric Press.

Mehta, M. (1990). A comparative study of family-based and patients-based behavioral management in obsessive-compulsive disorder. *British Journal of Psychiatry, 157,* 133–135.

Melges, F. T. (1982). *Time and the inner future*. New York: Wiley.

Merluzzi, T. V., & Boltwood, M. D. (1989). Cognitive assessment. In A. Freeman, K. Simon, L. Beutler, & H. Arkowitz (Eds.), *Comprehensive handbook of cognitive therapy* (pp. 135–176). New York: Plenum.

Meyer A. (1957). *Psychobiology: A science of man*. Springfield, IL: Charles C Thomas.

Miller, S., Duncan, B. L., & Hubble, M. A. (1997). *Escape from Babel*. New York: Norton.

Miller, W. R., & Rollnick, S. (1991). *Motivational interviewing*. New York: Guilford.

Miller, W. R., & Rollnick, S. (2002). *Motivational interviewing* (2nd ed.). New York: Guilford.

Miller, W. R., Taylor, C. A., & West, J. C. (1980). Focused versus broad-spectrum behavior therapy for problem drinkers. *Journal of Consulting and Clinical Psychology, 48,* 590–601.

Milrod, B., Busch, F., Cooper, A., & Shapiro, T. (1997). *Manual of panic-focused psychodynamic psychotherapy*. Washington, DC: American Psychiatric Press.

Minuchin, S. (1974). *Families and family therapy*. Cambridge, MA: Harvard University Press.

Minuchin, S., & Fishman, H. C. (1981). *Family therapy techniques*. Cambridge, MA: Harvard University Press.

Minuchin, S., Montalvo, B., Guerney, B. G., Rosman, B. L., & Schumer, F. (1967). *Families of the slums*. New York: Basic.

Moos, R. (1990). Depressed outpatients' life contexts, amount of treatment and treatment outcome. *Journal of Nervous and Mental Diseases, 178*, 105–112.

Moras, K., & Strupp, H. H. (1982). Pretherapy interpersonal relations, patient's alliance and outcome of brief therapy. *Archives of General Psychiatry, 39*, 405–409.

Morin, C. M., Bastien, C., Guary, B., Radouco-Thomas, M., Leblanc, J., & Vallieres, A. (2004). Randomized clinical trial of supervised tapering and cognitive behavior therapy to facilitate benzodiazepine discontinuation in older adults with chronic insomnia. *American Journal of Psychiatry, 161*, 332–342.

Mowrer, O. H. (1948). Learning theory and the neurotic paradox. *American Journal of Orthopsychiatry, 18*, 571–610.

Murkoff, H. (2002). *What to expect when you are expecting*. New York: Workman.

Myers, L. J., Speight, S. L., Highlen, P. S., Cox, C. I., Reynolds, A., Adams, E., Hanley, C. P. (1991). Identity development and world view: Toward an optimal conceptualization. *Journal of Counseling & Development, 70*, 54–63

Nathan, P. E., & Gorman, J. M. (Eds.). (1998). *A guide to treatments that work*. New York: Oxford University.

National Institute on Drug Abuse (2004a). *A record of achievement*. Vol 19(1).

National Institute on Drug Abuse (2004b). *2003 survey reveals increase in prescription drug abuse, sharp drop in abuse of hallucinogens*. Vol. 19(4), p. 14.

National Institute on Drug Abuse (2004c). *In chronic drug abuse, acute dopamine surge may erode resolve to abstain*. Vol. 19(1), pp. 1, 6.

National Institute on Drug Abuse (2005a, March 8). *NIDA InfoFacts: Costs to Society*. Retrieved June 4, 2005, from www.nida.gov/Infofacts/costs.html.

National Institute on Drug Abuse (2005b, March 8). *NIDA InfoFacts: Drug Addiction Treatment Medications*. Retrieved June 4, 2005, from www.nida.gov/Infofacts/treatmed.html.

National Institute on Drug Abuse (2005c, March 8). *NIDA InfoFacts: Drug Addiction Treatment Methods*. Retrieved June 4, 2005, from www.nida.gov/Infofacts/treatmeth.html.

National Institute on Drug Abuse (2005d, April 12). *NIDA InfoFacts: Marijuana*. Retrieved June 4, 2005, from www.nida.gov/Infofacts/marijuana.html.

National Institute on Drug Abuse (2005e, April 21). *NIDA InfoFacts: Heroin*. Retrieved June 4, 2005, from www.nida.gov/Infofacts/heroin.html.

National Institute on Drug Abuse (2005g, April 22). *NIDA InfoFacts: Crack and Cocaine*. Retrieved June 4, 2005, from www.nida.gov/Infofacts/cocaine.html.

National Institute on Drug Abuse (2005h). Brief strategic family therapy for adolescent drug abuse. *Brief Strategic Family Therapy: An Overview*. Retrieved June 15, 2005, from www.nida.nih.gov/TXManuals/bsft/BSFT2.html.

Nelson-Jones, R. (2000). *Introduction to counseling skills*. Thousand Oaks, CA: Sage

Norcross, J. C., Hedges, M., & Castle, P. H. (2002). Psychologists conducting psychotherapy in 2001: A study of the Division 29 membership. *Psychotherapy: Theory/Research/Practice/Training, 39*, 97–102.

O'Hanlon, B., & Hulley, L. (2003) The good, the bad, and the ugly. *Psychotherapy Networker, 27*(1), 26–31.

Oliver, J. M., & Simmons, M. E. (1985). Affective disorders and depression as measured by the Diagnostic Interview Schedule and the Beck Depression Inventory in an unselected adult population. *Journal of Clinical Psychology, 41*, 469–477.

O'Neil, J. M. (1981). Patterns of gender role conflict and strain: Sexism and fear of femininity in men's lives. *Personnel and Guidance Journal, 60*, 203–210.

O'Neil, J.M., Good, G.E., & Holmes, S. (1995). Fifteen years of theory and research on men's gender role conflict: New paradigms for empirical research. In R. Levant & W. Pollack (Eds.), *A new psychology of men* (pp. 164–206). New York: Basic Books.

Parkes, C. M. (1987). *Bereavement: Studies of grief in adult life* (2nd ed.). Madison: International Universities Press.

Parkes, C. M. (1988). Bereavement as a psychosocial transition: Processes of adaptation to change. *Journal of Social Issues, 44*(3), 53–65.

Parlett, M., & Hemming, J. (1996). Gestalt therapy. In W. Dryden (Ed.), *Handbook of individual psychotherapy* (pp. 123–141). London: Sage.

Parloff, M. B., Waskow, I. E., & Wolfe, B. E. (1978). Research on therapist variables in relationship to process and outcome. In S. L. Garfield & A. E. Bergin (Eds.), *Handbook of psychotherapy and behavior change* (pp. 232–282). New York: Wiley.

Patel, V. (2001). Cultural factors and international epidemiology: Depression and public health. *British Medical Bulletin* 57, 33–45.

Patton, M. J., & Meara, N. M. (1992). *Psychoanalytic counseling*. New York: Wiley.

Pauk, W. (2001). *How to study in college*. Boston: Houghton Mifflin.

Pavlov, I. P. (1928). *Lectures on conditioned reflexes* (Vol. I). London: Lawrence & Wishart.

Paykel, E., Scott, J., Teasdale, J., Johnson, A. L., Garland, A., Moore, R., Jenaway, A. Cocnwall, P. L., Hayhurst, H., Abbott, R. & Pope, M. (1999). Prevention of relapse in residual depression by cognitive therapy: A controlled trial. *Archives of General Psychiatry, 56*, 829–835.

Pederson, P. B. (1991). Multiculturalism as a fourth force in counseling [Special issue]. *Journal of Counseling and Development, 70*.

Pekarik, G., & Finney-Owen, K. (1987). Outpatient clinic therapist attitudes and beliefs relevant to client dropout. *Community Mental Health Journal, 23*, 120–130.

Pelissler, B., & Jones, N. (2005). A review of gender differences among substance abusers. *Crime & Delinquency, 51*(3), 343–372.

Perls, F. (1973). *The Gestalt approach and eye witness to therapy*. Palo Alto, CA: Science and Behavior Books.

Persons, J. B., Burns, D. D., & Perloff, J. M. (1988). Predictors of dropout and outcome in cognitive therapy for depression in a private practice setting. *Cognitive Therapy & Research, 12*, 557–575.

Peters, R. H., Strozier, A. L., Murrin, M. R., & Keanrs, W. D. (1997). Treatment of substance-abusing jail inmates: Examination of gender differences. *Journal of Substance Abuse Treatment, 14*(4), 339–349.

Phillips, M. L., Drevets, W. C., Rouch, S. L., & Lane, R. (2003). Neurobiology of emotion perception I: The neural basis of normal emotion perception. *Biological Psychiatry, 54,* 504–514.

Philpot, C. L. (2005). Family therapy for men. In G. Good & G. Brooks (Eds.), *The new handbook of psychotherapy and counseling with men: A comprehensive guide to settings, problems, and treatment approaches* (pp. 278–288). San Francisco: Jossey-Bass.

Piccinelli, M., & Wikinson. G. (2000). Gender differences in depression: A critical review. *The British Journal of Psychiatry, 177,* 486–492.

Ponterotto, J. & Pedersen, P. (1993). *Preventing prejudice: A guide for counselors and educators.* Newbury Park, CA: Sage.

Pope, K., and Tabachnick, B. (1993). Therapists' anger, hate, fear, and sexual feelings: National survey of therapist responses, client characteristics, critical events, formal complaints, and training. *Professional Psychology: Research and Practice, 24,* 142–152.

Powell, J. (1995). *Will the real me please stand up?: Twenty-five guidelines for good communication.* Notre Dame, IN: Thomas More Assn.

Prochaska, J. O., DiClemente, C. C., & Norcorss, J. D. (1992). In search of how people change: Applications to addictive behavior. *American Psychologist, 47,* 1102–1114.

Prochaska, J. O., & Norcross, J. C. (2002). Stages of change. In J. C. Norcross (Ed.), *Psychotherapy relationships that work* (pp. 303–314). Oxford, UK: Oxford University Press.

Prochaska, J. O., & Norcross, J. C. (2003). *Systems of psychotherapy: A transtheoretical analysis* (5th ed.). Pacific Grove, CA: Brooks/Cole.

Prosky, P. (1991). Marital life. *Family Therapy, 18,* 129–143.

Rabinowitz, F. E., Good, G. E., & Cozad, L. (1989). Rollo May: A man of meaning and myth. *Journal of Counseling and Development, 67,* 436–441.

Rauch, S. L., & Jenike, M. A. (1998). Pharmacological treatment of obsessive-compulsive disorder. In P. E. Nathan & J. M. Gorman (Eds.), *A guide to treatments that work* (pp. 358–377). New York: Oxford University Press.

Rauch, S. L., Shin, L. M., & Wright, C. I. (2003). Neuroimaging studies of amygdala function in anxiety disorders. *Annals of New York Academy of Science, 985,* 389–410.

Real, T. (1997). *I don't want to talk about it: Overcoming the secret legacy of male depression.* New York: Scribner.

Regier, D. A., Farmer, M. E., Rae, D. S., Locke, B. Z., Keith, S. J., Judd, L. L., & Goodwin, F. K. (1990). Comorbidity of mental disorders with alcohol and other drug abuse. Results from the Epidemiologic Catchment Area (ECA) Study. *Journal of the American Medical Association, 264*(19), 2511–2518.

Reibel, D. K., Greeson, J. M., Brainard, G. C., & Rosenzweig, S. (2001). Mindfulness-based stress reduction and health-related quality of life in a heterogeneous patient population. *General Hospital Psychiatry, 23*, 183–192.

Reik, T. (1948). *Listening with the third ear*. New York: Grove.

Richert, A. (1983). Differential prescription for psychotherapy on the basis of client role preferences. *Psychotherapy: Theory, Research, and Practice, 20*, 321–329.

Roback, H. B. (2000). Adverse outcomes in group psychotherapy: Risk factors, prevention, and research directions. *Journal of Psychotherapy Practice & Research, 9*(3), 113–122.

Rogers, C. R. (1951). *Client centered psychotherapy*. Boston: Houghton-Mifflin.

Rogers, C. R. (1957). The necessary and sufficient conditions of therapeutic personality change. *Journal of Counseling Psychology, 22*, 95–1103.

Rogers, C. R. (1961). *On becoming a person*. Boston, Houghton-Mifflin.

Rogers, C. R. (1980). *A way of being*. Boston: Houghton Mifflin.

Rogers, C. R., & Wallen, J. L. (1946). *Counseling with returned servicemen*. New York: McGraw-Hill.

Rosenbaum, M. (1977). Premature interruption of psychotherapy: Continuation of contact by telephone and correspondence. *American Journal of Psychiatry, 134*, 200–202.

Rounsaville, B. J., Chevron, E. S., Prusof, B. A., Elkin, I., Imber, S., Sotsky, S., & Watkins, J. (1987). The relation between specific and general dimensions of the psychotherapy process in interpersonal psychotherapy of depression. *Journal of Consulting and Clinical Psychology, 55*, 379–384.

Roy-Byrne, P. P., & Cowley, D. S. (1998). Pharmacological treatment of panic, generalized anxiety, and phobic disorders. In P. E. Nathan & J. M. Gorman (Eds.), *A guide to treatments that work* (pp. 319–339). New York: Oxford University Press.

Safran, J. D. (1993). Breaches in the therapeutic alliance: An arena for negotiating authentic relatedness. *Psychotherapy, 30*, 11–24.

Safran, J. D., & Muran, J. C. (2000). *Negotiating the therapeutic alliance: A relationship guide*. New York: Guilford.

Santrock, J. W. (2001). *Educational psychology*. Boston: McGraw-Hill.

Schneider, F. R., & Siris, S. D. (1987). A review of psychoactive substance use and abuse in schizophrenia: Patterns of drug choice. *Journal of Psychiatry, 165*, 13–21.

Schwartz, J. M. (1997). *Brain lock: Free yourself from obsessive-compulsive behavior*. New York: Harper Collins.

Schwartz, J. (2001). *"The relationship cure" is manual for emotional connection* [News release]. Retrieved December 1, 2004, from www.washington.edu/newsroom/news/2001archive/05–01archive/ko 50701.html.

Scott, J. (2004). Treatment outcome studies. In S. Johnson & R. Leahy (Eds.), *Psychological treatment of bipolar disorders* (pp. 226–241). New York: Guilford.

Seltzer, L. F. (1986). *Paradoxical strategies in psychotherapy*. New York: Wiley.

Sevel, J., Cummins, L., & Madrigal, C. (1999). *Social work skills demonstrated: Beginning direct practice CD-ROM with student manual*. Boston: Allyn and Bacon.

Shaffer, H. J., & Robbins, M. (1995). Psychotherapy for addictive behavior: A stage-change approach to meaning making. In A. M. Washton (Ed.), *Psychotherapy and substance abuse: A practitioner's handbook*, (pp. 103–123). New York: Guilford.

Shapiro, D. A., Rees, A., Barkham, M., Hardy, G., Reynolds, S., & Startup, M. (1995). Effects of treatment duration and severity of depression on the maintenance of gains following cognitive-behavioural and psychodynamic-interpersonal psychotherapy. *Journal of Consulting and Clinical Psychology, 63*, 378–387.

Shapiro, F. (1995). *Eye movement desensitization and reprocessing: Basic principles, protocols and procedures*. New York: Guilford.

Shea, M. T., Elkin, I., & Sotsky, S. M. (1999). Patient characteristics associated with successful treatment. In D. S. Janowsky (Ed.), *Psychotherapy indications and outcomes* (pp. 71–90). Washington, DC: American Psychopathological Association.

Sherman, R., & Fredman, N. (1986). *Handbook of structural techniques in marriage and family therapy*. New York: Brunner/Mazel.

Sherman, R., Oresky, P., & Rountrees, Y. (1991). *Solving problems in couples and family therapy*. New York: Brunner/Mazel.

Shoben, E. J., Jr. (1962). The counselor's theory as a personal trait. *Personnel and Guidance Journal, 40*, 617–621.

Shwed, H. S. (1980). When a psychiatrist suddenly dies . . . making provisions for patients [Roche reprint]. *Frontiers of Psychiatry, 10*, 4–5.

Sifneos, P. (1972). *Short term psychotherapy and emotional crisis*. Cambridge: Harvard University Press.

Sikes, C., & Sikes, V. (2003). EMDR: Why the controversy? *Traumatology, 9*, 169–181.

Sim, K., Gwee, K. P., & Bateman, A. (2005). Case formulation in psychotherapy: Revitalizing its usefulness as a clinical tool. *Academic Psychiatry 29*, 289–292.

Simon, F. B., Stierlin, H., Wynne, L. C. (1985). *The language of family therapy. A systemic vocabulary and sourcebook*. New York: Family Process Press.

Simpson, D. D., Joe, G. W., Rowan-Szal, G. A. (1997). Drug abuse treatment retention and process effects on follow-up outcomes. *Drug and Alcohol Dependence, 47*(3), 227–235.

Slovenko, R. (1991). Undue familiarity or undue damages? *Psychiatric Annals, 21*, 598–610.

Smith, D. E., & Seymour, R. B. (2003). Addictions counseling. In J. L. Ronch, W. Van Ornum, & N. C. Stilwell (Eds.), *The counseling sourcebook. A practical reference on contemporary issues* (pp. 383–398). New York: Crossroad Publishing Company.

Smith, K. J., Subich, L. M., & Kalodner, C. (1995). The transtheoretical model's stages and processes of change and their relation to premature termination. *Journal of Counseling Psychology, 42*, 34–39.

Smith, M. L., Glass, C. V., & Miller, T. (1980). *The benefits of psychotherapy*. Baltimore: Johns Hopkins Press.

Smith, R. L., & Stevens-Smith, P. (1992). Basic techniques in marriage and family counseling and therapy. *ERIC Digest*, Identifier: ED350526. Ann Arbor, MI: ERIC Clearinghouse on Counseling and Personnel Services.

Snarch, D. (1998). *Passionate marriage: Love, sex, and intimacy in emotionally committed relationships*. New York: Henry Holt.

Snyder, D. K., & Wills, R. M. (1989). Behavioral versus insight-oriented marital therapy: Effects on individual and interpersonal functioning. *Journal of Consulting and Clinical Psychology, 57*, 39–46.

Sotsky, S. M., Glass, D. R., Shea, M. T., Pilkonis, P. A., Collins, J. F., Elkin, I., Watkins, J. T., Imber, S. D., Leber, W. R., Moyer, J., &

Oliveri, M. E. (1991). Patients' predictors of response to psychotherapy and pharmacotherapy: Findings in the NIMH Treatment of Depression Collaborative Research Program. *American Journal of Psychiatry, 148*, 997–1008.

Spanier, C., Frank, E., McEachran, A. B., Grochocinski, V. J., & Kupfer, D. J. (1996). The prophylaxis of depressive episodes in recurrent depression following discontinuation of drug therapy: Integrating psychological and biological factors. *Psychological Medicine, 26*, 461–475.

Spradlin, S. (2003). *Don't let your emotions run your life*. Oakland, CA: New Harbinger.

St. Clair, M. (2000). *Object relations and self-psychology: An introduction* (3rd ed.). Belmont, CA: Wadsworth.

Steffen, J. J., & Karoly, P. (1980). Toward a psychology of therapeutic persistence. In P. Karoly & J. J. Steffen (Eds.), *Improving the long-term effects of psychotherapy* (pp. 181–203). New York: Gardner.

Steinberg, K. L., Roffman, R. A., Carroll, K. M., Kabela, E., Kadden, R., Miller, M., Duresky, D., & the Marijuana Treatment Project Research Group (2002). Tailoring cannabis dependence treatment for a diverse population. *Addiction, 97*(Suppl. 1), 135–42.

Strachey, J. (Ed. & Trans.). (1953). *The standard edition of the complete works of Sigmund Freud* (Vols. 1–24). London: Hogarth Press.

Strong, S. R. (1968). Counseling: An interpersonal influence process. *Journal of Counseling Psychology, 15*, 215–224.

Strupp, H., & Binder, J. (1984). *Psychotherapy in a new key*. New York: Basic.

Stuart, R. (1980). *Helping couples change*. New York: Guildford.

Sudak, D. (2006). *Cognitive behavior therapy in clinical practice*. Philadelphia: Lippincott, Williams, and Wilkins.

Sue, D. W., Arrendondo, P., & McDavis, J. R. (1992). Multicultural counseling competencies and standards: A call to the profession. *Journal of Counseling and Development, 70*, 477–486.

Sue, D. W., & Sue, D. (2003). *Counseling the culturally diverse: Theory and practice* (4th ed.). New York: John Wiley & Sons.

Sue, D. W., & Torino, G. C. (2005). Racial-cultural competence: Awareness, knowledge, and skills. In R. T. Carter (Ed.), *Handbook of racial-cultural psychology and counseling* (pp. 3–18). Hoboken, NJ: Wiley.

Sullivan, H. S. (1953). *The Interpersonal theory of psychiatry*, New York: W. W. Norton.

Sullivan, H. S. (1972) *Personal psychopathology*. New York: W. W. Norton.

Sullivan, G. (1996). Behavior therapy. In W. Dryden (Ed.), *Handbook of individual psychotherapy* (pp. 283–304). London: Sage.

Szapocznik, J., & Kurtines, W. M. (1993). Family psychology and cultural diversity: Opportunities for theory, research, and application. *American Psychologist 48*, 400–407.

Thorne, B. (1996). Person-centered therapy. In W. Dryden (Ed.), *Handbook of individual psychotherapy* (pp. 121–145). London: Sage.

Tichenor, V., & Hill, C. E. (1989). A comparison of six variables of working alliance. *Psychotherapy: Theory, Research, and Practice, 41*, 165–180.

Truax, C. B. (1966). Reinforcement and nonreinforcement in Rogerian psychotherapy. *Journal of Abnormal Psychology, 71*, 1–7.

Trull, T. J., Widiger, T. A., Lynam, D. R., & Costa, P. T., Jr. (2003). Borderline personality disorder from the perspective of general personality functioning. *Journal of Abnormal Psychology, 112*, 193–202.

Turkington, D., Dudley, R., Warman, D. M., & Beck, A. T. (2004). Cognitive-behavioral therapy for schizophrenia: A review. *Journal of Psychiatric Practice, 10*, 5–16.

U.S. Department of Health and Human Services (2005). Administration for children & families. *The Health Marriage Initiative: Premarital and Marriage Education*. Retrieved July 15, 2005, from www2.acf.hhs.gov/healthymarriage/about/factsheets_premarital_edu.html#mission.

Valasquez, M. M., Maurer, G. G., Crouch, C., & DiClemente, C. C. (2001). *Group treatment for substance abuse: A stages of change therapy manual*. New York: Guilford.

Viamontes, G. I., Beitman, B. D., Viamontes, C. T., & Viamontes, J. A. (2005). Neural circuits for self-awareness: Evolutionary origins and implementation in the human brain. In B. D. Beitman & J. Nair (Eds.), *Self-awareness deficits in psychiatric patients* (pp. 24–111). New York: Norton.

Viamontes, G. I. (in press). *An atlas of neurobiology: How the brain creates the self*. New York: Norton.

Visher, E. B., & Visher, J. S. (1991). *How to win as a stepfamily*. New York: Taylor & Francis.

Wachtel, E. (1999). *We love each other but . . . . Simple secrets to strengthen your relationship and make love last*. New York: St. Martin's Griffen.

Wachtel, E., & Wachtel, P. (1986). *Family dynamics in individual psychotherapy: A guide to clinical strategies.* New York: Guilford.

Walsh, B., & Heppner, M. J. (2006). *Handbook of career counseling of women.* Hillsdale, NJ: Erlbaum.

Walsh, F., & McGoldrick, M. (Eds.) (2004). *Living beyond loss: Death in the family* (2nd ed.). New York: W. W. Norton.

Walter, J. L., & Peller, J. E. (1992). *Becoming solution-focused in brief therapy.* New York: Brunner/Mazel.

Wampold, B. (2001). *The great psychotherapy debate.* Mahwah, NJ: Erlbaum.

Wampold, B., Ahn, H., & Coleman, H. L. K. (2001). Medical model as metaphor: Old habits die hard. *Journal of Counseling Psychology, 48,* 268–273.

Warshaw, R. (1998). *I never called it rape.* New York: Harper Collins.

Watkins, J. T., Leber, W. R., Imber, S. D., Collins, J. F., Elkin, I., Pilkonis, P. A., Sotsky, S. M., Shea, M. T., & Glass, D. R. (1993). Temporal course of change of depression. *Journal of Consulting & Clinical Psychology, 61,* 858–64.

Watkins, K., Shaner, A., & Sullivan, G. (1999). The role of gender in engaging the dually diagnosed in treatment. *Community Mental Health Journal, 35*(2), 115–126.

Watzlawick, P. (1977). *How real is real: Confusion, disinformation, communication.* New York: Vintage-Random.

Watzlawick, P., Beavin, J. H., & Jackson, D. D. (1967). *Pragmatics of human communication.* New York: Norton.

Weighill, V. E., Hodge, J., & Peck, D. F. (1983). Keeping appointments with clinical psychologists. *The British Journal of Clinical Psychology, 22,* 143–144.

Westen, D., Novotny, C. M., & Thompson-Brenner, H. (2004). The empirical status of empirically supported psychotherapies: Assumptions, findings and reporting in controlled clinical trials. *Psychological Bulletin, 130,* 631–663.

Whitaker, C. A., & Malone, T. P. (1981). *The roots of psychotherapy.* New York: Brunner/Mazel.

White, M. (2000). *Reflections on narrative practice: Essays and interviews.* Adelaide, South Australia: Dulwich Centre.

White, M., & Epston, D. (1990). *Narrative means to therapeutic ends.* New York: W. W. Norton.

Wiggins, J. S. (1982). Circumplex models of interpersonal behavior in clinical psychology. In P. C. Kendall & J. N. Butcher (Eds.), *Handbook of research methods in clinical psychology* (pp. 183–221). New York: Wiley.

Winnicott, D. W. (1949). Hate in the countertransference. *International Journal of Psychoanalysis, 30*, 69–74.

Winnicott, D. W. (1953). Transitional objects and transitional phenomena. *International Journal of Psychoanalysis, 34*, 89–97.

Winnicott, D.W. (1965). Failure of expectable environment on child's mental functioning. *International Journal of Psychoanalysis, 46*, 81–87.

Winnicott, D. W. (1971). *Therapeutic consulations in child psychiatry.* London: Hogarth.

Wohl, J. (1989). Integration of cultural awareness into psychotherapy. *American Journal of Psychotherapy 4–3*, 343–355.

Wolman, B. B. (1968). *The unconscious mind: The meaning of Freudian psychology.* Englewood Cliffs, NJ: Prentice-Hall.

Wolpe J. (1958). *Psychotherapy by reciprocal inhibition.* Stanford, CA: Stanford University

Wolpe, J. (1973). *The practice of behavior therapy.* New York: Pergamon.

Worden, J. W. (1991). *Grief counseling and grief therapy.* New York: Springer.

Worell, J., & Remer, P. (2003). *Feminist perspectives in therapy: Empowering diverse women.* Hoboken, NJ: Wiley.

Yalom, I. (1980). *Existential psychotherapy.* New York: Basic.

Yates, A. J. (1970). *Behavior therapy.* New York: Wiley.

Yehuda, R., Marshall, R., & Giller, E. L. (1998). Psychopharmacological treatment of post-traumatic stress disorder. In P. E. Nathan & J. M. Gorman (Eds.), *A guide to treatments that work* (pp. 411–445). New York: Oxford University Press.

Zilbergeld, B. (1999). *The new male sexuality* (Rev. ed.). New York: Mass Market.

Index